MUSIC
An Appreciation
Sixth Brief Edition

Roger Kamien

Zubin Mehta Chair in Musicology, Emeritus
The Hebrew University of Jerusalem

 **Higher Education**

Boston   Burr Ridge, IL   Dubuque, IA   Madison, WI   New York   San Francisco   St. Louis
Bangkok   Bogotá   Caracas   Kuala Lumpur   Lisbon   London   Madrid   Mexico City
Milan   Montreal   New Delhi   Santiago   Seoul   Singapore   Sydney   Taipei   Toronto

For Anita, David, Joshua, and Adina

The **McGraw·Hill** Companies

Mc Graw Hill **Higher Education**

Published by McGraw-Hill, a business unit of The McGraw-Hill Companies, Inc., 1221 Avenue of the Americas, New York, NY, 10020. Copyright © 2008 by The McGraw-Hill Companies, Inc. All rights reserved. No part of this publication may be reproduced or distributed in any form or by any means, or stored in a database or retrieval system, without the prior written consent of The McGraw-Hill Companies, Inc., including, but not limited to, in any network or other electronic storage or transmission, or broadcast for distance learning. Some ancillaries, including electronic and print components, may not be available to customers outside the United States.

This book is printed on acid-free paper.

1 2 3 4 5 6 7 8 9 0 DOW/DOW 0 9 8 7

ISBN   978-0-07-340134-8 (student edition)
MHID: 0-07-340134-X
ISBN   978-0-07-332637-5 (annotated instructor's edition)
MHID: 0-07-332637-2

Editor in Chief: *Emily Barrosse*
Publisher: *Lisa Moore*
Senior Sponsoring Editor: *Christopher Freitag*
Senior Development Editor: *Nancy Crochiere*
Executive Marketing Manager: *Pamela Cooper*
Project Managers: *Cathy Iammartino
    and Christina Gimlin*
Manuscript Editor: *Susan Gamer*
Art Director: *Jeanne Schreiber*
Designer: *Cassandra J. Chu*
Text Designer: *Ellen Pettengell*

Cover Designer: *Cassandra J. Chu*
Art Editor: *Emma C. Ghiselli*
Photo Research Coordinator: *Sonia Brown*
Cover Image: © *Joshua Kamien*
Lead Media Project Manager: *Marc Mattson*
Production Supervisors: *Jason I. Huls
    and Richard DeVitto*
Media Producer: *Jocelyn Spielberger*
Composition: *10/12 Palatino by Thompson Type*
Printing: *45 # Pub Matte, R. R. Donelley & Sons*

Acknowledgments: The Acknowledgments section for this book begins on page A-1 and is considered an extension of the copyright page.

Library of Congress Cataloging-in-Publication Data

Kamien, Roger
    Music : an appreciation / Roger Kamien.—6th brief ed.
      p. cm.
    Includes index.
    ISBN-13: 978-0-07-340134-8 (softcover : alk. paper)
    ISBN-10: 0-07-340134-X
    1. Music appreciation.   I. Title.
MT90.K34 2007
780—dc22   2007921891

The Internet addresses listed in the text were accurate at the time of publication. The inclusion of a Web site does not indicate an endorsement by the authors or McGraw-Hill, and McGraw-Hill does not guarantee the accuracy of the information presented at these sites.

www.mhhe.com

About the Author

Roger Kamien was born in Paris in 1934 and was brought to the United States at the age of six months. He received his B.A. in music from Columbia College in New York, and his M.A. and Ph.D in musicology from Princeton University. He studied piano with Nadia Reisenberg and Claudio Arrau. During 1957–1959, he returned to Paris as a Fulbright scholar, for research on eighteenth-century music.

Professor Kamien taught music history, theory, and literature for two years at Hunter College and then for twenty years at Queens College of the City University of New York, where he was coordinator of the music appreciation courses. During this time he was also active as a pianist, appearing both in the United States and in Europe. In 1983, he was appointed to the Zubin Mehta Chair of Musicology at the Hebrew University of Jerusalem.

In addition to *Music: An Appreciation*, Dr. Kamien was the editor of *The Norton Scores* and one of the coauthors of *A New Approach to Keyboard Harmony* and a contributor to *The Cambridge Companion to Beethoven*. He has also written articles and reviews for journals including *Music Forum, Beethoven Forum, Musical Quarterly, Journal of Music Theory, Music Theory Spectrum, Journal of Musicology,* and *Journal of the American Musicological Society*.

In recent years, he has appeared as a piano soloist in twenty-six countries on five continents. He frequently performs together with his wife, the conductor-pianist Anita Kamien, who has also contributed in many ways to *Music: An Appreciation*. The Kamiens have three children and seven grandchildren.

ALSO BY THE AUTHOR

Music: An Appreciation—Ninth Edition

Contents

Preface

As a performer, teacher, and musicologist, I work to bring music to life in a variety of ways. *Music: An Appreciation, Sixth Brief Edition,* grew out of my involvement in various aspects of music. I have aimed to write a book that is concise yet clear, accurate, and engaging—useful both for study and in the classroom. This text provides an approach to perceptive listening and an introduction to musical elements, forms, and stylistic periods. Its discussions of composers' lives, individual styles, and representative works aim not merely to impart facts but also to stimulate curiosity and enthusiasm. The book was written to increase readers' love of music as well as to enhance their listening skills. The features outlined below have proved appealing to students and instructors alike.

Organization

- Part I of the book examines the elements of music both in general terms and with reference to illustrative pieces that are attractive, brief, and representative of a variety of periods. Notation is used sparingly in this part—usually in connection with familiar tunes like *Home on the Range,* which allow students first to analyze music that they probably have known since childhood.
- Parts II through VI deal with specific periods of music history from the Middle Ages to the present; jazz, music for stage and screen, and rock are considered within Part VI. Nonwestern music is surveyed in Part VII.
- Each of Parts II to VI begins with a richly illustrated part opener that discusses the main stylistic, cultural, and historical trends of the period. These part openers include timelines that place musical events within their cultural and historical context.
- A Glossary with Example Locator is provided as an appendix at the end of the book. A quick guide to the CD audio recordings is provided on the inside front and back covers of the book.

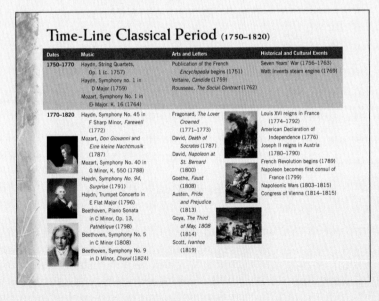

Time-Line Classical Period (1750–1820)

Dates	Music	Arts and Letters	Historical and Cultural Events
1750–1770	Haydn, String Quartets, Op. 1 (c. 1757) Haydn, Symphony no. 1 in D Major (1759) Mozart, Symphony No. 1 in E♭ Major, K. 16 (1764)	Publication of the French *Encyclopedia* begins (1751) Voltaire, *Candide* (1759) Rousseau, *The Social Contract* (1762)	Seven Years' War (1756–1763) Watt invents steam engine (1769)
1770–1820	Haydn, Symphony No. 45 in F Sharp Minor, *Farewell* (1772) Mozart, *Don Giovanni* and *Eine kleine Nachtmusik* (1787) Mozart, Symphony No. 40 in G Minor, K. 550 (1788) Haydn, Symphony No. 94, *Surprise* (1791) Haydn, Trumpet Concerto in E Flat Major (1796) Beethoven, Piano Sonata in C Minor, Op. 13, *Pathétique* (1798) Beethoven, Symphony No. 5 in C Minor (1808) Beethoven, Symphony No. 9 in D Minor, *Choral* (1824)	Fragonard, *The Lover Crowned* (1771–1773) David, *Death of Socrates* (1787) David, *Napoleon at St. Bernard* (1800) Goethe, *Faust* (1808) Austen, *Pride and Prejudice* (1813) Goya, *The Third of May, 1808* (1814) Scott, *Ivanhoe* (1819)	Louis XVI reigns in France (1774–1792) American Declaration of Independence (1776) Joseph II reigns in Austria (1780–1790) French Revolution begins (1789) Napoleon becomes first consul of France (1799) Napoleonic Wars (1803–1815) Congress of Vienna (1814–1815)

Flexibility

Music: An Appreciation, Sixth Brief Edition takes a chronological approach but can be adapted easily to individual teaching methods. Each stylistic period is subdivided into short, relatively independent sections that can be studied in any order; some could even be omitted. While music examples are offered throughout the book, discussions of the pieces require no knowledge of musical notation. The examples provide visual aids for those who want them; students may prefer simply to read the text and skip the details of notation.

Using the Book

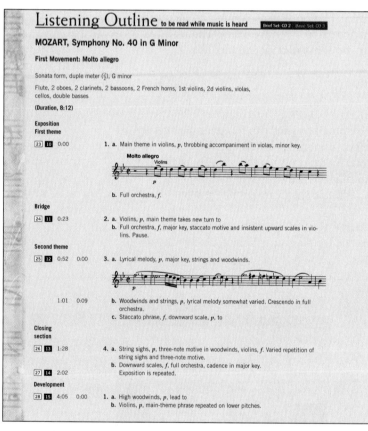

Listening Outlines

One of the outstanding features of *Music: An Appreciation* is the use of Listening Outlines to be followed while the pieces are heard. A Listening Outline focuses attention on musical events as they unfold and is easy to follow because it describes what students can readily hear. Listening Outlines develop students' listening skills and reinforce their understanding of musical forms and elements. These outlines are useful for outside listening assignments as well as for classroom work. Every piece with a Listening Outline in the text is included on the Basic Set of compact discs available with the text, and many pieces are included on the Brief Set. Additionally, every Listening Outline from the text is presented in an interactive format on the book's Online Learning Center at www.mhhe.com/kamien6.

Vocal Music Guides

The study of music with vocal texts—such as songs, choruses, and operas—is aided in this book by Vocal Music Guides. In a Vocal Music Guide, the sung text appears with marginal notes that indicate the relationship between words and music and help the listener follow the thought, story, or drama. These vocal music guides include extended **excerpts from opera librettos,** making it unnecessary for instructors to supply them to the class. Every piece with a Vocal Music

Guide in the text is included on the Basic CD Set, and many pieces are included on the Brief CD Set. In addition, both sets of CDs now include a bonus CD-ROM featuring **video excerpts**—with English subtitles—of outstanding performances of **three of the operas** discussed in the text.

Musical Terms and Example Locator

Within the text, important musical terms are defined simply and appear in *bold italic* type. Terms and definitions also appear in the Glossary and Example Locator provided as an Appendix. The Glossary and Example Locator allows readers to combine a review of musical terms with instant reference to clear musical examples of these terms (elements, forms, genres, and compositional techniques). These examples come from the works included on the Basic and Brief CD sets available with *Music: An Appreciation.*

Recordings

A listening program produced by Sony and featuring the highest quality recordings of leading performers and ensembles is available for use with *Music: An Appreciation.* The recordings are available as

- A Basic Set of 9 CDs, including 8 audio CDs and one bonus CD-ROM with video clips from three operas. The CDs contain the music from all the Listening Outlines and Vocal Music Guides. The bonus CD-ROM includes scenes (with English subtitles) from three operas discussed in the text: Mozart's *Don Giovanni,* Puccini's *La Bohème,* and Berg's *Wozzeck.*

- A Brief Set of 5 CDs, including 4 audio CDs and one CD-ROM containing both audio selections and the 3 video opera clips.

The CD sets are internally tracked, so the student or instructor can locate specific themes or sections within a composition at the push of a button.

Using the Recordings with the Text

So that the recordings can be used easily, notes in the text margins refer the reader to the appropriate CD and track number. References to the Brief Set and Basic Set are given in the forms shown here in the margin.

The boxed numbers are CD track numbers. Track numbers for the Basic Set are in dark boxes and track numbers for the Brief Set are in white boxes.

Brief Set:
CD 2 23

Listening Outlines and Vocal Music Guides include indications of time elapsed. For example, the indication 2:36 means that 2 minutes and 36 seconds have elapsed since the beginning of the piece. New to this edition are timings that also indicate how much time has elapsed since the start of a new track.

Basic Set:
CD 3

Topics within the text that can be enriched by materials available on the text Web site are indicated by global Web icons placed in the margins of the text.

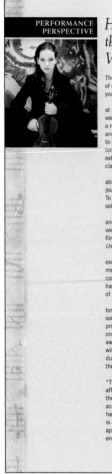

PERFORMANCE PERSPECTIVE

Hilary Hahn, Violinist, Playing the First Movement of Mendelssohn's Violin Concerto in E Minor, Op. 64

Though still in her twenties, Hilary Hahn is one of the most prominent concert violinists of our time. In 1999, when she was nineteen, *Time* Magazine called her "America's best" young classical musician.

As with most concert artists, Hahn's extraordinary musical talent was recognized at a very early age. When not quite four, she began studying violin, and at age ten she was accepted to the Curtis Institute of Music in Philadelphia. At sixteen, she signed a recording contract, made her debut at Carnegie Hall with the Philadelphia Orchestra, and completed the requirements for her bachelor of music degree. However, she chose to delay her graduation from Curtis for three years: "I loved the school, so I stayed as long as I could. There were a lot of classes that interested me that I hadn't taken yet; for extra electives, I enrolled in poetry- and fiction- writing workshops and several literature classes, in addition to continuing with German."

For Hahn, "communicating music to people is something that I feel very lucky to be able to do." She writes her own liner notes for her recordings and maintains an online journal (on her Web site, HilaryHahn.com) of her experiences in cities where she performs. To expand children's musical horizons, Hahn often plays in grade schools. "I always play solo Bach, a slow and a fast movement. The music casts a spell. They really like it."

Hahn enjoys music in a wide range of styles, from blues and world music to trip-hop and classical. Her prizewinning recordings include works by Mendelssohn, Bach, Beethoven, and Bernstein, and she performs on the sound track of the M. Night Shyamalan film *The Village*, as well as on an album by Austin alt-rockers . . . *And You Will Know Us by the Trail of Dead.*

Hahn learned the Mendelssohn Violin Concerto when she was eleven and performed excerpts with the Curtis Orchestra the following year. (Her performance of the first movement of the concerto is included in the CD Sets.) "Not long after, I performed the entire concerto with a chamber orchestra in Florida, and since then the Mendelssohn concerto has been a staple of my repertoire." For Hahn, the first movement of the concerto is full of "lyricism, fire, drama, and contrast."

Hahn observes that performing a concerto requires close cooperation with the conductor and members of the orchestra. "Sometimes the conductor and I will disagree about something and meet in the middle. There's a system of give-and-take, opinions, and compromise—though as a musician, you try to never be compromised or compromise someone else's interpretation. Musicians inevitably interact with each other, so we have to be aware of what the others are doing. For example, if I share a solo line with the flute, I will pay attention to how the flutist plays the line so that it sounds like a duet. The conductor coordinates some of that, but in a concerto, the minutiae are really decided by the musicians, by listening to each other and reacting to the musical ideas that we hear."

For Hahn, playing before a live audience is very different from recording in a studio. "The audience influences performing to a large extent because the presence of people affects the way the concert hall sounds. The energy in the hall is hard to describe, but there is a different feeling when you know people are there to absorb the music (both acoustically and psychologically). It's quite energizing and inspiring. In recording, you have a limited time and an empty hall—any tiny noise can ruin a take, so no audience is allowed in the studio—and you have to get it right, so that situation takes a different approach. I try to keep the feeling as similar as possible, though, by imagining an audience listening in the hall, or in their car, or to their stereo."

New Features in the Sixth Brief Edition

Performance Perspective

The *Sixth Brief Edition* includes "Performance Perspective," features designed to heighten readers' awareness of the vital role played by performers in making music come alive. This book now highlights several musicians whose recorded performances appear on the CD Sets. Often using the performers' own words, these discussions shed light on a wide range of issues, including the emotions evoked by music, the nature of interpretative decisions, historically accurate performance, and the ways in which recordings have heightened the impact of performers. The performers discussed are the pianist-author Roger Kamien, conductor Andrew Parrott, violinist-conductor Jeanne Lamon, pianist-conductor Murray Perahia, violinist Hilary Hahn, tenor Luciano Pavarotti, cellist Yo-Yo Ma, blues singer Bessie Smith, and rock guitarist Carlos Santana.

Revised and Expanded Material

The section on music in the Middle Ages has been revised in light of recent scholarship.

The sections on jazz and rock have been updated, expanded, and thoroughly revised with the assistance of Professor Scott Lipscomb of Northwestern University, the coauthor of *Rock and Roll: Its History and Stylistic Development, Fourth Edition.* These updates and revisions acknowledge the importance of jazz and rock for today's generation of students.

Increased Coverage of Latin American Musicians

In the *Sixth Brief Edition* I have responded to reviewers' requests for more coverage of Latin American musicians by including a discussion of the Argentinian tango composer Astor Piazzolla and his attractive piece *Fugata,* as well as a Performance Perspective feature on the guitarist Carlos Santana, who fuses rock with Latin and African rhythms and elements of jazz and the blues.

Supplements

Support for Students

The Online Learning Center at www.mhhe.com/kamien6 includes a wide variety of materials to enhance the use of this text.

New "Listening Room" software provides a visual illustration of every Listening Outline and Vocal Music Guide in the text. With written narration coordinated to the music, students can navigate through the various parts of each musical selection with ease.

Additional Recordings allow students to experience recordings of the work of some composers discussed in the text, but not included in the CD sets.

An Interactive Elements section provides visual and audio examples of the concepts covered in Part I of the text. Animated demonstration activities allow students to experience musical elements in action.

The Instruments section provides video demonstrations of all the instruments in an orchestra; an interactive instrument lab in which you can make your own music using the instruments on screen; and an animated, interactive version of Benjamin Britten's *Young Person's Guide to the Orchestra.*

Chapter-specific materials help students prepare and study. These include multiple-choice quizzes, chapter summaries, and Web exercises.

Interactive activities help students understand some of the common forms heard in concert settings, like *Concerto Grosso, Fugue, Minuet, Sonata, Rondo,* and *Theme and Variations.*

Six Interactive Timelines present an in-depth and informative view of specific time periods, including events in music, history, and arts and letters. Audio examples of the work of various composers are also included.

A Concert-Goer's Guide will help students understand and enjoy concert performances and provide tips for writing concert reports.

A **Student Study Guide and Workbook** is available for purchase. The Study Guide provides study materials, projects, and listening activities. Contact your local McGraw-Hill sales representative or go to www.mhhe.com for more details.

Support for Instructors

Your local McGraw-Hill representative can provide you with details on the teaching and learning package for this book. If you are not sure who your representative is, you can find him or her by visiting www.mhhe.com, and using the Rep Locator feature available on the home page.

Instructor's Edition on the Online Learning Center at http://www.mhhe .com/kamien6—This handy resource provides all of the text support materials you will need to organize your lectures and prepare tests, including:

- *Instructor's Manual:* includes objectives and lecture topics for each part.

- *Test Bank:* includes a wealth of test questions for use with the text.

- *EZ Test Computerized Test Bank:* McGraw-Hill's EZ Test is a flexible and easy-to-use electronic testing program. The program allows instructors to create tests from book-specific items. It accommodates a wide range of question types, and instructors may add their own questions. Multiple versions of the test can be created, and any test can be used with course management systems. The program is available for Windows and Macintosh environments.

- PowerPoint Slides

The **Classroom Performance System (CPS)** is a revolutionary wireless response system that engages students while gathering important assessment data. CPS units include easy-to-use software for creating and delivering quiz questions and assessments to your class. Each student simply responds with his or her individual wireless response pad. Responses are tabulated instantly. Go to http://www.mhhe.com/cps/ for further details.

Acknowledgments

Over the course of fifteen editions of the brief and basic versions of *Music: An Appreciation,* many wonderful reviewers, colleagues, and friends have contributed immeasurably to the growth and improvement of the text. By now, they are too numerous to thank by name. However, I want to express my particular gratitude to those instructors around the country who provided guidance for the current edition: Jeanne Belfy, *Boise State University;* Dominique Bellon, *Arizona State University;* Gail Flemming, *Southwestern Illinois College;* William Hinkle, *Seminole Community College;* Martha Horst, *East Carolina University;* David Johansen, *Southeastern Louisiana University;* Dorothy Keyser, *University of North Dakota;* Peter Knapp, *Long Beach City College;* Greg McLean, *Georgia Perimeter College;* Charlotte F. Pipes, *Nicholls State University;* Catherine Roche-Williams, *The University of Louisiana;* Carol Shansky, *Bergen Community College;* Anna Thibeault, *Georgia Southern University;* Janette Tilley, *City University of New York;* and Suzanne Wong, *Fullerton College.*

Additionally, I would like to thank Professor John d'Armand for his numerous and very helpful suggestions.

My deep thanks go to Professor Scott Lipscomb, for his help with the sections on jazz, rock, the American musical, and film music; to Professor Anne Stone, for her critical reading of sections on medieval and renaissance music; and to Professor Roger Vetter, for his assistance with *Ompeh,* a song from Ghana that he recorded. I value the help of Pedro R. Aponte and Ilka Vasconcelos Araujo with the discussions of Latin American music and Astor Piazzolla and the help of Ronen Verbit with the discussion of film music. I am grateful to Dr. Adena Portowitz for class-testing the Listening Outline for Symphony No. 3 in F Major by Brahms. The violinists Jeanne Lamon and Hilary Hahn, the conductor Andrew Parrott, and the pianist Murray Perahia, featured in Performance Perspective boxes, were extraordinarily generous in sharing with me their insights on musical performance.

I want to express my thanks for the expert assistance of my sponsoring editor at McGraw-Hill, Chris Freitag, and the development editor, Nancy Crochiere.

I am grateful for the superb work of Sue Gamer, the copyeditor, Cathy Iammartino, project manager, Srdjan Savanovic, the designer, and David Tietz, the photo researcher. I'd like to thank Tom Laskey at Sony Music Special Products for his efforts to provide an outstanding package of CD recordings.

My wife, the conductor-pianist Anita Kamien, has contributed to every aspect of this book. She clarified ideas, helped choose representative pieces, and worked tirelessly to improve the Listening Outlines. Her advice and encouragement were essential to the completion of *Music: An Appreciation, Sixth Brief Edition.*

Roger Kamien

Elements

"Rhythm and harmony find their way into the inward places of the soul ..."

PLATO

I

All musical elements come together when people play or sing.

Music plays a vital role in human society. It provides entertainment and emotional release, and it accompanies activities ranging from dances to religious ceremonies. Music is heard everywhere: in auditoriums, churches, homes, elevators, and sports arenas, and on the street.

Recorded performance was a sensational innovation of the twentieth century. Thanks to modern technology, living rooms, cars, or jogging paths function as new kinds of concert halls where we can hear what we want, as often as we want.

Live performances provide a special excitement. In a live performance, artists put themselves on the line; training and magnetism must overcome technical difficulties to involve the listener's emotions. What is performed, how it sounds, how the artist feels about it that

Informal music making is a source of pleasure for players and listeners.

evening—all this exists for a fleeting moment and can never be repeated. An audience responds to the excitement of such a moment, and feel-

ings are exchanged between stage and hall.

Our response to a musical performance or an artist is subjective and rooted in deep feeling. Even professional critics can differ strongly in their evaluations of a performance. There is no one "truth" about what we hear and feel. Does the performer project a concept, an overall idea, or an emotion? Do some sections of a piece, but not others, communicate something to you? Can you figure out why? It's up to us as listeners to evaluate performances of music. Alert and repeated listening will enhance our ability to compare performances and judge music so that we can fully enjoy it.

People listen to music in many different ways. Music can be a barely perceived background or a totally absorbing experience. Part I

The audience at an outdoor concert in Atlanta, Georgia. Whether in a public park or a concert hall, live performances have a special electricity.

of this book, Elements, introduces concepts that can contribute to your enjoyment of a wide range of musical styles. For example, awareness of tone color—the quality that distinguishes one instrument from another—can heighten your pleasure when a melody passes from a clarinet to a trumpet. Perceptive, aware listening makes any musical experience more intense and satisfying.

Aerosmith lead singer Steven Tyler. The exchange between singer and audience contains something magical, direct, and spellbinding.

The use of computers and electronics has revolutionized the way we create, play, and listen to music.

Music making transcends boundaries of many kinds. Pictured here are musicians playing in a gamelan, an ensemble found in Indonesia.

1 Sound: Pitch, Dynamics, and Tone Color

Sounds bombard our ears every day—the squeaks and honks of traffic, a child's laugh, the bark of a dog, the patter of rain. Through sounds we learn what's going on; we need them to communicate. By listening to the speech, cries, and laughter of others, we learn what they think and how they feel. But silence, an absence of sound, also communicates. When we hear no sound in the street, we assume no cars are passing. When someone doesn't answer a question or breaks off in the middle of a sentence, we quickly notice, and we draw conclusions from the silence.

Sounds may be perceived as pleasant or unpleasant. Fortunately, we can direct our attention to specific sounds, shutting out those that don't interest us. At a party, for instance, we can choose to ignore the people near us and focus instead on a conversation across the room. Actually, we shut out most sounds, paying attention only to those of interest. The composer John Cage (1912–1992) may have meant to show this with his "composition" entitled *4'33"*, in which a musician sits at a piano for 4 minutes and 33 seconds—and does nothing. The silence forces the people in the audience to direct their attention to whatever noises, or sounds, they themselves are making. In a sense, the audience "composes" this piece. To get the effect, listen to the sounds that fill the silence around you right now.

What are these sounds that we hear? What *is* "sound"? What causes it, and how do we hear it?

Sound begins with the vibration of an object, such as a table that is pounded or a string that is plucked. The vibrations are transmitted to our ears by a medium, which is usually air. As a result of the vibrations, our eardrums start vibrating too, and *impulses,* or signals, are transmitted to the brain. There the impulses are selected, organized, and interpreted.

Music is part of this world of sound, an art based on the organization of sounds in time. We distinguish music from other sounds by recognizing the four main properties of musical sounds: *pitch, dynamics* (loudness or softness), *tone color,* and *duration.* We'll look now at the first three of these properties of musical sound. Duration—the length of time a musical sound lasts—is discussed in Section 3, "Rhythm."

Pitch: Highness or Lowness of Sound

Pitch is the relative highness or lowness that we hear in a sound. When you sing the beginning of *The Star-Spangled Banner,* for example, the pitch on *see* is higher than the pitch on *say:*

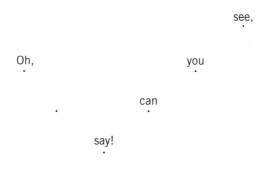

The pitch of a sound is decided by the *frequency* of its vibrations—that is, their speed, which is measured in cycles per second. The faster the vibrations, the higher the pitch; the slower the vibrations, the lower the pitch. All other things being equal, smaller objects vibrate faster and have higher pitches: thus plucking a short string produces a higher pitch than plucking a long string.

In music, a sound that has a definite pitch is called a ***tone.*** It has a specific frequency, such as 440 cycles per second. The vibrations of a tone are regular and reach the ear at equal time intervals. By contrast, noiselike sounds (such as a squeal of brakes and a clash of cymbals) have an indefinite pitch and are produced by irregular vibrations.

Two tones will sound different when they have different pitches. The "distance" in pitch between any two tones is called an ***interval.*** When tones are separated by the interval called an ***octave,*** they sound very much alike. Sing the opening of *The Star-Spangled Banner* again. Notice that the tone you produce on *see* sounds like your tone on *say*, even though it's higher. An octave lies between them. The vibration frequency of the *say* tone is exactly half that of the *see* tone. If the *say* tone were 440 cycles per second, the *see* tone—an octave higher—would be 880 cycles per second. A tone an octave lower than the *say* tone would be half of 440, or 220 cycles per second. When sounded at the same time, two tones an octave apart blend so well that they seem almost to merge into one tone.

The octave is important in music. It is the interval between the first and last tones of the familiar scale:

If you sing this, starting with the low *do* and ending on the high *do*, which "duplicates" it, you will fill the octave with seven different pitches, rather than sliding up like a siren. This group of seven tones (they are produced by the white keys of a piano) was the basis of western music for centuries. Eventually, five more pitches were added (the black keys on the piano), making twelve tones in all, each of which is "duplicated" in higher and lower octaves. (In nonwestern music, the octave may be divided into a different number of tones.)

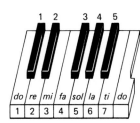

Seven different tones are produced by the white keys of the piano.

The distance between the lowest and highest tones that a voice or an instrument can produce is called its ***pitch range*** or simply its ***range.*** The range of an average untrained voice is about $1\frac{1}{2}$ octaves; a piano's range is more than 7 octaves.

The organization of pitch is a composer's first resource. In Sections 5 and 6, where melody and harmony are explored, we will look at how pitch is organized. For now, we'll simply observe that composers can create a special mood in their music by using very low or very high pitches. For example, low pitches can intensify the sadness of a funeral march; high pitches can make a dance sound lighter; and a steady rise in pitch often increases musical tension.

Though most music we know is based on definite pitches, indefinite pitches—such as those made by a bass drum or by cymbals—are important as well. Some percussion instruments, such as gongs, cowbells, and wood blocks, come in different sizes and therefore produce higher or lower indefinite pitches. Contrasts between higher and lower indefinite pitches play a vital role in twentieth-century and twenty-first-century western music and in musical cultures around the world.

Dynamics

Degrees of loudness or softness in music are called ***dynamics***—our second property of sound. Loudness is related to the amplitude of the vibration that produces the sound. The harder a guitar string is plucked (the farther it moves from the fingerboard), the louder its sound. When instruments are played more loudly or more softly, or when there is a change in how many instruments are heard, a dynamic change results; such a change may be made either suddenly or gradually. A gradual increase in loudness often creates excitement, particularly when the pitch rises too. On the other hand, a gradual decrease in loudness can convey a sense of calm.

A performer can emphasize a tone by playing it more loudly than the tones around it. We call an emphasis of this kind an ***accent.*** Skillful, subtle changes of dynamics add spirit and mood to performances. Sometimes these changes are written in the music; often, though, they are not written but are inspired by the performer's feelings about the music.

When notating music, composers have traditionally used Italian words, and their abbreviations, to indicate dynamics. The most common terms are:

Term	Abbreviation	Meaning
pianissimo	*pp*	very soft
piano	*p*	soft
mezzo piano	*mp*	moderately soft
mezzo forte	*mf*	moderately loud
forte	*f*	loud
fortissimo	*ff*	very loud

For extremes of softness and loudness, composers use ***ppp*** or ***pppp*** and ***fff*** or ***ffff***. The following notations indicate gradual changes in dynamics:

Symbol	Term	Meaning
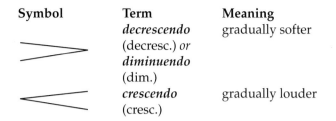	*decrescendo* (decresc.) *or* *diminuendo* (dim.)	gradually softer
	crescendo (cresc.)	gradually louder

Like many elements of music, a dynamic indication is not absolutely precise. A tone has a dynamic level—is soft or loud—in relation to other tones around it. The loudest sound of a single violin is tiny compared with the loudest sound of an entire orchestra, and even tinier compared with an amplified rock group. But it can be considered fortissimo (very loud) within its own context.

Tone Color

We can tell a trumpet from a flute even when they are playing the same tone at the same dynamic level. The quality that distinguishes them—our third property of sound—is called **tone color** or **timbre** (pronounced *tam'-ber*). Tone color is described by words like *bright, dark, brilliant, mellow,* and *rich.*

Changes in tone color create variety and contrast: for example, the same melody will have different expressive effects when it is played by one instrument and then another, or a new tone color may be used to highlight a new melody. Tone color also contributes to continuity; it is easier to recognize the return of a melody if the same instruments play it each time. And specific instruments can reinforce a melody's emotional impact—in fact, composers often invent melodies for particular instruments.

A practically unlimited variety of tone colors is available to composers: instruments (see Section 2) can be combined in various ways, and modern electronic techniques now allow composers to invent entirely new tone colors.

Listening Outlines, Vocal Music Guides, and the Properties of Sound

Reading about pitch, dynamics, and tone color without hearing music is too abstract. To understand and recognize the properties of sound, we must *listen for them.* In this book, listening outlines (for instrumental music) and vocal music guides (for music with vocal texts) will help focus your attention on musical events as they unfold. These outlines and guides must be read *as you listen to the music;* otherwise, their value to you is limited.

In a *listening outline,* each item describes some musical sound. It may point out dynamics, instruments, pitch level, or mood. (Remember, though, that indications of mood in music are subjective. What one person calls "triumphant," for instance, someone else may call "determined.") In a *vocal music guide,* the vocal text appears with brief marginal notes that indicate the relationship between words and music and help the listener follow the thought, story, or drama.

The outlines and guides are preceded by descriptions of the music's main features. Within the guide or outline, CD track numbers appear at the left along with indications of total elapsed time and time within a track. The outlines include instrumentation, notes about our recordings, and the duration of selections in our recordings.

Before you listen to a piece of music, you will find it helpful to glance over the entire listening outline or vocal music guide. Then, while hearing one passage, look ahead to learn what's next. For example, in the listening outline for the second scene of Igor Stravinsky's ballet *The Firebird*, the first item (1a) is "Slow melody in French horn, soft (*p*), quivering string accompaniment." While listening to the music described by item 1a, glance at item 1b: "Violins, soft, melody an octave higher. Flutes join."

Sometimes, not all the instruments playing are listed; instead, only those that are prominent at a given moment are shown. For example, item 2a in the listening outline for *The Firebird* reads "Brasses, very loud (*ff*), melody in quick detached notes, timpani." Although other instruments can be heard, this description focuses attention on the instruments that play the melody.

Following are our first two listening outlines.

The Firebird, Scene 2 (1910), by Igor Stravinsky

Brief Set:
CD 1 [1]

Basic Set:
CD 1 [8]

In the second—and final—scene of the ballet *The Firebird*, Igor Stravinsky (1882–1971) repeats one melody over and over, creating variety and contrast through changes of dynamics, tone color, and rhythm. During this scene, the hero triumphs and becomes engaged to a beautiful princess.

The second scene begins softly but becomes increasingly grand as the music gradually grows louder (crescendo), more instruments play, and the melody is repeated at higher pitches. After this slow buildup to a climax, there's a sudden quiet as all the instruments but the strings stop playing. A quick crescendo then leads to a brilliant concluding section.

Listening Outline to be read while music is heard   Brief Set: CD 1   Basic Set: CD 1

STRAVINSKY, *The Firebird*, Scene 2

Piccolo, 3 flutes, 3 oboes, English horn, 3 clarinets, bass clarinet, 3 bassoons, contrabassoon, 4 French horns, 6 trumpets, tuba, timpani, triangle, cymbals, bass drum, 3 harps, 1st violins, 2d violins, violas, cellos, double basses

(Duration, 3:06)

[1] [8]	0:00		**1. a.**	Slow melody in French horn, soft (*p*), quivering string accompaniment.
	0:29		**b.**	Violins, soft, melody an octave higher. Flutes join.
	0:43		**c.**	Grows louder (crescendo) as more instruments enter.
	1:03		**d.**	Violins and flutes, loud (*f*), melody at even higher octave, crescendo to
	1:17		**e.**	Full orchestra, melody very loud (*ff*), timpani (kettledrums).
	1:34		**f.**	Suddenly very soft (*pp*), strings, quick crescendo to
[2] [9]	1:41	0:00	**2. a.**	Brasses, very loud (*ff*), melody in quick detached notes, timpani.
	2:04	0:23	**b.**	Melody in slower, accented notes, brasses, *ff*, timpani, music gradually slows.
	2:35	0:54	**c.**	High held tone, *ff*, brass chords, extremely loud (*fff*), lead to sudden *pp* and crescendo to extremely loud close.

C-Jam Blues (1942), by Duke Ellington and His Famous Orchestra

Brief Set:
CD 1 ⬚3⬚

Basic Set:
CD 1 ■10■

A succession of different tone colors contributes to the variety within *C-Jam Blues* (1942), as performed by Duke Ellington and His Famous Orchestra. A repeated-note melody is played first by the piano and then by saxophones. Then we hear solos by the violin, cornet, tenor saxophone, trombone, and clarinet. These solos are improvised by the players. Each instrument is first heard alone and then heard with accompaniment. The cornet and trombones are played with mutes, devices inserted into the instrument to alter its sound. *C-Jam Blues* ends climactically when the full band is heard for the first time.

Listening Outline to be read while music is heard

Brief Set: CD 1   Basic Set: CD 1

ELLINGTON, *C-Jam Blues*

Piano (Duke Ellington), violin (Ray Nance), 2 trumpets (Wallace Jones, Ray Nance), cornet (Rex Stewart), 2 trombones (Joe "Tricky Sam" Nanton, Lawrence Brown), valve trombone (Juan Tizol), clarinet (Barney Bigard), 2 alto saxophones (Johnny Hodges, Otto Hardwick), 2 tenor saxophones (Barney Bigard, Ben Webster), baritone saxophone (Harry Carney), guitar (Fred Guy), bass (Junior Raglin), percussion (Sonny Greer)

⬚3⬚	■10■	0:00	1. Piano, repeated-note melody, accompanied by bass, guitar, drums.
⬚4⬚	■11■	0:17	2. Saxophones, repeated-note melody, accompanied by rhythm section (piano, bass, guitar, percussion).
⬚5⬚	■12■	0:33	3. Violin alone, then accompanied by rhythm section.
⬚6⬚	■13■	0:54	4. Muted cornet alone, then accompanied by rhythm section.
⬚7⬚	■14■	1:15	5. Tenor saxophone alone, then accompanied by rhythm section.
⬚8⬚	■15■	1:37	6. Muted trombone alone, then accompanied by rhythm section.
⬚9⬚	■16■	1:59	7. Clarinet alone, then accompanied by band.
⬚10⬚	■17■	2:20	8. Full band.

2 Performing Media: Voices and Instruments

Voices

Throughout history, singing has been the most widespread and familiar way of making music. Singers seem always to have had a magnetic appeal, and the exchange between singer and audience contains a bit of magic—something direct and spellbinding. The singer becomes an instrument with a unique ability to fuse words and musical tones.

For many reasons, it is difficult to sing well. In singing we use wider ranges of pitch and volume than in speaking, hold vowel sounds longer, and need a greater supply and control of breath. Air from the lungs is controlled by the lower abdominal muscles and the diaphragm. The air makes the vocal cords vibrate, and the lungs, throat, mouth, and nose produce the desired sound. The pitch of the tone varies with the tension of the vocal cords; the tighter they are, the higher the pitch.

The range of a singer's *voice* depends on both physical makeup and training. Professional singers can command 2 octaves or even more, whereas an untrained voice is usually limited to about $1\frac{1}{2}$ octaves. Men's vocal cords are longer and thicker than women's, and this difference produces a lower range. The classification of voice ranges for women and men follows, arranged from highest to lowest; the four basic voice ranges are soprano, alto, tenor, and bass:

Women	**Men**
soprano	*tenor*
mezzo-soprano	*baritone*
alto (or contralto)	*bass*

Methods and styles of singing vary from culture to culture, and even within a culture: for instance, in the west, classical, popular, jazz, folk, and rock music are all sung differently.

Until the late 1600s, most of the music of western culture was vocal. Since then, instrumental music has rivaled vocal music in importance; but composers have continued to write vocal works—both solo and choral—with and without instrumental accompaniment (which can range from a single guitar or piano to an entire orchestra).

Musical Instruments

An *instrument* may be defined as any mechanism—other than the voice—that produces musical sounds. Western instruments are usually classified in six broad categories: *string* (such as guitar and violin); *woodwind* (flute, clarinet); *brass* (trumpet, trombone); *percussion* (bass drum, cymbals); *keyboard* (organ, piano); and *electronic* (synthesizer).

An instrument is often made in different sizes that produce different ranges. For instance, there are soprano, alto, tenor, baritone, and bass saxophones. The tone color of a single instrument may vary according to the *register*—the part of its total range—in which it is played. A clarinet, for example, sounds dark and rich in its low register but brilliant and piercing in its high register. Most instruments have a wider range than the voice: many command 3 or 4 octaves, and some have 6 or 7. Instruments also produce tones more rapidly than the voice. When writing for a specific instrument, a composer must consider its range, its dynamics, and how quickly it produces tones.

People around the world use musical instruments that vary greatly in construction and tone color, and instruments have had many functions at different times and in different cultures. They may provide entertainment; they may accompany song, dance, ritual, and drama; they have sometimes been considered sacred or thought to have magical power; they have been used for communication; and they have even been status symbols.

A symphony orchestra.

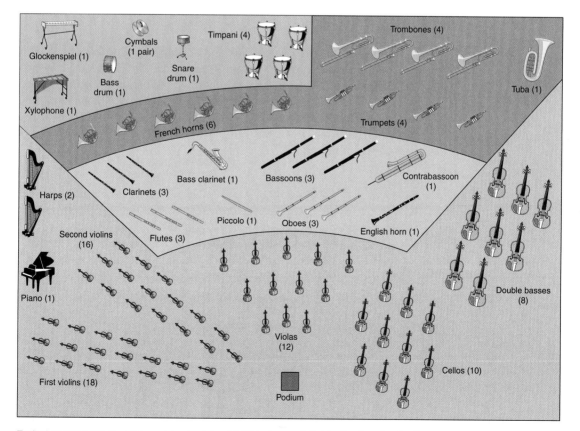

Typical seating plan for a large orchestra (about 100 instrumentalists), showing the distribution of instruments.

Instruments' popularity rises and falls with changing musical tastes and requirements. Today, only a fraction of all known instruments are used; but interest in music of earlier times has led to the resurrection of instruments like the harpsichord (an ancestor of the piano) and the recorder (a relative of the flute). In fact, modern musicians are flexible and far-ranging in their choice of instruments: some classical and rock composers are using nonwestern instruments, and some jazz musicians are turning to classical instruments while classical composers are using instruments associated with jazz.

Compositions are written for solo instruments and combinations of two or more instruments up to orchestras with over 100 musicians. A group may include instruments of only one category (say, strings) or several categories. Modern symphony orchestras have string, woodwind, brass, percussion, and sometimes keyboard instruments (see the illustrations on p. 11); bands consist mainly of brass, woodwind, and percussion instruments.

Orchestras and bands—as well as choruses—are usually led by a *conductor,* who coordinates the performers and shapes the interpretation of a musical composition. Many conductors hold a thin stick called a *baton* in one hand to beat time and indicate pulse and tempo. With the other hand they control the balance among the instruments—or voices—so that the most important musical ideas will be brought out. In an orchestra, the principal first violinist, the *concertmaster,* plays solo violin passages and coordinates the bowing of string instruments.

Instruments commonly used for western music are described in this chapter, by categories. Nonwestern instruments are discussed in Part VII.

String Instruments

The *violin, viola, cello* (*violoncello*), and *double bass* (sometimes called simply a *bass*) form the symphony orchestra's string section. They vary in tone color as well as in size and range: the violin is the smallest and has the highest range; the double bass is the largest and has the lowest range. For symphonic music the strings are usually played with a *bow,* a slightly curved stick strung tightly with horsehair (see the illustration below). Symphonic strings may also be plucked with the finger.

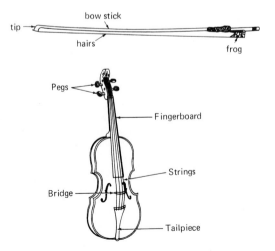

Violin and bow.

Of all the instrumental groups, the strings have the greatest versatility and expressive range. They produce many tone colors and have wide ranges of pitch and dynamics. String players can produce tones that are brilliant and rapid or slow and throbbing; they can control tone as subtly as a singer. Orchestral works tend to rely more on the strings than on any other group. Even with their differing tone colors, the four string instruments blend beautifully. Here it will be helpful to consider the construction and tone production of the string instruments; in this regard, the violin can represent the entire family.

The hollow wooden body of the violin supports four strings made of gut or wire. The strings stretch, under tension, from a *tailpiece* on one end over a wooden *bridge* to the other end, where they are fastened around wooden *pegs*. The bridge holds the strings away from the *fingerboard* so that they can vibrate freely; the bridge also transmits the strings' vibrations to the *body*, which amplifies and colors the tone. Each string is tuned to a different pitch by tightening or loosening the pegs. (The greater the tension, the higher the pitch.)

The musician makes a string vibrate by drawing the bow across it with the right hand. The speed and pressure of the bow stroke control the dynamics and tone color of the sound produced. Pitch is controlled by the musician's left hand. By pressing a string against the fingerboard, the player varies the length of its vibrating portion and so changes its pitch. This is called *stopping* a string (because the vibrations are stopped at a certain point along the string's length). Thus a range of pitches can be drawn from each of the four strings.

Basically the viola, cello, and double bass are made in the same manner as the violin and produce sound by similar means. How the string instruments are played—what string performance techniques are used—determines which of many musical effects they will produce. The techniques used most frequently are listed here.

Pizzicato (plucked string): The musician plucks the string, usually with a finger of the right hand. In jazz, the double bass is typically played mainly as a plucked instrument, rather than being bowed.

Double stop (two notes at once): By drawing the bow across two strings, a string player can sound two notes at once. And by rotating the bow rapidly across three strings *(triple stop)* or four strings *(quadruple stop)*, the player can sound three or four notes almost—though not quite— together.

Vibrato: The string player can produce a throbbing, expressive tone by rocking the left hand while pressing the string down. This causes small pitch fluctuations, which make the tone warmer.

Mute: The musician can veil or muffle the tone by fitting a clamp (mute) onto the bridge.

Tremolo: The musician rapidly repeats tones by quick up-and-down strokes of the bow. This can create a sense of tension, when loud; or a shimmering sound, when soft.

Harmonics: Very high-pitched tones, like a whistle's, are produced when the musician lightly touches certain points on a string.

Although the violin, viola, cello, and double bass are similar, they, like members of any family, also have their differences. The photographs in this section show why each adds something distinctive to the orchestra's total sound.

Strings

The violin is often used as a solo instrument. In the orchestra, the violins are divided into first and second violins, with the first violins frequently playing the main melody. The violinist shown here is Gil Shaham.

The body of the viola is about 2 inches longer than the violin, and thus the viola's range is somewhat lower. Its tone color is darker, thicker, and a little less brilliant than the violin's. The violist here is Nokuthula Ngwenyama.

Although eighteenth-century composers generally used the cello in its bass and baritone registers, later composers exploited its upper registers as well. The cellist shown here is Yo-Yo Ma.

The double bass (or bass) has a very heavy tone and is less agile than other string instruments. Generally played with a bow in symphonic music, in jazz and popular music it is commonly played by plucking the strings as shown here. The bassist is Tarus Mateen.

The harp—with forty-seven strings stretched on a triangular frame—has a wide range of 6 octaves. The harpist plucks the strings with the fingers of both hands.

The guitar has six strings, which are plucked with the fingers or strummed with a plectrum or pick. The frets on the fingerboard mark the places where the strings must be pressed with the fingers of the other hand. John Williams is the guitarist shown here.

Some string instruments are not played with a bow but are plucked instead, either with the fingers or with a *plectrum* (plural, *plectra*)—a small wedge. The most important of these are the *harp* and the *guitar.* The harp is the only plucked string instrument that has gained wide acceptance in the symphony orchestra.

Woodwind Instruments

The woodwind instruments are so named because they were traditionally made of wood. During the twentieth century, however, piccolos and flutes came to be made of metal. The sounds of woodwinds are generated by a vibrating air column in a tube. All the woodwinds have little holes along their length that are opened and closed by the fingers or by pads controlled by a key mechanism. By opening and closing these holes, a woodwind player changes the length of the vibrating air column and so varies the pitch.

The main woodwind instruments of the symphony orchestra are as follows, arranged in four families, in approximate order of range from highest (piccolo) to lowest (contrabassoon). (Only the two most frequently used instruments of each family are listed.)

Flute Family	Clarinet Family	Oboe Family	Bassoon Family
piccolo			
flute	*clarinet*	*oboe*	
		English horn	
	bass clarinet		*bassoon*
			contrabassoon

A woodwind instrument (unlike a string instrument) can produce only one note at a time. In symphonic music, woodwinds are frequently given melodic solos.

Woodwind instruments are great individualists and differ more in tone color than the strings do. Their unique sounds result largely from the way vibrations are produced. The flute and piccolo are played by blowing across the edge of the mouth hole (the *recorder,* a relative of the flute, has a "whistle" mouthpiece); but the rest of the woodwinds have a *reed*—a thin piece of cane that is set vibrating by a stream of air.

In *single-reed woodwinds* (such as the clarinet and the bass clarinet), the reed is fastened over a hole in the mouthpiece and vibrates when the player blows into the instrument. (*Saxophones*—instruments that are used mainly in jazz and music for band—are also single-reed woodwinds.) In *double-reed woodwinds* (oboe, English horn, bassoon, and contrabassoon), two pieces of cane are held between the player's lips. Tone colors differ greatly not only between single-reed and double-reed woodwinds but also among the various registers of each woodwind instrument. In general, low registers of the woodwinds tend to be breathy and thick, and their top registers more penetrating.

Woodwinds

The piccolo—whose name is short for *flauto piccolo,* or small flute—is half the size of the flute and plays an octave higher. The piccolo's high register is shrill and whistlelike.

The flute has a high range and is extremely agile, capable of producing a rapid succession of tones. Its tone is full and velvety in the low register and bright and sparkling at the top. Shown here is the flutist James Galway.

The oboe has a nasal, intense, expressive tone. Because the oboe's pitch is difficult to adjust, the entire orchestra is tuned to its A.

The recorder, like the flute and piccolo, has no reed. The recorder's tone resembles a flute's but is softer and gentler. It is commonly found in five sizes: sopranino, soprano, alto, tenor, and bass.

The English horn is neither English nor a horn, but simply a low, or alto, oboe.

The clarinet can produce tones very rapidly and has a wide range of dynamics and tone color. Pictured here is Benny Goodman.

The tone of the bassoon is deeply nasal.

The bass clarinet is larger than the clarinet and has a much lower range.

The contrabassoon can produce the lowest pitch in the orchestra.

The saxophone has a single-reed mouthpiece like a clarinet, but its tube is made of brass. Its tone is rich, husky, and speechlike. Shown here is the jazz saxophonist Sonny Rollins.

Brass Instruments

From high register to low, the main instruments of the orchestra's brass section are the **trumpet, French horn** (sometimes called simply a *horn*), **trombone,** and **tuba.** Other brasses, such as the *cornet, baritone horn,* and *euphonium,* are used mainly in concert and marching bands.

The brasses are played by blowing into a cup- or funnel-shaped mouthpiece. The vibrations come from the musician's lips and are amplified and colored in a coiled tube that is flared at the end to form a *bell.* Pitch is regulated both by varying lip tension and by using *slides* and *valves* to change the length of the tube (the longer the tube, the lower the pitch); the trombone uses a slide that is pulled in or pushed out, and the trumpet, French horn, and tuba have three or four valves to divert air through various lengths of tubing. (Valves came into use in the mid-nineteenth century, making these instruments much more flexible and allowing them to produce many more tones.) Brass players can alter the tone color of their instruments by inserting a **mute** into the bell. Mutes for brass instruments come in different shapes and are made of wood, plastic, or metal. They are most common in jazz, where they create a variety of effects, including a buzzing sound, a mellowing of the tone, and the comical "wah-wah."

Brasses are powerful instruments, often used at climaxes and for bold, heroic statements. Since the late nineteenth century, they are frequently given rapid solo passages as well. Today, brass instruments are very popular, owing to ensembles such as the Canadian Brass and soloists like the trumpeter Wynton Marsalis.

Brass

The trumpet sounds brilliant, brassy, and penetrating. The trumpeter shown here is Wynton Marsalis.

The French horn has a tone that is less brassy, more mellow, and more rounded than the trumpet's.

The trombone has a tone that combines the brilliance of a trumpet with the mellowness of a French horn.

The thick, heavy tone of the tuba is used to add weight to the lowest register of an orchestra or band.

Percussion Instruments

Most percussion instruments are struck by hand, with sticks, or with hammers, though some are shaken or rubbed. Percussion instruments of *definite pitch* produce tones; those of *indefinite pitch* produce noiselike sounds.

Definite Pitch	Indefinite Pitch
timpani (kettledrums)	*snare drum (side drum)*
glockenspiel	*bass drum*
xylophone	*tambourine*
celesta	*triangle*
chimes	*cymbals*
	gong (tam-tam)

In percussion instruments, vibrations are set up in stretched membranes (like the calfskin or plastic of the kettledrum) or in plates or bars (metal, wooden, etc.). Extremely loud sounds can be made by some percussion instruments like the bass drum or cymbals. In a symphony orchestra, one percussionist may play several different instruments.

Percussion instruments have long been used to emphasize rhythm and to heighten climaxes. But until about 1900, they played a far less important role in western music than strings, woodwinds, or brasses. Twentieth-century composers were more willing to exploit the special colors of the percussion group and occasionally wrote entire pieces to show it off, such as *Ionisation* (1931) by Edgard Varèse. Jazz, rock, and Latin-American musicians have, of course, made good use of percussion instruments. Yet, for all these explorations, western musicians barely approach the incredibly varied use of percussion found in Africa and Asia, where subtle changes of rhythm, tone color, and dynamics are used with great imagination.

Percussion

The timpani (kettledrums) are the only orchestral drums of definite pitch. A calfskin or plastic head is stretched over a hemispherical copper shell. Varying the tension of the head using adjustable screws around the head or a pedal changes the pitch of the timpani. One percussionist generally plays two to four timpani, each tuned to a different pitch.

The xylophone consists of a set of wooden bars that are struck with two hard hammers to produce a dry, wooden tone.

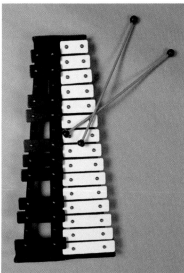

The metal bars of the glockenspiel (orchestral bells) are struck with two hammers to produce a tone that is bright and silvery.

The bass drum—the largest of the orchestral drums—is almost 3 feet in diameter.

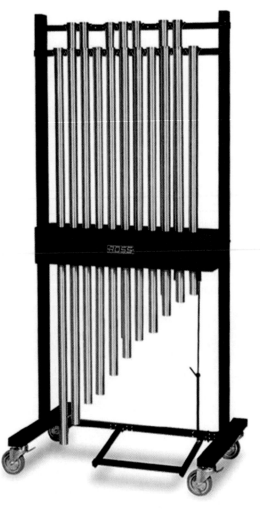

Chimes are a set of metal tubes hung from a frame. They are struck with a hammer and sound like church bells.

The celesta looks like a small upright piano, but its sounding mechanism is like a glockenspiel's. Metal bars are struck by hammers that are controlled by a keyboard. The celesta's tone is tinkling and graceful.

The dry rattling sound of the snare drum (or side drum) is produced by the vibration of snares—strings which are tightly stretched against the bottom head. The snare drum is often used in marches.

The triangle is struck with a metal beater and makes a tinkling, bell-like sound.

When struck by a beater, the gong (or tam-tam) produces long-lasting sounds that can seem solemn, mysterious, or frightening.

The tambourine is often used to create a Spanish or Italian effect. The player shakes it or strikes it with the knuckles.

Cymbals are round brass plates. They usually are struck together with a sliding motion, and their sound penetrates like a sharp crash.

Keyboard Instruments

The piano, harpsichord, organ, and accordion are the best-known keyboard instruments. Though they are quite different from each other, each has a keyboard that allows several tones to be played at once quickly and easily.

The *piano* was invented around 1700 and mechanically perfected by the 1850s. It produces sound through vibrating strings held under tension by an iron frame: striking a key causes a felt-covered hammer to hit a string (the harder the pianist strikes the key, the louder the sound); releasing the key causes a felt damper to come down on the string and end the tone. Pianos have two or three pedals: the *damper pedal* lets the pianist sustain a tone after releasing the key; the *una corda pedal (soft pedal)* veils the sound; the *sostenuto* pedal (which not all pianos have) sustains some tones but not others.

Pianos are exceptionally versatile; the eighty-eight keys span more than 7 octaves, the dynamic range is very broad, and the pianist can play many notes at once, including a melody and its accompaniment. Today, the piano is very popular as a solo instrument, for accompaniments, and in ensembles, including the symphony orchestra.

The *harpsichord* was important from about 1500 to 1775 (when it was gradually replaced by the piano) and was revived in the twentieth century for performance of early music and in some new works. It has strings plucked by small wedges called *plectra,* controlled by one or two keyboards.

The *pipe organ* was most prominent from 1600 to 1750 (when it was known as the "king of instruments") but is still in wide use today, particularly in religious services. It has a very wide range of pitch, dynamics, and tone color. There are several keyboards (including a pedal keyboard) that control valves from which air is blown across or through openings in the pipes; different sets of

Keyboard

The piano is exceptionally versatile. Shown here is the pianist Evgeny Kissin.

The harpsichord has plucked strings controlled by one or two keyboards.

A pipe organ has many sets of pipes controlled from several keyboards and pedals. The organist varies the sound by selecting different combinations of the pipes.

pipes—each with a particular tone color—are brought into play by pulling knobs called *stops;* dynamics are changed by adding or reducing the number of pipes, moving from one keyboard to another, or opening and closing shutters around some of the pipes.

The *accordion* has free steel reeds controlled by a treble keyboard with piano keys (played by the right hand) and a bass keyboard with buttons (played by the left hand). Air from a bellows makes the reeds vibrate.

Electronic Instruments

Electronic instruments produce or amplify sound through electronic means; they were invented as early as 1904 but have had a significant impact on music only since 1950. Today, electronic and computer technologies are developing rapidly, changing continually, and increasingly blending together. Electronic instruments for performing and composing music include amplified instruments, such as the electric piano, organ, and guitar; tape studios; synthesizers; computers; and various "hybrid" technologies.

The *tape studio* was the main tool of composers of electronic music during the 1950s. (In Part VI, we'll study Edgard Varèse's *Poème électronique,* which was created in a tape studio.) The raw material in tape studios consisted of recorded sounds of definite and indefinite pitch which might be electronic or from "real life"—flutes, birdcalls, etc. The composer manipulated these in various ways: by speeding them up or slowing them down, altering their pitch and duration, giving them echoes, filtering them to change tone color, mixing them, and editing the tape (as by cutting and splicing) to play them in any desired order. Rhythm could be fully controlled, because the duration of a sound depended only on the length of a tape segment. However, tape splicing and rerecording were difficult, inaccurate, and time-consuming processes, and many composers of the 1960s turned to synthesizers, which appeared around 1955.

Synthesizers are systems of electronic components that generate, modify, and control sound. They can generate a huge variety of musical sounds and noises, and the composer has complete control over pitch, tone color, loudness, and duration. Most synthesizers can be "played" by means of a keyboard—an addition to the mechanisms of the tape studio.

Synthesizers vary in size and capacity. The mid-1950s saw the invention of the RCA Mark II synthesizer, an enormous (and unique) vacuum-tube synthesizer occupying an entire wall of the Columbia-Princeton Electronic Music Center in

Today's electronic music studios create a wide range of sounds with the use of computers, synthesizers, digital recorders, and a variety of electronic effects and filters.

New York City. During the 1960s and 1970s, smaller, less expensive transistorized synthesizers such as the Moog and Buchla were developed; these were installed in electronic music studios at universities and advertising agencies, played in live rock concerts and concerts of electronic music, and used to create film and television scores. Highly sophisticated synthesizers using computer capabilities have now been developed, and several different technologies are in use.

Analog synthesis—the earliest of the synthesizer technologies, which predominated until about 1980—uses a mixture of complex sounds that are shaped by filtering. Like all analog technology, analog synthesis is based on representing data in terms of measurable physical quantities, in this case sound waves.

Digital frequency modulation (FM) synthesis, invented by John Chowning, was patented by Yamaha and has been associated with Yamaha instruments. Like all digital technology, it is based on representing physical quantities—here, points on sound waves—as numbers.

Effects devices, which include reverberators, echo devices, and stereo splitters, are often integrated into synthesizers and the synthesis process. They are used in almost all recorded music (especially popular music) and in some live music.

Sampling is considered a synthesizer technology, since it involves placing brief digital recordings of live sounds under the control of a synthesizer keyboard; but although the sounds can be modified during playback, no actual synthesis is present. Sampling can be seen as an advanced form of composing by tape splicing: it lets the composer record short segments of sounds (the "samples") digitally and then manipulate them. Sampling has been integrated into relatively inexpensive computer-linked keyboards and is one of the most important aspects of today's electronic music making.

A significant development in synthesizing technology is known as *musical instrument digital interface (MIDI):* this is a standard adopted by manufacturers for interfacing synthesizer equipment. MIDI has allowed the device actually played on to be separated from tone generation; thus there are now keyboards that look, feel, and play like a piano; wind controllers played like a woodwind instrument; and string controllers played like a violin or a cello. Also, control signals can be fed to and from a MIDI instrument into and out of a personal computer, and users can store and edit music and convert to and from musical notation.

Historically, **computers** were the third means of producing sounds on audiotape; they were developed for this purpose after the tape studio and synthesizers. Computers are used both as control devices to drive MIDI equipment and for direct digital synthesis.

The 1970s and 1980s saw the development of small computers with which composers could instantly hear music they programmed; since then, computers have become even more sophisticated. Computers are used for music synthesis (mainly to produce sounds not otherwise obtainable), to help composers write scores (following rules selected by the composer), to store samples of audio signals, to control synthesizing mechanisms, and so on. In **computer music**, some or all of the sounds are generated and manipulated by computer.

Obviously, it is not entirely possible (or particularly useful) to consider modern electronic music devices and processes separately: the distinction between synthesizer technology and computer technology is not clear-cut. To increase the variety of sound and the composer's control over it, today's electronic music studios contain and integrate a wide variety of equipment, including tape recorders, synthesizers, computers, and devices for mixing and filtering sound.

All this equipment enables the composer to exploit the entire spectrum of sound as never before. But the quality of the music produced still depends on the imagination and organizing power of the human mind.

The Young Person's Guide to the Orchestra, Op.* 34 (1946), by Benjamin Britten

Brief Set:
CD 1 [11]

Basic Set:
CD 1 **18**

Benjamin Britten (1913–1976), an English composer, wrote the attractive *Young Person's Guide to the Orchestra* in 1946 as an introduction to the instruments of the orchestra. He used a theme by Henry Purcell, a great English composer of the seventeenth century. (A *theme* is a melody used as the basis for a musical composition.) The majestic theme is first presented by the full orchestra and then by each section of the orchestra in turn: woodwinds, brasses, strings, and percussion. Thirteen *variations,* or varied repetitions of the theme, are then heard. Each highlights a different instrument. Together, they vary in dynamics, speed, and tone color, as well as mood. The variations follow each other without pause and last from about 30 seconds to 1 minute. (Variation 13, however, which features many percussion instruments, lasts almost 2 minutes.) Woodwind, string, and brass instruments are generally presented from highest to lowest in range.

Variation 13 is followed immediately by a concluding section beginning with a lively new tune played by an unaccompanied piccolo. Then other instruments enter, each playing the same tune. After woodwind, string, brass, and percussion instruments have had their turn, the brasses bring back the main theme and provide an exciting ending.

---

*The abbreviation *op.* stands for *opus,* Latin for *work.* An opus number is a way of identifying a piece or set of pieces. Usually, within a composer's output, the higher a composition's opus number, the later it was written.

Listening Outline to be read while music is heard

Brief Set: CD 1   Basic Set: CD 1

BRITTEN, *The Young Person's Guide to the Orchestra*

Piccolo, 2 flutes, 2 oboes, 2 clarinets, 2 bassoons, 4 horns, 2 trumpets, 3 trombones, tuba, timpani, bass drum, snare drum, cymbals, tambourine, triangle, Chinese block, xylophone, castanets, gong, whip, 1st violins, 2d violins, violas, cellos, double basses

(Duration, 17:23)

Theme

[11] **18**	0:00	**a.**	Full orchestra
[12] **19**	0:41	**b.**	Woodwind section

13	20	1:11	**c.** Brass section
14	21	1:42	**d.** String section
15	22	2:07	**e.** Percussion section
16	23	2:26	**f.** Full orchestra

Woodwinds

17	24	3:00	**Variation 1:** Flutes and piccolo
18	25	3:30	**Variation 2:** Oboes
19	26	4:33	**Variation 3:** Clarinets
20	27	5:16	**Variation 4:** Bassoons

Strings

21	28	6:13	**Variation 5:** Violins
22	29	6:58	**Variation 6:** Violas
23	30	7:38	**Variation 7:** Cellos
24	31	8:34	**Variation 8:** Double basses
25	32	9:32	**Variation 9:** Harp

Brasses

26	33	10:23	**Variation 10:** French horns
27	34	11:03	**Variation 11:** Trumpets
28	35	11:38	**Variation 12:** Trombones and tuba

Percussion

29	36	12:39	**Variation 13: a.** Timpani (kettledrums); bass drum and cymbals
30	37	13:06	**b.** Tambourine and triangle; snare drum (side drum) and Chinese block (a hollow wooden block that is struck with a drumstick)
31	38	13:28	**c.** Xylophone
32	39	13:40	**d.** Castanets and gong
33	40	13:49	**e.** Whip (two hinged pieces of wood that are slapped against each other)
34	41	13:54	**f.** Entire percussion section; xylophone and triangle

Concluding section

35	42	14:32	0:00	**a.** Unaccompanied piccolo, lively new tune, tune played in turn by flutes, oboes, clarinets, and bassoons, crescendo.
		15:42	1:10	**b.** Lively tune played in turn by 1st violins, *p*; 2d violins, violas, cellos, double basses, woodwinds accompany, crescendo; quick decrescendo introduces
		16:11	1:39	**c.** Harp, lively tune, crescendo in strings and woodwinds.
		16:22	1:50	**d.** Lively tune played in turn by French horns, *ff*, trumpets, trombones and tuba, orchestra accompanies.
		16:41	2:09	**e.** Percussion, *f*, accompanied by orchestra, *p*, crescendo to
		16:50	2:18	**f.** Main theme in brasses, *ff*, together with lively tune in high woodwinds and strings. Full orchestra, percussion, long-held closing chord, *fff*.

Rhythm

Rhythm is basic to life. We see it in the cycle of day and night, the four seasons, the rise and fall of tides. More personally, we find it in our heartbeats, and we feel it when we breathe and walk. The essence of rhythm is a recurring pattern of tension and release, or expectation and fulfillment. This rhythmic alternation seems to pervade the flow of time. Time, as we live it, has fantastic diversity; each hour has 60 minutes, but how different one hour may seem from another!

Rhythm is the lifeblood of music, too. In its widest sense, ***rhythm*** is the flow of music through time. Rhythm has several interrelated aspects, which we'll consider in turn: beat, meter, accent and syncopation, and tempo.

Beat

When you clap your hands or tap your foot to music, you are responding to its beat. ***Beat*** is a regular, recurrent pulsation that divides music into equal units of time. Beats can be represented by marks on a time line (see the illustration). In music, such beats occur as often as every $\frac{1}{4}$ second or as seldom as every $1\frac{1}{2}$ seconds. Sometimes the beat is powerful and easy to feel, as in marches or rock music. Or it may be barely noticeable, suggesting floating or aimlessness.

Beats

Time

Beats can be shown as a series of marks on a time line.

The pulse of music is communicated in different ways. Sometimes the beat is explicitly pounded out—by a bass drum in a marching band, for instance. At other times, however, the beat is sensed rather than actually heard.

Sing the beginning of the song *America* up to the words *Land where my fathers died:*

My	coun-	try	'tis		of	thee,	Sweet	land	of	lib-		er-	ty,
|	|	|	|		|		|	|	|	|	|		|

Of	thee	I	sing.			Land (etc.)
|	|	|	|	|	|	|

Each of the marks represents a beat. Did you notice that you automatically held *sing* for 3 beats? You *sensed* the beat because you were aware of it and expected it to continue.

Beats form the background against which the composer places notes of varying length, and they are the basic unit of time by which all notes are measured. Notes last a fraction of a beat, or an entire beat, or more than a beat. In the example from *America,* the syllables, or notes, range from $\frac{1}{2}$ beat for *of* to 3 beats for *sing.*

Combinations of different note lengths create rhythm. Earlier, **rhythm** was defined as the flow of music through time; more specifically, it can be defined as the particular arrangement of note lengths in a piece of music. Rhythm is an essential feature of a melody's "personality." Indeed, we might be able to recognize *America* merely by clapping out its rhythm without actually singing the tones. The *beat* of *America* is an even, regular pulsation. But its *rhythm* flows freely, sometimes matching the beat, sometimes not.

Meter

In music, some beats feel stronger or more stressed—that is, more emphasized— than others, and we find repeated patterns of a strong beat plus one or more weaker beats. The organization of beats into regular groups is called **meter.** A group containing a fixed number of beats is called a **measure.** The first, or stressed, beat of the measure is called the **downbeat.** There are several types of meter, based on the number of beats in a measure.

When a measure has 2 beats, it is said to be in **duple meter;** we count **1**–2, **1**–2, etc., as in the following example (the vertical lines indicate the measures):

Ma- ry	had a	lit- tle	lamb,	lit- tle	lamb,	lit- tle	lamb
1	2	|**1**	2	|**1**	2	|**1**	2 |

A pattern of 3 beats to the measure is known as **triple meter;** we count **1**–2–3, **1**–2–3, etc. *America* is in triple meter:

My	coun-	try,	'tis		of	thee,	
1	2	3	| **1**	2		3 |	
Sweet	land	of	lib-		er-	ty,	
1	2	3	| **1**	2		3 |	
Of	thee	|	sing.				
1	2	3	| **1**	2		3 |	

Quadruple meter has 4 beats to the measure. As usual, the downbeat is strongest, but there is another, slighter stress on the third beat; we count **1**–2–*3*–4, **1**–2–*3*–4, etc. In the following example, the first word is on the **upbeat,** an unaccented pulse preceding the downbeat:

Mine eyes have seen the glo- ry	of the	com- ing	of	the	Lord;	He is
|**1**	2	*3*	4	| **1**	2	*3*	4 |

Sextuple meter has 6 rather quick beats to the measure. The downbeat is strongest, but the fourth beat also has a stress; we count **1**–2–3–*4*–5–6. Actually, the measure is subdivided into two 3-beat groups, **1**–2–3/*4*–5–6, so that sextuple meter is a combination of duple and triple meter. For example:

Oh,	give	me	a	home	where the buf-	fa- lo	roam,	where the
| **1**	2	3	*4*	5	6	|**1**	2	3	*4*	5	6	|

Quintuple meter (5 beats to the measure) and *septuple meter* (7 beats to the measure) also combine duple and triple meter. In quintuple meter, for example, the measure is subdivided into 2- and 3-beat groups: **1**–2–**3**/**4**–5 or **1**–2/**3**–4–5. These meters occur frequently in twentieth-century music but only occasionally in earlier music.

Accent and Syncopation

An important aspect of rhythm is how individual notes are stressed. One way to emphasize a note is by giving it a dynamic **accent,** that is, by playing it more loudly than the notes around it. A note can also be emphasized by being held longer or being higher in pitch than nearby notes.

When an accented note comes where we would normally not expect it, the effect is known as **syncopation.** A syncopation occurs when an "off-beat" note is accented (that is, when the stress comes *between* beats). In the following example, syncopation occurs on the accented *my,* which comes between beats 1 and 2:

Give	**my**	re-	gards	to	Broad-		way	
1	2	3	4	|1	2	3	4	|

A syncopation also occurs when a weak beat is accented (as in 1–**2**–3–4 and 1–2–3–**4**). It creates rhythmic excitement and is one of the most characteristic features of jazz.

Tempo

Tempo—the speed of the beat—is the basic pace of the music. We associate fast tempos with energy, drive, and excitement, and slow tempos with solemnity, lyricism, or calmness.

A *tempo indication* is usually given at the beginning of a piece. As with dynamics, the terms that show tempo are usually in Italian:

Term	Meaning
largo	very slow, broad
grave	very slow, solemn
adagio	slow
andante	moderately slow, a walking pace
moderato	moderate
allegretto	moderately fast
allegro	fast
vivace	lively
presto	very fast
prestissimo	as fast as possible

Tempo indications are often made more specific by qualifiers, such as *molto (much)* and *non troppo (not too much):* thus *allegro molto* means *very fast* and *allegro non troppo* means *not too fast.* The same tempo is not always used throughout a piece. Gradual speeding up may be indicated by **accelerando** *(becoming faster),* and slowing down by **ritardando** *(becoming slower).*

All these terms (again, like dynamics) are relative and approximate; different performers interpret them differently, and there is no one "right" tempo for a piece. This is true even though, since about 1816, composers have been able to indicate tempo by a metronome setting. A *metronome* is a device that ticks or flashes a light at any desired musical speed, and a metronome setting indicates the exact number of beats per minute.

Music Notation

We use written words to express our thoughts and communicate with others when we cannot be with them. In music, ideas are also written down, or *notated*, so that performers can play pieces unknown to them. **Notation** is a system of writing music so that specific pitches and rhythms can be communicated. It is explained here—very briefly—primarily to help you recognize rising and falling melodic lines and long and short notes so that you can follow the music examples in this book. (You will find it helpful to review the material on pitch in Section 1, and rhythm in Section 3.)

Notating Pitch

With music notation, we can indicate exact pitches by the upward or downward placement of symbols—called *notes*—on a *staff*. A **note** is an oval. (Its duration is indicated by whether it is black or white or has a *stem* and *flags*, as will be explained later, under "Notating Rhythm.") A **staff** (plural, *staves*) is a set of five horizontal lines. Notes are positioned either on the lines of the staff or between them, in the spaces; the higher a note is placed on the staff, the higher its pitch:

If a pitch falls above or below the range indicated by the staff, short, horizontal *ledger lines* are used:

Seven of the twelve pitches (tones) that fill the octave in western music are named after the first seven letters of the alphabet: A, B, C, D, E, F, G. This sequence is repeated over and over to represent the "same" tones in higher and lower octaves, and it corresponds to the white keys of the piano. The other five tones of the octave correspond to the black keys of the piano and are indicated by one of the same seven letters plus a *sharp sign* (♯) or a *flat sign* (♭) (see the illustration on page 34). Thus the pitch between C and D may be called C sharp (C♯; higher than C) or D flat (D♭; lower than D). A *natural sign* (♮) is used to cancel a previous sharp or flat sign.

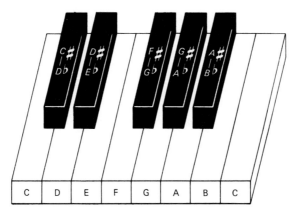

The twelve pitches of the octave and their positions on the piano keyboard.

A *clef* is placed at the beginning of the staff to show the pitch of each line and space. The two most common clefs are the *treble clef,* used for relatively high ranges (such as those played by a pianist's right hand), and the *bass clef,* used for relatively low ranges (played by the pianist's left hand):

Treble Clef

Bass Clef

Keyboard music calls for a wide range of pitches to be played by both hands; for such music, the *grand staff*—a combination of the treble and bass staves—is used. The following illustration shows how the notes on the grand staff are related to the piano keyboard. Note that the C nearest to the middle of the keyboard is called *middle C.*

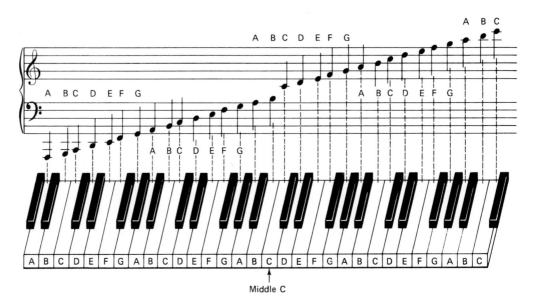

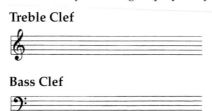

Notes on the grand staff and their positions on the piano keyboard.

Notating Rhythm

Music notation does not indicate the exact duration of tones; instead, it shows how long one tone lasts in relation to the others in the same piece. A single note on the staff lasts longer or shorter depending on how it looks—on whether it is white or black and has a *stem* or *flags.*

The chart below shows the relationships of the duration symbols:

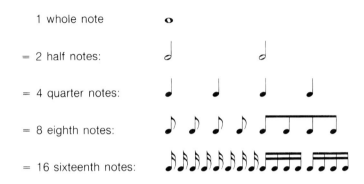

One whole note lasts as long as 2 half notes or 4 quarter notes, and so on. As shown, the flags of several eighth notes or sixteenth notes in succession are usually joined by a horizontal *beam.*

To lengthen the duration of a tone (and add rhythmic variety), we can make it a *dotted note;* adding a dot (·) to the right of a note increases its duration by half. Thus, 1 quarter note ordinarily equals 2 eighth notes, but 1 dotted quarter note equals 3 eighth notes:

Frequently, a dotted note is followed by a note that is much shorter; this long-short pattern, called *dotted rhythm,* strongly emphasizes the beat (and is therefore often used in marches).

A *tie* (⌢) is another way to lengthen the duration of a note. When two notes in a row are the same pitch and are connected by a tie, the first note is lengthened by the duration of the second. In the following example, the tone on *dell* lasts as long as 1 dotted quarter note plus 1 quarter note; the two tied notes become one continuous sound:

We can also add rhythmic variety by shortening the duration of a note. One method is the *triplet,* three notes of equal duration notated as a group within a curved line and the number 3. Such a group lasts only as long as if it were two notes of equal value:

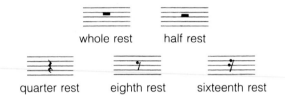

Notating Silence (Rests)

Duration of silence is notated by using a symbol called a *rest.* Rests are pauses; their durations correspond to those of notes:

whole rest   half rest

quarter rest   eighth rest   sixteenth rest

Notating Meter

A *time signature* (or *meter signature*) shows the meter of a piece. It appears at the beginning of the staff at the start of a piece (and again later if the meter changes) and consists of two numbers, one on top of the other. The upper number tells how many beats fall in a measure; the lower number tells what kind of note gets the beat (2 = a half note, for instance, and 4 = a quarter note). Thus a $\frac{2}{4}$ time signature shows that there are 2 beats to the measure (duple meter) and a quarter note gets 1 beat. Duple meter may also be shown as $\frac{2}{2}$ (or by its symbol, ¢); quadruple meter is usually $\frac{4}{4}$ (or c). The most common triple meter is $\frac{3}{4}$.

The Score

An orchestral *score* shows the music for each instrumental or vocal category in a performing group; often, a score will show more than twenty different staves of notation (see the illustration on the next page).

A page from the orchestra score of Tchaikovsky's *Romeo and Juliet*.

Melody

For many of us, music means melody. Though it is easier to recognize than define, we do know that a *melody* is a series of single notes that add up to a recognizable whole. A melody begins, moves, and ends; it has direction, shape, and continuity. The up-and-down movement of its pitches conveys tension and release, expectation and arrival. This is the melodic curve, or line.

As you get further into the music explored in this book, you'll find a wealth of melodies: vocal and instrumental, long and short, simple and complex. This section will help you sort them out by introducing some terms and basic melodic principles.

A melody moves by small intervals called *steps* or larger ones called *leaps*. A **step** is the interval between two adjacent tones in the *do-re-mi* scale (from *do* to *re*, *re* to *mi*, etc.). Any interval larger than a step is a **leap** (*do* to *mi*, for example). Besides moving up or down by a step or leap, a melody may simply repeat the same note. A melody's range—the distance between its lowest and highest tones—may be wide or narrow; melodies written for instruments tend to have a wider range than those for voices, and they frequently have wide leaps and rapid notes that would be difficult to sing. Often the highest tone of a melody will be the **climax**, or emotional focal point.

Note durations as well as pitches contribute to the distinctive character of a melody, and the specific order of long and short notes is important. A well-known melody can be almost unrecognizable if it is not sung or played in proper rhythm.

How the tones are performed can also vary the effect of a melody: they may be sung or played in a smooth, connected style called **legato** or in a short, detached style called **staccato.**

Many melodies are made up of shorter parts called **phrases.** Phrases may have similar pitch and rhythm patterns that help unify the melody, or they may contrast, furnishing variety. They often appear in balanced pairs (a phrase of rising pitches, say, followed by one of falling pitches). In analyzing music, letters are customarily used to represent sections of a piece: lowercase letters (a, b, etc.) for phrases and other relatively short sections, and capital letters (A, B, etc.) for longer sections. If two sections, such as phrases, differ significantly, we use different letters: a b. If one exactly repeats another, the letter is repeated: a a. If one section is a varied repetition of a previous section, the repeated letter has a prime mark: a a'. A repetition of a melodic pattern at a higher or lower pitch is called a **sequence.**

A resting place at the end of a phrase—a point of arrival—is called a **cadence;** it may be partial, setting up expectations (an **incomplete cadence**), or it may give a sense of finality (a **complete cadence**).

Now let's consider some examples of familiar melodies, starting with *Row, Row, Row Your Boat* (a b):

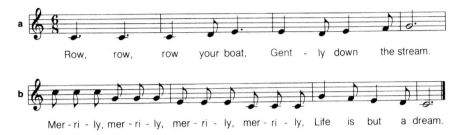

Sing it only up to the word *stream*. Notice that on *stream* the melody comes to a resting place, which ends the first phrase (a); but it seems incomplete, as though it had posed a question. Now sing the rest—the second phrase (b), beginning on *merrily*—and notice how it ends conclusively and seems to answer the question. Thus the first phrase ends with an incomplete cadence and the second with a complete cadence. Each phrase is the same length, a formula typical of many melodies called *tunes;* the two phrases create a feeling of symmetry and balance, one beginning with repeated notes and then moving upward by step, the second moving downward by leap and then by step. The climax comes on the first *merrily*.

Next, sing the nursery tune *Mary Had a Little Lamb* (a a'):

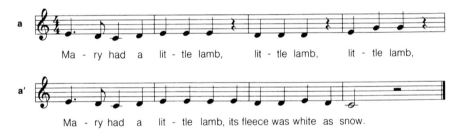

It also has two balancing phrases, the first phrase (a) ending with an incomplete cadence and the second with a complete cadence. But here the second phrase (a') begins exactly like the first before proceeding to a different, more conclusive ending. Melodic repetition, both exact and (as here) varied, plays an important unifying role in music.

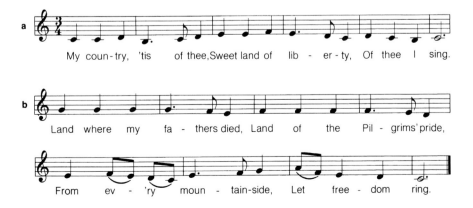

The singer-songwriter Avril Lavigne blends melody and harmony by accompanying herself on the guitar.

Our final example, *America* (a b), has phrases that are *not* of equal length: the second phrase (starting from *Land*) is longer than the first and creates a feeling of continuation rather than balance or symmetry. An interesting aspect of *America* is the way a repeated rhythmic pattern (for *My country, 'tis of thee, Sweet land of liberty, Land where my fathers died,* and *Land of the Pilgrims' pride*) unifies the melody. *America* also contains a sequence: the melody for *Land of the Pilgrims' pride* is simply a repetition a little lower of the preceding *Land where my fathers died.*

These three melodies are complete in themselves. Frequently, however, a melody will serve as a starting point for a more extended piece of music and, in stretching out, will go through all kinds of changes. This kind of melody is called a ***theme***.

Harmony

When folksingers accompany themselves on a guitar, they add support, depth, and richness to the melody; we call this *harmonizing*. Most music in western culture is a blend of melody and harmony (much nonwestern music, on the other hand, emphasizes melody and rhythm rather than harmony).

Harmony refers to the way chords are constructed and how they follow each other. A **chord** is a combination of three or more tones sounded at once. Essentially, a chord is a group of simultaneous tones, and a melody is a series of individual tones heard one after another. As a melody unfolds, it gives clues for harmonizing, but it does not always dictate a specific series—or *progression*—of chords; a melody may be harmonized in several musically convincing ways. Chord progressions enrich a melody by adding emphasis, surprise, suspense, or finality. New chords and progressions continually enter the language of music, but the basic chordal vocabulary has remained fairly constant. We'll look now at a few principles of harmony.

Consonance and Dissonance

Some chords are considered stable and restful, others unstable and tense. A stable tone combination is a **consonance;** consonances are points of arrival, rest, and resolution. An unstable tone combination is a **dissonance;** its tension demands an onward motion to a stable chord. Thus dissonant chords are "active"; traditionally, they have been considered harsh and have expressed pain, grief, and conflict. A dissonance has its **resolution** when it moves to a consonance. When a resolution is delayed or is accomplished in surprising ways—when the composer plays with our sense of expectation—a feeling of drama or suspense is created.

Consonance and dissonance exist in varying degrees; some consonant chords are more stable than others, and some dissonant chords are tenser than others. Also, dissonance has come to be used more and more freely over the centuries, so that a chord considered intolerably harsh at one time may later come to seem mild.

The Triad

A great variety of chords are used in music. Some consist of three different tones; others have four, five, or even more. The simplest, most basic chord is the **triad** (pronounced *try'-ad*), which has three tones; to indicate that the three tones are played at one time, it is notated:

A triad is made up of alternate tones of the scale, such as the first *(do)*, third *(mi)*, and fifth *(sol)*. The bottom tone is called the *root;* the others are a third and a fifth

Roger Kamien, Pianist, Playing Chopin's Prelude in E Minor

Without a performer, music would remain soundless on a page. Unlike books and paintings, music speaks to us through a re-creator, a musician who makes the printed notes sound. A composition, even a familiar one, can be a new experience each time it's performed.

It's the job of the performer to bring life to the printed symbols laid out by the composer. Just how loud is a chord marked *f*? How fast is a section labeled *allegro*? No matter how many specific indications of pitch, rhythm, or dynamics appear on a page, much has to be decided by the performer. Like actors, performers mold their interpretations through subtle timings and inflections.

To illustrate the role of the performer, I would like to share with you some of the decisions involved in my performance of Chopin's Prelude in E Minor, Op. 28, No. 4, included in the CD Sets (see the discussion and listening outline on pages 43–44). For me, the Prelude in E Minor is an emotional journey from the profound grief of the beginning, through a climactic outburst of despair, to a final acceptance of death. My tempo is very slow (largo), as Chopin indicates, but not excessively so. To emphasize the changes in color of the long notes in the melody, which return obsessively, I play each one at a slightly different dynamic level. In the pulsating accompanying chords, I stress the dissonant tones, either by subtly lengthening them, or by playing them a little louder than the consonant tones. To intensify the climax that grows out of the return of the opening melody, I momentarily quicken the tempo, as Chopin indicates. Toward the end of the Prelude, I give extra time to the pause following the questioning dissonant chord, thus heightening expectancy before the final low cadence.

You may find it interesting to compare my recorded performance of Chopin's Prelude in E Minor with those by two other pianists. How do the three performances differ in expression, tempo, dynamic range, and relationship between melody and accompaniment? All three pianists have played the same notes, and yet they have made three different statements. That is what *molding an interpretation* means.

above the root. (From *do* to *mi* in the scale is an interval of a third; from *do* to *sol* is the interval of a fifth.)

A triad built on the first, or tonic, note of the scale *(do)* is called the **tonic chord** *(do-mi-sol)*; it is the main chord of a piece, the most stable and conclusive, and traditionally would begin and end a composition. Next in importance is the triad built on the fifth note of the scale *(sol)*, the **dominant chord** *(sol-ti-re)*. The dominant chord is pulled strongly toward the tonic chord—it sets up tension that is resolved by the tonic, and the progression from dominant to tonic gives a strong sense of conclusion. This has great importance in music. The progression from the dominant to the tonic chord (often used at the end of a phrase, a melody, or an entire piece) is called a **cadence.** (As noted in Section 5, this term also means a resting point at the end of a phrase.)

Broken Chords (Arpeggios)

When the individual tones of a chord are sounded one after another, it is called a **broken chord,** or **arpeggio.** *The Star-Spangled Banner* begins with a broken chord:

In this example, the notes of the tonic chord are heard in succession rather than together.

Throughout this book, the importance of harmony will be more and more apparent. It helps give music variety and movement; and its effects are endless, varying with the style of a particular era and the desires of individual composers.

Prelude in E Minor for Piano, Op. 28, No. 4 (1839), by Frédéric Chopin

Brief Set:

CD 1 36

Basic Set:

CD 1 52

Chopin's harmony makes a vital contribution to the brooding quality of this miniature lasting around 2 minutes. Without the pulsating chords of its accompaniment, the melody might seem aimless and monotonous. It hardly moves, alternating obsessively between a long note and a shorter one right above it. But the returning long note seems to change in color, because each time there is a different dissonant chord below it. The dissonant chords underscore the melancholy of this prelude, which is meant to be played *espressivo* (*expressively*).

In the middle of the prelude, a return of the opening melody leads to a brief but passionate climax with a crescendo, faster rhythm, and an acceleration of tempo (accelerando). The agitation rapidly subsides as we again hear returning long notes in the melody. Toward the end of the piece, a mildly dissonant chord is followed by a brief pause. This silence is filled with expectancy, as we wait for the dissonance to resolve. Finally the tension is released in the three solemn chords of the closing cadence.

Listening Outline to be read while music is heard

Brief Set: CD 1   Basic Set: CD 1

CHOPIN, Prelude in E Minor for Piano

Largo, Duple meter ($\frac{2}{2}$), E minor

Piano

(Duration, 2:16)

| 36 | 52 | 0:00 | **1.** Sad melody with obsessively returning long notes, accompanied by pulsating dissonant chords, *p*, |

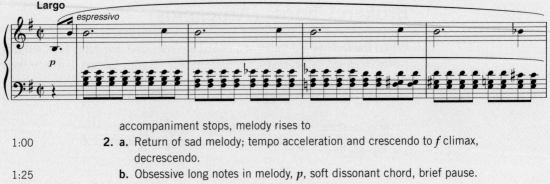

accompaniment stops, melody rises to

1:00   **2. a.** Return of sad melody; tempo acceleration and crescendo to *f* climax, decrescendo.

1:25   **b.** Obsessive long notes in melody, *p*, soft dissonant chord, brief pause.

1:56   **c.** Final cadence of three low chords.

7 Key

Almost all familiar melodies are built around a central tone toward which the other tones gravitate and on which the melody usually ends. To feel this gravitational pull (which is rooted in cultural conditioning), sing *America* (page 39), pausing for a few seconds between *freedom* and *ring;* you will probably feel uneasy until you supply the last tone. This central tone is the **keynote,** or **tonic.** A keynote can be any of the twelve tones of the octave; when, for example, a piece is in the key of C, the tonic or keynote is C.

Key involves not only the central tone but also a central chord and scale. *Chord* was defined in Section 6 above; the basic chord of a piece in C is a tonic triad with C as its root, or bottom tone. A *scale* is made up of the basic pitches of a piece of music arranged in order from low to high or high to low. A piece in the key of C has a basic scale, *do-re-mi-fa-sol-la-ti-do,* with C as its *do,* or tonic. Key, then, refers to the presence of a central note, scale, and chord within a piece, and all the other tones are heard in relationship to them. Another term for key is **tonality.** After 1900, some composers abandoned tonality; but even today much of the music we hear is tonal.

The Major Scale

The basic scales of western music from the late 1600s to 1900 were the *major* and *minor,* and they continue to be widely used today.

The *major scale*—the familiar *do-re-mi*, etc.—has two kinds of intervals in a specific pattern: the *half step,* the smallest interval traditionally used in western music; and the *whole step,* twice as large as the half step. The illustrations show the pattern of whole and half steps in the major scale and a major scale with C as the beginning tone.

Pattern of whole and half steps making up the major scale.

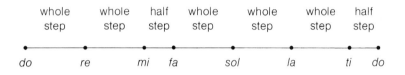

The C major scale uses only the white keys of the piano (the half steps come between E and F and between B and C, which are not separated by black keys). We can construct similar major scales by starting the same pattern of intervals on any of the twelve tones of the octave (thus there are twelve possible major scales); the other major scales use one or more black keys of the piano, but the pattern sounds the same.

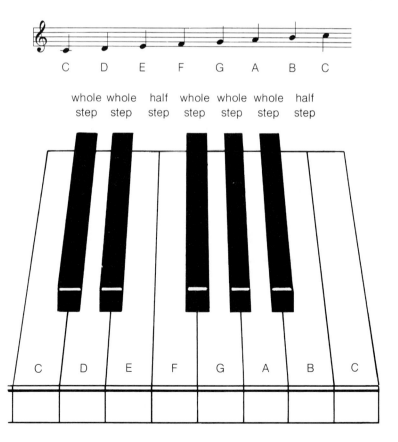

Major scale beginning on C.

The Minor Scale

Along with the major scale, the minor scale is fundamental to western music. The *minor scale*—like the major—consists of seven different tones and an eighth tone that duplicates the first an octave higher, but it differs from the major scale in its pattern of intervals, or whole and half steps. Since (again, like the major) it can begin on any of the twelve tones of the octave, there are twelve possible minor scales. Here is a comparison between a major and a minor scale both starting on C.*

C Major Scale

whole step		whole step		half step		whole step		whole step		whole step		half step	
C		D		E	F		G		A		B	C	

C Minor Scale

whole step		half step		whole step		whole step		half step		whole step		whole step	
C		D	E♭		F		G	A♭		B♭			C	

The crucial difference is that in the minor scale there is only a half step between the second and third tones; this greatly changes the sound of the scale and the mood of music using it. Music based on minor scales tends to sound serious or melancholy; also, the tonic triad built from a minor scale is a minor chord, which sounds darker than a major chord.

Joshua Fought the Battle of Jericho is a tune based on a minor scale:

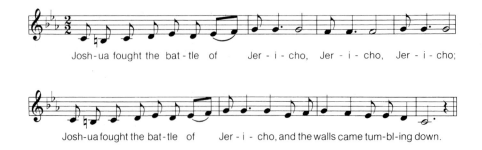

Josh-ua fought the bat-tle of Jer - i - cho, Jer - i - cho, Jer - i - cho;

Josh-ua fought the bat-tle of Jer - i - cho, and the walls came tum-bl-ing down.

---

*The minor scale shown in the example is the *natural minor,* one of three minor scales. The other two kinds are the *harmonic minor* and the *melodic minor* scales. The three types of minor scales have slight variations in their patterns of intervals, but all can begin on any tone of the octave, and all will produce a sound that contrasts with the major scale as described here.

The Key Signature

When a piece of music is based on a major scale, we say that it is in a **major key;** when it is based on a minor scale, it is said to be in a **minor key.** Thus a piece based on (for example) a major scale with D as its keynote is in the key of D major; a piece based on a minor scale with the keynote F is in the key of F minor. Each major and minor scale has a specific number of sharps or flats, from none to seven; and to indicate the key of a piece, a **key signature**—consisting of sharp and flat signs following the clef at the beginning of the staff—is used. To illustrate, here is the key signature for D major, which contains two sharps:

Key signatures make it unnecessary to put a sharp or flat sign before every sharped or flatted note in the piece.

The Chromatic Scale

The twelve tones of the octave—*all* the black and white keys in one octave on the piano—form the **chromatic scale.** The tones of the chromatic scale (unlike those of the major or minor scale) are all the same distance apart, one half step:

The word *chromatic* comes from the Greek *chroma, color;* and the traditional function of the chromatic scale is to color or embellish the tones of the major and minor scales. The chromatic scale does not define a key, but it gives a sense of motion and tension. It has long been used to evoke grief, loss, or sorrow. In the twentieth century the chromatic scale became independent of major and minor scales and was used as the basis for entire compositions.

Modulation: Change of Key

Most short melodies remain in one key from start to end; but in longer pieces, variety and contrast are created by using more than one key. A shift from one key to another within the same piece is called a **modulation.**

A modulation is like a temporary shift in the center of gravity—it brings a new central tone, chord, and scale. Though modulations are sometimes subtle and difficult to hear, they produce subconscious effects that increase our enjoyment.

Tonic Key

No matter how often a piece changes key, there is usually one main key, called the *tonic* or *home key.* The tonic key is the central key around which the whole piece is organized. Traditionally, a piece would usually begin in the home key and practically always end in it. A composition in the key of C major, for example, would begin in the home key (C major), modulate to several other keys—say, G major and A minor—and finally conclude in the home key of C major. The other keys are subordinate to the tonic.

Modulating away from the tonic key is like visiting: we may enjoy ourselves during the visit, but after a while we're glad to go home. In music, modulations set up tension that is resolved by returning to the home key. For centuries, the idea of a central key was a basic principle of music. But after 1900, some composers wrote music that ignored the traditional system. The results of this revolutionary step are explored in Part VI, The Twentieth Century and Beyond.

Musical Texture

At any moment within a piece, we may hear one unaccompanied melody, several melodies, or one melody with harmony. The term *musical texture* describes these possibilities; it refers to how many different layers of sound are heard at once, whether they are melody or harmony, and how they are related to each other. Texture is described as transparent, dense, thin, thick, heavy, or light; and variations in texture create contrast and drama. We'll now look at three basic textures: *monophonic, polyphonic, and homophonic.*

Monophonic Texture

The texture of a single unaccompanied melodic line is *monophonic,* meaning literally *one sound.* If you sing alone, you make monophonic music. Performance of a single melodic line by more than one instrument or voice is playing or singing in *unison* and results in a fuller, richer-sounding monophonic texture.

Polyphonic Texture

Simultaneous performance of two or more melodic lines of relatively equal interest produces *polyphonic (many-sounding)* texture. In polyphony several melodic lines compete for attention, adding a dimension that has been compared to perspective in painting: each line enriches the others. The technique of combining several melodic lines into a meaningful whole is called ***counterpoint*** (and the term *contrapuntal texture* is sometimes used in place of *polyphonic texture*). To fully enjoy polyphony, you may have to hear a piece several times; it's often helpful to listen first for the top line, then for the bottom line, and then for the middle lines.

Polyphonic music often contains ***imitation,*** which occurs when a melodic idea is presented by one voice or instrument and then restated immediately by another. A *round*—a song in which several people sing the same melody but each starts at a different time—uses imitation; *Row, Row, Row Your Boat* is a familiar example:

Here, the imitation is "strict": each voice sings exactly the same melody. But in polyphonic texture imitation is often freer, with the imitating line starting like the first one but then going off on its own.

Homophonic Texture

When we hear one main melody accompanied by chords, the texture is ***homophonic.*** Attention is focused on the melody, which is supported and colored by sounds of subordinate interest. When harmonized by chords, *Row, Row, Row Your Boat* is an example of homophonic texture:

Accompaniments in homophonic music vary widely in character and importance, from subdued background chords to surging sounds that almost hide the main melody. When a subordinate line asserts its individuality and competes for the listener's attention, the texture is probably best described as being between homophonic and polyphonic.

Changes of Texture

Changing textures within a composition creates variety and contrast, as was noted above. A composer may, for instance, begin with a melody and a simple accompaniment and later weave the melody into a polyphonic web—or contrast a single voice with massive chords sung by a chorus. *Farandole* by Georges Bizet (1839–1875), from *L'Arlésienne* Suite No. 2, is a good example of textural variety.

Farandole from *L'Arlésienne* Suite No. 2 (1879), by Georges Bizet*

Brief Set:
CD 1 37

Basic Set:
CD 1 53

The *Farandole* comes from music by Georges Bizet (1838–1875) for the play *L'Arlésienne (The Woman from Arles)*, set in southern France. Two contrasting themes are heard in this exciting orchestral piece. The first, in minor, is a march

---

*L'Arlésienne Suites No. 1 and No. 2 are sets of pieces from the theater music composed by Bizet. Suite No. 2 was arranged by Bizet's friend Ernest Guiraud in 1879, after the composer's death.

theme adapted from a southern French folk song. The lively second theme, in major, has the character of the *farandole*, a southern French dance.

Many changes of texture contribute to the *Farandole's* exciting mood. The piece contains two kinds of homophonic texture: in one, the accompaniment and melody have the same rhythm; in the other, the rhythm of the accompaniment differs from that of the melody. The *Farandole* opens with the march theme and its accompaniment in the same rhythm. But when the lively dance theme is first presented, its accompanying chords do not duplicate the rhythm of the melody; instead, they simply mark the beat.

The *Farandole* also includes two kinds of polyphony: with and without imitation. Soon after the opening, the march theme is presented by the violins and then is imitated by the violas. At the end of the piece, polyphony results when the march and dance themes—previously heard in alternation—are presented simultaneously. In this concluding section, both themes are in major.

The *Farandole* also contains monophonic texture, which sets off the homophony and polyphony. Monophony is heard when the march theme is played by the strings in unison.

Listening Outline to be read while music is heard

Brief Set: CD 1   Basic Set: CD 1

BIZET, *Farandole* from *L'Arlésienne* Suite No. 2

Allegro deciso (forceful allegro), march tempo, quadruple meter ($\frac{4}{4}$), D minor

Piccolo, 2 flutes, 2 oboes, 2 clarinets, 2 bassoons, 4 French horns, 2 trumpets, 2 cornets, 3 trombones, timpani, tambourine, bass drum, cymbals, 1st violins, 2d violins, violas, cellos, double basses

(Duration, 3:08)

37 53 0:00   **1. a.** Full orchestra, *ff*, march theme; homophonic (accompaniment in same rhythm as melody), minor.

38 54 0:16   **b.**   Violins imitated by violas, march theme; polyphonic, minor.

39 55 0:33   **2. a.** High woodwinds, *ppp*, dance theme; faster tempo, homophonic (accompanying chords on beat), major; decorative rushes in violins, long crescendo to *ff* as dance theme is repeated.

ppp   *poco a poco crescendo* ————————————————————————————

	1:17		**b.** Full orchestra, *fff*, dance theme.

40 56   1:28   0:00   **3. a.** Strings only, *ff*, march theme in faster tempo; monophonic, minor.

1:39   0:11   **b.** High woodwinds, *ppp*, dance theme; homophonic.

1:45   0:17   **c.** Strings only, *ff*, continue march theme; monophonic, then homophonic as lower strings accompany melody.

1:56   0:28   **d.** High woodwinds, *ppp*, dance theme; homophonic. Crescendo to

41 57   2:19   **4.** Full orchestra, *fff*, dance and march themes combined; polyphonic, major. Homophonic ending.

9 Musical Form

The word *form* is associated with shape, structure, organization, and coherence. Form calls to mind the human body or the balanced arrangement of figures in a painting. **Form** in music is the organization of musical elements in time. In a musical composition, pitch, tone color, dynamics, rhythm, melody, and texture interact to produce a sense of shape and structure. All parts of the composition are interrelated. Our memory lets us perceive the overall form by recalling the various parts and how they relate to each other. The form becomes clearer as awareness and recall of these parts are developed through repeated listening. As listeners, we can respond more fully to the emotional power and meaning of a musical composition when we appreciate its form.

Techniques That Create Musical Form

Both in short tunes (such as those we explored in Section 5) and in much longer compositions, repetition, contrast, and variation are essential techniques. *Repetition* creates a sense of unity; *contrast* provides variety; and *variation,* in keeping some elements of a musical thought while changing others, provides both unity and variety.

Repetition

Musical repetition appeals to the pleasure we get in recognizing and remembering something, and the repetition of melodies or extended sections is a technique widely used for binding a composition together. The passage of time influences our reaction to repetition: when a musical idea returns, the effect is not duplication but balance and symmetry.

Contrast

Forward motion, conflict, and change of mood all come from contrast. Opposition—of loud and soft, strings and woodwinds, fast and slow, major and minor—propels and develops musical ideas. Sometimes such contrast is complete, but at other times the opposites have common elements that give a sense of continuity.

Variation

In the variation of a musical idea, some of its features will be retained while others are changed. For example, a melody might be restated with a different accompaniment, or its pitches might stay the same while its rhythm is changed. A whole composition can be created from variations on one idea.

Types of Musical Form

Composers have traditionally organized musical ideas by using certain forms or patterns, and listeners can respond more fully when they recognize these patterns. It's important to note, though, that two compositions having the same form may be different in every other respect. We'll look now at two basic types of musical form. (Remember, from Section 5, that lowercase letters represent phrases or short sections and capital letters represent longer sections.)

Three-Part (Ternary) Form: A B A

During the last few centuries *three-part form (A B A)* has probably been used most frequently. It can be represented as *statement* (A), *contrast* or departure (B), *return* (A). When the return of A is varied, the form is outlined A B A'. The contrast between A and B can be of any kind; A and B can be of equal or unequal length; and the way A returns after B differs from piece to piece—A may come unexpectedly, or it may be clearly signaled (if B comes to a definite end with a cadence and a pause), or there may be a transition smoothly linking the two.

The sections of an A B A composition can be subdivided; for example, as follows:

		A			B			A	
	a	b	a		c	d	c		a	b	a

In some pieces, a listener might mistake subsection b within the first A for the arrival of B; but as the music progresses, the greater contrast one hears with B will make it clear that b is a subsection. (For example, in Tchaikovsky's *Dance of the Reed Pipes,* studied below, the English horn melody in item 1*c* in the listening outline introduces a brief contrast within the A section, whereas the trumpet melody in item 2*a* brings a greater contrast and initiates the B section.)

Dance of the Reed Pipes from *Nutcracker* Suite (1892), by Peter Ilyich Tchaikovsky

Brief Set:
CD 1 42

Basic Set:
CD 1 58

The *Nutcracker* Suite is a set of dances from the fairy-tale ballet *The Nutcracker* by Peter Ilyich Tchaikovsky (1840–1893). *Dance of the Reed Pipes* is a particularly clear example of A B A' form. Section A features three flutes playing a staccato melody, which conveys a light, airy feeling and is repeated several times. Section B contrasts in tone color, melody, and key—it features a trumpet melody accompanied by brasses and cymbals. This melody moves by step within a narrow range, in contrast to the opening flute melody, which has a wide range and many leaps as well as steps. The F sharp minor key of the middle section contrasts with the D major key of the opening section. The concluding A′ section, in D major, is a shortened version of the opening A section.

Listening Outline to be read while music is heard

Brief Set: CD 1   Basic Set: CD 1

TCHAIKOVSKY, *Dance of the Reed Pipes* from *Nutcracker* Suite

Three-part (ternary) form: A B A′

Moderato assai (very moderate), duple meter ($\frac{2}{4}$), D major

3 flutes, 2 oboes, English horn, 2 clarinets, bass clarinet, 2 bassoons, 4 French horns, 2 trumpets, 3 trombones, tuba, timpani, cymbals, 1st violins, 2d violins, violas, cellos, double basses

(Duration, 2:05)

A

| 42 | 58 | 0:00 | | **1. a.** Low pizzicato strings, *p*, introduce |
| | | 0:03 | | **b.** 3 flutes, staccato melody in major, pizzicato strings accompany. Melody repeated. |

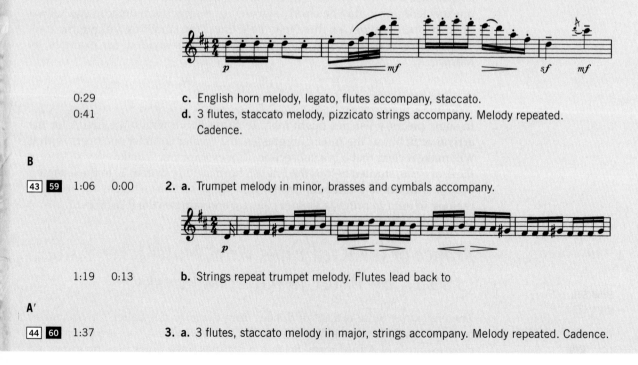

| | | 0:29 | | **c.** English horn melody, legato, flutes accompany, staccato. |
| | | 0:41 | | **d.** 3 flutes, staccato melody, pizzicato strings accompany. Melody repeated. Cadence. |

B

| 43 | 59 | 1:06 | 0:00 | **2. a.** Trumpet melody in minor, brasses and cymbals accompany. |

| | | 1:19 | 0:13 | **b.** Strings repeat trumpet melody. Flutes lead back to |

A′

| 44 | 60 | 1:37 | | **3. a.** 3 flutes, staccato melody in major, strings accompany. Melody repeated. Cadence. |

Two-Part (Binary) Form: A B

A composition divided into two large sections is in ***two-part form (A B).*** Two-part form gives a sense of *statement* (A) and *counterstatement* (B). If either of its large sections is immediately repeated, or if both are, the form might be represented by A A B, A B B, or A A B B. As in three-part form, differences between A and B may be of any kind, and the two sections may be equal or unequal in length and may have subsections. The B section almost always returns to the home key and gives a sense of finality.

Contradance No. 7 in E Flat Major from Twelve Contradances for Orchestra (1801), by Ludwig van Beethoven

Brief Set:

CD 1 45

Basic Set:

CD 1 61

The contradance is a lively dance in duple meter. Beethoven's Contradance No. 7 in E Flat Major (1801) is part of a set of Twelve Contradances for Orchestra meant for ballroom use in Vienna. Previously, Beethoven used this contradance in the finale of his ballet *Prometheus* (1801). He must have been particularly fond of this music because he later used it as the theme of his *Eroica* Variations for Piano, Op. 35 (1802; sometimes called the *Prometheus* Variations), and as the main theme of the finale of his Third Symphony (*Eroica*, 1803–1804).

The very brief Contradance in E Flat is in two-part (binary) form and is outlined A A B B, because each part is repeated. In parts A and B, which are each only eight bars in length, the first violins present the melody, while the other strings, clarinets, and French horns provide a mostly staccato accompaniment. Part A ends up in the air with an incomplete cadence, and part B ends conclusively with a complete cadence.

Part A consists of a soft lilting melodic phrase beginning with the repeated rhythm short-long, short-long. In contrast, part B begins energetically, with a rapid upward unaccompanied scale that leads to three loud repeated chords. A quieter repetition of the rapid upward scale introduces a soft, expectant sustained chord. Part B concludes with a new lilting phrase also based on the repeated rhythm short-long, short-long.

Listening Outline to be read while music is heard   Brief Set: CD 1   Basic Set: CD 1

BEETHOVEN, Contradance No. 7 in E Flat Major for Orchestra

Two-part (binary) form: A A B B

Duple meter ($\frac{2}{4}$), E flat major

2 clarinets, two French horns, 1st violins, 2d violins, cellos, basses

(Duration, 0:47)

A

45 **61** 0:00

1. 1st violins, *p*, lilting melody beginning with the rhythm short-long, short-long, other instruments accompany, incomplete cadence.

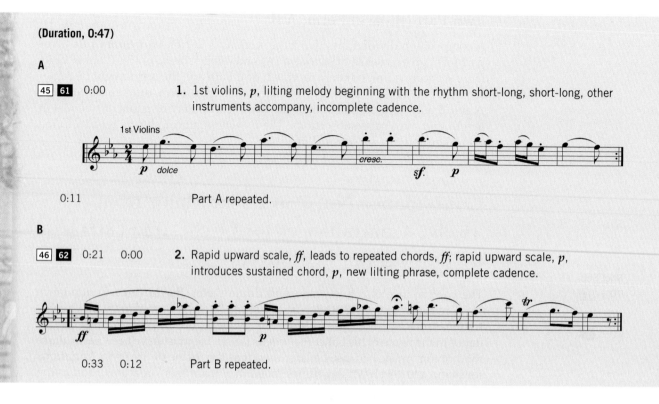

0:11   Part A repeated.

B

46 **62** 0:21   0:00

2. Rapid upward scale, *ff*, leads to repeated chords, *ff*; rapid upward scale, *p*, introduces sustained chord, *p*, new lilting phrase, complete cadence.

0:33   0:12   Part B repeated.

Listening for Form

The musical patterns covered in this section fall into clearly defined units. However, music is continuous in its flow and sometimes can't be subdivided quite so easily. Some music seems to fit none of the frequently used patterns. But such music is not formless—it has a unique form that can be discovered through repeated hearings.

Again, it's important to lean on memory when you listen to music. Spotting musical ideas when they occur is fine, but it's only the beginning. The goal is to put the related ideas together by recognizing and remembering them and by finding the relationships between them. Through alert, repeated listening their overall shape will be made clear, and your response to music will be more satisfying.

10 Musical Style

We use the word *style* in reference to everything from clothing to cooking, automobiles to paintings. In music, **style** refers to a characteristic way of treating the various musical elements: melody, rhythm, tone color, dynamics, harmony, texture, and form. The particular way these elements are combined can result in a distinctive or unique sound, and we can speak of the musical style of one composer, a group of composers, a country, or a period in history. Compositions created in the same part of the world or at about the same time are often similar in style, but individuals using the same musical vocabulary can create a personal manner of expression.

Musical styles change from one historical era to the next, but these changes are continuous, so that any boundary between one stylistic period and another is only approximate. Although there are some sudden turning points, even the most revolutionary new styles are usually foreshadowed in earlier compositions; and few changes of style sweep away the past entirely.

Western art music can be divided into the following stylistic periods:

Middle Ages (450–1450)
Renaissance (1450–1600)
Baroque (1600–1750)
Classical (1750–1820)
Romantic (1820–1900)
Twentieth century to 1945
1945 to the present

The following parts and sections describe the general features of each period and show how it differs from the preceding one. Awareness of the characteristics of a style will let you know what to listen for in a composition and help you recognize innovative or unique features.

Music is not created in a vacuum. To fully understand the style of a composition, one has to be aware of its function in society. Is a piece meant to provide entertainment in an aristocrat's castle, a concert hall, or a middle-class home? Is it designed to accompany singing, dancing, religious rites, or drama? Musical style is shaped by political, economic, social, and intellectual developments as well. And often, similar features of style can be found in different arts of the same period.

Music is probably as old as the human race; and we know—from art and other evidence—that it existed in ancient Egypt, Israel, Greece, and Rome, but hardly any notated music has survived from these civilizations. The first stylistic period to be considered in this book is the European Middle Ages, from which notated music has come down to us—allowing compositions created more than 1,000 years ago to come alive today.

qui non abiit in consilio
impiorum & in uia pecca
tor non stetit: & in cathe
dra pestilentie non sedit.
Sed in lege domini uo

The Middle Ages and Renaissance

II

"The man that hath no music in himself,

Nor is not mov'd with concord of sweet sounds,

Is fit for treasons, strategems and spoils."

WILLIAM SHAKESPEARE

1 Music in the Middle
Ages (450–1450)

2 Music in the Renaissance
(1450–1600)

A page from the Peterborough Psalter. Most medieval music was vocal, though a wide variety of instruments served as accompaniment.

Time-Line Middle Ages (450–1450)

Dates	Music	Arts and Letters	Historical and Cultural Events
450–1000	Earliest notated Gregorian chant manuscripts (c. 900)	*Beowolf* (c. 700) *Book of Kells* (c. 800)	Sack of Rome by Vandals (455) Reign of Pope Gregory I (the Great) (590–604) Charlemagne crowned Holy Roman emperor (800)
1000–1300	Troubadours and trouvères (c. 1100–1300) Hildegard of Bingen, *O successores* (c. 1150) School of Notre Dame (began c. 1170)	Beginning of Notre Dame Cathedral in Paris (1163) Thomas Aquinas, *Summa Theologica* (1273)	Norman Conquest (1066) First Crusade (1096–1099) Magna Carta signed (1215)
1300–1450	Guillaume de Machaut *Notre Dame* Mass (c. 1360)	Dante, *The Divine Comedy* (1321) Boccaccio, *Decameron* (1351) Chaucer, *The Canterbury Tales* (1387–1400)	Hundred Years' War (1337–1453) Black death (1347–1352) Joan of Arc executed by the English (1431)

Time-Line Renaissance (1450–1600)

Dates	Music	Arts and Letters	Historical and Cultural Events
1450–1500	Josquin Desprez, *Ave Maria . . . Virgo Serena* (c. 1475)	Botticelli, *La Primavera* (1477)	Fall of Constantinople (1453) Gutenberg Bible (1456) Columbus reaches America (1492)
1500–1600	Giovanni Pierluigi da Palestrina, *Pope Marcellus* Mass (1563) Thomas Weelkes, *As Vesta Was Descending* (1601)	Leonardo da Vinci, *Mona Lisa* (c. 1503) Michelangelo, *David* (1504) Raphael, *The School of Athens* (1505) Titian, *Venus and the Lute Player* (c. 1570) Shakespeare, *Romeo and Juliet* (1596)	Martin Luther's ninety-five theses, start of the Reformation (1517) Council of Trent (1545–1563) Elizabeth I, queen of England (1558–1603) Spanish Armada defeated (1588)

The Middle Ages (450–1450)

A thousand years of European history are spanned by the phrase *Middle Ages.* Beginning around 450 with the disintegration of the Roman empire, the early Middle ages were a time of migrations, upheavals, and wars. But the later Middle Ages (until about 1450) were a period of cultural growth: romanesque churches and monasteries (1000–1150) and gothic cathedrals (1150–1450) were constructed, towns grew, and universities were founded. The later Middle Ages also witnessed the crusades, a series of wars undertaken by European Christians—primarily between 1096 and 1291—to recover the holy city of Jerusalem from the Muslims.

During the Middle Ages there was a very sharp division among three main social classes: nobility, peasantry, and clergy. Nobles were sheltered within fortified castles surrounded by moats. During wars, noblemen engaged in combat as knights in armor, while noblewomen managed estates, ran households, and looked after the sick. In peacetime, nobles amused themselves with hunting, feasting, and tournaments. Peasants—the vast majority of the population—lived miserably in one-room huts. Many were serfs, bound to the soil and subject to feudal overlords. All segments of society felt the powerful influence of the Roman Catholic church. In this age of faith, hell was very real, and heresy was the gravest crime. Monks in monasteries held a virtual monopoly on learning; most people —including the nobility—were illiterate.

In the fourteenth century, an age of disintegration, Europe suffered through the Hundred Years' War (1337–1453) and the black death—or bubonic plague (around 1350)—which killed one-fourth of its population. By this time, both the feudal system and the authority of the church had been weakened. From 1378 to 1417, two rival popes claimed authority; and at one time there were three. Even devout Christians were confused. Literature of the time, such as Chaucer's *Canterbury Tales* (1387–1400) and Boccaccio's *Decameron* (after 1348), stressed graphic realism and earthly sensuality rather than virtue and heavenly rewards.

Architecture changed during the Middle Ages from the Romanesque style, seen in the eleventh-century nave at left, to the Gothic style of the thirteenth-century cathedral of Reims, at right.

Choir of cathedral of Reims. During the Middle Ages, religious teachings were imparted, and beliefs were strengthened, by biblical scenes depicted in stained-glass windows.

During the Middle Ages, artists were more concerned with religious symbolism than with lifelike representation. *Madonna and Child Enthroned* by an anonymous Byzantine artist of the thirteenth century.

The Renaissance (1450–1600)

The fifteenth and sixteenth centuries in Europe have come to be known as the Renaissance. People then spoke of a "rebirth," or "renaissance," of human creativity. It was a period of exploration and adventure—consider the voyages of Christopher Columbus (1492), Vasco da Gama (1498), and Ferdinand Magellan (1519–1522).

The Renaissance was an age of curiosity and individualism, too, as can be seen in the remarkable life of Leonardo da Vinci (1452–1519), who was a painter, sculptor, architect, engineer, and scientist—and a fine musician as well.

During the Renaissance, the dominant intellectual movement, which was called *humanism*, focused on human life and its accomplishments. Humanists were not concerned with an afterlife in heaven or hell. Though devout Christians, they were captivated by the cultures of ancient Greece and Rome. They became intoxicated with the beauty of ancient

During the Renaissance, the Virgin Mary was depicted as a beautiful, idealized young woman. Renaissance painters emphasized balance and used perspective to create an illusion of depth. *Madonna del Granduca* (c. 1505) by Raphael.

Renaissance sculptors and painters once again depicted the nude human body, which had been an object of shame and concealment during the Middle Ages. *David* (1504) by Michelangelo.

languages—Greek and Latin—and with the literature of antiquity. Humanism strongly influenced art throughout the Renaissance. Painters and sculptors were attracted to subjects drawn from classical literature and mythology. Once again they depicted the nude human body, a favorite theme of antiquity, but an object of shame and concealment during the Middle Ages. Medieval artists had been concerned more with religious symbolism than with lifelike representation. They had conceived of a picture as a flat, impenetrable surface on which

persons or objects were shown. Renaissance painters like Raphael (1483–1520) and Leonardo da Vinci were more interested in realism and used linear perspective, a geometrical system for creating an illusion of space and depth. During the Renaissance, painters no longer treated the Virgin Mary as a childlike, unearthly creature; they showed her as a beautiful young woman.

The Catholic church was far less powerful during the Renaissance than it had been during the Middle Ages, for the unity of Christendom was exploded by the Protestant

Reformation led by Martin Luther (1483–1546). No longer did the church monopolize learning. Aristocrats and the upper middle class now considered education a status symbol, and they hired scholars to teach their children. The invention of printing with movable type (around 1450) accelerated the spread of learning. Before 1450, books were rare and extremely expensive because they were copied entirely by hand. But by 1500, 15 million to 20 million copies of 40,000 editions had been printed in Europe.

Classical mythology was an important source of inspiration for Renaissance art. *La Primavera* (*Spring,* c. 1482) by Sandro Botticelli depicts Venus (center); the Three Graces and Mercury (left); and Flora, Spring, and Zephyrus (right).

Renaissance artists were strongly influenced by the cultures of ancient Greece and Rome. *The School of Athens* (1505) by Raphael, showing the Greek philosophers Aristotle and Plato (center). Plato is painted in the likeness of Leonardo da Vinci.

1 Music in the Middle Ages (450–1450)

Just as the cathedral dominated the medieval landscape and mind, so was it the center of musical life. Most important musicians were priests and worked for the church. An important occupation in thousands of monasteries was liturgical singing. Boys received music education in schools associated with churches and cathedrals. Women were not allowed to sing in church but did make music in convents. Nuns learned to sing, and some—like Hildegard of Bingen (1098–1179), abbess of Rupertsberg—wrote music for their choirs. With this preeminence of the church, it is not surprising that for centuries only sacred music was notated.

Most medieval music was vocal, though musicians also performed on a wide variety of instruments. Church officials required monks to sing with proper pronunciation, concentration, and tone quality. For example, Saint Bernard, the twelfth-century mystic and head of the abbey at Clairvaux in France, ordered his monks to sing vigorously, "pronouncing the words of the Holy Spirit with becoming manliness and resonance and affection; and correctly, that while you chant you ponder on nothing but what you chant."

The church frowned on instruments because of their earlier role in pagan rites. After about 1000, however, organs and bells became increasingly common in cathedrals and monastic churches. For three centuries or so, organs were played mainly on feast days and other special occasions. Sometimes the clergy complained about noisy organs that distracted worshipers. "Whence hath the church so many Organs," complained St. Aelred, a twelfth-century abbot. "To what purpose, I pray you, is that terrible blowing of Bellows, expressing rather the cracks of thunder than the sweetness of a Voyce?" St. Aelred criticized people who watch the organ as if "in a theater not a place of worship."

Today, we know relatively little about how medieval music sounded. Few medieval instruments have survived and music manuscripts of the time do not indicate tempo, dynamics, or names of instruments. In some kinds of medieval music, the notation indicates pitch, but not rhythm. Singers and instrumentalists often appear together in pictures and in literary descriptions, but it is not certain whether polyphonic music was performed with voices alone or with voices and instruments.

Gregorian Chant

For over 1,000 years, the official music of the Roman Catholic church has been *Gregorian chant,* which consists of melody set to sacred Latin texts and sung without accompaniment. (The chant is monophonic in texture.) The melodies of Gregorian chant were meant to enhance specific parts of religious services. They set the atmosphere for prayers and ritual actions. For centuries, composers have based original compositions on chant melodies. (Since the Second Vatican Council of 1962–1965, however, most Roman Catholic services have been celebrated in the native language of each country, and so today Gregorian chant is no longer common.)

Manuscript page with music from sixteenth-century Spain. The illustration within the initial R depicts the resurrection of Christ.

Gregorian chant conveys a calm, otherworldly quality; it represents the voice of the church, rather than of any single individual. Its rhythm is flexible, without meter, and has little sense of beat. The exact rhythm of chant melodies is uncertain, because precise time values were not notated. But its free-flowing rhythm gives Gregorian chant a floating, almost improvisational character. The melodies tend to move by step within a narrow range of pitches. Depending on the nature and importance of the text, they are simple or elaborate; some are little more than recitations on a single tone; others contain complex melodic curves.

Gregorian chant is named after Pope Gregory I (the Great), who reorganized the Catholic liturgy during his reign from 590 to 604. Although medieval legend credits Pope Gregory with the creation of Gregorian chant, we know that it evolved over many centuries. Some of its practices, such as the singing of psalms, came from the Jewish synagogues of the first centuries after Christ. Most of the several thousand melodies known today were created between A.D. 600 and 1300.

At first Gregorian melodies were passed along by oral tradition, but as the number of chants grew to the thousands, they were notated to ensure musical uniformity throughout the western church. (The illustration on page 66 is an example of medieval chant notation.) The earliest surviving chant manuscripts date from about the ninth century. The composers of Gregorian chant—like the sculptors who decorated early medieval churches—remain almost completely unknown.

Medieval monks and nuns spent several hours of each day singing Gregorian chant in two types of services, the office and the mass. Each type included both sung and spoken texts in Latin. The office consisted of eight services, the first before sunrise and the last at sunset. The mass, the highlight of the liturgical day, was a ritual re-enactment of the Last Supper. Some texts of the mass remained the same from day to day throughout most of the church year, while other texts were meant only for particular feasts, such as Christmas, Epiphany, or Easter.

The Church Modes

The "otherworldly" sound of Gregorian chant results partly from the unfamiliar scales used. These scales are called **church modes** (or sometimes simply *modes*). Like major and minor scales, church modes consist of seven different tones and an eighth tone that duplicates the first an octave higher. However, their patterns of whole and half steps are different. The church modes were the basic scales of western music during the Middle Ages and Renaissance and were used in secular as well as sacred music. Much western folk music follows the patterns of the church modes. For example, the sea chantey *What Shall We Do with the Drunken Sailor?* is in a mode called *Dorian*.

Alleluia: Vidimus Stellam (We Have Seen His Star)

Brief Set:
CD 1 47

Basic Set:
CD 1 63

An elaborate and jubilant Gregorian chant is the Alleluia from the Mass for Epiphany. The word *alleluia* is a Latinized form of the Hebrew *hallelujah (praise ye the Lord)*. In this chant (shown in medieval notation on page 68), many notes are sung to single syllables of text. The long series of tones on *ia* is a wordless expression of joy and religious ecstasy. The monophonic texture of the chant is varied by an alternation between a soloist and a choir singing in unison. The chant is in A B A form; the opening *alleluia* melody is repeated after a middle section that is set to a biblical verse.

Vocal Music Guide to be read while music is heard

Brief Set: CD 1   Basic Set: CD 1

ALLELUIA: VIDIMUS STELLAM

47 63 0:00
A

| Solo, opening phrase | *Alleluia.* | Hallelujah. |
| Choir, many tones on *ia* | *ia* | jah. |

48 64 0:24
B

| Choir | *Vidimus stellam ejus in Oriente et venimus cum muneribus adorare Dominum.* | We have seen his star in the east and are come with gifts to worship the Lord. |

49 65 1:44
A

| Choir, opening phrase with many tones on *ia* | *Alleluia.* | Hallelujah. |

Medieval chant notation for
Alleluia: Vidimus stellam.

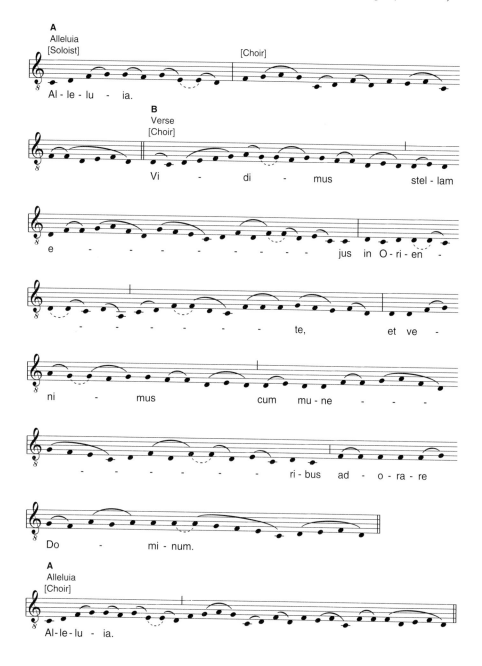

A
Alleluia
[Soloist]   [Choir]

Al - le - lu - ia.

B
Verse
[Choir]

Vi - di - mus   stel - lam

e - jus in O - ri - en -

- te, et ve -

ni - mus cum mu - ne -

- ri - bus ad - o - ra - re

Do - mi - num.

A
Alleluia
[Choir]

Al - le - lu - ia.

O successores (You successors), by Hildegard of Bingen

Brief Set:
CD 1 [50]

Basic Set:
CD 1 **66**

A late, highly expressive example of Gregorian chant is *O successores (You successors)* by the nun Hildegard of Bingen (1098–1179), abbess of Rupertsberg in Germany. Hildegard was one of the most creative and many-sided personalities of the Middle Ages. A visionary and mystic, she was active in religious and diplomatic affairs. She also wrote poetry and music; treatises on theology, science, and medicine; and a musical drama, *Ordo virtutum (Play of the Virtues)*, which is the earliest known morality play. She was the first woman composer from whom a large number of works—monophonic sacred songs—have survived.

The chant *O successores* was composed to be sung by the nuns in Hildegard's convent. It is in praise of the holy confessors who are successors of Christ. (Christ is referred to as *lion* and *lamb* in the text.) Hildegard explained that the words came to her in a vision: "Then I saw the lucent sky, in which I heard different kinds of music. . . . I heard the praises of the joyous citizens of heaven, steadfastly persevering in the ways of truth."

The chant is notated in the manuscript as a single melodic line, without accompaniment. However, in our recording the performers have added a drone accompaniment. A *drone* consists of one or more long, sustained tones accompanying a melody. In *O successores*, two simultaneous sustained notes at the interval of a fifth are played on a fiddle, a medieval bowed string instrument. It may well be that such an accompaniment accords with medieval performance practice.

The melody is sung by a women's choir and is made up of several different phrases. This chant usually has one to four notes to each syllable; only at the end are many notes sung on the final syllable. The melody creates a sense of progression and growth as it moves gradually through a wide pitch range (an octave and a sixth). At first, the melody seems calm as it proceeds primarily by step within a low register. However, beginning with the word *sicut* there are several ascents to high notes and wide upward leaps of a fifth (on the words *et*, *vos*, *qui*, and *semper*). The climactic tone (on the important word *officio*, *service*) is reserved for the concluding phrase, which gently descends by step (on the word *agni*, *lamb*) to the original low register. *O successores* seems more speechlike than *Alleluia: Vidimus stellam*, in which many tones are sung to single syllables of text. Hildegard's chant has a larger pitch range, more wide leaps, and a greater feeling of motion toward a climax near the end.

Vocal Music Guide to be read while music is heard Brief Set: CD 1   Basic Set: CD 1

HILDEGARD OF BINGEN, *O successores*

50 66		
Low register	*O successores fortissimi leonis*	You successors of the mightiest lion
	inter templum et altare—	between the temple and the altar—
	dominantes in ministratione eius—	you the masters in his household—
Melody rises and falls	*sicut angeli sonant in laudibus,*	as the angels sound forth praises
	et sicut adsunt populis in adiutorio,	and are here to help the nations,
	vos estis inter illos,	you are among those
	qui haec faciunt,	who accomplish this,
	semper curam habentes	forever showing your care
Climax on *officio*, long descent on *agni*	*in officio agni.*	in the service of the lamb.

Many secular songs in the Middle Ages dealt with love. The illustration shows the German poet-composer Frauenlob (c. 1255–1318) with a group of musicians.

Secular Music in the Middle Ages

Despite the predominance of Gregorian chant throughout the Middle Ages, there was also much music outside the church. The pleasures of secular music and dance are vividly evoked by the thirteenth-century theologian Henri de Malines, as he reminisced about his life as a young student in Paris. "This servant of God gladly heard music performed upon reed instruments, pipes, and every kind of musical instrument." Henri "knew how to play a fiddle, bringing together in harmonious fashion, a melodious touching of the strings and drawing of the bow. He was familiar with and willingly sang all kinds of monophonic songs in various languages." Henri created poems and melodies and was a "merry and amorous leader . . . of dances in wooded places, arranging parties and games, and interspersing the sport of dancing with others."

The first large body of secular songs surviving in decipherable notation was composed during the twelfth and thirteenth centuries by French nobles called *troubadours* and *trouvères*. Among the best-known of these poet-musicians were the troubadour Guillaume IX, duke of Aquitaine, from southern France; and the trouvère Chastelain de Couci, from northern France. During this age of chivalry, knights gained great reputations as musical poets. Many of the songs they sang have been preserved because nobles had clerics write them down. These songs were usually performed by court minstrels, and most of them deal with love; but there are also songs about the Crusades, dance songs, and spinning songs. In southern France, there were women troubadours—such as Beatriz de Dia—who addressed their songs to men.

Some 1,650 troubadour and trouvère melodies have been preserved. The notation does not indicate rhythm, but it's likely that many had a regular meter with a clearly defined beat. They thus differ from the free, nonmetrical rhythm of Gregorian chant.

During the Middle Ages, wandering minstrels (or *jongleurs—juggler* comes from this French word) performed music and acrobatics in castles, taverns, and town squares. They were without civil rights and on the lowest social level, with prostitutes and slaves, and only a lucky few found steady work in the service of the nobility. But they were an important source of information in a time when there were no newspapers. They usually sang songs written by others and played instrumental dances on harps, fiddles (as noted above, these were bowed string instruments), and lutes (plucked string instruments).

Estampie (Thirteenth Century)

Brief Set:
CD 1 51

Basic Set:
CD 1 67

The *estampie,* a medieval dance, is one of the earliest surviving forms of instrumental music. In the manuscript for this estampie, a single melodic line is notated and, as usual, no instrument is specified. In our recording, the melody is played on a *rebec* (a bowed string instrument) and a *pipe* (a tubular wind instrument). Since medieval minstrels probably improvised modest accompaniments to dance tunes, the performers have added a drone—two simultaneous, repeated notes at the interval of a fifth, played on a *psaltery* (a plucked or struck string instrument). The estampie is in triple meter and has a strong, fast beat.

The Development of Polyphony: Organum

For centuries, western music was basically monophonic, having a single melodic line. But sometime between 700 and 900, the first steps were taken in a revolution that eventually transformed western music. Monks in monastery choirs began to add a second melodic line to Gregorian chant. In the beginning, this second line was improvised, not written down; it duplicated the chant melody at a different pitch. The two lines were in parallel motion, note against note, at the interval of a fourth or a fifth. (The interval from *do* to *fa* is a fourth; from *do* to *sol* is a fifth.)

Sit glo - ri - a Do - mi - ni in se - cu - la

Medieval music that consists of Gregorian chant and one or more additional melodic lines is called **organum.** Between 900 and 1200, organum became truly polyphonic, and the melody added to the chant became more independent. Instead of moving strictly parallel to the chant, it developed a melodic curve of its own. Sometimes this line was in contrary motion to the chant, moving up as the original melody moved down. The second line became even more independent around 1100, when the chant and the added melody were no longer restricted to a note-against-note style. Now the two lines could differ rhythmi-

The cathedral of Notre Dame in Paris.

cally as well as melodically. The chant, on the bottom, was generally sung in very long notes while the added melody, on top, moved in shorter notes.

Medieval listeners must have been startled to hear religious music in which the added melody was more attractive than the chant. In fact, at times the chant tones were so slow and dronelike that the original melody was hardly recognizable. Still, the chant represented the authority of the church. And respect for the church was so great that for centuries most polyphonic music was created by placing new melodic lines against known chants.

School of Notre Dame: Measured Rhythm

After 1150, Paris—the intellectual and artistic capital of Europe—became the center of polyphonic music. The University of Paris attracted leading scholars, and the cathedral of Notre Dame (begun in 1163) was the supreme monument of gothic architecture. Two successive choirmasters of Notre Dame, Leonin and Perotin, are among the first notable composers known by name. They and their followers are referred to as the *school of Notre Dame.*

From about 1170 to 1200, the Notre Dame composers developed rhythmic innovations. Earlier polyphonic music was probably performed in the free, unmeasured rhythms of Gregorian chant. But the music of Leonin and Perotin used *measured rhythm,* with definite time values and clearly defined meter. For the first time in music history, notation indicated precise rhythms as well as pitches. At first the new notation was limited to only certain rhythmic patterns, and the beat had to be subdivided into threes, the symbol of the Trinity. Despite these limitations, much fine polyphonic music was composed during the late twelfth century and the thirteenth century.

Modern listeners sometimes find medieval polyphony hollow and thin, probably because it has relatively few triads, which in later periods became the basic consonant chords. The triad contains two intervals of a third; medieval music theorists considered this interval a dissonance. (An interval of a third separates *do* and *mi*, and *mi* and *sol*.) But as the Middle Ages advanced, triads and thirds were used more often, and polyphonic music gradually became fuller and richer by our standards.

Fourteenth-Century Music: The "New Art" in France

As we have seen in the opening to Part II (page 61), the fourteenth century was an age of disintegration that witnessed the Hundred Years' War, the catastrophic plague known as the black death, and a weakening of the feudal system and of the Catholic church. Literary works of the fourteenth century stressed sensuality more than virtue.

Given this atmosphere, it's not surprising that secular music became more important than sacred music in the fourteenth century. Composers wrote polyphonic music that was *not* based on Gregorian chant, including drinking songs and pieces in which birdcalls, barking dogs, and shouting hunters were imitated.

By the early fourteenth century, a new system of music notation had evolved, and a composer could specify almost any rhythmic pattern. Now beats could be subdivided into two as well as three. Syncopation—rarely used earlier—became an important rhythmic practice. Changes in musical style in the fourteenth century were so profound that music theorists referred to French and Italian music as the *new art* (*ars nova* in Latin). As contrasting examples of fourteenth-century music, we'll study a love song and a mass by Guillaume de Machaut, the foremost French composer of the time.

Guillaume de Machaut

Guillaume de Machaut (about 1300–1377), who was famous as both a musician and a poet, was born in the French province of Champagne. He studied theology and spent much of his life in the service of various royal families. Around 1323, he became secretary and chaplain to John, king of Bohemia, whom he accompanied on trips and military campaigns throughout Europe. In his later years he lived mainly in Reims, where he served as a church official.

Machaut traveled to many courts and presented beautifully decorated copies of his music and poetry to noble patrons. These copies make Machaut one of the first important composers whose works have survived. The decline of the church in the fourteenth century is reflected in Machaut's output, which consists mainly of courtly love songs for one to four performers. We'll consider, first, one of his love songs, and then the *Notre Dame* Mass, the best-known composition of the fourteenth century.

Puis qu'en oubli sui de vous (Since I am forgotten by you; around 1363)

Brief Set:
CD 1 52

Basic Set:
CD 1 70

When he was about sixty, Machaut fell in love with Peronne, a beautiful young noblewoman. For several years they exchanged poems and letters, but the difference in age eventually proved too great and their relationship ended in mutual disappointment. Machaut immortalized their love in his greatest narrative poem, *Le Livre Dou Voir Dit* (*The Book of the True Poem*, 1363–1365). Along with the narrative, the *Voir Dit* contains lyric poems and letters by Machaut and Peronne as well as nine musical compositions, including the song *Puis qu'en oubli sui de vous* (*Since I am forgotten by you*).

This melancholy work expresses Machaut's "farewell to joy," since he has been forgotten by his beloved. The song consists of a vocal melody and two accompanying parts in an exceptionally low pitch range. Since these lower parts have no texts in the medieval manuscript, it is not certain whether they are meant to be sung or to be played by instruments. In our recording, they are performed by two solo voices.

Puis qu'en oubli sui de vous is a *rondeau*, one of the main poetic and musical forms in fourteenth- and fifteenth-century France. The poem has eight lines, each ending either with the syllable *mis* or *mant* (see the French text in the Vocal Music Guide below). Lines 1–2 constitute the poetic refrain, which returns as lines 7–8; line 1 appears again as line 4.

The music consists of two phrases, a and b. (These phrases are indicated to the left of the French text in the Vocal Music Guide.) Phrase a is used for lines ending with *mis.* It begins with long notes, pauses in the middle, and ends with an incomplete cadence.

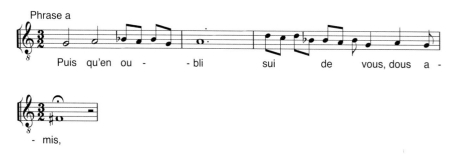

Phrase b is set to lines ending with *mant.* It begins with short notes, flows continuously, and ends with a complete cadence.

The endings of both phrases contain syncopation, a rhythmic feature of fourteenth-century music. This heartfelt song re-creates the vanished world of chivalry.

Vocal Music Guide to be read while music is heard | Brief Set: CD 1   Basic Set: CD 1 |

MACHAUT, *Puis qu'en oubli*

| 52 | 70 | **a.** *Puis qu'en oubli sui de vous dous amis* | Since I am forgotten by you, sweet friend, |
| | | **b.** *Vie amoureuse et joie a dieu commant* | I say farewell to joy and a life of love. |

a. *Mar vi le jour que m'amour en vous mis*
a. *Puis qu'en oubli sui de vous dous amis*

Ill-fated was the day I placed my love in you,
Since I am forgotten by you, sweet friend.

a. *Mais ce tenray que je vous ay promis*
b. *C'est que jamais n'aray nul autre amant*

But what I have promised you I will maintain,
Which is that I shall never have any other lover.

a. *Puis qu'en oubli sui de vous dous amis*
b. *Via amoureuse et joie a dieu command*

Since I am forgotten by you, sweet friend.
I say farewell to joy and a life of love.

Notre Dame Mass (Mid-Fourteenth Century)

Machaut's *Notre Dame* Mass, one of the finest compositions known from the Middle Ages, is also of great historical importance: it is the first polyphonic treatment of the mass ordinary by a known composer.

The **mass ordinary** consists of texts that remain the same from day to day throughout the church year. The five sung prayers of the ordinary are the Kyrie, Gloria, Credo, Sanctus, and Agnus Dei. Since the fourteenth century, these five texts have often been set to polyphonic music and have inspired some of the greatest choral works. (In the service, the Kyrie and Gloria were sung in succession, whereas the Credo, Sanctus, and Agnus Dei were separated by liturgical activity and by other texts sung as Gregorian chant.) In each age, composers have responded to the mass in their own particular style. This centuries-old tradition of the mass gives invaluable insight into the long span of music and its changing styles.

The *Norte Dame* Mass is written for four voice parts. How Machaut wanted his mass to be performed in unknown, but it is likely that four solo voices were employed. In our recording, the four voice parts are sung by two tenors and two basses. The *Notre Dame* Mass was probably composed in the early 1360s for performance at the cathedral of Reims. We'll examine the Agnus Dei of the mass as an example of fourteenth-century polyphony.

Agnus Dei

Brief Set:
CD 1 [53]

Basic Set:
CD 1 **71**

Machaut's music for the Agnus Dei—a prayer for mercy and peace—is solemn and elaborate. It is in triple meter. Complex rhythmic patterns contribute to its intensity. The two upper parts are rhythmically active and contain syncopation, a characteristic of fourteenth-century music. The two lower parts move in longer notes and play a supporting role.

The Agnus Dei is based on a Gregorian chant, which Machaut furnished with new rhythmic patterns and placed in the tenor, one of the two lower parts. Since the chant, or cantus firmus, is rhythmically altered within a polyphonic web, it is more a musical framework than a tune to be recognized. The harmonies of the Agnus Dei include stark dissonances, hollow-sounding chords, and full triads.

Like the chant melody on which it is based, the Agnus Dei is in three sections. It may be outlined as follows:

Agnus Dei (I)	Agnus Dei (II)	Agnus Dei (III)
A	B	A

Andrew Parrott Conducting the Agnus Dei *from Machaut's* Notre Dame *Mass*

Like musical styles, performance styles change from generation to generation. A wide range of performance practices coexist during every historical period. Today, for example, some musicians choose to use modern instruments when performing works of the eighteenth century and the early nineteenth century. They believe that modern instruments can convey the composer's message more effectively than early instruments. Keyboard artists, for instance, will play Bach on a twentieth-century concert grand piano rather than on a harpsichord, because their audiences are used to a much wider range of dynamics and are hearing the performance in larger halls.

Other musicians today play a composition as they think it was performed during the composer's lifetime. They will play on replicas of old instruments and use early performance techniques (as described in treatises of the period). The size of a vocal or instrumental group will be reduced to what was available in a church in 1360 or a castle in 1760. Their quest for historical accuracy can be difficult because concrete evidence about early performance practice—such as the participation of instruments in medieval polyphony—is often sparse.

The English conductor and musicologist Andrew Parrott is an outstanding representative of musicians who advocate historically-informed performance. "For music of the past to become immediate and present," writes Parrott, "it seems to me that there is no better way than for performers today to do their utmost to understand the workings of their predecessors' craft. Rewards are unpredictable and may be subtle or even disturbing but are always to the music's advantage."

His performance in 1983 of Machaut's complete *Notre Dame* Mass—the Agnus Dei is included in the CD Sets—pioneered the use of four unaccompanied solo voices for this work. Earlier recorded performances of the *Notre Dame* Mass usually employed instruments to perform or double some of the voice parts. According to Parrott, "liturgical polyphony of the fourteenth century seems to have been the preserve of soloists, not of choirs, and apart from organ and bells, instruments had no place in liturgical music making."

Parrott wants listeners to imagine themselves "just behind the high altar of Reims cathedral," where the *Notre Dame* Mass was first performed. He attempts to approximate the original performances by asking the singers to pronounce the Latin text as probably was done in fourteenth-century France. Parrott's recording of the complete *Notre Dame* Mass also includes the parts of the mass that were sung in Gregorian chant for the high mass on the feast of the Nativity of the Virgin, as it was celebrated during Machaut's lifetime. In this way, the polyphony of Machaut's music contrasts brilliantly with the monophonic texture of the surrounding Gregorian chant.

The same text appears in each section, except for a change from *miserere nobis (have mercy on us)* to *dona nobis pacem (grant us peace)* in the concluding Agnus Dei (III). A and B are similar in mood, rhythm, and texture and end with the same hollow-sounding chord. The division into three sections is thought to symbolize the Trinity. In Machaut's time, music was meant to appeal to the mind as much as to the ear.

Vocal Music Guide to be read while music is heard   Brief Set: CD 1   Basic Set: CD 1

MACHAUT, Agnus Dei from *Notre Dame* Mass

53 71 0:00 **A**	*Agnus Dei, qui tollis peccata mundi: miserere nobis.*	Lamb of God, who taketh away the sins of the world, have mercy on us.
54 72 0:57 **B**	*Agnus Dei, qui tollis peccata mundi: miserere nobis.*	Lamb of God, who taketh away the sins of the world, have mercy on us.
55 73 2:01 **A**	*Agnus Dei, qui tollis peccata mundi: dona nobis pacem.*	Lamb of God, who taketh away the sins of the world, grant us peace.

2 Music in the Renaissance (1450–1600)

The Renaissance in music occurred between about 1450 and 1600. (Some historians place the beginning of the Renaissance as early as 1400, however.) As in the other arts, the horizons of music were greatly expanded. The invention of printing widened the circulation of music, too, and the number of composers and performers increased.

In keeping with the Renaissance ideal of the "universal man," every educated person was expected to be trained in music. "I am not pleased with the courtier if he be not also a musician," Castiglione wrote in *The Book of the Courtier* (1528). Shakespeare's stage directions call for music over 300 times, and his plays are full of beautiful tributes to music:

The man that hath no music in himself,
Nor is not mov'd with concord of sweet sounds,
Is fit for treasons, stratagems and spoils.

(The Merchant of Venice)

As in the past, musicians worked in churches, courts, and towns. Church choirs grew in size. (The Papal Choir in Rome increased from ten singers in 1442 to twenty-four in 1483.) Although polyphonic church music in the Middle Ages was usually sung by several soloists, during the Renaissance it was performed by an entire (male) choir. The church remained an important patron of music, but musical activity gradually shifted to the courts. Kings, princes, and dukes competed for the finest composers. A single court might have ten to sixty musicians, including singers as well as instrumentalists. Women functioned as virtuoso singers at several Italian courts during the late Renaissance. A court music director would compose secular pieces to entertain the nobility and sacred works for the court chapel. The nobility often brought their musicians along when traveling from one castle to another.

Renaissance town musicians played for civic processions, weddings, and religious services. In general, musicians enjoyed higher status and pay than ever before. Composers were no longer content to remain unknown; like other artists, they sought credit for their work.

Many leading Renaissance composers came from the low countries (Flanders), an area which now includes parts of the Netherlands, Belgium, and northern France. These Flemish composers were regarded highly and held important positions throughout Europe, especially in Italy, which became the leading music center in the sixteenth century. Other countries with a vibrant musical life in the Renaissance were Germany, England, and Spain.

Characteristics of Renaissance Music

Words and Music

In the Renaissance, as in the Middle Ages, vocal music was more important than instrumental music. During the Renaissance, though, the humanistic interest in language influenced vocal music in a new way. As a result, an especially close relationship was created between words and music. Renaissance composers wrote music to enhance the meaning and emotion of the text. "When one of the words expresses weeping, pain, heartbreak, sighs, tears, and other similar things, let the harmony be full of sadness," wrote Gioseffo Zarlino, a music theorist of the sixteenth century. By contrast, medieval composers had been relatively uninterested in expressing the emotions of a text.

Renaissance composers often used *word painting,* musical representation of specific poetic images. For example, the words *descending from heaven* might be set to a descending melodic line, and *running* might be heard with a series of rapid notes. Yet despite this emphasis on capturing the emotion and imagery of a text, Renaissance music may seem calm and restrained to us. While there *is* a wide range of emotion in Renaissance music, it is usually expressed in a moderate, balanced way, with *no* extreme contrasts of dynamics, tone color, or rhythm.

Texture

The texture of Renaissance music is chiefly polyphonic. A typical choral piece has four, five, or six voice parts of nearly equal melodic interest. Imitation among the voices is common: each presents the same melodic idea in turn, as in a round. Homophonic texture, with successions of chords, is also used, especially in light music, like dances. The texture may vary within a piece to provide contrast and bring out aspects of the text as it develops.

Renaissance music sounds fuller than medieval music. The bass register was used for the first time, expanding the pitch range to more than 4 octaves. With this new emphasis on the bass line came richer harmony. Renaissance music sounds mild and relaxed, because stable, consonant chords are favored; triads occur often, while dissonances are played down.

Renaissance choral music did not need instrumental accompaniment. For this reason, the period is sometimes called the "golden age" of unaccompanied— *a cappella*—choral music. Even so, on special occasions instruments were combined with voices. Instruments might duplicate the vocal lines to reinforce the sound. But parts specified for instruments are rarely found in Renaissance choral music.

Rhythm and Melody

In Renaissance music, rhythm is more a gentle flow than a sharply defined beat. This is because each melodic line has great rhythmic independence: when one singer is at the beginning of his or her melodic phrase, the others may already be in the middle of theirs. This technique makes singing Renaissance music both a pleasure and a challenge, for each singer must maintain an individual rhythm. But pitch patterns in Renaissance melodies are easy to sing. The melody usually moves along a scale with few large leaps.

Sacred Music in the Renaissance

The two main forms of sacred Renaissance music are the motet and the mass. They are alike in style, but a mass is a longer composition. The Renaissance *motet* is a polyphonic choral work set to a sacred Latin text other than the ordinary of the mass. The Renaissance *mass* is a polyphonic choral composition made up of five sections: Kyrie, Gloria, Credo, Sanctus, and Agnus Dei.

Josquin Desprez and the Renaissance Motet

Josquin Desprez (about 1440–1521), a contemporary of Leonardo da Vinci and Christopher Columbus, was a master of Renaissance music. Like many other Flemish composers, he had an international career. Josquin was born in the province of Hainaut—today part of Belgium—and spent much of his life in Italy, serving in dukes' private chapels and in the Papal Choir at Rome. In later years, he worked for Louis XII of France and held several church posts in his native land.

Josquin's compositions, which include masses, motets, and secular vocal pieces, strongly influenced other composers and were praised enthusiastically by music lovers. Martin Luther, for example, remarked: "God has His Gospel preached also through the medium of music; this may be seen from the compositions of Josquin, all of whose works are cheerful, gentle, mild, and lovely; they flow and move along and are neither forced nor coerced and bound by rigid and stringent rules, but, on the contrary, are like the song of the finch."

Ave Maria . . . Virgo Serena
(Hail, Mary . . . Serene Virgin; c. 1475)

Brief Set:

CD 1 56

Basic Set:

CD 1 74

Josquin's four-voice motet *Ave Maria . . . virgo serena* is an outstanding Renaissance choral work. This Latin prayer to the Virgin is set to delicate and serene music. The opening uses polyphonic imitation, a technique typical of the period.

The short melodic phrase on *Ave Maria* is presented by the soprano voice and then imitated in turn by the alto, tenor, and bass. The next two words, *gratia plena (full of grace),* have a different melody, which also is passed from voice to voice. Notice that each voice enters while the preceding one is in the middle of its melody. This overlapping creates a feeling of continuous flow. Josquin adapted the melody for the opening phrases from a Gregorian chant, but the rest of the motet was not based on a chant melody.

Josquin skillfully varies the texture of this motet; two, three, or four voices are heard at one time. In addition to the imitation among individual voices, there is imitation between pairs of voices: duets between the high voices are imitated by the two lower parts. Sometimes the texture almost becomes homophonic, as at the words *Ave, vera virginitas.* Here, also, is a change from duple to triple meter, and the tempo momentarily becomes more animated. But soon the music returns to duple meter and a more peaceful mood. *Ave Maria* ends with slow chords that express Josquin's personal plea to the Virgin: *O Mother of God, remember me. Amen.*

Vocal Music Guide to be read while music is heard | Brief Set: CD 1 | Basic Set: CD 1 |

JOSQUIN, *Ave Maria . . . Virgo Serena*

56 74 0:00	Each soprano phrase imitated in turn by alto, tenor, and bass. Duple meter.	*Ave Maria gratia plena dominus tecum, virgo serena.*	Hail Mary, full of grace, the Lord is with thee, serene Virgin.
0:49	High duet imitated by three lower voices.	*Ave, cuius conceptio,*	Hail, whose conception,
	All four voices. Increased rhythmic animation reflects "new joy."	*solemni plena gaudio, coelestia terrestria nova replet laetitia.*	full of great jubilation, fills Heaven and Earth with new joy.
1:32	High duet imitated by low duet. Soprano phrase imitated by alto, tenor, and bass.	*Ave, cuius nativitas nostra fuit solemnitas, ut lucifer lux oriens verum solem praeveniens.*	Hail, whose birth brought us joy, as Lucifer, the morning star, went before the true sun.
2:17	High duet imitated by low duet. High duet. Low duet.	*Ave, pia humilitas, sine viro fecunditas, cuius annuntiatio nostra fuit salvatio.*	Hail, pious humility, fruitful without a man, whose Annunciation brought us salvation.
57 75 2:50	Triple meter.	*Ave, vera virginitas, immaculata castitas, cuius purificatio nostra fuit purgatio.*	Hail, true virginity, immaculate chastity, whose purification brought our cleansing.
58 76 3:16	Duple meter, high duets imitated by lower voices.	*Ave praeclara omnibus angelicis virtutibus, cuius assumptio nostra glorificatio.*	Hail, glorious one in all angelic virtues, whose Assumption was our glorification.
	Brief pause. Sustained chords.	*O mater Dei, memento mei. Amen.*	O Mother of God, remember me. Amen.

Palestrina and the Renaissance Mass

During the sixteenth century, Italian composers attained the excellence of such earlier Flemish musicians as Josquin Desprez. Among the most important Italian Renaissance composers was Giovanni Pierluigi da Palestrina (about 1525–1594), who devoted himself to music for the Catholic church. His career thus centered in Rome, where he held important church positions, including that of music director for St. Peter's.

Palestrina's music includes 104 masses and some 450 other sacred works; it is best understood against the background of the Counter-Reformation. During

A miniature showing a mass at the court of Phillip the Good in Burgundy.

the early 1500s, the Catholic church was challenged and questioned by the Protestants and, as a result, sought to correct abuses and malpractices within its structure, as well as to counter the move toward Protestantism. This need to strengthen the church led to the founding of the Jesuit order (1540) and the convening of the Council of Trent (1545–1563), which considered questions of dogma and organization.

During its deliberations, the council discussed church music, which many felt had lost its purity. Years before, the scholar Desiderius Erasmus (about 1466–1536) had complained: "We have introduced an artificial and theatrical music into the church, a bawling and agitation of various voices, such as I believe have never been heard in the theaters of the Greeks and Romans. . . . Amorous and lascivious melodies are heard such as elsewhere accompany only the dances of courtesans and clowns." At the council sessions, church music was attacked because it used secular tunes, noisy instruments, and theatrical singing. Some complained that complex polyphony made it impossible to understand the sacred texts; they wanted only monophonic music—Gregorian chant—for the mass. The council finally decreed that church music should be composed not "to give empty pleasure to the ear," but to inspire religious contemplation.

The restraint and serenity of Palestrina's works reflect this emphasis on more spiritual music. For centuries, church authorities have regarded his masses as models of church music because of their calmness and "otherworldly" quality. Even today, the technical perfection of his style is a model for students of counterpoint.

Pope Marcellus Mass (1562–1563)

Palestrina's *Pope Marcellus* Mass, his most famous mass, was long thought to have convinced the Council of Trent that polyphonic masses should be kept in Catholic worship. While we now know that this work did *not* play that role, it does reflect the council's desire for a clear projection of the sacred text. It is dedicated to Pope Marcellus II, who reigned briefly in 1555 while Palestrina was a singer in the Papal Choir.

The *Pope Marcellus* Mass is written for an a cappella choir of six voice parts: soprano, alto, two tenors, and two basses. We'll focus on the first section of the mass, the Kyrie.

Kyrie

Brief Set:

CD 1 59

Basic Set:

CD 1 77

The Kyrie has a rich polyphonic texture. Its six voice parts constantly imitate each other, yet blend beautifully. This music sounds fuller than Josquin's *Ave Maria*, in part because six voices are used rather than four. The elegantly curved melodies summon the spirit of Gregorian chant. They flow smoothly and can be sung easily. Upward leaps are balanced at once by downward steps, as in the opening melody:

Soprano

Ky - rie e - lei - - - - son,

The Kyrie of the *Pope Marcellus* Mass is written in three different sections:

1. *Kyrie eleison.*   Lord, have mercy.
2. *Christe eleison.*   Christ, have mercy.
3. *Kyrie eleison.*   Lord, have mercy.

This text is short, and words are repeated with different melodic lines to express calm supplication. The rhythm flows continuously to the end of each section, when all voices come together on sustained chords. Each of the three sections begins in a thin texture with only some of the voices sounding; but as the other voices enter, the music becomes increasingly full and rich. In our recording, the third section sounds climactic because it is performed in a somewhat faster tempo and at a louder dynamic level than the first two sections.

Vocal Music Guide to be read while music is heard | Brief Set: CD 1 | Basic Set: CD 1

PALESTRINA, *Kyrie* from *Pope Marcellus* Mass

59 77	0:00		Tenor quickly imitated in turn by three other voice parts; remaining two voice parts join. Voices imitate each other and repeat words. Sustained chord, pause end section.	1. *Kyrie eleison.*	Lord, have mercy.
60 78	1:35		Three voice parts begin at same time; other three voice parts join in turn. Voices imitate each other. Sustained chord, pause.	2. *Christe eleison.*	Christ, have mercy.
61 79	3:29	0:00	Soprano phase quickly imitated in turn by three lower voice parts; two other voice parts join. Voices imitate each other.	3. *Kyrie eleison.*	Lord, have mercy.
	4:35	1:06	Sustained chord ends *Kyrie*.		

Secular Music in the Renaissance

Vocal Music: The Renaissance Madrigal

During the Renaissance, secular vocal music became increasingly popular. Throughout Europe, music was set to poems in various languages, including Italian, French, Spanish, German, Dutch, and English.

The development of music printing helped spread secular music, and thousands of song collections became available. Music was an important leisure activity; every educated person was expected to play an instrument and read notation. The Elizabethan composer Thomas Morley describes the embarrassment of being unable to participate in after-dinner music making: "But supper being ended, and Musicke bookes (according to the custome) being brought to the tables, the mistresse of the house presented me with a part, earnestly requesting me to sing. But when, after many excuses, I protested unfainedly that I could not: every one began to wonder. Yea, some whispered to others, demanding how I was brought up."

Renaissance secular music was written for groups of solo voices and for solo voice with the accompaniment of one or more instruments. Word painting—musical illustration of a text—was common. Composers delighted in imitating natural sounds such as birdcalls and street cries. In a famous piece entitled *La Guerre (The War)*, the Frenchman Clément Janequin (about 1485–1560) vividly imitated battle noises, drumbeats, and fanfares. Secular music contained more rapid shifts of mood than sacred music did. As Morley advised one composer, "You must in your music be wavering like the wind, sometimes wanton, sometimes drooping, sometimes grave and staid; . . . and the more variety you show the better shall you please."

An important kind of secular vocal music during the Renaissance was the *madrigal,* a piece for several solo voices set to a short poem, usually about love. A madrigal, like a motet, combines homophonic and polyphonic textures. But it uses word painting and unusual harmonies more often.

The Renaissance madrigal originated in Italy around 1520, during a creative explosion in Italian poetry. Madrigals were published by the thousands in sixteenth-century Italy, where they were sung by cultivated aristocrats. Among the many Italian madrigalists were Luca Marenzio (1553–1599) and Carlo Gesualdo (about 1560–1613), the infamous prince of Venosa who had his wife and her lover murdered after finding them together in bed.

In 1588—the year of the defeat of the Spanish armada—a volume of translated Italian madrigals was published in London. This triggered a spurt of madrigal writing by English composers, and for about thirty years there was a steady flow of English madrigals and other secular vocal music. The time of Queen Elizabeth (1533–1603) and William Shakespeare (1564–1616) was as much a golden age in English music as it was in English literature. The impetus for both arts arose in Italy. But the English madrigal became lighter and more humorous than its Italian model, and its melody and harmony were simpler.

As Vesta Was Descending (1601), by Thomas Weelkes

Brief Set:
CD 1 62

Basic Set:
CD 1 80

Among the finest English madrigalists was Thomas Weelkes (about 1575–1623), an organist and church composer. Weelkes's *As Vesta Was Descending* comes from *The Triumphes of Oriana* (1601), an anthology of English madrigals written to honor Queen Elizabeth, who was often called Oriana. The text of this six-voice madrigal pictures Vesta (the Roman goddess of the hearth) coming down a hill with her attendants, "Diana's darlings." (Diana was the Roman goddess of chastity, hunting, and the moon.) At the same time, the "maiden queen," Oriana (Elizabeth), is climbing the hill with her shepherd gallants. Vesta's attendants desert her and race down the hill to join Oriana.

As Vesta Was Descending has the light mood typical of English madrigals. Word painting is plentiful. For example, the word *descending* is sung to downward scales, and *ascending* to upward ones.

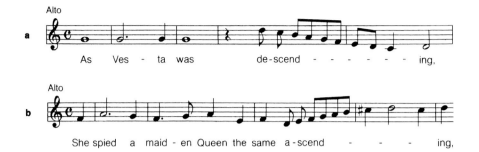

When Vesta's attendants run down the hill, "first *two* by *two*, then *three* by *three together*, leaving their goddess all *alone*," we hear first *two* voices, then *three* voices, then *six* voices, and finally a *solo* voice. In the extended concluding section, "*Long live fair Oriana*," a joyous phrase is imitated among the voices. And in the bass this phrase is sung in long notes, with the longest note on the word *long*.

Vocal Music Guide to be read while music is heard   Brief Set: CD 1   Basic Set: CD 1

WEELKES, *As Vesta Was Descending*

62 80	
Descending scales.	As Vesta was from Latmos hill *descending*,
Ascending scales.	she spied a maiden queen the same *ascending*,
	attended on by all the shepherds swain,
Rapid descending figures.	to whom Diana's darlings came *running down* amain.
Two voices, three voices; all voices.	First *two* by *two*, then *three* by *three together*,
Solo voice.	leaving their goddess *all alone*, hasted thither,
	and mingling with the shepherds of her train
	with mirthful tunes her presence entertain.
	Then sang the shepherds and nymphs of Diana,
Brief joyful phrase imitated among voices; long notes in bass.	*Long* live fair Oriana!

Instrumental Music

Though still subordinate to vocal music, instrumental music did become more important during the Renaissance. Traditionally, instrumentalists accompanied voices or played music intended for singing. Even in the early 1500s instrumental music was largely adapted from vocal music. Instrumental groups performed

An illustration from a book of hours produced in Tours, France, c. 1530–1535.

polyphonic vocal pieces, which were often published with the indication *to be sung or played.* Soloists used the harpsichord, organ, or **lute** (a versatile plucked string instrument with a body shaped like half a pear) to play simple arrangements of vocal works.

During the sixteenth century, however, instrumental music became increasingly emancipated from vocal models. More music was written specifically for instruments. Renaissance composers began to exploit the particular capacities of the lute or organ for instrumental solos. They also developed purely instrumental forms, such as theme and variations.

Much of this instrumental music was intended for dancing, a popular Renaissance entertainment. Every cultivated person was expected to be skilled in dance, which was taught by professional dancing masters. Court dances were often performed in pairs. A favorite pair was the stately *pavane,* or *passamezzo,* in duple meter, and the lively *galliard,* in triple meter. Dance music was performed by instrumental groups or by soloists like harpsichordists and lutenists. A wealth of dance music published during the sixteenth century has come down to us.

Renaissance musicians distinguished between loud outdoor instruments like the trumpet and the *shawm* (a double-reed ancestor of the oboe), and soft indoor instruments like the lute and the *recorder* (an early flute). The many instruments used in the Renaissance produced softer, less brilliant sounds than we hear from instruments today; most came in families of from three to eight instruments, ranging from soprano to bass. Among the most important Renaissance instruments were recorders, shawms, *cornetts* (wooden instruments with cup-shaped mouthpieces), *sackbuts* (early trombones), lutes, *viols* (bowed string instruments), organs, *regals* (small organs with reed pipes), and harpsichords. Often several members of the same instrumental family were played together, but Renaissance composers did not specify the instruments they wanted. A single work might be performed by recorders, viols, or several different instruments, depending on what was available. Today's standardized orchestra did not exist. Large courts might employ thirty instrumentalists of all types. On state occasions such as a royal wedding, guests might be entertained by woodwinds, plucked and bowed strings, and keyboard instruments all playing together.

Passamezzo and Galliard, by Pierre Francisque Caroubel, from *Terpsichore* (1612), by Michael Praetorius

This Passamezzo and Galliard illustrate the Renaissance practice of pairing contrasting court dances in duple and triple meter. These dances come from *Terpsichore,* a collection of over 300 dance tunes arranged for instrumental ensemble by Michael Praetorius (1571–1621), a German composer and theorist. (Terpsichore was the Greek muse, or goddess, of dance.) A few dances in the collection, including the Passamezzo and Galliard studied here, were composed by the French violinist Pierre Francisque Caroubel (1576–1611). Both dance types originated in Italy and were popular during the sixteenth century and the early seventeenth century.

Basic Set:
CD 1 **82**

A passamezzo is a stately dance in duple meter. The one studied here is written for six unspecified instrumental parts. In our recording it is performed by a large Renaissance band that includes bowed strings (violins, violas, cello, double bass); plucked strings (harps, archlute—a lute with additional strings—and theorbo, a bass lute); woodwinds (recorders and curtal, a double-reed instrument); brasses (cornetts, sackbuts); keyboard instruments (organ, regal, harpsichord); and timpani. The passamezzo consists of three brief sections (a, b, c), each ending with a cadence and a brief pause. In our recording, each section is immediately repeated with louder dynamics and fuller instrumentation: a a' b b' c c'. The carefree Galliard has essentially the same melody as the preceding Passamezzo, but its meter is triple rather than duple.

Basic Set:
CD 1 **83**

At the very beginning, the composer artfully conceals this similarity by placing a competing melody over the main melody. The Galliard's rhythm is delightfully irregular because the triple meter often changes to sextuple meter with quick beats (**1**-2-3-**4**-5-6).

This Galliard is written for five unspecified instrumental parts. In our recording, the Galliard is performed by a smaller and softer Renaissance band than the one used for the Passamezzo. The ensemble includes bowed strings (violins, violas, cello, double bass); plucked strings (archlute, theorbo); woodwinds (recorders, curtal); and harpsichord. Like the Passamezzo, the Galliard consists of three short sections (a, b, c), each ending with a cadence and a brief pause. In this recording, the performers immediately repeat each section with a slightly larger group of instruments, and then play all three sections successively with the fuller instrumentation: a a' b b' c c' a' b' c'.

The Baroque Period

III

"The figured bass is the most perfect foundation of music, being played with both hands in such a manner that the left hand plays the notes written down while the right adds consonances and dissonances, in order to make a well-sounding harmony to the Glory of God and the permissible delectation of the spirit."

JOHANN SEBASTIAN BACH

During the baroque period, voices were accompanied by melodic lines designed for instruments. In *The Concert* (c. 1626–1627), by Hendrick Ter Brugghen, a singer is accompanied by a flutist and a lute player.

Time-Line Baroque Period (1600–1750)

Dates	Music	Arts and Letters	Historical and Cultural Events
1600–1680	Monteverdi, *Orfeo* (1607) Monteverdi, *The Coronation of Poppea* (1642) 	Shakespeare, *Hamlet* (1600) Cervantes, *Don Quixote* (1605) Gentileschi, *Judith Slaying Holofernes* (1613) Bernini, *David Slaying Goliath* (1623) Poussin, *Mars and Venus* (1630) Rubens, *Descent from the Cross* (1612–15) Rembrandt, *Self-Portrait* (1659) Milton, *Paradise Lost* (1667)	Jamestown founded (1607) King James Bible (1611) Galileo confirms that earth revolves around the sun (1610) Thirty Years' War (1618–1648) Louis XIV reigns in France (1643–1715)
1680–1750	Purcell, *Dido and Aeneas* (1689) Corelli, Trio Sonata in A Minor, Op. 3, No. 10 (1689)  Bach, Organ Fugue in G Minor *(Little Fugue)* (c. 1709) Bach, *Brandenburg* Concerto No. 5 in D Major (c. 1721) Vivaldi, *La Primavera (Spring),* Concerto for Violin and Orchestra, Op. 8, No. 1 (1725) Bach, Cantata No. 140: *Wachet auf, ruft uns die Stimme* (1731) Handel, *Messiah* (1741)	Locke, *Essay Concerning Human Understanding* (1689) Watteau, *The Embarkation for Cythera* (1717) Defoe, *Robinson Crusoe* (1719) Swift, *Gulliver's Travels* (1726)	Newton, *Principia Mathematica* (1687) Witchcraft trials in Salem, Massachusetts (1692) Louis XV reigns in France (1715–1774) Frederick the Great reigns in Prussia (1740–1786)

The Baroque Style (1600–1750)

Though the word *baroque* has at various times meant bizarre, flamboyant, and elaborately ornamented, modern historians use it simply to indicate a particular style in the arts. An oversimplified but useful characterization of baroque style is that it fills space—canvas, stone, or sound—with action and movement. Painters, sculptors, and architects became interested in forming a total illusion, like a stage setting. Artists such as Caravaggio, Gentileschi, Bernini, Rubens, and Rembrandt exploited their materials to expand the dramatic potential of color, depth, and contrasts of light and dark; they wanted to create totally structured worlds.

Such a style was very well suited to the wishes of the aristocracy, who also thought in terms of completely integrated structures. In France, for example, Louis XIV held court in the palace of Versailles, a magnificent setting that fused baroque painting, sculpture, architecture, and garden design into a symbol of royal wealth and power.

The aristocracy was enormously rich and powerful during the seventeenth and eighteenth centuries. While most of the population barely managed to survive, European rulers surrounded themselves with luxury. There were many such rulers. Germany, for example, was divided into about 300 territories, each governed separately. Kings and princes proclaimed their greatness by means of splendid palaces and magnificent court entertainments like balls, banquets, ballets, operas, and plays. Indeed, entertainment was a necessity; most courtiers did no real work and tried to avoid boredom as much as possible.

The baroque period (1600–1750) is also known as the "age of absolutism" because many rulers exercised absolute power over their

Judith Slaying Holofernes (c. 1612–1613) by the Italian painter Artemisia Gentileschi (1593–1652). Baroque artists emphasized motion and drama.

Bernini's *David Slaying Goliath* (1623) fills space with action and movement. It is far more dynamic than Michelangelo's *David* shown on page 63.

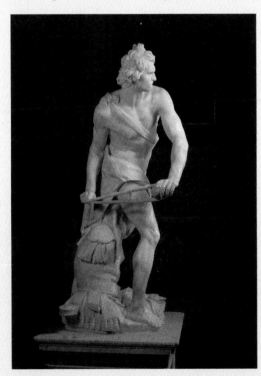

subjects. In Germany, for example, the duke of Weimar could throw his court musician Johann Sebastian Bach into jail for a month because Bach stubbornly requested to leave his job.

Along with the aristocracy, religious institutions powerfully shaped the baroque style. Churches used the emotional and theatrical qualities of art to make worship more attractive and appealing. During the baroque period, Europe was divided into Catholic and Protestant areas: France, Spain, Italy, and the Austrian empire were primarily Catholic; England, Holland, Denmark, Sweden, and parts of Germany were Protestant.

The middle class, too, influenced the development of the baroque style. In the Netherlands, for example, prosperous merchants and doctors commissioned realistic landscapes and scenes from everyday life.

It is also helpful to think of baroque style against the backdrop of scientific discoveries during the seventeenth and eighteenth centuries. The work of Galileo (1564–1642) and Newton (1642–1727) represented a new approach to science based on the union of mathematics and experiment; they discovered mathematical laws governing bodies in motion. Such scientific advances led to new inventions and the gradual improvement of medicine, mining, navigation, and industry during the baroque era.

Mars and Venus (c. 1630) by the French painter Nicholas Poussin. The subject matter, harmonious colors, and balanced composition reflect Poussin's love of classical antiquity and Renaissance art.

The Flemish painter Peter Paul Rubens used diagonal motion and theatrical lighting in *Descent from the Cross* (1612–15). Baroque artists became interested in forming a total illusion, like a stage setting. Often baroque painting and baroque opera were created for the nobility and were designed to display magnificent extravagance.

Self-Portrait (1659) by Rembrandt van Rijn. Rembrandt's use of light and dark contributes to the poetry, drama, and psychological truth of his portraits.

The Palace of Versailles, in France, fused baroque architecture, sculpture, and painting into a symbol of royal wealth and power.

Baroque Music (1600–1750)

In music, the baroque style flourished during the period from 1600 to 1750. The two giants of baroque composition were George Frideric Handel and Johann Sebastian Bach. Bach's death in 1750 marks the end of the period. Other baroque masters—Claudio Monteverdi, Henry Purcell, Arcangelo Corelli, Antonio Vivaldi—were largely forgotten until the twentieth century. But the appearance of long-playing records in the late 1940s spurred a "baroque revival" that made these long-forgotten musicians familiar to many music lovers.

The baroque period can be divided into three phases: early (1600–1640), middle (1640–1680), and late (1680–1750). Though the baroque music best known today comes from the latest phase, the earliest was one of the most revolutionary periods in music history. Monteverdi (1567–1643), for instance, strove to create unprecedented passion and dramatic contrast in his works. In Italy, especially, music was composed for texts conveying extreme emotion, and the text ruled the music. With this stress on drama and text, it is not surprising that Italian composers of the early baroque created opera—a drama sung to orchestral accompaniment. Their melodic lines imitated the rhythms and inflections of speech.

Early baroque composers favored homophonic texture over the polyphonic texture typical of Renaissance music. They felt that words could be projected more clearly by using just one main melody with a chordal accompaniment. But note that this new emphasis on homophonic texture characterizes only the *early* baroque; by the *late* baroque period, polyphonic texture returned to favor.

To depict the extreme emotions in their texts, early baroque composers used dissonance with a new freedom. Never before were unstable chords so prominent and emphatic. Contrasts of sound were stressed—one or more solo singers against a chorus, or voices against instruments. In Renaissance choral music, instruments—if used at all—duplicated a singer's melody. But in the early baroque, voices were accompanied by melodic lines designed for instruments.

During the middle phase of the baroque (1640–1680), the new musical style spread from Italy to practically every country in Europe. The medieval or church modes—scales that had governed music for centuries—gradually gave way to major and minor scales. By about 1680, major or minor scales were the tonal basis of most compositions. Another feature of the middle baroque phase was the new importance of instrumental music. Many compositions were written for specific instruments, the violin family being most popular.

We will focus mainly on the late baroque period (1680–1750), which produced most of the baroque music heard today. Many aspects of harmony—including an emphasis on the attraction of the dominant chord to the tonic—arose in this period. During the late baroque, instrumental music became as important as vocal music for the first time. Early baroque composers had emphasized homophonic texture; late baroque composers gloried in polyphony. Let's look more closely at some features of late baroque style. (From now on the word *baroque* will pertain to the late baroque phase.)

Characteristics of Baroque Music

Unity of Mood

A baroque piece usually expresses one basic mood: what begins joyfully will remain joyful throughout. Emotional states like joy, grief, and agitation were represented—at the time, these moods were called *affections*. Composers molded a musical language to depict the affections; specific rhythms or melodic patterns were associated with specific moods. This common language gives a family resemblance to much late baroque music.

The prime exception to this baroque principle of unity of mood occurs in vocal music. Drastic changes of emotion in a text may inspire corresponding changes in the music. But even in such cases, one mood is maintained at some length before it yields to another.

Rhythm

Unity of mood in baroque music is conveyed, first of all, by continuity of rhythm. Rhythmic patterns heard at the beginning of a piece are repeated throughout it. This rhythmic continuity provides a compelling drive and energy—the forward motion is rarely interrupted. The beat is emphasized far more in baroque music than in most Renaissance music, for example.

Melody

Baroque melody also creates a feeling of continuity. An opening melody will be heard again and again in the course of a baroque piece. And even when a melody is presented in varied form, its character tends to remain constant. There is a continuous expanding, unfolding, and unwinding of melody. This sense of directed motion is frequently the result of a melodic sequence, that is, successive repetition of a musical idea at higher or lower pitch levels. Many baroque melodies sound elaborate and ornamental, and they are not easy to sing or remember. A baroque melody gives an impression of dynamic expansion rather than of balance or symmetry. A short opening phrase is often followed by a longer phrase with an unbroken flow of rapid notes.

Dynamics

Paralleling continuity of rhythm and melody in baroque music is continuity of dynamic level: the volume tends to stay constant for a stretch of time. When the dynamics do shift, the shift is usually sudden, like physically stepping from one level to another. This alternation between loud and soft is called **terraced dynamics.** *Gradual* changes through crescendo and decrescendo, though occasionally used, are *not* prominent features of baroque music. However, singers and instrumentalists no doubt made some subtle dynamic inflections for expressive purposes.

The main keyboard instruments of the baroque period were the organ and harpsichord, both well suited for continuity of dynamic level. An organist or harpsichordist could not obtain a crescendo or decrescendo by varying finger pressure, as pianists today can. A third keyboard instrument, the *clavichord,* could make gradual dynamic changes, but only within a narrow range—from about *ppp* to *mp*. (The clavichord produced sound by means of brass blades striking the strings. It was usually not used in large halls, since its tone was too weak. But for home use by amateurs it was ideal; its cost was low and its expressive sound satisfying. It had especially wide popularity in Germany.)

Texture

We've noted that late baroque music is predominantly polyphonic in texture: two or more melodic lines compete for the listener's attention. Usually, the soprano and bass lines are the most important. Imitation between the various lines, or "voices," of the texture is very common. A melodic idea heard in one voice is likely to make an appearance in the other voices as well.

However, not all late baroque music was polyphonic. A piece might shift in texture, especially in vocal music, where changes of mood in the words demand musical contrast. Also, baroque composers differed in their treatment of musical texture. Bach inclined toward a consistently polyphonic texture, whereas Handel used much more contrast between polyphonic and homophonic sections.

Chords and the Basso Continuo (Figured Bass)

Chords became increasingly important during the baroque period. In earlier times, there was more concern with the beauty of individual melodic lines than with chords formed when the lines were heard together. In a sense, chords were mere by-products of the motion of melodic lines. But in the baroque period chords became significant in themselves. As composers wrote a melodic line, they thought of chords to mesh with it. Indeed, sometimes they composed a melody to fit a specific chord progression. This interest in chords gave new prominence to the bass part, which served as the foundation of the harmony. The whole musical structure rested on the bass part.

The new emphasis on chords and the bass part resulted in the most characteristic feature of baroque music, an accompaniment called the *basso continuo,* or *figured bass.* This is made up of a bass part together with numbers (figures) which specify the chords to be played above it. The *continuo*—to use the common abbreviation for *basso continuo*—is usually played by at least two instruments: an organ or a harpsichord and a low melodic instrument like a cello or bassoon. With the left hand, the organist or harpsichordist plays the bass part, which is also performed by the cellist or bassoonist. With the right hand, the keyboard player improvises chords or even a melodic line, following the indications of the numbers. These numbers specify only a basic chord, not the exact way in which the chord should be played. Thus the performer is given a great deal of freedom. (This shorthand system is similar in principle to the chord indications found on the modern song sheets from which jazz pianists improvise.) Shown on page 99 is the beginning of the continuo part of Bach's *Brandenburg* Concerto No. 5, first movement (studied in Section 3), and one possible performance or "realization" of this part by a harpsichordist.

Basso Continuo Part

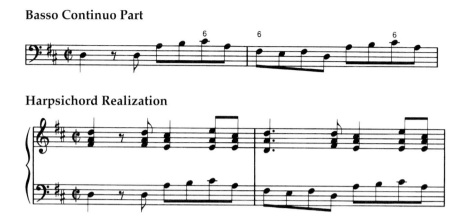

Harpsichord Realization

The basso continuo offered the advantage of emphasizing the all-important bass part, besides providing a steady flow of chords. Practically, the use of numbers, rather than chords with all their notes written out, saved time for busy baroque composers. It also saved paper at a time when paper was expensive.

Words and Music

Like their Renaissance predecessors, baroque composers used music to depict the meaning of specific words. *Heaven* might be set to a high tone, and *hell* to a low tone. Rising scales represented upward motion; descending scales depicted the reverse. Descending chromatic scales were associated with pain and grief. This descriptive musical language was quite standardized: a lament for a lost love might call forth the same descending chromatic scale used to depict suffering in the *Crucifixus* of the mass.

Baroque composers often emphasized words by writing many rapid notes for a single syllable of text; this technique also displayed a singer's virtuosity. The individual words and phrases of a text are repeated over and over as the music continuously unfolds.

The Baroque Orchestra

During the baroque period, the orchestra evolved into a performing group based on instruments of the violin family. By modern standards, the baroque orchestra was small, consisting of from ten to thirty or forty players. Its instrumental makeup was flexible and could vary from piece to piece. At its nucleus were the basso continuo (harpsichord plus cello, double bass, or bassoon) and upper strings (first and second violins and violas). Use of woodwind, brass, and percussion instruments was variable. To the strings and continuo could be added recorders, flutes, oboes, trumpets, horns, trombones, or timpani. One piece might use only a single flute, while another would call for two oboes, three trumpets, and timpani. Trumpets and timpani joined the orchestra mainly when the music was festive. This flexibility contrasts with the standardized orchestra of later periods, consisting of four sections: string, woodwind, brass, and percussion.

The baroque trumpet (like the early French horn) had no valves but was given rapid, complex melodic lines to play in a high register. Because the instrument was difficult to play and had a traditional association with royalty, the trumpeter was the aristocrat of the baroque orchestra. When prisoners of war were exchanged, trumpeters, if they had been captured, were treated like military officers.

Bach, Handel, Vivaldi, and others chose their orchestral instruments with care and obtained beautiful effects from specific tone colors. They loved to experiment with different combinations of instruments. However, in the baroque period tone color was distinctly subordinate to other musical elements—melody, rhythm, and harmony. Composers frequently rearranged their own or other composers' works for different instruments. A piece for string orchestra might become an organ solo, losing little in the process. Often, one instrument was treated like another. An oboe would play the same melody as the violins, or the flute and trumpet would imitate each other for extended sections of a piece.

Baroque Forms

It has been noted that a piece of baroque music—particularly instrumental music—usually has unity of mood. Yet many baroque compositions include a set of pieces, or movements, that contrast. A *movement* is a piece that sounds fairly complete and independent but is part of a larger composition. Usually, each movement has its own themes, comes to a definite end, and is separated from the next movement by a brief pause. Thus, a baroque composition in three movements may contain contrasts between a fast and energetic opening, a slow and solemn middle, and a conclusion that is quick, light, and humorous.

All the forms described in Part I, Section 9—"Musical Form"—appear in baroque music. Three-part form (A B A), two-part form (A B), and continuous or undivided form are all common. We'll consider examples of these and other forms in the sections that follow.

Regardless of form, baroque music features contrasts between bodies of sound. Often there is a quite regular alternation between a small and a larger group of instruments, or between instruments and voices with instrumental accompaniment. This exploration of contrasting sounds was pursued with great imagination and provides a key to the understanding and enjoyment of baroque music.

2 Music in Baroque Society

Before 1800, most music was written to order, to meet specific demands that came mainly from churches and aristocratic courts. Opera houses and municipalities also required a constant supply of music. In every case, the demand was for *new* music; audiences did not want to listen to pieces in an "old-fashioned" style.

Music was a main source of diversion in the courts of the aristocracy. One court might employ an orchestra, a chapel choir, and opera singers—the size of the musical staff depending on the court's wealth. Bach directed about eighteen players in the orchestra of a small German court in 1717; but a large court might

During the baroque period, musicians often played with amateurs in music clubs or university music societies, getting together in private homes, coffeehouses, and taverns. *The Concert* by Nicholas Tournier (1590–1639) shows one such gathering.

have more than eighty performers, including the finest opera singers of the day. The music director supervised performances and composed much of the music required, including operas, church music, dinner music, and pieces for court concerts. This overworked musician also was responsible for the discipline of the other musicians, and for the upkeep of the instruments and the music library.

The music director's job had good and bad features. Pay and prestige were quite high, and anything the composer wrote would be performed. But no matter how great, the composer was still a servant who could neither quit nor even take a trip without the patron's permission. Like everyone in baroque society, musicians had to curry favor with the aristocracy.

It is in this light that we must understand dedications like the one which Bach addressed to a nobleman along with his *Brandenburg* Concertos: "Begging Your Highness most humbly not to judge their imperfection with the rigor of the fine and delicate taste which the whole world knows Your Highness has for musical pieces; but rather to infer from them in benign Consideration the profound respect and the most humble obedience which I try to show Your Highness." Yet sometimes musicians formed personal friendships with their patrons, as did Arcangelo Corelli, who thus gained a private apartment in a palace.

Some rulers were themselves good musicians. Frederick the Great, king of Prussia during the mid-eighteenth century, was a flutist and good composer, as well as a feared general. At his nightly court concerts, Frederick played his own works and some of the hundreds of pieces supplied by his flute teacher, Johann Quantz. (Quantz was "granted the privilege" of shouting "Bravo!" after a royal performance.)

Churches also needed music, and church music was often very grand. Along with an organ and a choir, many baroque churches had an orchestra to accompany services. Indeed, it was in church that most ordinary citizens heard music. There were few public concerts, and the populace was rarely invited to the palace. The music director of a church, like the music director at a court, had to produce a steady flow of new music and was also responsible for the musical training of choristers in the church school. Fine church music contributed to the prestige of a city, and cities often competed to attract the best musicians.

Still, church musicians earned less and had lower status than court musicians. Their meager income was supplemented by allotments of firewood and grain and by irregular fees for weddings and funerals. They suffered a financial pinch when a "healthy wind" blew and there were fewer funerals than usual, a situation Bach once complained about.

Large towns employed musicians for a variety of functions—to play in churches, in processions, in concerts for visiting dignitaries, and for university graduations. These town musicians often played with amateurs in music clubs or university music societies, getting together at private homes, coffeehouses, and taverns.

Some baroque musicians earned money by writing operas for commercial opera houses; such houses were located mainly in Italy. In Venice, a city of 125,000 people, six opera companies performed simultaneously between 1680 and 1700. In London, Handel became music director of a commercial opera company in 1719. Backed by English nobles, this company was a corporation with shares listed on the London stock exchange. When the company went bankrupt in 1728, Handel formed his own company, for which he wrote operas and served as conductor, manager, and impresario. In filling these many roles, Handel became one of the first great "freelance" musicians.

How did one become a musician in the baroque period? Often the art was handed from father to son; many leading composers—such as Bach, Vivaldi, Purcell, Couperin, and Rameau—were sons of musicians. Sometimes boys were apprenticed to a town musician and lived in his home. In return for instruction, the boys did odd jobs, such as copying music. Many baroque composers began their studies as choirboys, learning music in the choir school. In Italy, music schools were connected with orphanages. (*Conservatory* comes from the Italian for *orphans' home.*) There, orphans, foundlings, and poor children—boys and girls—were given thorough musical training, and some became the most sought-after opera singers and instrumentalists in Europe. Eminent composers such as Vivaldi were hired to teach and direct concerts in these schools. Vivaldi's all-female orchestra in Venice was considered one of the finest ensembles in Italy. During the baroque period, women were not permitted to be employed as music directors or as instrumentalists in court or opera orchestras. Nevertheless, a number of women—including Francesca Caccini, Barbara Strozzi, and Elisabeth-Claude Jacquet de la Guerre—succeeded in becoming respected composers.

To get a job, musicians usually had to pass a difficult examination, performing and submitting compositions. Sometimes there were nonmusical job requirements, too. An applicant might be expected to make a "voluntary contribution" to the town's treasury, or even to marry the daughter of a retiring musician. Bach and Handel turned down the same job because one of the conditions was marriage to the organist's daughter. Italian musicians held the best posts in most European courts and were frequently paid twice as much as local musicians.

Composers were an integral part of baroque society, working for courts, churches, towns, and commercial opera houses. Though they wrote their music to fit specific needs, its quality is so high that much of it has become standard in today's concert repertoire.

3 The Concerto Grosso and Ritornello Form

We've seen that the contrast between loud and soft sounds—between relatively large and small groups of performers—is a basic principle of baroque music. This principle governs the concerto grosso, an important form of orchestral music in the late baroque period. In a *concerto grosso,* a small group of soloists is pitted against a larger group of players called the *tutti* *(all).* Usually, between two and four soloists play with anywhere from eight to twenty or more musicians for the tutti. The tutti consists mainly of string instruments, with a harpsichord as part of the basso continuo. A concerto grosso presents a contrast of texture between the tutti and the soloists, who assert their individuality and appeal for attention through brilliant and fanciful melodic lines. The soloists were the best and highest-paid members of the baroque orchestra, because their parts were more difficult than those of the other players. Concerti grossi were frequently performed by private orchestras in aristocratic palaces.

A concerto grosso consists of *several movements that contrast in tempo and character.* Most often there are three movements: (1) fast, (2) slow, (3) fast. The opening movement is usually vigorous and determined, clearly showing the contrast between tutti and soloists. The slow movement is quieter than the first, often lyrical and intimate. The last movement is lively and carefree, sometimes dancelike.

The first and last movements of concerti grossi are often in *ritornello form,* which is based on alternation between tutti and solo sections. In ritornello form the tutti opens with a theme called the *ritornello* *(refrain).* This theme, always played by the tutti, returns in different keys throughout the movement. But it usually returns in fragments, not complete. Only at the end of the movement does the entire ritornello return in the home key. Although the number of times a ritornello (tutti) returns varies from piece to piece, a typical concerto grosso movement might be outlined as follows:

1. a. Tutti (f), ritornello in home key
   b. Solo
2. a. Tutti (f), ritornello fragment
   b. Solo
3. a. Tutti (f), ritornello fragment
   b. Solo
4. Tutti (f), ritornello in home key

In contrast to the tutti's ritornello, the solo sections offer fresh melodic ideas, softer dynamics, rapid scales, and broken chords. Soloists may also expand short melodic ideas from the tutti. The opening movement of Bach's *Brandenburg* Concerto No. 5 is a fine example of ritornello form in the concerto grosso.

Brandenburg Concerto No. 5 in D Major (about 1721), by Johann Sebastian Bach

With his set of six *Brandenburg* Concertos, Bach gave immortality to a German aristocrat, the margrave of Brandenburg. Bach met the margrave in 1718, when he was music director for another patron. The margrave loved music and asked Bach to send him some original compositions. About three years later, Bach sent him the *Brandenburg* Concertos with the flattering dedication quoted in Section 2, probably hoping for money or favors in return. (We don't know whether he got any.) These concertos had actually been composed for, and performed by, the orchestra of Bach's employer, the prince of Cöthen. Each of the concertos is written for a different and unusual combination of instruments.

Brandenburg Concerto No. 5 uses a string orchestra and a group of soloists consisting of a flute, a violin, and a harpsichord. This was the first time that a harpsichord had been given the solo role in a concerto grosso. In 1719, the prince of Cöthen had bought a new harpsichord; Bach probably wanted to show off this instrument (as well as his own skill as a keyboard player), and so he gave it a solo spot. The tutti is written for violins, violas, cellos, and double bass. During the tutti sections the solo violinist plays along, as does the harpsichordist, who realizes the figured bass.

The *Brandenburg* Concerto No. 5 has three movements: (1) fast, (2) slow, (3) fast. We'll focus on the first movement.

First Movement:
Allegro

Brief Set:

CD 1 63

Basic Set:

CD 2 1

The allegro movement opens with the ritornello, which is an almost continuous flow of rapid notes. After the ritornello ends—clearly—the soloists present short melodic ideas, the flute and violin imitating each other playfully. The appearance of the soloists brings a lower dynamic level and a new tone color—the flute. After a while, the tutti returns loudly with a brief fragment of the ritornello, only to give way again to the soloists. This alternation between brief, relatively loud ritornello fragments in the tutti and longer, softer solo sections continues throughout the movement.

The soloists' music tends to be brilliant, fanciful, and personal as compared with the more vigorous and straightforward tutti sections. Solo sections are also more polyphonic in texture than the tutti and stress imitation between the flute and violin. The soloists play new material of their own or varied fragments from the ritornello. These solo sections build tension and make the listener anticipate the tutti's return. Listen especially for the suspenseful solo section that begins with a new theme in minor and ends with long notes in the flute.

Only the harpsichord plays during the long final solo section. And it is spectacular! Bach builds a tense high point for the movement through irresistible rhythm and dazzling scale passages that require a virtuoso's skill. His audience must have marveled at this brilliant harpsichord solo within a concerto grosso. Audiences are still dazzled by it.

Listening Outline to be read while music is heard   Basic Set: CD 2   Brief Set: CD 1

BACH, *Brandenburg* Concerto No. 5

First movement: Allegro

Ritornello form, duple meter ($\frac{2}{2}$), D major

Flute, violin, harpsichord (solo group); string orchestra, continuo (tutti)

(Duration, 9:58)

Tutti

| 63 | 1 | 0:00 | | **1. a.** Strings, *f*, ritornello. |

Solo

| 64 | 2 | 0:20 | | **b.** Flute, violin, harpsichord, major key. |

Tutti

| 65 | 3 | 0:44 | 0:00 | **2. a.** Strings, *f*, ritornello fragment. |

Solo

| | | 0:49 | 0:05 | **b.** Flute, violin, harpsichord, varied ritornello fragment. |

Tutti

| | | 1:09 | 0:25 | **3. a.** Strings, *f*, ritornello fragment. |

Solo

1:16	0:32	**b.** Violin, flute, harpsichord.

Tutti

1:36	0:52	**4. a.** Strings, *f*, ritornello fragment, minor.

Solo

1:42	0:58	**b.** Harpsichord, flute, violin.

Tutti

2:23	1:39	**5. a.** Strings, *f*, ritornello fragment, major.

Solo

2:30	1:46	**b.** Flute, harpsichord, violin, varied ritornello fragment, *pp*.
66 4 2:55	0:00	**c.** New theme in minor, *pp*, tossed between flute and violin.

Tension mounts, long notes in flute lead to

Tutti

4:11	1:16	**6. a.** Strings, *f*, ritornello fragment, major.

Solo

4:16	1:21	**b.** Violin, flute, harpsichord.

Tutti

5:01	2:06	**7. a.** Strings, *f*, longer ritornello fragment.

Solo

5:12	2:17	**b.** Violin, harpsichord, flute, varied ritornello fragment.

Tutti

5:40	2:45	**8. a.** Strings, *f*, ritornello fragment.

Solo

5:47	2:52	**b.** Violin and flute play carefree idea with rapid harpsichord scales in background.
67 5 6:24	0:00	**c.** Long harpsichord solo featuring virtuoso display. Mounting tension resolved in

Tutti

9:32	3:08	**9.** Strings, *f*, ritornello.

4 The Fugue

One cornerstone of baroque music is the fugue, which can be written for a group of instruments or voices, or for a single instrument such as an organ or a harpsichord. A *fugue* is a polyphonic composition based on one main theme, called a *subject.* Throughout a fugue, different melodic lines, or *"voices,"* imitate the subject. The top melodic line—whether sung or played—is the soprano voice and the bottom is the bass. A fugue usually consists of three, four, or five voices. Though the subject remains fairly constant throughout, it takes on new meanings when shifted to different keys or combined with different melodic and rhythmic ideas.

The form of a fugue is extremely flexible; in fact, the only constant feature of fugues is how they begin—the subject is almost always presented in a single, unaccompanied voice. By thus highlighting the subject, the composer tells us what to remember and listen for. In getting to know a fugue, try to follow the subject through the different levels of texture. After its first presentation, the subject is imitated in turn by all the remaining voices. For example, the top voice may announce the subject and then the lower voices imitate it in turn. However, the subject may be announced by *any* voice—top, bottom, or middle—and the order in which the remaining voices imitate it is also completely flexible.

This may seem reminiscent of a round such as *Row, Row, Row Your Boat,* but in a fugue the game of follow the leader (exact imitation of the subject) does not continue indefinitely. *After a voice has presented the subject, it is free to go its own way with different melodic material.* A fugue's opening differs from a round's in another way: in a round, each voice presents the melody on the same pitches. If the melody begins with the pitches C-D-E, each successive voice will begin with these same pitches, whether at a higher or lower register. However, in the opening of a fugue, *the subject is presented in two different scales.* The first time, it is based on the notes of the *tonic* scale. But when the second voice presents the subject, it is in the *dominant* scale—five scale steps higher than the tonic—and is called the *answer.* A subject beginning with the notes C-D-E, for example, would be imitated by an answer five steps higher, G-A-B. This alternation of subject and answer between the two scales creates variety. The following diagram shows the alternation of subject and answer in the opening section of a fugue in four voices:

Soprano	Subject _____ . . . . etc.	
Alto	Answer _____ . . . . etc.	
Tenor	Subject _____ . . . . etc.	
Bass	Answer _____ . . . . etc.	

In many fugues, the subject in one voice is accompanied throughout in another voice by a different melodic idea called a *countersubject.* A constant companion, the countersubject always appears with the subject, sometimes below it, sometimes above it.

After the opening of a fugue, when each voice has taken its turn at presenting the subject, a composer is free to decide how often the subject will be presented, in which voices, and in which keys. Between presentations of the subject, there are often transitional sections called *episodes,* which offer either new material or fragments of the subject or countersubject. Episodes do *not* present the subject in its entirety. They lend variety to the fugue and make reappearances of the subject sound fresh. Bach called one composer of fugues "pedantic" because he "had not shown enough fire to reanimate the theme by episodes."

Several musical procedures commonly appear in fugues. One is *stretto,* in which a subject is imitated before it is completed; one voice tries to catch the other. Another common procedure is *pedal point* (or *organ point*), in which a single tone, usually in the bass, is held while the other voices produce a series of changing harmonies against it. (The term is taken from organ music, where a sustained low tone is produced by the organist's foot on a key of the pedal keyboard.)

A fugue subject can be varied in four principal ways:

1. It can be turned upside down, a procedure known as *inversion.* If the subject moves *upward* by leap, the inversion will move *downward* the same distance; if the subject moves *downward* by step, the inversion will move *upward* by step. In inversion, each interval in the subject is reversed in direction.
2. The subject may be presented *retrograde,* that is, by beginning with the last note of the subject and proceeding backward to the first.
3. The subject may be presented in *augmentation,* in which the original time values are lengthened.
4. The subject may appear in *diminution,* with shortened time values.

A fugue usually conveys a single mood and a sense of continuous flow. Fugues may be written as independent works or as single movements within larger compositions. Very often an independent fugue is introduced by a short piece called a *prelude.*

Bach and Handel each wrote hundreds of fugues; their fugues represent the peak among works in the form. In the baroque period, as a friend of Bach's observed, "Skill in fugue was so indispensable in a composer that no one could have attained a musical post who had not worked out a given subject in all kinds of counterpoint and in a regular fugue." Fugal writing continued into the nineteenth and twentieth centuries. It is not used as frequently today as in the baroque period; yet to this day, as part of their training, musicians study how to write fugues.

Brief Set:
CD 1 [68]

Basic Set:
CD 2 [14]

Organ Fugue in G Minor
(*Little Fugue;* about 1709),
by Johann Sebastian Bach

One of Bach's best-known organ pieces is the *Little Fugue* in G Minor, so called to differentiate it from another, longer fugue in G minor. The opening section of the *Little Fugue* corresponds to the diagram on page 107. Each of the fugue's four voices takes its turn presenting the tuneful subject, which is announced in the top voice and then appears in progressively lower voices, until it reaches the bass, where it is played by the organist's feet on the pedal keyboard. Like many baroque melodies, the subject gathers momentum as it goes along, beginning with relatively long time values (quarter notes) and then proceeding to shorter ones (eighth and sixteenth notes). The answer in the alto voice is accompanied by a lively countersubject in the soprano that moves in short time values. During the rest of the fugue, the countersubject appears with the subject and answer, sometimes in a higher voice, sometimes in a lower voice.

After the opening section, the subject appears five more times, each time preceded by an episode. The first episode uses both new material and a melodic idea from the countersubject. This episode contains downward sequences, which are melodic patterns repeated in the same voice but at lower pitches.

For harmonic contrast, Bach twice presents the subject in major keys rather than minor. The final statement of the subject—in minor—exploits the powerful bass tones of the pedal keyboard. Though the fugue is in minor, it ends with a major chord. This was a frequent practice in the baroque period; major chords were thought more conclusive than minor chords.

Listening Outline to be read while music is heard

Brief Set: CD 1   Basic Set: CD 2

BACH, Organ Fugue in G Minor *(Little Fugue)*

Fugue, quadruple meter ($\frac{4}{4}$), G minor

Organ

(Duration, 4:04)

68 14   0:00   **1. a.** Subject, soprano voice alone, minor key.

0:18   **b.** Answer in alto, countersubject in running notes in soprano.

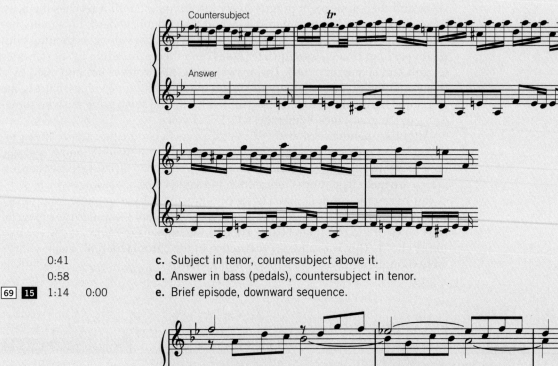

0:41   **c.** Subject in tenor, countersubject above it.
0:58   **d.** Answer in bass (pedals), countersubject in tenor.
[69] [15] 1:14   0:00   **e.** Brief episode, downward sequence.

1:24   0:10   **2. a.** Subject begins in tenor, continues in soprano, accompanied by sustained tone in bass; subject leads to
1:43   0:29   **b.** Brief episode, running notes in a downward sequence.
[70] [16] 1:52   0:00   **3. a.** Subject in alto, major key; countersubject in soprano; subject leads to
2:08   0:16   **b.** Episode in major, upward leaps and running notes.
2:20   0:28   **c.** Subject in bass (pedals), major key, countersubject and long trill above it.
2:37   0:45   **d.** Longer episode, downward sequence; begins in major, ends in minor.
2:54   1:02   **4. a.** Subject in soprano, minor key, countersubject below it.
3:10   1:18   **b.** Most extended episode, running notes in a downward sequence; upward sequences lead to sustained high tones, which usher in
3:40   1:48   **c.** Subject in bass (pedals), countersubject in soprano. Fugue ends with major chord.

5 The Elements of Opera

The baroque era witnessed the development of a major innovation in music—
opera, or drama that is sung to orchestral accompaniment. This unique fusion
of music, acting, poetry, dance, scenery, and costumes offers a theatrical experi-

ence of overwhelming excitement and emotion. Since its beginnings in Italy around 1600, opera has spread to many countries, and it remains a powerful form of musical theater today. In Section 6, we'll look closely at opera in the baroque period; but first, a general discussion of opera is in order.

In an opera, characters and plot are revealed through song, rather than the speech used in ordinary drama. Once we accept this convention, opera offers us great pleasure; its music both delights the ear and heightens the emotional effect of the words and story. Music makes even a complicated plot believable by depicting mood, character, and dramatic action. The flow of the music carries the plot forward. In opera, the music *is* the drama.

Opera demands performers who can sing and act simultaneously. On stage are star solo singers, secondary soloists, a chorus, and sometimes dancers—all in costume. Besides the chorus of professional singers, there may be "supers" (supernumeraries, or "extras"), who don't sing but who carry spears, fill out crowds, drink wine, or do other things that add to the effect. Scenery, lighting, and stage machinery are intricate and are used to create illusions of fires, floods, storms, and supernatural effects. In the orchestra pit are the instrumentalists and the conductor, whose awesome responsibility it is to hold everything together. The personnel for a large opera—from conductor to stage director and assorted vocal coaches, rehearsal accompanists, technicians, and stagehands—may reach a startling total of several hundred people.

The capacity of this combined force to create spectacle and pageantry accounts for much of opera's appeal. Historically, opera has been associated with high social status. It originated in the courts of kings and princes (who could afford it) and long continued as a form of aristocratic entertainment. But as opera became more concerned with "real" people and less with royal figures, it attracted popular audiences. Today, radio and television broadcasts, videos, DVDs, and recordings have changed opera's image as an exotic and expensive diversion for the very rich. Millions of people from every economic background know opera for what it is: a powerful and pleasurable emotional experience.

The creation of an opera results from the joint efforts of a composer and a dramatist. The *libretto*—that is, the text—of the opera is usually written by the *librettist,* or dramatist, and set to music by the composer. But composers often collaborate with dramatists to ensure that the texts meet their musical needs. W. H. Auden once said that a good libretto "offers as many opportunities as possible for the characters to be swept off their feet by placing them in situations which are too tragic or too fantastic for words. No good opera plot can be sensible, for people do not sing when they are feeling sensible." And that is true— opera characters are people overwhelmed by love, lust, hatred, and revenge. They wear fantastic disguises and commit extraordinary acts of violence. Yet the music makes them human and real. It evokes the haughtiness of a countess or the simplicity of a peasant girl. It creates a dramatic entrance for an outraged father, depicts the tension behind sword thrusts in a duel, and portrays the bleakness of a winter dawn. A great opera composer is a master of musical timing and characterization and has a keen sense of theater, knowing just when to have a character sing a simple phrase or a soaring melody, when to provide a stirring chorus or a graceful dance. Through the music, the composer paces the drama, controlling the speed of gestures, entrances, exits, and stage movements.

Some operas are serious, some comic, some both. Operas may contain spoken dialogue, but most are entirely sung. (Spoken dialogue is used mainly in comic opera, where stage action must be performed quickly for the most humorous effect.) Since it normally takes longer to sing than to speak words, the text of a 3-hour opera is shorter than that of a 3-hour play. The librettist allows time for the composer's musical elaboration.

The range of characters found in opera is broad and varied; gods, empresses, dukes, servants, priests, prostitutes, peasants, clowns, and cowboys all make appearances. Opera soloists must create all these characters and so need acting skill as well as vocal artistry. During rehearsals, the stage director coaches the singers to move well, gesture meaningfully, and identify with their characters.

As noted in Section 2 of Part I, Elements, the basic voice ranges are soprano, alto, tenor, and bass. These are divided more finely in opera. Some of the *voice categories of opera* are as follows:

Coloratura soprano	Very high range; can execute rapid scales and trills
Lyric soprano	Rather light voice; sings roles calling for grace and charm
Dramatic soprano	Full, powerful voice; is capable of passionate intensity
Lyric tenor	Relatively light, bright voice
Dramatic tenor	Powerful voice; is capable of heroic expression
Basso buffo	Takes comic roles; can sing very rapidly
Basso profondo	Very low range, powerful voice; takes roles calling for great dignity

Like a play, an opera has from one to five acts subdivided into scenes. A single act presents a variety of vocal and orchestral contrasts. For example, a tenor solo might be followed by a duet for soprano and bass, and then by a chorus or an orchestral interlude. A section may end definitely—and provide an opportunity for applause—or it may be linked with the next section to form a continuous flow of music within the act.

The main attraction for many opera fans is the *aria,* a song for solo voice with orchestral accompaniment. It's an outpouring of melody that expresses an emotional state. In an aria, *I love you* might be sung ten times to accommodate the expansion of the idea. Often the action stops while the character's feelings are revealed through music. An aria usually lasts several minutes. It is a complete piece with a definite beginning, high point, and end. If the performance of an aria is brilliant, the audience responds with an ovation at its conclusion. This breaks the dramatic flow but allows the audience to release its feelings through applause and shouts of *bravo!* or *brava!*

Opera composers often lead into an aria with a *recitative,* a vocal line that imitates the rhythms and pitch fluctuations of speech. In a recitative (from the Italian word for *recite*), words are sung quickly and clearly, often on repeated tones. There is usually only one note to each syllable in a recitative—as opposed to an aria, where one syllable may be stretched over many notes. Recitative is used for monologues and dialogues that connect the more melodic sections of the opera. It carries the action forward and presents routine information quickly.

Besides arias, the soloists in an opera will sing compositions for two or more singers: duets (for two singers), trios (for three), quartets (for four), quintets (for five), and sextets (for six). When three or more singers are involved, the composition is called an *ensemble.* In a duet or ensemble, the performers either face the audience or move through action that develops the plot. Each character expresses his or her own feelings. Conflicting emotions like grief, happiness, and anger can be projected simultaneously when different melodies are combined. This special blend of feelings is the glory of opera and is possible only through music; it cannot be duplicated in spoken drama.

An opera *chorus* generates atmosphere and makes comments on the action. Its members might be courtiers, sailors, peasants, prisoners, ballroom guests, and so on. Their sound creates a kind of tonal background for the soloists.

Rising just over the edge of center stage is the prompter's box. In this cramped space, invisible to the audience, is the *prompter,* who gives cues and reminds the singers of words or pitches if they momentarily forget—as can happen. Occasional memory lapses are inevitable with so much activity on stage.

Dance in opera is generally incidental. It provides an ornamental interlude that contrasts with and relaxes the thrust of the plot. By and large, dance is used as part of the setting—in a ballroom, at a country fair, in a pagan court—while the soloists, downstage, advance the action of the plot and work out their destinies.

The nerve center of an opera in performance is the orchestra pit—a sunken area directly in front of the stage. An opera orchestra has the same instruments as a full symphony orchestra, but usually it has a smaller string section. Covered lights attached to the players' music stands leave the orchestra in a deep shadow that doesn't interfere with the audience's view of the stage. The orchestra not only supports the singers but depicts mood and atmosphere and comments on the stage action. During the performance, the conductor shapes the entire work. He or she sets tempos, cues in singers, and indicates subtle dynamic gradations.

Most operas open with a purely orchestral composition called an *overture* or a *prelude.* Since the eighteenth century, the music for an overture has been drawn from material heard later in the opera. The overture is thus a short musical statement that involves the audience in the overall dramatic mood. Orchestral introductions to acts in the opera other than the first are always called *preludes.* Because overtures and preludes, like arias, are complete compositions, they frequently appear on symphony orchestra programs.

Should opera be translated? This question has long aroused controversy, and the battle continues. Most of the best-loved operas are in Italian, German, or French. Champions of translations into English argue that an audience should be able to understand the plot as it develops. Why tell jokes in a comic opera if they can't be understood? On the other hand, a composer takes pains to make a special fusion of pitch and the original words. This results in a tonal color that seems absolutely right. But no matter how well a singer articulates, some words are bound to be lost, whatever the language. For example, a sung melody can stretch one vowel over many notes; it takes a while to get to the end of a word. If the melody is placed in a soprano's highest range, the listener is really aware only of the silvery vowel and not of the word as a whole. Some operas seem to work well in translation; others don't. Much depends on the style of the opera and on the sensitivity of the translator.

In many recent opera productions, a translation of the libretto appears either above the stage or on a small screen in front of each viewer. These devices have also been a source of controversy. Their advocates say that they provide the best of both worlds, since they allow an opera to be sung in the original language while the audience is enabled to understand the words. But their opponents feel that these devices detract from the music and the action on stage.

Before you attend a live opera performance, in any language and with or without supertitles, it's a good idea to read the libretto or synopsis of the plot. Even better, watch a video or DVD, or listen to a recording while following the libretto. This way, you will be freer at the performance to appreciate the quality of production and interpretation.

Opera in the Baroque Era

Opera was born in Italy. Its way was prepared by musical discussions among a small group of nobles, poets, and composers who began to meet regularly in Florence around 1575. This group was known as the **Camerata** (Italian for *fellowship* or *society*) and included the composer Vincenzo Galilei, father of the astronomer Galileo.

The Camerata wanted to create a new vocal style modeled on the music of ancient Greek tragedy. Since no actual dramatic music had come down to them from the Greeks, they based their theories on literary accounts that had survived. It was believed that the Greek dramas had been sung throughout in a style that was midway between melody and speech. The Camerata wanted the vocal line to follow the rhythms and pitch fluctuations of speech. Because it was modeled after speech, the new vocal style became known as *recitative (recited)*. It was sung by a soloist with only a simple chordal accompaniment. The new music was therefore homophonic in texture. Polyphony was rejected by the Camerata because different words sounding simultaneously would obscure the all-important text.

Euridice by Jacopo Peri is the earliest opera that has been preserved. It was composed for the wedding of King Henri IV of France and Marie de' Medici and was performed in Florence in 1600. Seven years later Monteverdi composed *Orfeo*—the first *great* opera—for the court of the Gonzaga family in Mantua. Both these operas are based on the Greek myth of Orpheus's descent into hades to bring back his beloved Eurydice.

Much baroque opera was composed for ceremonial occasions at court and was designed as a display of magnificence and splendor. The subject matter was drawn from Greek mythology and ancient history. Not only were aristocratic patrons of the baroque fascinated by the classical civilizations of Greece and Rome, but they identified with Greek and Roman heroes and divinities. Opera did indeed reflect the creative urge of composer and librettist, but it also was a way to flatter the aristocracy. The radiant appearance of Apollo (god of poetry, music, and the sun) might symbolize a prince's enlightened rule.

The first public opera house opened in Venice in 1637; now anyone with the price of admission could attend an opera performance. Between 1637 and 1700 there were seventeen opera houses in Venice alone, as well as many in other

Much baroque opera was designed to display magnificent extravagance. Pietro Domenico Olivero's painting of the Royal Theater, Turin (1740), shows a performance of Francesco Feo's opera *Arsace.*

Italian cities—ample evidence that opera had been born in the right place at the right time. Hamburg, Leipzig, and London had public opera houses by the early 1700s, but, on the whole, public opera outside Italy took longer to develop.

Venetian opera became a great tourist attraction. An English traveler wrote in 1645 about the opera and its "variety of scenes painted and contrived with no less art of perspective, and machines for flying in the air, and other wonderful motions; taken together, it is one of the most magnificent and expensive diversions the wit of man can invent." The stage machinery of baroque opera bordered on the colossal; stage effects might include gods descending on clouds or riding across the sky in chariots, ships tossing, boulders splitting. And set design was an art in itself. Painters turned backdrops into cities with arches and avenues that stretched into the distant horizon.

Baroque opera marked the rise of virtuoso singers. Chief among these was the *castrato,* a male singer who had been castrated before puberty. (Castration of boy singers was common in Italy from 1600 to 1800; it was usually done with the consent of impoverished parents who hoped their sons would become highly paid opera stars.) A castrato combined the lung power of a man with the vocal range of a woman. His agility, breath control, and unique sound (which was not like a woman's) intrigued listeners. Castrati received the highest fees of any musicians. With their soprano or alto vocal ranges, they played male roles such as Caesar and Nero—baroque audiences evidently were more interested in vocal virtuosity than dramatic realism. Some baroque operas cannot be performed today, because contemporary singers aren't able to manage the fiendishly difficult castrato parts.

During the late baroque, operas consisted largely of arias linked by recitatives. These recitatives were usually accompanied only by a basso continuo, in which case they are called *secco recitatives.* At emotional high points and moments of tension, however, they might be supported by the orchestra; they are then called *accompanied recitatives.*

All action stopped during the aria, when the singer faced the audience, expressed the feelings of the character, and displayed vocal virtuosity. The form of a typical late baroque aria is A B A. An aria in A B A form is called a *da capo aria:* after the B section, the term *da capo* is written; this means *from the beginning* and indicates a repetition of the opening A section. However, the repetition was usually not literal, because the singer was expected to embellish the returning melody with ornaments.

By combining virtuosity, nobility, and extravagance, baroque opera perfectly expressed the spirit of a grand age.

7 Claudio Monteverdi

Claudio Monteverdi (1567–1643), one of the most important composers of the early baroque era, was born in Cremona, Italy. He served at the court of Mantua for twenty-one years, first as a singer and violist, then as music director. For this court Monteverdi created the earliest operatic masterpiece, *Orfeo* (*Orpheus,* 1607). Though widely recognized as a leading composer in Mantua, Monteverdi received little pay or respect: "I have never suffered greater humiliation," he wrote, "than when I had to go and beg the treasurer to obtain what was due me."

Life improved for Monteverdi in 1613, when he was appointed music director at St. Mark's in Venice, the most important church position in Italy. He stayed at St. Mark's for thirty years, until his death in 1643. There he composed not only the required sacred music but also secular music for the aristocracy. He wrote operas for San Cassiano in Venice, the first public opera house in Europe. At the age of seventy-five, Monteverdi wrote his last opera, *L'incoronazione di Poppea* (*The Coronation of Poppea,* 1642).

Monteverdi is a monumental figure in the history of music. His works form a musical bridge between the sixteenth and seventeenth centuries and greatly influenced composers of the time. All his music—madrigals, church music, opera—is for voices, ordinarily supported by a basso continuo and other instruments.

Portrait of Claudio Monteverdi (c. 1640) by Bernardo Strozzi.

Monteverdi wanted to create music of emotional intensity. He felt that earlier music had conveyed only moderate emotion, and he wanted to extend its range to include agitation, excitement, and passion. To achieve this intensity, he used dissonances with unprecedented freedom and daring. And to evoke the angry or warlike feelings in some of his texts, he introduced new orchestral effects, including pizzicato and tremolo.

Monteverdi was the first composer of operatic masterpieces. Only three of the twelve operas he wrote are preserved, but they truly blend music and drama. His vocal lines respond marvelously to the inflections of Italian while maintaining melodic flow.

Orfeo (Orpheus, 1607)

Fittingly enough, Monteverdi's first opera is about Orpheus, the supremely gifted musician of Greek myth. Orpheus, son of the god Apollo, is ecstatically happy after his marriage to Eurydice. But his joy is shattered when his bride is killed by a poisonous snake. Orpheus goes down to hades hoping to bring her back to life. Because of his beautiful music, he is granted this privilege—on the condition that he not look back at Eurydice while leading her out of hades. During a moment of anxiety, however, Orpheus does look back, and Eurydice vanishes. Nonetheless, there is a happy ending, of sorts. Apollo pities Orpheus and brings him up to heaven, where he can gaze eternally at Eurydice's radiance in the sun and stars.

Orfeo was composed in 1607 for the Mantuan court, and no expense was spared to make it a lavish production. There were star soloists, a chorus, dancers, and a large orchestra of about forty players. The aristocratic audience was wildly enthusiastic and recognized the historic significance of the performance.

Monteverdi creates variety in *Orfeo* by using many kinds of music—recitatives, arias, duets, choruses, and instrumental interludes. He uses the opera orchestra to establish atmosphere, character, and dramatic situations. With the simplest of musical means, Monteverdi makes his characters come alive. Through vocal line alone he quickly characterizes the hero's joy and despair. Monteverdi sets

Orpheus and Euridice (c.1625), by Jacopo Vignali. The painting depicts Orpheus leading Eurydice out of hades while a winged demon reaches out to her from behind.

his text in a very flexible way, freely alternating recitatives with more melodious passages, depending on the meaning of the words.

We'll now consider one well-known passage from this opera, Orpheus's recitative *Tu se' morta (You are dead)*.

Act II
Recitative: *Tu se' morta (You are dead)*

Brief Set:
CD 1 71

Basic Set:
CD 2 17

Monteverdi's mastery of the then-novel technique of recitative is shown in *Tu se' morta*, sung by Orpheus after he is told of Eurydice's death. Orpheus resolves to bring her back from hades, and he bids an anguished farewell to the earth, sky, and sun. His vocal line is accompanied only by a basso continuo played by a small portable organ and a bass lute. (In modern performances, other instruments are sometimes substituted.)

The texture is homophonic: the accompaniment simply gives harmonic support to the voice. The vocal line is rhythmically free, with little sense of beat or meter, and its phrases are irregular in length. This flexible setting of text is meant to suggest the passionate speech of an actor declaiming his lines.

Monteverdi frequently uses word painting, the musical representation of poetic images that was favored by baroque composers. For example, words like *stelle (stars)* and *sole (sun)* are sung to climactic high tones, whereas *abissi (abysses)* and *morte (death)* are sung to somber, low tones. Three times during the recitative the melodic line rises to a climax and then descends. Through such simple means, Monteverdi makes Orpheus's passion seem very real.

Vocal Music Guide to be read while music is heard Brief Set: CD 1 Basic Set: CD 2

MONTEVERDI, *Tu se' morta* from *Orfeo*

71 17

Tu se' morta, se' morta, mia vita, — You are dead, you are dead, my dearest,

ed io respiro; tu se' da me partita, — And I breathe; you have left me,
se' da me partita per mai più, — You have left me forevermore,
mai più non tornare, ed io rimango— — Never to return, and I remain—
no, no, che se i versi alcuna cosa ponno, — No, no, if my verses have any power,

Low tone on *abissi.* *n'andrò sicuro a' più profondi abissi,* — I will go confidently to the deepest abysses,

e, intenerito il cor del re de l'ombre, — And, having melted the heart of the king of shadows,

High tone on *stelle.* *meco trarotti a riverder le stelle,* — Will bring you back to me to see the stars again,

o se ciò negherammi empio destino, — Or, if pitiless fate denies me this,

Low tone on *morte.* *rimarrò teco in compágnia di morte.* — I will remain with you in the company of death.

High tone *on* *sole.* *Addio terra, addio cielo, e sole, addio.* — Farewell earth, farewell sky, and sun, farewell.

Henry Purcell

Henry Purcell (about 1659–1695), called the greatest of English composers, was born in London; his father was a musician in the king's service. At about the age of ten, Purcell became a choirboy in the Chapel Royal, and by his late teens his extraordinary talents were winning him important musical positions. In 1677, at about eighteen, he became composer to the king's string orchestra; two years later he was appointed organist of Westminster Abbey; and in 1682, he became an organist of the Chapel Royal. During the last few years of his short life, Purcell was also active composing music for plays.

Acclaimed as *the* English composer of his day, Purcell, who died at thirty-six, was buried beneath the organ in Westminster Abbey. He was the last native English composer of international rank until the twentieth century.

Purcell mastered all the musical forms of late-seventeenth-century England. He wrote church music, secular choral music, music for small groups of instruments, songs, and music for the stage. His only true opera is *Dido and Aeneas* (1689), which many consider the finest ever written to an English text. His other dramatic works are spoken plays with musical numbers in the form of overtures, songs, choruses, and dances.

Few composers have equaled Purcell's handling of the English language. His vocal music is faithful to English inflection and brings out the meaning of the

Henry Purcell.

text. Purcell developed a melodious recitative that seems to grow out of the English language. His music is filled with lively rhythms and a fresh melodic style that captures the spirit of English folk songs. He treated the chorus with great variety and was able to obtain striking effects through both simple homophonic textures and complex polyphony. His music is spiced with dissonances that seemed harsh to the generation of musicians who followed him. Some of Purcell's finest songs use a variation form found in many baroque works—a ground bass.

Ground Bass

Often in baroque works, a musical idea in the bass is repeated over and over while the melodies above it change. The repeated musical idea is called a ***ground bass,*** or ***basso ostinato*** (*obstinate* or *persistent bass*). The ground bass pattern may be as short as four notes or as long as eight measures. In this type of variation form, the constant repetition of the bass pattern gives unity, while the free flow of the melodic lines above it results in variety.

Composers have used a ground bass in both vocal and instrumental music. We'll hear a ground bass in Purcell's opera *Dido and Aeneas.*

Dido and Aeneas (1689)

Purcell's *Dido and Aeneas,* a masterpiece of baroque opera, was written for students at a girls' boarding school. It lasts only an hour, is scored only for strings and harpsichord continuo, and requires no elaborate stage machinery or virtuoso soloists. Most of its solo roles are for women. Purcell used many dances in *Dido and Aeneas,* because the director of the school was a dancing master who wanted to display the students' accomplishments. The chorus plays a prominent role, both participating in the action and commenting on it.

The libretto of *Dido and Aeneas,* by Nahum Tate, was inspired by the *Aeneid,* an epic poem by the Roman poet Virgil (70–19 b.c.). The opera's main characters are Dido, queen of Carthage; and Aeneas, king of the defeated Trojans. After the destruction of his native Troy, Aeneas has been ordered by the gods to seek a site for building a new city. He sets out on the search with twenty-one ships. After landing at Carthage, a north African seaport, Aeneas falls in love with Dido. A sorceress and two witches see this as an opportunity to plot Dido's downfall. (In Purcell's time, people really believed in witches: nineteen supposed "witches" were hanged in Massachusetts in 1692, three years after *Dido's* first performance.) A false messenger tells Aeneas that the gods command him to leave Carthage immediately and renew his search. Aeneas agrees but is desolate at the thought of deserting Dido.

In the last act, which takes place at the harbor, Aeneas's sailors sing and dance before leaving, and the witches look on in glee. An emotional scene follows between Aeneas and Dido, who enters with her friend Belinda. Dido calls Aeneas a hypocrite and refuses his offer to stay. After he sails, Dido sings a noble, deeply tragic lament and kills herself. The opera concludes with the mourning of the chorus.

Now let's look at *Dido's Lament.*

Act III:
Dido's Lament

Brief Set:
CD 1 [72]

Basic Set:
CD 2 **18**

A melodic recitative accompanied only by the basso continuo sets the sorrowful mood for *Dido's Lament,* the climax of the opera. This aria is built on a chromatically descending ground bass that is stated eleven times. (In the baroque period, such chromatic ground basses were commonly used to show grief.) As shown in the music example on page 122, Dido's melody moves freely above this repeated bass line, creating touching dissonances with it.

Dido's repeated *Remember me* reaches the highest note of the aria and haunts the listener. The emotional tension is sustained in the orchestral conclusion, where a chromatically descending violin melody movingly expresses Dido's tragedy.

Vocal Music Guide to be read while music is heard   Brief Set: CD 1   Basic Set: CD 2

PURCELL, *Dido's Lament*

[72] **18** 0:00
Recitative, descending melody, basso continuo accompanies.

Thy hand, Belinda, darkness shades me,
On thy bosom let me rest;
More I would but Death invades me;
Death is now a welcome guest.

73 **19** 0:56
Dido's Lament (aria), low strings introduce chromatically descending ground bass.

Upper strings join.

Orchestral conclusion, violin melody descends chromatically.

When I am laid, am laid in earth, may my wrongs create
No trouble, no trouble in thy breast.
Remember me! But ah! forget my fate.

9 The Baroque Sonata

Instrumental music gained importance rapidly and dramatically during the baroque period. One of the main developments in instrumental music was the **sonata,** a composition in several movements for one to eight instruments. (In later periods, the term *sonata* took on a more restricted meaning.)

Composers often wrote **trio sonatas,** so called because they had three melodic lines: two high ones and a basso continuo. The word *trio* is somewhat misleading, because the "trio" sonata actually involves *four* instrumentalists. There are two high instruments (commonly, violins, flutes, or oboes) and two instruments for the basso continuo—a keyboard instrument (organ or harpsichord) and a low instrument (cello or bassoon).

The sonata originated in Italy but spread to Germany, England, and France during the seventeenth century. Sonatas were played in palaces, in homes, and even in churches—before, during, or after the service. Sometimes composers differentiated between the *sonata da chiesa (church sonata),* which had a dignified character and was suitable for sacred performance; and the *sonata du camera (chamber sonata),* which was more dancelike and was intended for performance at court.

Trio Sonata in A Minor, Op. 3, No. 10 (1689), by Arcangelo Corelli

Arcangelo Corelli (1653–1713), the most prominent Italian violinist and composer of string music around 1700, was also an eminent teacher who laid the foundations of modern violin technique; he wrote only instrumental music—sixty sonatas and twelve concertos, all for strings.

Corelli's Trio Sonata in A Minor, Op. 3, No. 10, is written for two violins and basso continuo. The violins play the two upper lines in the same high register and are the center of attention; they seem to be rivals, taking turns at the melodic ideas, intertwining, and sometimes rising above each other in pitch. The basso continuo is for organ and cello or *theorbo* (bass lute), a plucked string instrument that is capable of producing chords as well as the bass line. Though the bass line is subordinate to the two upper voices, it is not merely an accompaniment. It imitates melodic ideas presented by the violins.

The sonata consists of four short movements:

1. Fast
2. Fast
3. Slow
4. Fast

All are in the same minor key, but they differ in meter, mood, and tempo. Each movement alone has only a single basic mood, as is typical in baroque instrumental music.

Basic Set:
CD 2 20

The lively opening movement is in quadruple meter and features dotted rhythms. It is played twice, each time ending with an incomplete cadence on the dominant that creates a feeling of expectancy.

Basic Set:
CD 2 21

The second movement, a vigorous allegro, is fuguelike and also in quadruple meter. Fugal second movements were characteristic of baroque trio sonatas. The subject begins with a pervasive repeated-note motive.

This subject is introduced by the first violin and then is successively imitated in lower registers by the second violin and the cello (doubled by the organ). The second movement, like the first, ends with an incomplete cadence on the dominant that creates expectancy.

The third movement is songlike and soulful, a very brief adagio in triple meter. It opens with a descending leap in the first violin that is immediately imitated a step higher by the second violin. In this movement, the performers vary the tone color by using the plucked string sounds of the theorbo as part of the basso continuo.

The longest and most brilliant movement of this sonata is the concluding allegro, a dancelike piece in quadruple meter in which each beat is subdivided into three. This fourth movement is in two-part form, and each part is repeated: A A B B. Section B is three times as long as section A. At the end of section B, Corelli calls for the only dynamic change in the sonata: the concluding phrase is repeated more softly, like an echo.

Antonio Vivaldi

Antonio Vivaldi (1678–1741), a towering figure of the late Italian baroque, was born in Venice; his father was a violinist at St. Mark's Cathedral. Along with his musical training, Vivaldi prepared for the priesthood. He took holy orders at the age of about twenty-five, but poor health caused him to leave the ministry after a year. Because of his religious background and his red hair, Vivaldi was known as the "red priest" *(il prete rosso).*

For most of his life, Vivaldi was a violin teacher, composer, and conductor at the music school of the Pietà, an institution for orphaned or illegitimate girls in

Antonio Vivaldi.

Venice. Every Sunday and holiday, about forty young women presented a concert of orchestral and vocal music in the chapel. They were placed in a gallery, "hid from any distinct view of those below by a lattice of ironwork." It was for this all-female group—considered one of the finest orchestras in Italy—that Vivaldi composed many of his works. He also wrote for Venetian opera houses and sometimes took leave to visit foreign courts.

Vivaldi was famous and influential as a virtuoso violinist and composer. Bach arranged some of his concertos. Emperor Charles VI, a passionate music lover, was said to have talked longer to Vivaldi "alone in fifteen days, than he talked to his ministers in two years."

But Vivaldi's popularity waned shortly before his death in 1741, and he died in poverty. Although he had been acclaimed during his lifetime, he was almost forgotten for 200 years after his death. The baroque revival of the 1950s established his reputation among modern music lovers.

Although Vivaldi composed operas and fine church music, he is best known for his 450 or so concerti grossi and solo concertos. A *solo concerto* is a piece for a *single* soloist and an orchestra. Vivaldi exploited the resources of the violin as well as other instruments. (There are Vivaldi concertos for solo flute, piccolo, cello, bassoon, and even mandolin.) His fast movements feature tuneful themes in vigorous rhythms, and his slow movements have impassioned, lyrical melodies that would be appropriate in an opera aria.

La Primavera (Spring), Concerto for Violin and String Orchestra, Op. 8, No. 1, from *The Four Seasons* (1725)

Vivaldi's most popular work is the concerto *La Primavera (Spring)* from *The Four Seasons,* a set of four solo concertos for violin, string orchestra, and basso continuo. Each of these concertos depicts sounds and events associated with one of the seasons, such as the birdsongs heard in spring and the gentle breezes of summer. The descriptive effects in the music correspond to images and ideas found in the sonnets that preface each of the four concertos. To make his intentions absolutely clear, Vivaldi placed lines from the poems at the appropriate passages in the musical score and even added such descriptive labels as *sleeping goatherd* and *barking dog.* The concertos *Spring, Summer, Autumn,* and *Winter* are examples of baroque *program music,* or instrumental music associated with a story, poem, idea, or scene. They are forerunners of the more elaborate program music that developed during the romantic period.

Spring was as popular in Vivaldi's time as it is in ours and was a special favorite of Louis XV, king of France. Once, when the violinist Guignon gave a concert at the court, the king asked for *Spring* as an encore. This posed a problem, since the king's orchestra was not present. Rising to the occasion, a group of nobles at the court volunteered to accompany the violin soloist. A newspaper in Paris reported that "this beautiful piece of music was performed perfectly."

Like most of Vivaldi's concertos, *Spring* has three movements: (1) fast, (2) slow, (3) fast. The first and last movements are both in ritornello form.

First Movement:
Allegro

Spring has come, and joyfully,
The birds greet it with a happy song.
And the streams, fanned by gentle breezes,
Flow along with a sweet murmur.
Covering the sky with a black cloak,
Thunder and lightning come to announce the season.
When these have quieted down, the little birds
Return to their enchanting song.

Basic Set:

CD 2 22

Brief Set:

CD 2

The allegro, in E major, opens with an energetic orchestral ritornello depicting the arrival of spring. Each of the ritornello's two phrases is played loudly and then repeated softly, in the terraced dynamics typical of baroque music. After the ritornello, the movement alternates between extended solo sections containing musical tone painting and brief tutti sections presenting part of the ritornello theme. In the first solo section, birdsongs are imitated by high trills and repeated notes played by the violin soloist and two violins from the orchestra. (A *trill* is an ornament consisting of the rapid alternation of two tones that are a whole or half step apart.) In the second descriptive episode, murmuring streams are suggested by soft running notes in the violins. The next solo section contains string tremolos and rapid scales representing thunder and lightning. Following the storm, the ritornello appears in minor instead of in major. All the pictorial passages in this movement provide contrasts of texture and dynamics between returns of the ritornello theme. The allegro's tunefulness, rhythmic vitality, and light, homophonic texture evoke the feeling of springtime.

Listening Outline to be read while music is heard   Basic Set: CD 2   Brief Set: CD 2

VIVALDI, *La Primavera*, from *The Four Seasons*

First Movement: Allegro

Ritornello form, quadruple meter ($\frac{4}{4}$), E major

Solo violin, string orchestra, harpsichord (basso continuo)

(Duration, 3:38)

Spring
has come

| 1 | 22 | 0:00 |

1. a. Tutti, ritornello opening phrase, *f*, repeated *p*.

Closing phrase with syncopations, *f*, repeated *p*, major key.

**Song of
the birds**

| 2 | 23 | 0:31 | 0:00 | **b.** Solo violin joined by two violins from orchestra, high trills and repeated notes. |
| | | 1:06 | 0:35 | **2. a.** Tutti, ritornello closing phrase, *f*. |

**Murmuring
streams**

| 3 | 24 | 1:14 | 0:00 | **b.** Violins, *p*, running notes, cellos, *p*, running notes below sustained tones in violins. |
| | | 1:38 | 0:24 | **3. a.** Tutti, ritornello closing phrase, *f*. |

**Thunder
and lightning**

| 4 | 25 | 1:46 | 0:00 | **b.** String tremolos, *f*, upward rushing scales introduce high solo violin, brilliant virtuoso passages answered by low string tremolos. |
| | | 2:15 | 0:29 | **4. a.** Tutti, ritornello closing phrase in minor key, *f*. |

**Song of
the birds**

5	26	2:23	0:00	**b.** Solo violin joined by two violins from orchestra, high repeated notes and trills, minor key.
		2:43	0:20	**5. a.** Tutti, ritornello opening phrase varied, *f*, ends in major key.
		2:55	0:32	**b.** Solo violin, running notes accompanied by basso continuo.
		3:11	0:48	**6.** Tutti, ritornello closing phrase, *f*, repeated *p*, major key.

Second Movement:
Largo e pianissimo sempre (very slow and very soft throughout)

> And then, on a pleasant meadow covered with flowers,
> Lulled by the soft murmuring of leaves and branches,
> The goatherd sleeps, his faithful dog at his side.

**Brief Set:
CD 2 6**

**Basic Set:
CD 2 27**

The peaceful slow movement, in C sharp minor, is much quieter than the energetic opening movement. It uses only the solo violin and the orchestral violins and violas, omitting the cellos, basses, and harpsichord. A tender, expansive melody for the solo violin depicts the goatherd's slumber, while a soft, rocking figure in the violins suggests the rustling of leaves. The violas imitate the barking of the goatherd's "faithful dog" with a repeated-note figure in short-long rhythm. The tranquillity of this pastoral scene is evoked by the movement's unchanging texture, rhythm, and dynamic level.

In the recorded performance of this movement on our CD sets, the violin soloist Jeanne Lamon decorates the melody with ornaments, or embellishing

Jeanne Lamon, Violinist, Plays and Conducts Vivaldi's Spring Concerto

One of the leading performers on the baroque violin is Jeanne Lamon, who conducts and directs the Canadian period-instrumental group Tafelmusik. During the past few decades, many performers of baroque music have chosen to use baroque instruments—originals and reproductions—rather than the later counterparts. Baroque instruments differ somewhat from their later counterparts in construction and in the way they are played. Baroque violins, for example, usually have strings of gut rather than metal. The strings are held under less tension and produce sounds that are softer and less brilliant.

Jeanne Lamon, who was raised in New York state, began to play the violin at age 7 and later studied music at Brandeis University in Boston. After graduating, she studied baroque violin in the Netherlands, a center for the performance of early music. In 1973, she returned to North America, where she performed as soloist and concertmaster with many ensembles. Under her direction since 1981, Tafelmusik has made many award-winning recordings, including Vivaldi's *The Four Seasons* and Bach's *Brandenburg* Concertos.

In Lamon's performance of Vivaldi's *Spring* Concerto—included in the CD Sets—she conducts from the concertmaster's seat, playing the solo violin part at the same time. She points out that "most orchestral music of the baroque was led by the first violinist or the harpsichordist. This suits the music very well, as do the original instruments. It is in many ways easier for string players to follow a violinist than a conductor."

As we have seen, Vivaldi's *Spring* Concerto contains episodes suggesting birdsongs and murmuring streams. Lamon believes that such passages pose special problems for the performer: "How rhythmically strict should an imitation of birds be? How literally would Vivaldi have wished it to be played? Should the birdcalls be played as literally as possible, or should we take whatever freedom we see fit to make them as realistic as we can? I chose a middle ground, probably a bit more strict than free, but with the intention of applying humor and charm to this music. I see it not as literal music, but as playful and evocative."

In the peaceful second movement, Lamon enriches the written solo violin melody with decorative tones. She points out that she "chose to ornament in a way that was comfortable for me as a player and reflected the mood of the musical picture." The second movement poses special interpretive problems for the conductor. "The biggest challenge in this movement, writes Lamon, "is the viola part, which imitates dogs barking and is indicated *ff e strappato* ("very loud and ripped"). If we really do this, we hear nothing else, but the polite version where the violas play softly and roundly doesn't sound at all like dogs." Lamon's solution is to have the violists play *forte* rather than *fortissimo.* She thinks that Vivaldi marked the part *fortissimo* because he was "frustrated that his violists were playing too softly and without any edge or roughness (barking). Our violists are much meatier players perhaps!"

How can the performer breathe new life into such a well-known work as Vivaldi's *Spring* Concerto? Lamon answers that "our challenge as performers is to keep sometimes very familiar works 'new' and fresh by remembering what was new and fresh about them . . . when they were heard for the first time, what surprised the audience, what was innovative, shocking, humorous."

notes. During the baroque period, performers were often expected to add embellishments not indicated in the printed music. Vivaldi's notated melody and the decorated version of the melody you hear in the recording are shown in the following music examples.

(a) Notated melody

(b) Ornamented melody

a)

b)

Third Movement:
Danza pastorale (Pastoral Dance)

> To the festive sounds of country bagpipes,
> Dance nymphs and shepherds in their beloved fields,
> When spring appears in all its brilliance.

Brief Set:
CD 2 [7]

Basic Set:
CD 2 **27**

Like the first movement, the concluding *Danza pastorale (Pastoral Dance)*, in E major, alternates between tutti and solo sections. The playful ritornello theme, with its dotted rhythms, suggests nymphs and shepherds dancing in the fields. Sustained tones in the lower strings imitate the drone of country bagpipes. The sections for solo violin contain brilliant passages with many melodic sequences, which are typical of baroque style.

The following outline will clarify the movement's ritornello form:

28 [7]	0:00		1. a.	Tutti, ritornello, lilting melody in major.
	0:27		b.	Solo violin accompanied by basso continuo.
29 [8]	0:49	0:00	2. a.	Tutti, varied ritornello in minor.
	1:17	0:28	b.	Solo violin joined by violin from orchestra, major.
	1:47	0:58	c.	Solo violin, staccato, accompanied by violins, faster rhythms.
30 [9]	2:08	0:00	3. a.	Tutti, ritornello, major, varied in minor.
	2:39	0:31	b.	Solo violin accompanied by sustained tone in cellos and basses, minor.
	3:02	0:54	4.	Tutti, ritornello in major.

11 Johann Sebastian Bach

The masterpieces of Johann Sebastian Bach (1685–1750) mark the high point of baroque music. Bach came from a long line of musicians and passed on this musical heritage; four of his sons were also composers. He was born in Eisenach, Germany, and began his musical career as a church organist and then as court organist and later concertmaster of the court orchestra in Weimar.

His most lucrative and prestigious post was as court conductor for the prince of Cöthen—more important, this was the first position in which he was not involved with church or organ music. For six years (1717–1723) he directed

Though recognized as the most eminent organist, harpsichordist, improviser, and master of the fugue, Bach was by no means considered the greatest composer of his day; his music was largely forgotten and remained unpublished for years after his death.

and composed for the prince's small orchestra; the *Brandenburg* Concertos grew out of this productive period.

Bach's next position was as cantor (director of music) of St. Thomas Church in Leipzig, with responsibility for the four main municipal churches. Bach remained here for the last twenty-seven years of his life. He rehearsed, conducted, and usually composed an extended work for chorus, soloists, and orchestra for each Sunday and church holiday and was responsible for the musical education of some fifty-five students in the St. Thomas school. He also became director of the Leipzig Collegium Musicum, a student organization that gave weekly concerts at a coffeehouse. An eminent teacher of organ and composition, he gave organ recitals and was often asked to judge the construction of organs. In his last years, his eyesight deteriorated, yet he continued to compose, conduct, and teach; when he died in 1750, he had become completely blind.

Bach was a deeply religious man—a Lutheran—who wrote the letters *J. J.,* standing for *Jesu Juva (Jesus help),* at the beginning of each of his sacred compositions and *S. D. G.* for *Soli Deo Gloria (to God alone the glory)* at the end. His love of music was so great that as a young man he would walk up to 30 miles to hear a famous organist. He was married twice and had twenty children, of whom nine survived him and four (as noted above) became well-known musicians.

Bach was by no means considered the greatest composer of his day, though he was recognized as the most eminent organist, harpsichordist, and improviser (*improvisation* is the term used for music created at the same time as it is performed). He was little known outside Germany; and by the time of his maturity, the baroque style had started to go out of fashion and many people thought his works too heavy, complex, and polyphonic. His music was largely forgotten for years after his death, though a few later composers were aware of his genius; but in 1829 Felix Mendelssohn presented the *St. Matthew Passion,* and Bach's music has been the daily bread of every serious musician since then.

Bach's Music

Bach created masterpieces in every baroque form except opera. Throughout, he fused technical mastery with emotional depth. The excellence and number of his compositions for orchestra, small groups, and various solo instruments show how prominent instrumental music had become in the baroque period. His vocal music—the bulk of his output—was written mostly for the Lutheran church and was often based on familiar hymns. But his personal style was drawn from Italian concertos and French dance pieces as well as German church music.

Bach's works are unique in their combination of polyphonic texture and rich harmony and are used as models by music students today. Baroque music leans toward unity of mood, and this is particularly true of Bach, who liked to elaborate a single musical idea in a piece, creating unity by an insistent rhythmic drive. By his time, there was little difference in style between sacred and secular music; he often created sacred music simply by rearranging secular works, and his church music uses operatic forms like aria and recitative. Sometimes he composed music to demonstrate what could be done with a specific form (his *Art of the Fugue,* for example) or a particular instrument (for instance, his six suites for solo cello). His *Well-Tempered Clavier,* a collection of forty-eight preludes and fugues, two in each major key and each minor key, was composed to explore and demonstrate a system of tuning (the title means, roughly, *The Well-Tuned Keyboard Instrument*).

The Baroque Suite

Instrumental music has always been closely linked with dancing; in the past, much of it was written for use in palace ballrooms. During the Renaissance, dances often came in pairs—a dignified dance in quadruple meter was often followed by a lively one in triple meter. In the baroque period and later, music was written that—while meant for listening, not dancing—was related to specific dance types in tempo, meter, and rhythm.

Baroque composers wrote **suites,** which are sets of dance-inspired movements. Whether for solo instruments, small groups, or orchestra, a baroque suite is made up of movements that are all written in the same key but differ in tempo, meter, and character. The dancelike movements also have a variety of national origins: the moderately paced *allemande* (from Germany) might be followed by a fast *courante* and a moderate *gavotte* (from France), a slow and solemn *sarabande* (from Spain), and a fast *gigue* (jig, from England and Ireland). Suites were played in private homes, at court concerts, or as background music for dinner and outdoor festivities.

Dance pieces have a diverse past. Some began as folk dances; others sprang from aristocratic ballrooms. Even the character of a dance might show dramatic evolution. The slow, solemn sarabande grew out of a sexually suggestive song and dance that a sixteenth-century moralist condemned as "so lascivious in its words, so ugly in its movements, that it is enough to inflame even very honest people." In the seventeenth century, however, the sarabande became respectable enough to be danced by a cardinal at the French court.

The movements of a suite are usually in two-part form with each section repeated; that is, in the form A A B B. The A section, which opens in the tonic key and modulates to the dominant, is balanced by the B section, which begins in the dominant and returns to the tonic key. Both sections use the same thematic material, and so they contrast relatively little except in key.

Suites frequently begin with a movement that is *not* dance-inspired. One common opening is the French overture, which is also the type of piece heard at the beginning of baroque oratorios and operas. Usually written in two parts, the **French overture** first presents a slow section with dotted rhythms that is full of dignity and grandeur. The second section is quick and lighter in mood, often beginning like a fugue. Sometimes part of the opening section will return at the end of the overture.

The suite was an important instrumental form in the baroque. Even compositions not called "suite" often have several dance-inspired movements. Music influenced by dance tends to have balanced and symmetrical phrases of the same length, because formal dancing has a set of steps in one direction symmetrically balanced by a similar motion in the opposite direction.

Bach wrote four suites for orchestra. We don't know exactly when they were composed, but it seems likely that the Collegium Musicum performed them in a Leipzig coffeehouse.

Suite No. 3 in D Major (1729–1731), by Johann Sebastian Bach

First Movement: Overture

Suite No. 3 in D Major—scored for two oboes, three trumpets, timpani, strings, and basso continuo—opens with a majestic French overture, which exploits the bright sounds of trumpets. After a slow opening section with dotted rhythms, we hear the energetic fast section. This begins like a fugue, with an upward-moving theme introduced by the first violins and then imitated by the other instruments.

The fast section is like a concerto grosso in its alternation of solid tutti passages with lightly scored passages highlighting the first violins. After the fast section, there is a return to the slow tempo, dotted rhythms, and majestic mood of the opening return.

Basic Set:
CD 2 **38**
Section A
38 0:00
Section B
39 0:14

Second Movement: Air

The second movement, the air, contains one of Bach's best-loved melodies. It is scored for only strings and continuo and is serene and lyrical, in contrast to the majestic and then bustling French overture. The title suggests that the movement is written in the style of an Italian aria. Like the opening movement, the air is not related to dance. It is in A A B B form, with the B section twice as long as the A section. The air combines a steadily moving bass (which proceeds in upward and downward octave leaps) with a rhapsodic and rhythmically irregular melody in the violins.

Third Movement: Gavotte

All the movements that follow the overture and the air are inspired by dance, beginning with the gavotte, which is written in duple meter and in a moderate tempo and uses the full orchestra again. It may be outlined as follows: gavotte I (A A B B); gavotte II (C C D D); gavotte I (A B). Notice the contrast between the sections for full orchestra and those without trumpets and timpani.

Brief Set:
CD 2 ☐10

Basic Set:
CD 2 **40**

Section A
☐10 **40** 0:00
Section B
☐11 **41** 0:16

Basic Set:
CD 2 **42**
Section A
42 0:00
Section B
43 0:49

Fourth Movement: Bourrée

The bourrée is an even livelier dance, also in duple meter; it is the shortest movement of the suite. Its form is A A B B. Section A uses the full orchestra, including trumpets and timpani. Section B is three times as long as section A and alternates loud tutti passages with softer passages for strings and oboes.

Fifth Movement: Gigue

The suite concludes with a rollicking gigue in $\frac{6}{8}$ time, which is also in the form A A B B. Here, Bach's manner is simple and direct. Listen for the splendid effect when timpani and trumpets periodically join the rest of the orchestra.

 The Chorale and Church Cantata

In Leipzig in Bach's time, the Lutheran church service on Sunday was the social event of the week: it started at seven in the morning and lasted about 4 hours. The sermon alone could take an hour.

Music was a significant part of the Lutheran service. While most religious services today use no more than a chorus and organ, Bach's church had a small orchestra of fourteen to twenty-one players to accompany the twelve or so men and boys of the choir. The service was filled with music; a single composition might last half an hour.

Lutheranism stressed direct communication between the believer and Christ; to further this communication, the rite was largely in the vernacular—German. Each service included several hymns, or chorales. The *chorale,* or hymn tune, was sung to a German religious text. Chorales were easy to sing and remember, having only one note to a syllable and moving in steady rhythm. They were tunes that had been composed in the sixteenth and seventeenth centuries or had been adapted from folk songs and Catholic hymns. The members of the congregation had sung these tunes since childhood, and each tune carried religious associations. Congregational singing of chorales was an important way for people to participate directly in the service. These melodies were often harmonized for church choirs. The hymn melody was sung in the top part, and the tones of the supporting harmonies were sung in the three lower parts.

New church music was often based on traditional melodies written as far back as two centuries earlier. Before the congregation began to sing a hymn, the organist might play a *chorale prelude,* a short composition based on the hymn tune that reminded the congregation of the melody. By using traditional tunes in their works, composers could involve the congregation and enhance the religious associations.

The Church Cantata

The principal means of musical expression in the Lutheran service, and one which used chorales, was the church *cantata. Cantata* originally meant a piece that was *sung,* as distinct from a sonata, which was *played.* Many kinds of cantatas were being written in Bach's day, but we shall focus only on the cantata designed for the Lutheran service in Germany in the early 1700s. It was usually written for chorus, vocal soloists, organ, and a small orchestra. It had a German religious text, either newly written or drawn from the Bible or familiar hymns. In the Lutheran services, there were different Gospel and Epistle readings for each Sunday and holiday, and the cantata text was related to them. In a sense, the cantata was a sermon in music that reinforced the minister's sermon, also based on the readings. The cantata of Bach's day might last 25 minutes and include several different movements—choruses, recitatives, arias, and duets. In its use of aria, duet, and recitative, the cantata closely resembled the opera of the time and thus is typical of the baroque fusion of sacred and secular elements in art and music.

The cantor, or music director, had to provide church cantatas for every Sunday and holiday. Bach wrote about 295; about 195 are still in existence. In his first few years as cantor in Leipzig, he composed cantatas at the staggering rate of almost three a month. During the remaining twenty-five years of his tenure, he was inclined to reuse cantatas, and so his output dropped.

Cantata No. 140: *Wachet auf, ruft uns die Stimme (Awake, a Voice Is Calling Us; 1731)*, by Johann Sebastian Bach

Wachet auf, ruft uns die Stimme (Cantata No. 140), one of Bach's best-known cantatas, is based on a chorale which was then about 130 years old and widely familiar. The melody has the form A A B, and the last movement of the cantata presents it unadorned. (The text of the chorale is translated on page 140.)

Last movement:
Brief Set:
CD 2 [15]

Basic Set:
CD 2 **50**

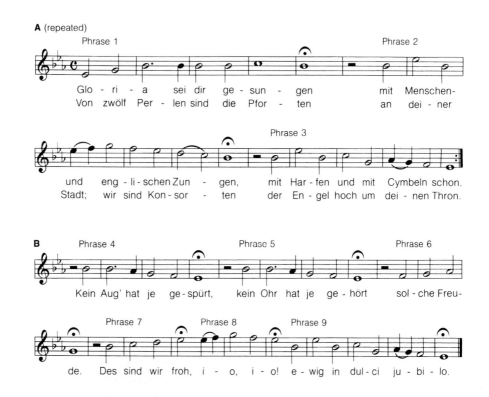

There are nine melodic phrases, of which the first three (making up section A) are repeated immediately. The last phrase of section A (phrase 3) reappears at the end of section B (phrase 9) and beautifully rounds off the chorale.

Now let's consider movements 1, 4, and 7, which use the chorale in different ways.

First Movement: Chorus and Orchestra

Basic Set:
CD 2 **44**

The opening movement is scored for chorus and a small orchestra of two oboes, English horn, French horn, strings, and basso continuo (organ, bassoon, and cello). In the chorale text of the first movement, watchmen on the towers of Jerusalem call on the wise virgins (Christians) to awake because the bridegroom (Christ) is coming. The movement opens with an orchestral ritornello that may have been intended to suggest a procession or march. As shown in the following music example, there are dotted rhythms (long-short, long-short), a rising figure with syncopation, and a series of rising scales.

At the ritornello's closing cadence the sopranos enter and sing the first phrase of the chorale in long notes. Soon the three lower voices engage in an imitative dialogue based on a new motive in shorter note values. Throughout, the orchestra continues to play still shorter notes.

Thus there are three layers of sound: the chorale phrases in long notes in the soprano; the imitative dialogue in shorter note values in the three lower voices; and the ever-busy orchestra playing motives from the ritornello in even shorter notes. The chorale (in the soprano) is presented not as a continuous whole but rather phrase by phrase, with breaks between. After each phrase, the voices pause while the orchestra continues to play interludes made up of either the whole ritornello or sections from it. Sometimes the motives in the three lower voices illustrate the text, as when they have rising scale figures at the word *hoch (high)* and exclamations at the repeated *wo (where)*.

Once during the movement, the three lower voices become emancipated from the soprano and jubilantly sing a melody in rapid notes on *Alleluja*. This, perhaps, is the most exciting moment in the movement.

44 0:00 Orchestral ritornello.			
45 0:28 0:00 Brief orchestral interlude.	*Wachet auf, ruft uns die Stimme*	"Awake," the voice of watchmen
0:49 0:21 Rising scales in lower voices depict *hoch* (*high*). Brief orchestral interlude.	*der Wächter sehr hoch auf der Zinne*	calls us from high on the tower,
	wach auf, du Stadt Jerusalem!	"Awake, you city of Jerusalem!"
1:32 1:04 Orchestral ritornello.		
2:00 1:32 Brief orchestral interlude.	*Mitternacht heisst diese Stunde;*	Midnight is this very hour;
Brief orchestral interlude.	*sie rufen uns mit hellem Munde:*	they call to us with bright voices:
	wo seid ihr klugen Jungfrauen?	"Where are you, wise virgins?"
3:04 2:36 Long orchestral interlude.		
Brief orchestral interlude.	*Wohl auf, der Bräut'gam kömmt,*	Take cheer, the Bridegroom comes,
	steht auf, die Lampen nehmt!	arise, take up your lamps!
46 3:56 0:00 *Altos, jubilant melody in rapid notes. Imitation by tenors, then basses.*	*Alleluja!*	Hallelujah!

4:22	0:26	*Alleluja!*	Hallelujah!

Sopranos, chorale in long notes.

Orchestral interlude.

Macht euch bereit	Prepare yourselves

Orchestral interlude.

zu der Hochzeit	for the wedding,

Brief orchestral interlude.

5:14	1:18	*ihr müsset ihm entgegen gehn.*	you must go forth to meet him.

Orchestral ritornello.

Fourth Movement: Tenor Chorale

Brief Set:
CD 2 ⌊12⌋

Basic Set:
CD 2 ⌊47⌋

The fourth movement is scored for tenors; violins and violas in unison; and basso continuo. The chorale returns in this movement, the most popular of the cantata. Bach liked this section so much that toward the end of his life he re-arranged it as a chorale prelude for organ. With miraculous ease, he sets two contrasting melodies against each other. First we hear the unison strings supported by the continuo playing the ritornello—a warm, flowing melody that Bach may have intended as a dancelike procession of the maidens as they "all follow to the joyful hall and share in the Lord's supper." This melody is repeated and varied throughout while the tenors sing the chorale against it.

The chorale moves in faster rhythmic values than in the opening movement, but here, too, it is broken into component phrases linked by the instrumental melody. It's helpful to listen several times to this movement, focusing first on the rapid rhythms of the graceful string melody; then on the sturdy, slower rhythms of the chorale; and finally on all lines at once.

Vocal Music Guide to be read while music is heard | Brief Set: CD 2 Basic Set: CD 2

BACH, *Wachet auf, ruft uns die Stimme*

Fourth Movement

| 12 | 47 | 0:00 |
String ritornello.

| 13 | 48 | 0:39 | 0:00 |

Zion hört die Wächter singen,	Zion hears the watchmen singing,
das Herz tut ihr vor Freuden springen,	for joy her very heart is springing,
sie wachet und steht eilend auf.	she wakes and rises hastily.

Ritornello.

| | 1:52 | 1:13 |

Ihr Freund kommt von Himmel prächtig,	From heaven comes her friend resplendent,
von Gnaden stark, von Wahrheit mächtig,	sturdy in grace, mighty in truth,
Ihr Licht wird hell, ihr Stern geht auf.	her light shines bright, her star ascends.

Ritornello.

| 14 | 49 | 2:46 | 0:00 |

| *Nun komm, du werte Kron,* | Now come, you worthy crown, |
| *Herr Jesu, Gottes Sohn.* | Lord Jesus, God's own Son. |

| | 3:04 | 0:18 |

| *Hosianna!* | Hosanna! |

Ritornello in minor.

| | 3:28 | 0:42 |

| *Wir folgen all' zum Freudensaal* | We all follow to the joyful hall |
| *und halten mit das Abendmahl.* | and share the Lord's supper. |

Ritornello.

Seventh Movement: Chorale

Brief Set:
CD 2 [15]

Basic Set:
CD 2 **50**

Bach rounds off Cantata No. 140 by bringing back the chorale once more. For the first time since the first movement, all voices and instruments take part. Here the chorale is set in a relatively simple, homophonic texture for four voices, with the instruments simply doubling them, not playing melodies of their own. Now the chorale is heard as a continuous melody, without interludes between its phrases. The rich sound, full harmonies, and regular rhythms express praise of God, faith in him, and joy in being part of his kingdom. No doubt the congregation joined in the singing of the final chorale, which so firmly expressed their unity and belief.

Vocal Music Guide to be read while music is heard Brief Set: CD 2　Basic Set: CD 2

BACH, *Wachet auf, ruft uns die Stimme*

Seventh Movement

15 **50**

A

Gloria sei dir gesungen	Gloria be sung to you
mit Menschen- und englischen Zungen,	with men's and angel's tongues,
mit Harfen und mit Zimbeln schon.	with harps and beautiful cymbals.

A

Von zwölf Perlen sind die Pforten	Of twelve pearls are the gates
an deiner Stadt; wir sind Konsorten	at your city; we are consorts
der Engel hoch um deinen Thron.	of the angels high about your throne.

B

Kein Aug' hat je gespürt,	No eye has ever sensed,
kein Ohr hat je gehört	no ear has ever heard
solche Freude.	such a delight.
Des sind wir froh,	In this we rejoice,
io, io!	io, io,
ewig in dulci jubilo.	forever in sweet joy.

The Oratorio

Together with opera and the cantata, the oratorio stands as a major development in baroque vocal music. Like an opera, an *oratorio* is a large-scale composition for chorus, vocal soloists, and orchestra; it is usually set to a narrative text. Oratorio differs from opera in that it has no acting, scenery, or costumes. Most oratorios are based on biblical stories, but usually they are not intended for religious services. Today they are performed in either concert halls or churches.

An oratorio contains a succession of choruses, arias, duets, recitatives, and orchestral interludes. The chorus is especially important and serves either to comment on or to participate in the drama. A narrator's recitatives usually relate the story and connect one piece with another. Oratorios are longer than cantatas (they sometimes last over 2 hours) and have more of a story line.

Oratorios first appeared in early seventeenth-century Italy as musical dramatizations of biblical stories and were performed in prayer halls called *oratorios*. During the baroque period, the oratorio spread to other countries and assumed many forms. *Messiah,* by George Frideric Handel, has for decades been the best-known and most-loved oratorio.

George Frideric Handel

George Frideric Handel (1685–1759), a master of Italian opera and English oratorio, was born one month before J. S. Bach, in Halle, Germany. He was not from a musical family—his father wanted him to study law—but by the time he was nine, his musical talent was so outstanding that he was allowed to study with a local organist and composer. By eleven, he himself was able to compose and give organ lessons. At eighteen, he set out for Hamburg, where he was drawn to the renowned opera house, and became a violinist and harpsichordist in the orchestra. When he was twenty, one of his operas was successfully produced.

At twenty-one, Handel went to Italy; there he wrote widely acclaimed operas and mingled with princes, cardinals, and famous musicians. Returning to Germany in 1710, he took a well-paid position as music director for Elector Georg Ludwig of Hanover; but after a month he asked for a leave to go to London, where his opera *Rinaldo* was being produced. It was a triumph, and a year later Handel asked for another English leave—which was granted for a "reasonable time" that turned out to be the next half-century (1712–1759).

Handel became England's most important composer and a favorite of Queen Anne. He was the director of the Royal Academy of Music (a commercial opera company) and composed a number of brilliant operas for outstanding sopranos and castrati. When the Royal Academy folded, he formed his own company to

Handel's triple career as impresario, composer, and performer brought him success and fame but led to political infighting and two nervous breakdowns.

produce his works (for years, he had a triple career as impresario, composer, and performer). The company eventually went bankrupt and Handel suffered a breakdown; but he recovered and managed to continue producing operas on his own. To these he added his oratorios, opening a glowing new chapter in music history.

Late in life, Handel was still conducting and giving organ concerts, though he was almost blind. When he died in 1759, 3,000 mourners attended his funeral in Westminster Abbey. Handel was stubborn, wealthy, generous, and cultivated. But above all, he was a master composer whose dramatic sense has rarely been equaled.

Handel's Music

Handel shares Bach's stature among composers of the late baroque. Although he wrote a great deal of instrumental music—suites, organ concertos, concerti grossi—the core of his huge output consists of English oratorios and Italian operas.

His oratorios are usually based on stories from the Old Testament and have titles such as *Israel in Egypt* and *Joshua;* but they are not church music—they were for paying audiences in public theaters. Most have plots and characters, though they were performed without acting, scenery, or costumes. (*Messiah,* which deals with a New Testament subject and has no plot, is an exception.) The chorus is the focus of a Handel oratorio and is combined flexibly and imaginatively with the orchestra. Handel's music has more changes in texture than Bach's. He liked to combine two different melodic ideas polyphonically, and he achieved sharp changes of mood by shifting between minor and major keys.

Handel's thirty-nine Italian operas are less well known today than his oratorios; but after two centuries of neglect, they are being revived successfully by modern opera companies. Their arias—often written to display the virtuosity of singers—show his outstanding ability to evoke a mood or an emotion.

Messiah (1741)

Messiah lasts about 2½ hours and was composed in just twenty-four days. Handel wrote it before going to Ireland to attend performances of his own works that were being given to dedicate a concert hall. About five months after his arrival in Dublin (in 1742), Handel gave the first performance of *Messiah;* the occasion was a benefit for people in debtors' prisons. The rehearsals attracted wide attention: one newspaper commented that *Messiah* was thought "by the greatest Judges to be the finest Composition of Musick that ever was heard." Normally, the concert hall held 600 people; but to increase the capacity, women were asked not to wear hoopskirts, and men were asked to leave their swords at home.

Although the premiere was a success, the first London performance (1743) was poorly received, mainly because of religious opposition to the use of a Christian text in a theater. It took *Messiah* almost a decade to find popularity in London. Not until it was performed yearly at a benefit for a London orphanage did it achieve its unique status. A contemporary wrote that *Messiah* "fed the hungry, clothed the naked, fostered the orphan."

Messiah is in three parts. Part I starts with the prophecy of the Messiah's coming and makes celestial announcements of Christ's birth and the redemption of humanity through his appearance. Part II has been aptly described by one Handel scholar as "the accomplishment of redemption by the sacrifice of Jesus, mankind's rejection of God's offer and mankind's utter defeat when trying to oppose the power of the Almighty." Part III expresses faith in the certainty of eternal life through Christ as redeemer.

Unlike most of Handel's oratorios, *Messiah* is meditative rather than dramatic; it lacks plot action and specific characters. *Messiah* is Handel's only English oratorio that uses the New Testament as well as the Old. Charles Jennens, a millionaire and amateur literary man, compiled the text by taking widely separated passages from the Bible—Isaiah, Psalms, and Job from the Old Testament; Luke, I Corinthians, and the Book of Revelation from the New.

Over the years, Handel rewrote some movements in *Messiah* for different performers and performances. In Handel's own time, it was performed with a smaller orchestra and chorus than we are used to. Handel's own chorus included twenty singers, all male, and his small orchestra had only strings and continuo, with trumpets and timpani used in some sections. Today we sometimes hear arranged versions; Mozart made one, and still later versions are often played by orchestras of 100 and choruses of several hundred.

Messiah has over fifty movements, and Handel ensures variety by skillfully contrasting and grouping them. We will focus on two movements from Part I and the famous *Hallelujah* Chorus, which ends Part II.

Ev'ry Valley Shall Be Exalted
Aria for tenor, strings, and basso continuo
Andante

Brief Set:
CD 2 16

Basic Set:
CD 2 55

The aria *Ev'ry Valley Shall Be Exalted* is based on a verse from Isaiah (40:4) which describes the creation of a desert highway on which God will lead his people back to their homeland. Like many baroque arias, it opens and closes with a string ritornello. This aria is striking in its vivid word painting, so characteristic of baroque music. On a single syllable of *exalted (raised up)*, forty-six rapid notes form a rising musical line.

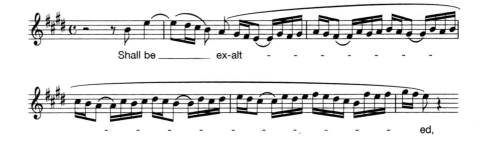

Notice, too, the rising and falling direction of the phrase *and every mountain and hill made low:*

and ev-'ry moun-tain and hill_____ made low;

The crooked straight is represented as follows:

the crook-ed __ straight,

In the line *and the rough places plain,* the word *plain (smooth or level),* is expressed by sustained tones and a long, legato melodic line.

Vocal Music Guide to be read while music is heard   Brief Set: CD 2   Basic Set: CD 2

HANDEL, *Ev'ry Valley Shall Be Exalted,* from *Messiah*

16 **55**   Orchestral ritornello.

Voice alone.	Ev'ry valley
Orchestra imitates voice.	
Ascending rapid notes on *exalted.*	Ev'ry valley shall be exalted,
High tone on *mountain.*	and ev'ry mountain
Low tone on *low.*	and hill made low,
Wavy melody on *crooked.*	the crooked straight,
Legato melody on *plain.*	and the rough places plain.
Orchestra alone, cadence.	
New word painting on	Ev'ry valley shall be exalted,
exalted, mountain, low.	and ev'ry mountain and hill
crooked, plain.	made low, the crooked straight,
	and the rough places plain.
Slow, ornamented	The crooked straight,
vocal cadence.	and the rough places plain.
Orchestral ritornello.	

For unto Us a Child Is Born
Chorus, strings, basso continuo

Basic Set:
CD 3 **1**

The twelfth movement, *For unto Us a Child Is Born,* is among Handel's most joyful music. This chorus is based on a verse from Isaiah (9:6) that celebrates the birth of a royal child whose names predict salvation. The texture is light, often with only one or two voices singing at a time. Handel uses a transparent polyphonic texture for the words *For unto us a Child is Born, unto us a Son is given*. He sets two contrasting ideas against each other. One voice part sings fifty-six rapid notes on the single syllable of *born* while another sings *unto us a Son is given*, with one note to each syllable.

1

2

The words *and the government shall be upon His shoulder* bring a new melodic idea in dotted rhythm:

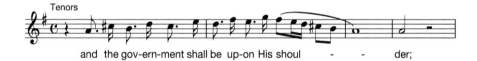

3

Handel keeps the dynamics subdued until the striking chordal outburst on *Wonderful, Counsellor*. This change from *p* to *ff* and from polyphonic to homophonic texture is a master's stroke.

For unto Us a Child Is Born divides into four sections, each with the same text and musical ideas. The first three sections all begin with a light texture, but the climactic final section uses the full chorus almost from the very beginning.

With such a close fusion of words and music, it may be disconcerting to learn that most of the melodic ideas in this chorus came from Handel's Italian duet for the words *No, I will not trust you, blind love, cruel Beauty! You are too treacherous, too charming a deity!* (The musical idea for *Wonderful* is new.) But remember that in Handel's time there was little difference in style between sacred and secular music. Amorous joy and religious joy could therefore be conveyed in the same manner.

> For unto us a Child is born, unto us a Son is given, and the government shall
> be upon His shoulder, and His Name shall be called: Wonderful, Counsellor, the
> Mighty God, the Everlasting Father, the Prince of Peace!

Hallelujah Chorus

Brief Set:
CD 2 17

Basic Set:
CD 3 4

The *Hallelujah* Chorus is one of the world's most famous choral pieces. In this vigorous chorus, Handel offers sweeping variety by making sudden changes among monophonic, polyphonic, and homophonic textures. The monophonic texture is very full-sounding as all the voices and instruments perform in unison at the proclamation *for the Lord God Omnipotent reigneth.* The texture becomes polyphonic when this majestic proclamation is set against joyful repeated exclamations of *Hallelujah* in quick rhythms. Polyphony gives way to homophony as the chorus sings *The kingdom of this world* to hymnlike music.

In the *Hallelujah* Chorus, words and phrases are repeated over and over, as has been common practice in choral music for several centuries. (In the following text, braces connect lines sung at the same time.) Handel took his text from the Revelation of St. John, which celebrates God as the almighty and everlasting ruler.

Vocal Music Guide to be read while music is heard | Brief Set: CD 3 Basic Set: CD 2

HANDEL, *Hallelujah* Chorus, from *Messiah*

17 4 Orchestral
introduction.

Chorus joins,
homophonic,
quick
exclamations.

Hallelujah!

18 5 Monophonic,
longer notes.

for the lord God Omnipotent reigneth;

Homophonic,
quick
exclamations.

Hallelujah!

Monophonic,
longer notes.

for the Lord God Omnipotent reigneth;

Homophonic,
quick
exclamations.

Hallelujah!

19 6 Longer-note
melody
against quick
exclamations,
polyphonic.

{ for the Lord God Omnipotent reigneth;
{ Hallelujah!

20 7 Hymnlike in
longer notes,
homophonic.

The kingdom of this world is become the Kingdom of our Lord
and of His Christ:

21 8	Bass melody, monophonic. Other voices imitate, polyphonic.	and He shall reign for ever and ever,
22 9	Long repeated tones against quick exclamations; phrases repeated at higher pitches.	{ King of Kings, and Lord of Lords, { for ever and ever, Hallelujah, Hallelujah!
	Polyphonic, imitation.	and He shall reign for ever and ever,
	Long repeated tones against quick exclamations.	{ King of Kings, and Lord of Lords, { for ever and ever, Hallelujah, Hallelujah!
	Polyphonic. Homophonic. Polyphonic.	and He shall reign for ever and ever, King of Kings, and Lord of Lords, and He shall reign for ever and ever,
	Quick exclamations.	{ King of Kings, and Lord of Lords, { for ever and ever, for ever and ever, Hallelujah, Hallelujah, Hallelujah, Hallelujah!
	Pause. Sustained chords, homophonic.	Hallelujah!

The Classical Period

IV

"I am never happier than when I have something to compose, for that, after all, is my sole delight and passion."

WOLFGANG AMADEUS MOZART

Wolfgang Amadeus Mozart was one of the most amazing child prodigies in the history of music. He is shown performing with his father and sister Nannerl in *Leopold Mozart and His Children* (1763–64), by Louis Carrogis, known as Carmontelle.

Time-Line Classical Period (1750–1820)

Dates	Music	Arts and Letters	Historical and Cultural Events
1750–1770	Haydn, String Quartets, Op. 1 (c. 1757) Haydn, Symphony no. 1 in D Major (1759) Mozart, Symphony No. 1 in E♭ Major. K. 16 (1764)	Publication of the French *Encyclopedia* begins (1751) Voltaire, *Candide* (1759) Rousseau, *The Social Contract* (1762)	Seven Years' War (1756–1763) Watt invents steam engine (1769)
1770–1820	Haydn, Symphony No. 45 in F Sharp Minor, *Farewell* (1772) Mozart, *Don Giovanni* and *Eine kleine Nachtmusik* (1787) Mozart, Symphony No. 40 in G Minor, K. 550 (1788) Haydn, Symphony *No. 94, Surprise* (1791) Haydn, Trumpet Concerto in E Flat Major (1796) Beethoven, Piano Sonata in C Minor, Op. 13, *Pathétique* (1798) Beethoven, Symphony No. 5 in C Minor (1808) Beethoven, Symphony No. 9 in D Minor, *Choral* (1824)	Fragonard, *The Lover Crowned* (1771–1773) David, *Death of Socrates* (1787) David, *Napoleon at St. Bernard* (1800) Goethe, *Faust* (1808) Austen, *Pride and Prejudice* (1813) Goya, *The Third of May, 1808* (1814) Scott, *Ivanhoe* (1819)	Louis XVI reigns in France (1774–1792) American Declaration of Independence (1776) Joseph II reigns in Austria (1780–1790) French Revolution begins (1789) Napoleon becomes first consul of France (1799) Napoleonic Wars (1803–1815) Congress of Vienna (1814–1815)

The Classical Era (1750–1820)

In looking at the baroque era, we found that the scientific methods and discoveries of geniuses like Galileo and Newton vastly changed people's view of the world. By the middle of the eighteenth century, faith in the power of reason was so great that it began to undermine the authority of the social and religious establishment. Philosophers and writers—especially Voltaire (1694–1778) and Denis Diderot (1713–1784)—saw their time as a turning point in history and referred to it as the "age of enlightenment." They believed in progress, holding that reason, not custom or tradition, was the best guide for human conduct. Their attacks on the privileges of the aristocracy and clergy reflected the outlook of the middle class, which was struggling for its rights.

The ideas of enlightenment thinkers were implemented by several rulers during the eighteenth century. For example, Emperor Joseph II of Austria, who reigned from 1780 to 1790, abolished serfdom, closed monasteries and convents, and eliminated the nobility's special status in criminal law. He discouraged elaborate religious ceremonies and decreed that burials be simple; though this decree was soon revoked, modest funerals became customary in Vienna. In 1791, Wolfgang Amadeus Mozart—one of the greatest composers of the classical period—was buried in a sack in an unmarked communal grave.

Violent political and social upheaval marked the seventy-year period from 1750 to 1820. These years were convulsed by the Seven Years' War, the American and French revolutions, and the Napoleonic Wars. Political and economic power shifted from the aristocracy and church to the middle class. Social mobility increased to a point that Napoleon could become emperor of France by his own genius rather than as a birthright. "Subversive" new slogans like *Liberty, equality, fraternity!* sprang from the people's lips. All established ideas were being reexamined, including the existence of God.

Revolutions in thought and action were paralleled by shifts in style in the visual arts. During the early eighteenth century, the heavy, monumental baroque style gave way to the more intimate *rococo* style, with

The rococo painter Jean-Honoré Fragonard showed the game of love in *The Lover Crowned* (1771–73).

Death of Socrates (1787) by Jacques-Louis David. By the late eighteenth century, the rococo style had been superseded by the neoclassical style, which attempted to recapture the "noble simplicity and calm grandeur" of ancient Greek and Roman art. Neoclassic artists, such as the French painter David, emphasized firm lines, clear structure, and moralistic subjects.

Monticello, Thomas Jefferson's home, shows the influence of ancient Greek and Roman architecture.

its light colors, curved lines, and graceful ornaments. The painters Antoine Watteau (1684–1721) and Jean-Honoré Fragonard (1732–1806) depicted an enchanted world peopled by elegant men and women in constant pursuit of pleasure. But by the later eighteenth century there was yet another change in taste, and rococo art was thought frivolous, excessively ornamented, and lacking in ethical content. The rococo style was superseded by the *neoclassical* style, which attempted to recapture the "noble simplicity and calm grandeur" of ancient Greek and Roman art. Neoclassical artists emphasized firm lines, clear struc-

Napoleon at St. Bernard (1800) by Jacques-Louis David. Beethoven originally planned to name his Third Symphony (*Eroica;* 1803–04) "Bonaparte," because he saw Napoleon as an embodiment of heroism; but when he learned that Napoleon had proclaimed himself emperor, Beethoven tore out the title page and later renamed the symphony "Heroic Symphony composed to celebrate the memory of a great man."

The Third of May, 1808 by the Spanish artist Francisco Goya. The classical period was a time of violent political and social upheaval, witnessing the American Revolution, the French Revolution, and the Napoleonic Wars. In 1814 Goya painted this vivid scene of the execution of Spanish hostages by Napoleon's soldiers.

ture, and moralistic subject matter. The painter Jacques-Louis David (1748–1825), who took part in the French Revolution, sought to inspire heroism and patriotism through his scenes of ancient Rome.

The artistic response to the decline of traditional power is evidenced further by the English painter William Hogarth (1697–1764), whose socially conscious paintings satirized the manners and morals of the British aristocracy and middle class; and by the Spanish painter Francisco Goya (1746–1828), who used his highly personal vision to create art that lashed out against hypocrisy, oppression, and inhumanity.

 # The Classical Style (1750–1820)

In music history, the transition from the baroque style to the full flowering of the classical is called the *preclassical* period; it extends from roughly 1730 to 1770. The shift in musical taste parallels a similar, earlier trend in the visual arts. It was developing even as Bach and Handel were creating baroque master-pieces. Among the important pioneers in this new style were Bach's sons Carl Philipp Emanuel (1714–1788) and Johann Christian (1735–1782). Around the middle of the eighteenth century, composers concentrated on simplicity and clarity, discarding much that had enriched late baroque music. Polyphonic tex-ture was neglected in favor of tuneful melody and simple harmony. Carl Philipp Emanuel Bach described music with strict polyphonic imitation as "dry and despicable pieces of pedantry." Mid-eighteenth-century composers entertained their listeners with music offering contrasts of mood and theme. The term *style galant (gallant style)* was applied to this light, graceful music. The *style galant* in music is comparable to the rococo style in art.

The term *classical* is confusing because it has so many different meanings. It may refer to Greek or Roman antiquity, or it may be used for any supreme accom-plishment of lasting appeal (as in the expression *movie classic*). Many people take *classical music* to mean anything that is *not* rock, jazz, folk, or popular music.

Music historians have borrowed the term *classical* from the field of art his-tory, where it is more appropriate. The painting, sculpture, and architecture of the late eighteenth and early nineteenth centuries were often influenced by Greek and Roman models. But the music of this period shows little direct rela-tionship to antiquity. The significant parallel between "classical" music and "neoclassical" art is a common stress on balance and clarity of structure. These traits can be found in the fully developed classical style in music, which we will focus on. The style flourished from about 1770 to 1820, and its master com-posers were Joseph Haydn (1732–1809), Wolfgang Amadeus Mozart (1756–1791), and Ludwig van Beethoven (1770–1827). First, we'll study the character-istics of their work.

Characteristics of the Classical Style

Contrast of Mood

Great variety and contrast of mood received new emphasis in classical music. Whereas a late baroque piece may convey a single emotion, a classical compo-sition will fluctuate in mood. Dramatic, turbulent music might lead into a care-free dance tune. Not only are there contrasting themes within a movement, but there may also be striking contrasts within a single theme.

Mood in classical music may change gradually or suddenly, expressing con-flicting surges of elation and depression. But the classical composer firmly con-trols such conflict and contrast. Masters like Haydn, Mozart, and Beethoven were able to impart unity and logic to music of wide emotional range.

Rhythm

Flexibility of rhythm adds variety to classical music. A classical composition has a wealth of rhythmic patterns, whereas a baroque piece contains a few patterns that are reiterated throughout. Baroque works convey a sense of continuity and perpetual motion, so that after the first few bars one can predict pretty well the rhythmic character of an entire movement. But the classical style also includes unexpected pauses, syncopations, and frequent changes from long notes to shorter notes. And the change from one pattern of note lengths to another may be either sudden or gradual.

Texture

In contrast to the polyphonic texture of late baroque music, classical music is basically homophonic. However, texture is treated as flexibly as rhythm. Pieces shift smoothly or suddenly from one texture to another. A work may begin homophonically with a melody and simple accompaniment but then change to a more complex polyphonic texture that features two simultaneous melodies or melodic fragments imitated among the various instruments.

Melody

Classical melodies are among the most tuneful and easy to remember. The themes of even highly sophisticated compositions may have a folk or popular flavor. Occasionally, composers simply borrowed popular tunes. (Mozart did, in his variations on the French song *Ah, vous dirai-je, Maman,* which we know as *Twinkle, Twinkle, Little Star.*) More often, they wrote original themes with a popular character.

Classical melodies often sound balanced and symmetrical because they are frequently made up of two phrases of the same length. The second phrase, in such melodies, may begin like the first, but it ends more conclusively. Such a melodic type, which may be diagrammed a a', is easy to sing (it is frequently found in nursery tunes such as *Mary Had a Little Lamb*). Baroque melodies, on the contrary, tend to be less symmetrical, more elaborate, and harder to sing.

Dynamics and the Piano

Classical composers' interest in expressing shades of emotion led to a widespread use of gradual dynamic change—crescendo and decrescendo. These composers did not restrict themselves to the terraced dynamics (abrupt shifts from loud to soft) characteristic of baroque music. Crescendos and decrescendos were an electrifying novelty; audiences sometimes rose excitedly from their seats.

During the classical period, the desire for gradual dynamic change led to the replacement of the harpsichord by the piano. By varying the finger pressure on the keys, a pianist can play more loudly or softly. Although the piano was invented around 1700, it began to replace the harpsichord only around 1775. Most of the mature keyboard compositions of Haydn, Mozart, and Beethoven were written for the piano, rather than for harpsichord, clavichord, and organ, which were featured in baroque music. The late-eighteenth-century piano—called a *fortepiano*—weighed much less than the modern piano and had thinner strings held by a frame made of wood rather than metal. Its pitch range was smaller, and its tone was softer and lasted a shorter time.

The End of the Basso Continuo

The basso continuo was gradually abandoned during the classical period. In Haydn's or Mozart's works, a harpsichordist did not need to improvise an accompaniment. One reason why the basso continuo became obsolete was that more and more music was written for amateurs, who had not mastered the difficult art of improvising from a figured bass. Also, classical composers wanted more control; they preferred to specify an accompaniment rather than trust the judgment of improvisers.

The Classical Orchestra

A new orchestra evolved during the classical period. Unlike the baroque orchestra, which could vary from piece to piece, it was a standard group of four sections: strings, woodwinds, brass, and percussion. In the late instrumental works of Mozart and Haydn, an orchestra might consist of the following:

Strings: 1st violins, 2d violins, violas, cellos, double basses
Woodwinds: 2 flutes, 2 oboes, 2 clarinets, 2 bassoons
Brass: 2 French horns, 2 trumpets
Percussion: 2 timpani

Notice that woodwind and brass instruments are paired and that clarinets have been added. Trombones were also used by Haydn and Mozart, but only in opera and church music, not in solely instrumental works.

The number of musicians was greater in a classical orchestra than in a baroque group, though practice varied considerably from place to place. Haydn directed a private orchestra of only twenty-five players from 1761 to 1790. But for public concerts in London in 1795, he led an orchestra of sixty.

Classical composers exploited the individual tone colors of orchestral instruments. Unlike baroque composers, they did not treat one instrument like another. Classical composers would not let an oboe duplicate the violin melody for the entire length of a movement. A classical piece has greater variety—and more rapid changes—of tone color. A theme might begin in the full orchestra, shift to the strings, and then continue in the woodwinds.

Each section of the classical orchestra had a special role. The strings were the most important section, with the first violins taking the melody most of the time and the lower strings providing an accompaniment. The woodwinds added contrasting tone colors and were often given melodic solos. Horns and trumpets brought power to loud passages and filled out the harmony, but they did not usually play the main melody. Timpani were used for rhythmic bite and emphasis. As a whole, the classical orchestra had developed into a flexible, colorful instrument to which composers could entrust their most powerful and dramatic musical conceptions.

Classical Forms

Instrumental compositions of the classical period usually consist of several movements that contrast in tempo and character. There are often four movements, arranged as follows:

1. Fast movement
2. Slow movement
3. Dance-related movement
4. Fast movement

Classical symphonies and string quartets usually follow this four-movement pattern, while classical sonatas may consist of two, three, or four movements. A *symphony* is written for orchestra; a *string quartet* for two violins, viola, and cello; and a *sonata* for one or two instruments. (The classical symphony, string quartet, and sonata are more fully described in Sections 3 to 7 and 9.)

In writing an individual movement of a symphony, string quartet, or sonata, a classical composer could choose from several different forms. One movement of a composition might be in A B A form, while another might be a theme and variations. The sections that follow will describe some forms used in classical movements, but now let's look at a few general characteristics of classical form.

Classical movements often contrast themes vividly. A movement may contain two, three, or even four or more themes of different character. This use of contrasting themes distinguishes classical music from baroque music, which often uses only one main theme. The classical composer sometimes provides a brief pause to signal the arrival of a new theme.

The larger sections of a classical movement balance each other in a satisfying and symmetrical way. Unstable sections that wander from the tonic key are balanced by stable sections that confirm it. By the end of a classical movement, musical tensions have been resolved.

Though we speak of the classical style, we must remember that Haydn, Mozart, and Beethoven were three individuals with dissimilar personalities. Haydn's and Mozart's works may sound similar at first, but deeper involvement reveals striking personal styles. Beethoven's music seems more powerful, violent, and emotional when compared with the apparently more restrained and elegant works of the earlier masters. But Haydn and Mozart also composed music that is passionate and dramatic. We'll see that all three composers used similar musical procedures and forms, yet their emotional statements bear the particular stamp of each.

2 Composer, Patron, and Public in the Classical Period

Haydn, Mozart, and Beethoven—three of the world's greatest composers—worked during a period of violent political and social upheaval, as we have seen in the opening of Part IV (page 151). Like everyone else, musicians were strongly affected by changes in society, and in the careers of the three classical masters we can trace the slow emancipation of the composer. First came Joseph Haydn (1732–1809), who was content to spend most of his life serving a wealthy aristocratic family. His contract of employment (1761) shows that he was considered a skilled servant, like a gardener or gamekeeper. He had to wear a uniform and "compose such music as His Highness shall order"—and was warned to "refrain from vulgarity in eating, drinking, and conversation." Wolfgang Amadeus Mozart (1756–1791), born just twenty-four years later, could not bear being treated as a servant; he broke from his court position and went to Vienna to try his luck as a freelance musician. For several years, he was very successful, but then his popularity declined; he died in debt. Ludwig van Beethoven (1770–1827) fared better than Mozart. Only a few years after Mozart's death, Beethoven was able to work as an independent musician in Vienna. His success was gained through a wider middle-class market for music and a commanding personality that prompted the nobility to give him gifts and treat him as an equal.

As the eighteenth century advanced, more people made more money. Merchants, doctors, and government officials could afford larger homes, finer clothes, and better food. But the prospering middle class wanted more than material goods; it also sought aristocratic luxuries like theater, literature, and music. In

Most of Haydn's music was composed for a wealthy aristocratic family. Shown here is a performance of a comic opera by Haydn in 1775 at the palace Eszterháza.

fact, during the classical period, the middle class had a great influence on music. Because palace concerts were usually closed to them, townspeople organized public concerts, where, for the price of admission, they could hear the latest symphonies and concertos. During the second half of the eighteenth century, public concerts mushroomed throughout Europe. In London, a concert series ran from 1765 to 1781, codirected by one of Bach's sons, Johann Christian Bach, who had settled in England. In Paris, around the same time, a concert organization called the *Concert des Amateurs* assembled a large orchestra, conducted during the 1770s by the Chevalier de Saint-Georges (1739–1799), a black composer and violinist who was a champion fencer as well.

But merchants and lawyers were not content to hear music only in concerts. They wanted to be surrounded by music at home. They felt that their sons and daughters deserved music lessons as much as the children of aristocrats did. Indeed, if middle-class children played instruments well enough, they might be invited to palaces and eventually marry into the aristocracy. In any event, the demand for printed music, instruments, and music lessons had vastly increased.

Composers in the classical period took middle-class tastes into account. They wrote pieces that were easy for amateur musicians to play and understand. They turned from serious to comic opera, from heroic and mythological plots dear to the nobility to middle-class subjects and folklike tunes. Their comic operas sometimes even ridiculed the aristocracy, and their dance movements became less elegant and courtly, more vigorous and rustic.

Serious composition was flavored by folk and popular music. The classical masters sometimes used familiar tunes as themes for symphonies and variations. Mozart was delighted that people danced to waltzes arranged from melodies in his operas. Haydn, Mozart, and Beethoven all wrote dance music for public balls in Vienna.

Vienna

Vienna was one of the music centers of Europe during the classical period, and Haydn, Mozart, and Beethoven were all active there. As the seat of the Holy Roman Empire (which included parts of modern Austria, Germany, Italy, Hungary, and the Czech Republic), it was a bustling cultural and commercial center with a cosmopolitan character. Its population of almost 250,000 (in 1800) made Vienna the fourth largest city in Europe. All three classical masters were born elsewhere, but they were drawn to Vienna to study and to seek recognition. In Vienna, Haydn and Mozart became close friends and influenced each other's musical style. Beethoven traveled to Vienna at sixteen to play for Mozart; at twenty-two, he returned to study with Haydn.

Aristocrats from all over the empire would spend winters in Vienna, sometimes bringing their private orchestras. Music was an important part of court life, and a good orchestra was a symbol of prestige. Many of the nobility were excellent musicians. For instance, Empress Maria Theresa had sung in palace musicales when she was young, Emperor Joseph II was a competent cellist, and Archduke Rudolf was Beethoven's longtime student of piano and composition.

Much music was heard in private concerts, where aristocrats and wealthy commoners played alongside professional musicians. Mozart and Beethoven often earned money by performing in these intimate concerts. The nobility frequently hired servants who could double as musicians. An advertisement in the *Vienna Gazette* of 1789 reads: "Wanted, for a house of the gentry, a man-servant who knows how to play the violin well."

In Vienna there was also outdoor music, light and popular in tone. Small street bands of wind and string players played at garden parties or under the windows of people likely to throw down money. A Viennese almanac reported that "on fine summer nights you may come upon serenades in the streets at all hours." Haydn and Mozart wrote many outdoor entertainment pieces, which they called *divertimentos* or *serenades.* Vienna's great love of music and its enthusiastic demand for new works made it the chosen city of Haydn, Mozart, and Beethoven.

3 Sonata Form

An astonishing amount of important music from the classical period to the twentieth century is composed in sonata form (sometimes called *sonata-allegro form*). The term **sonata form** refers to the form of a *single* movement. It should not be confused with the term *sonata,* which is used for a whole composition made up of *several* movements. The opening fast movement of a classical symphony, sonata, or string quartet is usually in sonata form. This form is also used in slow movements and in fast concluding movements.

A sonata-form movement consists of three main sections: the exposition, where the themes are presented; the development, where themes are treated in new ways; and the recapitulation, where the themes return. These three main sections are often followed by a concluding section, the coda (Italian for *tail*). Remember that these sections are all within *one movement.* A *single* sonata-form movement may be outlined as follows:

Exposition
First theme in tonic (home) key
Bridge containing modulation from home key to new key
Second theme in new key
Closing section in key of second theme

Development
New treatment of themes; modulations to different keys

Recapitulation
First theme in tonic key
Bridge
Second theme in tonic key
Closing section in tonic key

(Coda)
In tonic key

A fast movement in sonata form is sometimes preceded by a slow introduction that creates a feeling of expectancy.

Exposition

The *exposition* sets up a strong conflict between the tonic key and the new key, and between the first theme (or group of themes) and the second theme (or group of themes). It begins with the first theme in the tonic, or home, key. There follows a **bridge,** or *transition,* leading to the second theme, in a new key. The modulation from the home key to a new key creates a feeling of harmonic tension and forward motion. The second theme often contrasts in mood with the first theme. A closing section ends the exposition in the key of the second theme. At the end of a classical exposition there is usually a repeat sign (:|) to indicate that the whole exposition is to be played again.

Development

The *development* is often the most dramatic section of the movement. The listener may be kept off balance as the music moves restlessly through several different keys. Through these rapid modulations, the harmonic tension is heightened. In this section, themes are *developed,* or treated in new ways. They are broken into fragments, or **motives,** which are short musical ideas developed within a composition. A motive may take on different and unexpected emotional meanings. One fragment of a comic theme, for example, may be made to sound aggressive and menacing through changes of melody, rhythm, or dynamics. Themes can be combined with new ideas or changed in texture. A complex polyphonic texture can be woven by shifting a motive rapidly among different instruments. The harmonic and thematic searching of the development builds tension that demands resolution.

Recapitulation

The beginning of the *recapitulation* brings resolution, as we again hear the first theme in the tonic key. In the recapitulation, the first theme, bridge, second theme, and concluding section are presented more or less as they were in the exposition, with one crucial difference: all the principal material is now in the tonic key. Earlier, in the exposition, there was strong contrast between the first theme in the home key and the second theme and closing section in a new key; that tension is resolved in the recapitulation by presenting the first theme, second theme, and closing section all in the tonic key.

A movement in sonata form progresses from a stable situation toward conflict, to heightened tension, and then back to stability.

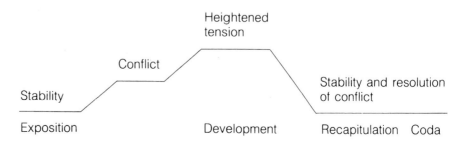

Coda

An even more powerful feeling of conclusion is attained by following the recapitulation with yet another section. The *coda* rounds off a movement by repeating themes or developing them further. It always ends in the tonic key.

The amazing durability and vitality of sonata form result from its capacity for drama. The form moves from a stable situation toward conflict (in the exposition), to heightened tension (in the development), and then back to stability and resolution of conflict (see the illustration on page 161). Sonata form is exceptionally flexible and capable of endless variation. It is not a rigid mold into which musical ideas are poured. Rather, it may be viewed as a set of principles that serve to shape and unify contrasts of theme and key. Haydn, Mozart, and Beethoven repeatedly used sonata form, yet each maintained individuality. Movements in sonata form may differ radically in character, in length, and in the number and treatment of themes. Sonata form is so versatile that it is no surprise to find its use spanning more than two centuries.

We'll now consider an excellent example of sonata form: the first movement of Symphony No. 40 by Wolfgang Amadeus Mozart.

Symphony No. 40 in G Minor, K. 550,* by Wolfgang Amadeus Mozart

First Movement:
Molto allegro

Brief Set:

CD 2 23

Basic Set:

CD 3 10

The rapid sonata-form opening movement of Mozart's Symphony No. 40 in G Minor, K. 550, conveys a feeling of controlled agitation. A throbbing accompaniment in the violas contributes to the tension of the opening theme, which begins softly in the violins. Dominating the violin melody is the rhythmic pattern short-short-long, first heard in the opening three-note motive.

*In the nineteenth century, Mozart's compositions (numbering more than 600) were cataloged chronologically by Ludwig von Köchel. Hence it is customary to refer to them by their "K." numbers.

The persistence of this rhythmic pattern gives the music a sense of urgency. Yet the melody is balanced and symmetrical. Questioning upward leaps are answered by downward scales, and the second phrase of the melody is a sequential repetition of the first, one step lower. The exposition continues with a bridge section that presents a new staccato motive played loudly by the violins.

The lyrical second theme, in B flat major, contrasts completely with the agitated G minor opening. Mozart exploits the expressive resources of tone color by dividing the theme between strings and woodwinds. In the closing section of the exposition, he uses a fragment from the opening theme to achieve a different emotional effect. The three-note motive now sounds gentle and plaintive as it is passed between clarinet and bassoon against a sighing string background.

In the development, the movement becomes feverish. The opening theme is led into different keys and is cut into smaller and smaller pieces. The development begins mysteriously as the opening phrase ends in an unexpected way and sinks lower and lower. Then a sudden explosion of polyphonic texture increases the excitement and complexity. Mozart brusquely shifts the opening phrase between low and high strings while combining it with a furious staccato countermelody. Soon after, he demolishes the opening phrase: we hear the beginning of the theme without its upward leap.

Then the final note is lopped off.

Finally, we are left with the irreducible minimum of the original theme, the three-note motive.

The tension resolves only with the entrance of the entire opening theme in the tonic key.

In the recapitulation, material from the exposition is given new expressive meaning. The bridge is expanded and made more dramatic. The lyrical second theme, now in G minor, is touching and sad.

Listening Outline to be read while music is heard

Brief Set: CD 2   Basic Set: CD 3

MOZART, Symphony No. 40 in G Minor

First Movement: Molto allegro

Sonata form, duple meter ($\frac{2}{2}$), G minor

Flute, 2 oboes, 2 clarinets, 2 bassoons, 2 French horns, 1st violins, 2d violins, violas, cellos, double basses

(Duration, 8:12)

Exposition
First theme

[23] **10** 0:00 **1. a.** Main theme in violins, *p*, throbbing accompaniment in violas, minor key.

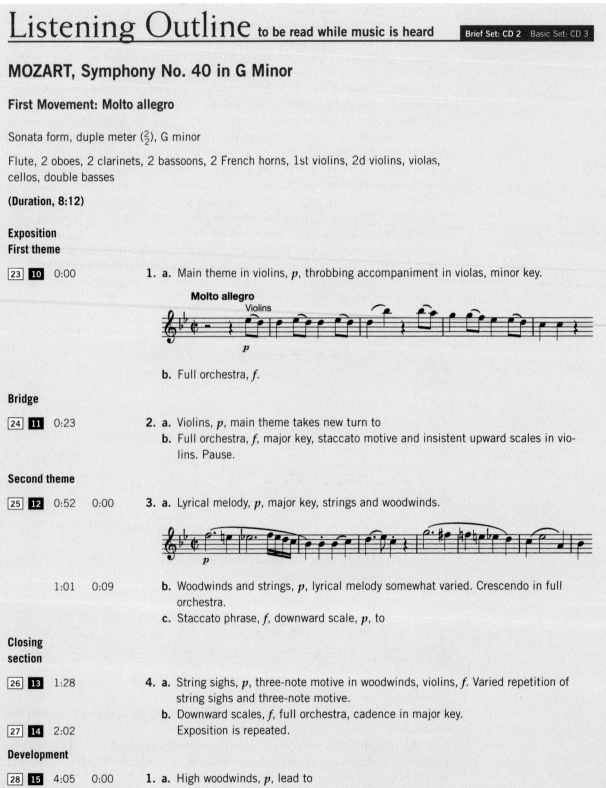

 b. Full orchestra, *f*.

Bridge

[24] **11** 0:23 **2. a.** Violins, *p*, main theme takes new turn to
 b. Full orchestra, *f*, major key, staccato motive and insistent upward scales in violins. Pause.

Second theme

[25] **12** 0:52 0:00 **3. a.** Lyrical melody, *p*, major key, strings and woodwinds.

 1:01 0:09 **b.** Woodwinds and strings, *p*, lyrical melody somewhat varied. Crescendo in full orchestra.
 c. Staccato phrase, *f*, downward scale, *p*, to

Closing section

[26] **13** 1:28 **4. a.** String sighs, *p*, three-note motive in woodwinds, violins, *f*. Varied repetition of string sighs and three-note motive.
 b. Downward scales, *f*, full orchestra, cadence in major key.

[27] **14** 2:02 Exposition is repeated.

Development

[28] **15** 4:05 0:00 **1. a.** High woodwinds, *p*, lead to
 b. Violins, *p*, main-theme phrase repeated on lower pitches.

4:21	0:16	**2.**	Sudden *f*, full orchestra, main-theme phrase combined with rapid countermelody
4:49	0:44	**3. a.**	Sudden *p*, high violins and woodwinds, three-note motive.
		b.	Sudden *f*, full orchestra, three-note motive.
		c.	Sudden *p*, high flutes and clarinets, three-note motive carried down to

Recapitulation
First theme

29 16	5:21	0:00	**1. a.**	Main theme in violins, *p*, throbbing accompaniment in violas, minor key.
			b.	Full orchestra, *f*.

Bridge

	5:46	0:25	**2. a.**	Violins, *p*, main theme takes new turn to
			b.	Full orchestra, *f*, staccato motive in violins and cellos. Insistent upward scales in violins, *f*. Pause.

Second theme

30 17	6:37	0:00	**3. a.**	Lyrical melody, p, minor key, strings and woodwinds.
	6:46	0:09	**b.**	Woodwinds and strings, *p*, lyrical melody somewhat varied. Crescendo in full orchestra.
			c.	Staccato phrase, *f*, downward scale, *p*, to

Closing
section

	7:19	0:42	**4. a.**	String sighs, *p*, three-note motive in woodwinds, violins, *f*. Varied repetition of string sighs and three-note motive.
			b.	Downward scales, *f*, full orchestra.

Coda

31 18	7:49		**1. a.**	Sudden *p*, main-theme motive in strings.
			b.	Full orchestra, *f*, cadence in minor key.

www.mhhe.com/kamien

Theme and Variations

The form called *theme and variations* was widely used in the classical period, either as an independent piece or as one movement of a symphony, sonata, or string quartet. In a **theme and variations**, a basic musical idea—the theme—is repeated over and over and is changed each time. This form may be outlined as theme (A)—variation 1 (A')—variation 2 (A")—variation 3 (A''"), and so on; each prime mark indicates a variation of the basic idea. (Another way of indicating variations is A1, A2, etc.)

Each variation, though usually about the same length as the theme, is unique and may differ in mood from the theme. Changes of melody, rhythm, harmony, accompaniment, dynamics, or tone color may be used to give a variation its own identity. The core melody may appear in the bass, or it may be repeated in a minor key instead of a major key. It may be heard together with a new melody. The variations may be connected to each other or separated by pauses. For the theme itself, a composer may invent an original melody or borrow someone else's. Beethoven once borrowed a little waltz tune and put it through thirty-three brilliant variations (the *Diabelli* Variations). More modest examples of theme and variations have as few as three variations.

Symphony No. 94 in G Major (*Surprise*; 1791), by Joseph Haydn

Second Movement: Andante

Brief Set:
CD 2 32

Basic Set:
CD 3 40

The second movement (andante) of Haydn's Symphony No. 94 in G Major (*Surprise* Symphony) is a theme and variations. The folklike, staccato theme begins softly but is punctuated by a sudden loud chord—this is the "surprise." There are four variations, in which the theme is changed in tone color, dynamics, rhythm, and melody. Sometimes the original melody is accompanied by a new one called a *countermelody.* Such combinations of two distinctive melodies result in a polyphonic texture. In one variation the theme is presented in minor instead of major. The last variation is followed by a closing section in which a gently dissonant accompaniment momentarily darkens the mood of the carefree theme.

The theme consists of two parts, sections a and b, each of which is repeated. This pattern is usually retained in the variations.

Listening Outline to be read while music is heard   Brief Set: CD 2   Basic Set: CD 3

HAYDN, Symphony No. 94 in G Major (*Surprise*)

Second Movement: Andante

Theme and variations, duple meter ($\frac{2}{4}$), C major

2 flutes, 2 oboes, 2 bassoons, 2 French horns, 2 trumpets, timpani, 1st violins, 2d violins, violas, cellos, double basses

(Duration, 6:14)

Theme
Section a

32 40   0:00   Violins, *p*, staccato theme.

Section a repeated, *pp*, with pizzicato string accompaniment. Surprise chord, *ff*.

Section b

Violins, *p*, continuation of theme.

Section b repeated with flute and oboe.

Variation 1

33 **41** 1:07

a. Theme begins, *f*, higher countermelody in violins, *p*. Section a repeated.

b. Violins, *p*, continuation of theme and higher countermelody. Section b repeated.

Variation 2

34 **42** 2:12

a. Theme in minor, *ff*, violin phrase in major, *p*. Section a repeated.

b. Violins, *f*, rapid downward scales, orchestra *f*. Violins alone, *p*, lead into

Variation 3

35 **43** 3:20

a. Oboe, *p*, theme in faster repeated notes, major key.

Flute and oboe, *p*, legato countermelody above staccato theme in violins, *p*.

b. Continuation of theme and countermelody. Section b repeated.

Variation 4

36 44   4:23

a. Theme in brasses and woodwinds, *ff*, fast notes in violins, *ff*. Violins, *p*, legato version of theme, dotted rhythm (long-short).

p dolce

b. Violins, *p*, continuation of theme, dotted rhythm. Full orchestra, *ff*, triumphant continuation of theme leads to suspenseful chord, *ff*, sudden *p*.

Closing Section

37 45   5:45

Theme in oboe, *p*, gently dissonant chords in strings, flute joins, *pp*, conclusion.

5 Minuet and Trio

The form known as ***minuet and trio,*** or ***minuet,*** is often used as the third movement of classical symphonies, string quartets, and other works. Like the movements of the baroque suite, the minuet originated as a dance. It first appeared at the court of Louis XIV of France around 1650 and was danced by aristocrats throughout the eighteenth century. The minuet was a stately, dignified dance in which the couple exchanged curtsies and bows.

The minuet movement of a symphony or string quartet is written for listening, not dancing. It is in triple meter($\frac{3}{4}$) and usually in a moderate tempo. The movement is in A B A form: minuet (A), trio (B), minuet (A). The trio (B) is usually quieter than the minuet (A) section and requires fewer instruments. It often contains woodwind solos. The trio section got its name during the baroque period, when a set of two dances would be followed by a repetition of the first dance. The second dance was known as a "trio" because it was usually played by three instruments. Classical composers did not restrict themselves to three instruments in the B sections of their minuets, but the name *trio* remained.

The A (minuet) section includes smaller parts a, b, and a′ (variation of a). In the opening A (minuet) section, all the smaller parts are repeated, as follows: a (repeated) ba′ (repeated). (In the musical score, the repeat sign ⦂ indicates each repetition.) The B (trio) section is quite similar in form: c (repeated) dc′ (repeated). At the close of the B (trio) section, the repetition of the entire A (minuet) section is indicated by the words ***da capo*** (*from the beginning*). This time, however, the minuet is played straight through without the repetitions: a ba′. The whole movement can be outlined like this:

Minuet	**Trio**	**Minuet**
A	B	A
a (repeated) ba′ (repeated)	c (repeated) dc′ (repeated)	a ba′

Basic Set:
CD 3 **49**

fiddler. The main theme, in minor, contrasts with the other themes, which are in major. Theme B is a lyrical legato melody, while theme C is playful, with quick upward rushes. At its final return, the main theme (A) has a faster tempo, prestissimo, and leads into a frenzied concluding section.

Listening Outline to be read while music is heard   Brief Set: CD 2 Basic Set: CD 3

BEETHOVEN, String Quartet in C Minor, Op. 18, No. 4

Fourth Movement: Rondo (Allegro)

Rondo form, duple meter ($\frac{2}{2}$), C minor

1st violin, 2d violin, viola, cello

(Duration, 4:08)

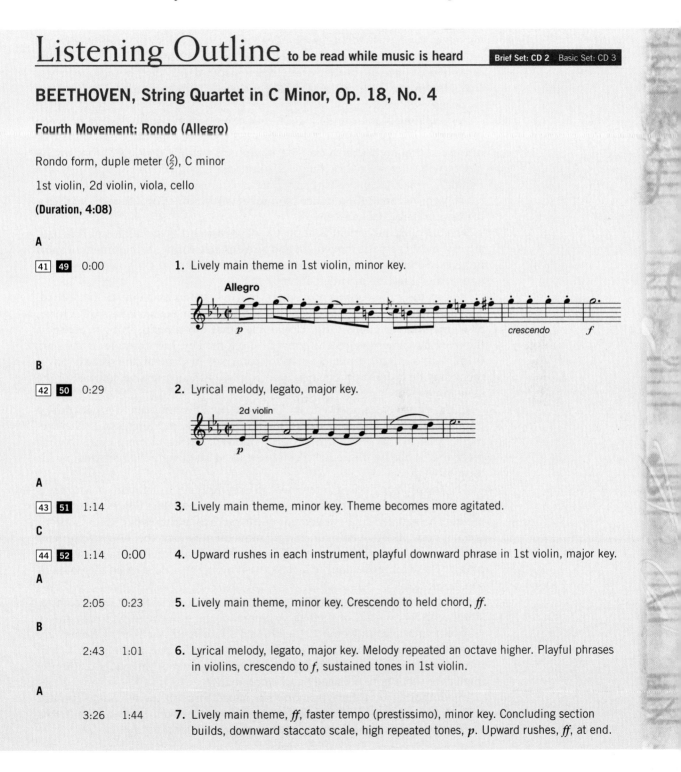

A

41 **49** 0:00

1. Lively main theme in 1st violin, minor key.

B

42 **50** 0:29

2. Lyrical melody, legato, major key.

A

43 **51** 1:14

3. Lively main theme, minor key. Theme becomes more agitated.

C

44 **52** 1:14   0:00

4. Upward rushes in each instrument, playful downward phrase in 1st violin, major key.

A

2:05   0:23

5. Lively main theme, minor key. Crescendo to held chord, *ff*.

B

2:43   1:01

6. Lyrical melody, legato, major key. Melody repeated an octave higher. Playful phrases in violins, crescendo to *f*, sustained tones in 1st violin.

A

3:26   1:44

7. Lively main theme, *ff*, faster tempo (prestissimo), minor key. Concluding section builds, downward staccato scale, high repeated tones, *p*. Upward rushes, *ff*, at end.

# The Classical Symphony

The great contribution of the classical period to orchestral music is the symphony. Haydn wrote at least 104 symphonies, Mozart over forty, and Beethoven nine. Most of Haydn's symphonies were composed for his employers, who required a steady flow of works for their palace concerts. Beethoven, on the other hand, wrote a symphony only when inspired. His symphonies are longer than Haydn's or Mozart's and were conceived for performance in large concert halls.

A *symphony* is an extended, ambitious composition usually lasting between 20 and 45 minutes, exploiting the expanded range of tone color and dynamics of the classical orchestra. A classical symphony usually consists of four movements, which evoke a wide range of emotions through contrasts of tempo and mood. A typical sequence is (1) a vigorous, dramatic fast movement; (2) a lyrical slow movement; (3) a dancelike movement (minuet or scherzo); and (4) a brilliant or heroic fast movement.

The opening movement is almost always fast and in sonata form. It is usually the most dramatic movement and stresses an exciting development of short motives. Sometimes a slow introduction leads to the opening fast movement and creates a feeling of anticipation.

It is in the slow second movement that we are most likely to find broad, songlike melodies. This movement, by and large, is in sonata form, A B A form, or theme-and-variations form. Unlike the other movements in the symphony, the slow movement is generally *not* in the tonic key. For example, if the first, third, and fourth movements are in the tonic key of C major, the second movement may be in F major. The new key points up the expressive contrast of the slow movement.

In the symphonies of Haydn and Mozart, the third movement is generally a minuet and trio, which may be in a moderate or fairly quick tempo. This movement varies in character from a courtly dance to a peasant romp or a vigorous piece that is hardly dancelike. Beethoven liked fast, energetic scherzos for his third movements.

The fourth, concluding movement of a symphony by Haydn or Mozart is fast, lively, and brilliant, but somewhat lighter in mood than the opening movement. (The agitated final movement of Mozart's Symphony No. 40 in G minor is not typical.) Beethoven's concluding movement tends to be more triumphant and heroic in character and is sometimes meant as the climax of the whole symphony. The final movement of a classical symphony is most often in sonata or sonata-rondo form.

In most classical symphonies, each movement is a self-contained composition with its own set of themes. A theme in one movement will only rarely reappear in a later movement. (Beethoven's Fifth and Ninth Symphonies are exceptions.) But a symphony is unified partly by the use of the same key in three of its movements. More important, the movements balance and complement each other both musically and emotionally.

The importance of the symphony has lasted through the twentieth century and into the twenty-first. Its great significance is reflected in such familiar terms as *symphonic music, symphony hall,* and *symphony orchestra.*

The Classical Concerto

A classical *concerto* is a three-movement work for an instrumental soloist and orchestra. It combines the soloist's virtuosity and interpretive abilities with the orchestra's wide range of tone color and dynamics. Emerging from this encounter is a contrast of ideas and sound that is dramatic and satisfying. The soloist is very much the star, and all of his or her musical talents are needed in this challenging dialogue.

The classical love of balance can be seen in the concerto: the soloist and orchestra are equally important. Between them, there's an interplay of melodic lines and a spirit of give-and-take. One moment the soloist plays the melody while the orchestra accompanies. Then the woodwinds may unfold the main theme against rippling arpeggios (broken chords) played by the soloist. Mozart and Beethoven—the greatest masters of the classical concerto—often wrote concertos for themselves to play as piano soloists; the piano is their favored solo instrument. Other solo instruments used in classical concertos include violin, cello, horn, trumpet, clarinet, and bassoon.

Like symphonies, concertos can last anywhere from 20 minutes to 45 minutes. But instead of the symphony's four movements, a classical concerto has three: (1) fast, (2) slow, and (3) fast. A concerto has no minuet or scherzo.

In the first movement and sometimes in the last movement, there is a special unaccompanied showpiece for the soloist, the **cadenza** (Italian for *cadence*). Near the end of the movement, the orchestra suspends forward motion by briefly sustaining a dissonant chord. This is indicated in the score by a *fermata* (⌒), a sign meaning *pause,* which is placed over the chord. The suspense announces the entry of the soloist's cadenza. For several minutes, the soloist, *without orchestra,* displays virtuosity by playing dazzling scale passages and broken chords. Themes of the movement are varied and presented in new keys. At the end of a cadenza, the soloist plays a long trill followed by a chord that meshes with the reentrance of the orchestra.

In the classical era, the soloist, who was often the composer, generally improvised the cadenzas. In this case, the score contained only the fermata, indicating where the cadenza should be inserted. But after the eighteenth century, the art of improvisation declined, and composers began to write cadenzas directly into the score. This gave them more control over their compositions.

Today, performers of eighteenth-century concertos may have a choice of cadenzas. For some concertos, composers wrote cadenzas for their own performance or for that of a student. Also, many nineteenth- and twentieth-century musicians later provided cadenzas for classical concertos. These are best when their style matches that of the concerto. For example, the cadenzas Beethoven composed for Mozart's D Minor Piano Concerto are so strong and so much in the spirit of the work that pianists still use them today.

A classical concerto begins with a movement in sonata form of a special kind, containing *two* expositions. The first is played by the orchestra, which presents several themes in the home key. This opening section sets the mood for the movement and leads us to expect the soloist's entrance. The second exposition begins with the soloist's first notes. Music for the solo entry may be powerful or quiet, but its effect is dramatic because suspense has been built. Together with the orchestra, the soloist explores themes from the first exposition and introduces new ones. After a modulation from the home key to a new key, the second exposition then moves to a development section, followed by the recapitulation, cadenza, and coda. The slow middle movement may take any one of several forms, but the finale is usually a quick rondo or sonata-rondo.

9 Classical Chamber Music

Classical *chamber music* is designed for the intimate setting of a room (chamber) in a home or palace, rather than for a public concert hall. It is performed by a small group of two to nine musicians, with one player to a part. Chamber music is lighter in sound than classical orchestral music. During the classical period, it was fashionable for an aristocrat or a member of the well-to-do middle class to play chamber music with friends and to hire professional musicians to entertain guests after dinner.

Chamber music is subtle and intimate, intended to please the performer as much as the listener. A chamber music group is a team. Each member is essential, and each may have an important share of the thematic material. Therefore much give-and-take is called for among the instruments. Chamber music does not need a conductor; instead, each musician must be sensitive to what goes on and coordinate dynamics and phrasing with the other musicians. In this respect, a chamber ensemble is like a small jazz group.

The most important form in classical chamber music is the **string quartet,** written for two violins, a viola, and a cello. Haydn, Mozart, and Beethoven wrote some of their most important music in this form. The string quartet can be compared to a conversation among four lively, sensitive, and intelligent people. It's not surprising that the string quartet evolved when conversation was cultivated as a fine art.

Like a symphony, a string quartet usually consists of four movements: (1) fast, (2) slow, (3) minuet or scherzo, (4) fast. (Sometimes the second movement is a minuet or a scherzo and the slow movement is third.)

Other popular forms of classical chamber music are the sonata for violin and piano, the piano trio (violin, cello, and piano), and the string quintet (two violins, two violas, and cello).

Today, as in the eighteenth century, much chamber music is performed by amateurs. By consulting the Internet or directory *Amateur Chamber Music Players,* one can find partners for chamber music almost anywhere in the United States.

10 Joseph Haydn

Joseph Haydn (1732–1809) was born in Rohrau, a tiny Austrian village. Until he was six, his musical background consisted of folk songs and peasant dances (which later had an influence on his style); but then his eager response to music

Haydn was a pathfinder for the classical style, a pioneer in the development of the symphony and string quartet.

was recognized and he was given training. At eight, he went to Vienna to serve as a choirboy in the Cathedral of St. Stephen.

When his voice changed, Haydn was dismissed, penniless, from St. Stephen's; he gave music lessons to children, struggled to teach himself composition, and took odd jobs (including playing violin in street bands). But gradually, aristocratic patrons of music began to notice his talent; and in 1761, when he was twenty-nine, his life changed for the better, permanently: he entered the service of the Esterházys, the richest and most powerful of the Hungarian noble families. For nearly thirty years, most of his music was composed for performances in the palaces of the family, especially Eszterháza—which contained an opera house, a theater, two concert halls, and 126 guest rooms.

As a highly skilled servant, Haydn was to compose all the music requested by his patron, conduct the orchestra, coach singers, and oversee the instruments and the music library. This entailed a staggering amount of work; there were usually two concerts and two opera performances weekly, as well as daily chamber music. Though today this sort of patronage seems degrading, it was taken for granted at the time and had definite advantages for composers: they received a steady income and their works were performed. Haydn was conscientious about his professional duties, concerned about his musicians' interest, and—despite an unhappy marriage—good-humored and unselfish.

Word spread about the Esterházys' composer, and Haydn's music became immensely popular all over Europe. In 1791–1792 and again in 1794–1795, Haydn went to London, and reports of the time say that his appearances there were triumphs. (The twelve symphonies he composed for these visits are now known as the *London symphonies.*) A servant had become a celebrity; Haydn was wined and dined by the aristocracy, given an honorary doctorate at Oxford, and received by the royal family.

In 1795, he returned to Vienna rich and honored. In his late sixties, he composed six masses and two oratorios—*The Creation* (1798) and *The Seasons* (1801)—which were so popular that choruses and orchestras were formed solely to present them. He died in 1809, at seventy-seven.

Haydn's Music

Haydn was a pathfinder for the classical style, a pioneer in the development of the symphony and the string quartet. Both Mozart and Beethoven were influenced by his style. His music, like his personality, is robust and direct; it radiates healthy optimism. Much of it has a folk flavor, and *The Creation* and *The Seasons* reflect his love of nature. Haydn was a master at developing themes; he could build a whole movement from a single main theme, creating contrasts of mood through changes in texture, rhythm, dynamics, and orchestration. The contagious joy that springs from his lively rhythms and vivid contrasts makes it clear why London went wild.

Haydn's 104 symphonies—along with his 68 string quartets—are considered the most important part of his enormous output. Many of them have nicknames, such as *Surprise* (No. 94), *Military* (No. 100), *Clock* (No. 101), and *Drum Roll* (No. 103).

Some scholars believe that Haydn invented the string quartet form. He began writing the first of his lifelong series of string quartets for a good reason—only three other musicians (two violinists and a cellist, in addition to Haydn as violist) were on hand during the summer of 1757, when he was invited to take part in chamber music performances at a castle.

Haydn's output also includes piano sonatas, piano trios, divertimentos, concertos, operas, oratorios, and masses. The variety in his works is astounding. He was a great innovator and experimenter who hated arbitrary "rules" of composition. "Art is free," he said. "The educated ear is the sole authority, . . . and I think that I have as much right to lay down the law as anyone."

Trumpet Concerto in E Flat Major (1796)

Haydn's Trumpet Concerto in E Flat Major has a remarkable history. After its premiere in 1800, it was forgotten for almost 130 years. It was first published only in 1929, but in the 1930s a phonograph recording brought it to a wide audience. Now, it may well be Haydn's most popular work.

Haydn wrote the concerto in 1796 for a friend, a trumpeter at the Viennese court who had recently invented a keyed trumpet that could produce a complete chromatic scale. The keyed trumpet was intended to replace the natural trumpet, which could produce only a restricted number of tones. But the keyed trumpet had a dull sound and was supplanted by the valve trumpet around 1840. Today, the concerto is performed on a valve trumpet. Like most concertos, it has three movements: (1) fast, (2) slow, (3) fast. We'll examine the third movement.

Third Movement: Allegro

Basic Set:
CD 3 `53`

The third movement is a dazzling sonata-rondo in which Haydn gives the trumpeter's virtuosity free rein. The movement combines the recurring main theme characteristic of rondo form with the development section found in sonata form. It may be outlined as A B A B′ A—development section—A B″—coda. Themes A and B are introduced by the orchestra and are then presented mainly by the trumpet, with orchestral support. The main theme, A, is a high-spirited melody that is well suited to the trumpet.

53 0:00

54 0:23

Theme B is playful; it contains a short, downward-moving phrase that is repeated several times.

Haydn's fondness for musical surprises is reflected in the coda, which contains sudden changes of dynamics, unexpected harmonic twists, and a suspenseful long pause.

11 Wolfgang Amadeus Mozart

Wolfgang Amadeus Mozart (1756–1791), one of the most amazing child prodigies in history, was born in Salzburg, Austria. By the age of six, he could play the harpsichord and violin, improvise fugues, write minuets, and read music perfectly at first sight. At age eight, he wrote a symphony; at eleven, an oratorio; at twelve, an opera.

Mozart's father, Leopold, a court musician, was eager to show him off. Between the ages of six and fifteen Mozart was continually on tour; he played for Empress Maria Theresa in Vienna, Louis XV at Versailles, George III in London, and innumerable aristocrats. On his trips to Italy he was able to master the current operatic style, which he later put to superb use.

When he was fifteen, Mozart returned to Salzburg—then ruled by a prince-archbishop. The archbishop was a tyrant who did not appreciate Mozart's music and refused to grant him more than a subordinate seat in the court orchestra. With his father's help, Mozart tried repeatedly but unsuccessfully over the next decade to find a position elsewhere.

Ironically, and tragically, Mozart won more acclaim as a boy wonder than as an adult musician. Having begun his professional life as an international celebrity, he could not tolerate being treated like a servant; he became insubordinate

Mozart was among the most versatile of all composers; he wrote masterpieces in all the musical forms of his time.

when the archbishop forbade him to give concerts or to perform at the houses of the aristocracy, and his relationship with his patron went from bad to worse. Moreover, his complete dependence on his father had given him little opportunity to develop initiative; and a contemporary observed that he was "too good-natured, not active enough, too easily taken in, too little concerned with the means that may lead him to good fortune."

When he was twenty-five, Mozart could stand it no more: he broke away from provincial Salzburg and became a freelance musician in Vienna. His first few years there were very successful. His German opera *Die Entführung aus dem Serail* (*The Abduction from the Seraglio,* 1782) was acclaimed; concerts of his own music were attended by the emperor and nobility; his compositions were published; pupils paid him high fees; and he formed a friendship with Haydn, who told Mozart's father, "Your son is the greatest composer that I know; he has taste and, what is more, the most profound knowledge of composition." In 1786 came his opera *Le Nozze di Figaro (The Marriage of Figaro).* Vienna loved it, and Prague was even more enthusiastic; "they talk of nothing but *Figaro,*" Mozart joyfully wrote. This success led an opera company in Prague to commission *Don Giovanni* the next year.

Although *Don Giovanni* was a triumph in Prague, its dark qualities and dissonance did not appeal to the Viennese, and Mozart's popularity in Vienna began to decline. Vienna was a fickle city in any case, and it found Mozart's music complicated and hard to follow. His pupils dwindled; the elite snubbed his concerts.

During the last year of his life—1791—Mozart was more successful. He received a commission for a comic opera, *Die Zauberflöte (The Magic Flute),* and while working on it was visited by a mysterious stranger who carried an anonymous letter commissioning a requiem, a mass for the dead. As Mozart's health grew worse, he came to believe that the requiem was for himself and rushed to finish it while on his deathbed. (In fact, the stranger was the servant of a nobleman who intended to claim the requiem as his own composition.) *The Magic Flute* was premiered to resounding praise in Vienna, but its success came too late. Mozart died shortly before his thirty-sixth birthday, leaving the Requiem unfinished. (It was completed by his friend and pupil Franz Süssmayer.)

Mozart's Music

Mozart was among the most versatile of composers and wrote masterpieces in all the musical forms of his time—symphonies, concertos, chamber music, operas. His music sings and conveys ease, grace, and spontaneity as well as balance, restraint, and proportion. Yet mysterious harmonies contrast with its lyricism, and it fuses elegance with power. His compositions sound effortless and were created with miraculous rapidity; for example, he completed his last three symphonies in six weeks.

Many of Mozart's concertos are among his greatest works. His piano concertos—composed mainly for his own performances—are particularly important; but he also wrote concertos for violin, horn, flute, bassoon, oboe, and clarinet.

Mozart was also a master of opera, with a supreme ability to coordinate music and stage action, a keen sense of theater, an inexhaustible gift of melody, and a genius for creating characters through tone. Most of his operas are comedies, composed to German or Italian librettos. His three masterpieces of Italian comic opera (all composed to librettos by Lorenzo da Ponte) are *The Marriage of Figaro* (1786), *Don Giovanni* (1787), and *Così fan tutte* (1790); his finest opera in German is *The Magic Flute* (1791). The comic operas have both humorous and serious characters—not mere stereotypes but individual human beings who think and feel. Emotions in his arias and ensembles continually evolve and change.

"I am never happier," Mozart once wrote, "than when I have something to compose, for that, after all, is my sole delight and passion." His delight and passion are communicated in his works, which represent late-eighteenth-century musical style at its highest level of perfection.

Don Giovanni (1787)

Don Giovanni (Don Juan) is a unique blend of comic and serious opera, combining seduction and slapstick with violence and the supernatural. The old tale of Don Juan, the legendary Spanish lover, had attracted many playwrights and composers before Mozart. Mozart's Don Giovanni is an extremely seductive but ruthless nobleman who will stop at nothing to satisfy his sexual appetite. Don Giovanni's comic servant, Leporello, is a grumbling accomplice who dreams of being in his master's place.

The Don attempts to rape a young noblewoman, Donna Anna; her father, the Commendatore (Commandant), challenges him to a duel. Don Giovanni kills

The Korean soprano Hei-Kyung Hong as Zerlina and the Welsh baritone Bryn Terfel as Don Giovanni in a production of *Don Giovanni* at the Metropolitan Opera.

the old man, causing Donna Anna and her fiancé, Don Ottavio, to swear revenge. Pursued by his enemies, Don Giovanni deftly engages in new amorous adventures. During one of them, he hides in a cemetery, where he sees a marble statue of the dead Commandant. The unearthly statue utters threatening words, but Don Giovanni brazenly invites it to dinner. When the statue appears at the banquet hall, it orders the Don to repent. Don Giovanni defiantly refuses and is dragged down to hell.

Act I:
Introduction

Brief Set:
CD 3 [1]
CD 5 video clip
Basic Set:
CD 3 **60**
C9 video clip

The overture leads directly into the action-packed opening scene. In breathless succession we witness Leporello keeping guard, Don Giovanni struggling with Donna Anna, the Commandant dueling with the Don, and the Commandant's agonized last gasps. Mozart's music vividly depicts the characters and pushes the action forward. (In the vocal music guide, braces indicate that characters sing at the same time. *Etc.* indicates that previous lines of text are repeated.)

Vocal Music Guide to be read while music is heard

MOZART, *Don Giovanni*

Act I: Introduction

☐1 ☐60 0:00
Orchestral
introduction,
molto allegro;
sudden fortes
suggest pacing
and abrupt turns.

(Late evening outside the Commandant's palace in Seville. Don Giovanni, concealing his identity, has stolen into Donna Anna's room for an amorous adventure. Leporello paces back and forth.)

Leporello

Notte e giorno faticar,	Night and day I slave
Per chi nulla sa gradir;	For one who does not appreciate it.
Piova e vento sopportar,	I put up with wind and rain,
Mangiar male e mal dormir!	Eat and sleep badly.
Voglio far il gentiluomo,	I want to be a gentleman
E non voglio più servir,	And to give up my servitude.
No, no, no, no, no, no,	No, no, no, no, no, no,
Non voglio più servir!	I want to give up my servitude.
O che caro galantuomo!	Oh, what a fine gentleman!
Voi star dentro colla bella	You stay inside with your lady
Ed io far la sentinella!	And I must play the sentinel!
Voglio far il gentiluomo, ecc.	Oh, what a fine gentleman, etc.
Ma mi par che venga gente . . .	But I think someone is coming!
Non mi voglio far sentir, ecc.	I don't want them to hear me, etc.

1:39
Orchestral
crescendo.

(Leporello hides to one side. Don Giovanni and Donna Anna come down the palace stairs struggling. The Don hides his face to prevent her from recognizing him.)

Donna Anna

Non sperar, se non m'uccidi.	There's no hope, unless you kill me
Ch'io ti lasci fuggir mai!	That I'll ever let you go!

Don Giovanni

Donna folle, indarno gridi:	Idiot! You scream in vain.
Chi son io tu non saprai.	Who I am you'll never know!

Donna Anna

Non sperar, ecc.	There's no hope, etc.

Don Giovanni

Donna folle! ecc.	Idiot! etc.

Leporello

Che tumulto! O ciel, che gridi!	What a racket! Heaven, what screams!
Il padron in nuovi guai.	My master in another scrape.

	Donna Anna
Gente! Servi! Al traditore!	Help! Everyone! The betrayer!
	Don Giovanni
Taci, e trema al mio furore!	Keep quiet! Beware my wrath!
	Donna Anna
Scellerato!	Scoundrel!
	Don Giovanni
Sconsigliata!	Fool!
	Donna Anna
Scellerato!	Scoundrel!
	Don Giovanni
Sconsigliata!	Fool!
	Leporello
Sta a veder che il malandrino	We will see if this rascal
Mi farà precipitar.	Will be the ruin of me!
	Donna Anna
Gente! Servi!	Help! Everyone!
	Don Giovanni
Taci, e trema!	Keep quiet!
	Donna Anna
Come furia disperata	Like a desperate fury
Ti saprò perseguitar! ecc.	I'll know how to pursue you! etc.
Scellerato! Gente! Servi!	Scoundrel! Help! Everyone!
Come furia disperata, ecc.	Like a desperate fury, etc.
	Don Giovanni
Questa furia disperata	This desperate fury
Mi vuol far precipitar! ecc.	Is aimed at destroying me!
Sconsigliata! Taci, e trema!	Fool! Keep quiet!
Questa furia disperata, ecc.	This desperate fury, etc.
	Leporello
Che tumulto! O ciel, che gridi!	What a racket! Heavens, what screams!
Sta a veder che il malandrino, ecc.	We will see if this rascal, etc.

2 **61** 3:05
String tremolo,
ff, shift to
minor key.

(Donna Anna hears the Commandant; she leaves Don Giovanni and goes
into the house. The Commandant appears.)

	Commandant
Lasciala, indegno! Battiti meco!	Leave her alone, wretch, and defend yourself.

Don Giovanni

Va, non mi degno di pugnar teco.　　　　Go away! I disdain to fight with you.

Commandant

Così pretendi da me fuggir?　　　　Thus you think to escape me?

Leporello

Potessi almeno di qua partir.　　　　If I could only get out of here!

Don Giovanni

Va, non mi degno, no!　　　　Go away! I disdain you!

Commandant

Così pretendi da me fuggir?　　　　Thus you think to escape me!

Leporello

Potessi almeno di qua partir!　　　　If I could only get out of here!

Commandant

Battiti!　　　　Fight!

Don Giovanni

Misero! Attendi, se vuoi morir!　　　　So be it, if you want to die!

Dueling music, upward sweeps in strings. Death blow, suspenseful, held chord.

(They duel. The Commandant is fatally wounded.)

3 62 4:09
Andante, *pp*, pathetic minor phrases.

Commandant

Ah, soccorso! son tradito!　　　　Help! I've been betrayed!
L'assassino m'ha ferito,　　　　The assassin has wounded me!
E dal seno palpitante　　　　And from my heaving breast
Sento l'anima partir.　　　　I feel my soul escaping!

Don Giovanni

Ah! già cade il sciagurato!　　　　Ah, already the wretch has fallen,
Affannosa e agonizzante　　　　And he gasps for air.
Già dal seno palpitante　　　　From his heaving breast I already
Veggo l'anima partir, ecc.　　　　See his soul escaping, etc.

Leporello

Qual misfatto! Qual eccesso!　　　　What a misdeed! What a crime!
Entro il sen dallo spavento　　　　I can feel my heart
Palpitar il cor mi sento!　　　　Beating hard from fright!
Io non sò che far, che dir, ecc.　　　　I don't know what to do or say, etc.
(The Commandant dies.)

4 63 5:19
Recitative,
harpsichord
accompanies.

Don Giovanni

Leporello, dove sei? Leporello, where are you?

Leporello

Son qui, per mia disgrazia. E voi? I'm here, unfortunately, and you?

Don Giovanni

Son qui. Over here.

Leporello

Chi è morto, voi, o il vecchio? Who's dead, you or the old man?

Don Giovanni

Che domanda da bestia! Il vecchio. What an idiotic question! The old man.

Leporello

Bravo! Due imprese leggiadre, Well done! Two misdeeds!
Sforzar la figlia, ed ammazzar First you raped the daughter, then
il padre! murdered the father!

Don Giovanni

L'ha voluto, suo danno. He asked for it; too bad for him.

Leporello

Ma Donn'Anna cosa ha voluto? And Donna Anna, did she ask for it too?

Don Giovanni

Taci, non mi seccar! Keep quiet and don't bother me.
Vien meco, se non vuoi qualche Now come along, unless you're
cosa ancor tu. anxious for something for yourself.

Leporello

Non vo' nulla, signor, non parlo I have no desires, sir, and no more to
più. say.

Act I:
Leporello's catalog aria (*Madamina*)

Basic Set:
CD 3 64

Not long after the opening scene, Leporello sings his famous "catalog" aria (*Madamina*) to Donna Elvira, a woman whom Don Giovanni had earlier seduced and deserted and who has now appeared on the scene. In mocking "consolation," Leporello tells her that she is but one of many and displays a fat catalog of his master's conquests. The music bubbles with Leporello's delight as he reels off the amazing totals: 640 in Italy, 231 in Germany, 100 in France, 91 in Turkey, and in Spain, 1,003! Mozart makes the most of comic description as Leporello proceeds to list the Don's seduction techniques for different types of women.

64 0:00
Allegro.

Madamina, il catalogo è questo
Delle belle, che amò il padron mio;
Un catalogo egli è, che ho fatt'io,
Osservate, leggete con me.

My dear lady, this is a list
Of the beauties my master has loved,
A list which I have compiled.
Observe, read along with me.

0:22
Staccato
woodwind
chuckles.

In Italia seicento e quaranta,

In Italy, six hundred and forty;

In Almagna duecento a trentuna,

In Germany, two hundred and thirty-one;

Cento in Francia, in Turchia
novantuna,

A hundred in France; in Turkey ninety-
one.

0:39
Longer notes.

Ma in Ispagna son già mille e tre!

In Spain already one thousand and three!

0:57
Shorter notes.

V'han fra queste contadine,
Cameriere, cittadine,
V'han contesse, baronesse,
Marchesine, principesse,
E v'han donne d'ogni grado,
D'ogni forma, d'ogni età!
In Italia seicento e quaranta, ecc.

Among these are peasant girls
Maidservants, city girls,
Countesses, baronesses,
Marchionesses, princesses,
Women of every rank,
Every shape, every age.
In Italy six hundred and forty, etc.

65 2:12   0:00
Andante con
moto, courtly
minuet.

Nella bionda egli ha l'usanza
Di lodar la gentilezza;

With blonds it is his habit
To praise their kindness;

2:32   0:20
Mock-heroic
flourish.

Nella bruna, la costanza;

In brunettes, their faithfulness;

2:42   0:30
Suave melodic
phrase.

Nella bianca la dolcezza;
Vuol d'inverno la grassotta,
Vuol d'estate la magrotta;

In the very blond, their sweetness.
In winter he likes fat ones,
In summer he likes thin ones.

3:05   0:53
Crescendo,
melody slowly
rises to high
held tone.

E la grande maestosa,

He calls the tall ones majestic.

<table>
<tr><td>3:28</td><td>1:16</td></tr>
</table>

Sprightly quick notes.	*La piccina è ognor vezzosa;*	The little ones are always charming.
	Delle vecchie fa conquista	He seduces the old ones
	Pel piacer di porle in lista.	For the pleasure of adding to the list.
	Sua passion predominante	His greatest favorite
	È la giovin principiante.	Is the young beginner.
	Non si picca se sia ricca,	It doesn't matter if she's rich,
	Se sia brutta, se sia bella,	Ugly, or beautiful;
	Se sia ricca, brutta, se sia bella;	If she is rich, ugly, or beautiful.
	Purchè porti la gonnella,	If she wears a petticoat,
	Voi sapctc quel che fa!	*You* know what he does.
	Purchè porti la gonnella, ecc.	If she wears a petticoat, etc.

Symphony No. 40 in G Minor, K. 550 (1788)

Symphony No. 40 in G Minor is the most passionate and dramatic of Mozart's symphonies. Although the work is classical in form and technique, it is almost romantic in emotional intensity. It staggers the imagination that Mozart could compose the G minor and two other great symphonies—No. 39 in E Flat and No. 41 in C *(Jupiter)*—during the short period of six weeks. They are his last three symphonies.

Like most classical symphonies, Symphony No. 40 in G minor has four movements: (1) fast, (2) slow, (3) minuet, (4) fast.

Brief Set:
CD 2 23

First Movement:
Molto allegro

Basic Set:
CD 3 10

Mozart opens his Symphony No. 40 in G Minor with the agitated movement already described in section 3.

Second Movement:
Andante

Basic Set:
CD 3 19

The mood of the andante hovers between gentleness and longing. The andante is written in sonata form and is the only movement of this symphony in major (it is in E flat). This movement develops from a series of gently pulsating notes in the opening theme.

Exposition
19 0:00

Development
20 3:39

Recapitulation
21 5:03

As the theme continues, the violins introduce an airy two-note rhythmic figure that will appear—with changes of dynamics and orchestration—in almost every section of the andante. The rhythmic figure will be, at different times, graceful, insistent, and forceful.

Later, Mozart uses the airy figures as a delicate countermelody to the repeated-note idea. Floating woodwinds interwoven with strings reveal Mozart's sensitivity to tone color as an expressive resource.

Third Movement:
Menuetto (Allegretto)

Basic Set:
CD 3 **22**

The minuet, in G minor, is serious and intense; it does not sound like an aristocratic dance. The form of the minuet is A B A:

Minuet	**Trio**	**Minuet**
A	B	A
a (repeated) ba' (repeated)	c (repeated) dc' (repeated)	a ba'

Section A
22 0:00

Powerful syncopations give a fierce character to section A (the minuet), which is predominantly loud and in minor.

Later, Mozart increases the tension through polyphonic texture and striking dissonances. At the end of section A, there is a sudden drop in dynamics; the flute, supported by oboes and a bassoon, softly recalls the opening melody of the minuet.

The trio section (B) brings a shift from minor to major, from fierce energy to graceful relaxation.

Section B
23 1:54

Return of section A
24 3:57

This change of mood is reinforced by a soft dynamic level and pastoral woodwind interludes. After the trio, a sudden forte announces the return of the fierce A section.

Fourth Movement:
Allegro assai (very fast)

Basic Set:
CD 3 **25**

First theme
25 0:00

The very fast finale, in sonata form, is unusually tense. Its opening theme, in the tonic key of G minor, offers brusque contrasts of dynamics and rhythm. A soft upward arpeggio (broken chord) alternates repeatedly with a loud rushing phrase.

Bridge
 0:27

Second theme
27 1:00

Excitement is maintained throughout the long bridge, which is based on the loud rushing phrase of the first theme. The bridge ends clearly with a brief pause, as do other sections in this movement.

The tender second theme, in the new key of B flat major, is a lyrical contrast to the brusque opening theme. It is softer, flows more smoothly, and uses longer notes.

Closing section
28 1:29

Development
29 1:49

The exposition closes with a loud passage of continuously rushing notes in the strings.

Mozart weaves almost the entire development section from the upward arpeggio of the first theme. During the opening few seconds, there is an eruption of violence as the orchestra in unison plays a variation of the arpeggio and a series of jagged downward leaps.

Recapitulation
First theme
30 3:03

Second theme
31 3:38

As the development continues, the texture becomes polyphonic and contrasts with the homophony of the exposition. Arpeggios press upon each other in quick imitation. Rapid shifts of key create restless intensity.

In the recapitulation, both the first and the second theme are in the tonic key, G minor. This minor key now adds a touch of melancholy to the tender second theme, which was heard in major before. The passion and violence of this movement foreshadow the romantic expression to come during the nineteenth century.

Piano Concerto No. 23 in A Major, K. 488 (1786)

Mozart's Piano Concerto in A Major—completed on March 2, 1786—dates from a very productive and successful period in his life. Between October 1785 and May 1786, he taught piano and composition; conducted operas; performed in concerts; and composed *The Marriage of Figaro*, the comic one-act opera *The Impressario,* two other great piano concertos (K. 482 in E Flat and K. 491 in C Minor), Quartet for Piano and Strings (K. 478), and *Masonic Funeral Music* (K. 477).

Mozart thought highly of the A Major piano concerto. In a letter to the court chamberlain of a prospective patron, he included it among "the compositions which I keep for myself or for a small circle of music-lovers and connoisseurs. . . ." Today, it is one of the best known of his piano concertos.

Like all classical concertos, this one has three movements. The grace of the opening movement (which we'll study) and the high spirits of the finale contrast with the melancholy of the middle movement. This concerto stresses poetry and delicacy rather than pianistic virtuosity or orchestral power. It is scored for an orchestra without trumpets or timpani and highlights the clarinets, flute, and bassoon. Mozart associated its key—A major—with tenderness, lyricism, and elegance.

First Movement: Allegro

Brief Set:

CD 3 5

Basic Set:

CD 4 1

The gentle opening movement blends lyricism with a touch of sadness, owing to many shifts between major and minor. Two main lyrical themes introduced by the orchestra in the first exposition are restated by the piano and orchestra in the second exposition. The development section is based on a new legato theme that is unexpectedly introduced by the orchestra after a dramatic pause. (In the listening outline, this is called the *development theme.*) Mozart creates a dramatic confrontation by juxtaposing fragments of this new theme, played by the woodwinds, with restless ideas in the piano and orchestra.

Toward the end of the allegro is a cadenza—an unaccompanied showpiece for the soloist. Exceptionally, Mozart notated the cadenza directly into the score, instead of leaving it to be improvised by the soloist. With its rapid sweeps up and down the keyboard, its alternation between brilliant and tender passages, and its concluding trill, this cadenza gives us some idea of how Mozart himself must have improvised.

Listening Outline to be read while music is heard

Brief Set: CD 3   Basic Set: CD 4

MOZART, Piano Concerto No. 23 in A Major

First Movement: Allegro

Sonata form, quadruple meter ($\frac{4}{4}$), A major

Solo piano, flute, 2 clarinets, 2 bassoons, 2 French horns, 1st violins, 2d violins, violas, cellos, double basses

(Duration, 11:36)

First
Exposition
First theme

5 1 0:00

1. a. Strings, *p*, gracious main melody, legato, major key,

staccato ascent.

0:16   **b.** Winds, *p*, repeat opening of main melody an octave higher. Strings, *f*, answered by winds; cadence to

Bridge

6 2 0:34   **2.** Full orchestra, *f*, vigorous bridge theme,

                    running notes in violins, *f*. Brief pause.

Second theme group

7 3 0:58 0:00   **3. a.** Violins, *p*, tender second theme, repeated notes in dotted rhythm.

                    b. Violins and bassoon, *p*, repeat second theme, flute joins.
                    c. Agitated rhythms in minor lead to
1:34 0:36   **d.** Full orchestra, *f*, major; winds alternate with violins, minor, crescendo to
                    e. Full orchestra, *f*, major, cadence. Brief pause.
                    f. High woodwind phrase, *p*, orchestral chords, *f*. Brief pause.

Second Exposition First theme

8 4 2:11 0:00   **1. a.** Piano solo, main melody, low strings join, violins introduce
                    b. Piano, varied repetition of main melody, rapid downward and upward scales.

Bridge

2:40 0:29   **2. a.** Full orchestra, *f*, bridge theme.
                    b. Piano, running notes, with string accompaniment. High staccato violins, high staccato winds, downward scale in piano. Brief pause.

Second theme group

3:11 1:00   **3. a.** Piano solo, second theme, dolce.
                    b. Violins and flute repeat second theme, piano joins.
3:42 1:31   **c.** Piano and orchestra.
3:53 1:42   **d.** Violins alternate with piano, minor.
                    e. Piano, major. Long passage of running notes in piano culminating in short trill closing into
4:25 2:14   **4.** Full orchestra, opening of bridge theme. Sudden pause.

Development

9 | 5 | 4:39 | 0:00   **1. a.** Strings, *p*, legato development theme.

        b. Piano solo, development theme embellished by rapid notes.

5:05 | 0:26   **2. a.** Clarinet, fragment of development theme in minor, answered by piano and staccato strings.

5:13 | 0:34   **b.** Flute, fragment of development theme in major, answered by piano and staccato strings.

5:21 | 0:42   **c.** High woodwinds, development theme fragment in minor answered by piano, strings join with development theme fragment.

5:33 | 0:54   **3.** Piano continues with running notes; clarinet and flute, imitations of development theme fragment.

5:48 | 1:09   **4.** Strings, minor, repeatedly alternate with piano and woodwinds.

6:10 | 1:31   **5.** Piano solo, orchestra joins. Long descents and ascents, rising chromatic scale leads into

Recapitulation
First theme

10 | 6 | 6:30 | 0:00   **1. a.** Strings, *p*, main melody, woodwinds join.

        b. Piano *p*, with woodwinds, ornamented repeat of main melody in higher octave; piano scales lead to

Bridge

7:00 | 0:30   **2. a.** Full orchestra, *f*, bridge theme.

        b. Piano, running notes, strings accompany; staccato violins, high staccato winds, upward scale in piano. Brief pause.

Second theme group

7:30 | 1:00   **3. a.** Piano solo, second theme.

        b. Winds repeat second theme an octave higher, piano joins.

8:00 | 1:30   **c.** Piano and orchestra.

8:12 | 1:42   **d.** Violins alternate with piano, minor.

8:20 | 1:50   **e.** Piano, major, running-note passage interrupted by brief pause.

8:35 | 2:05   **4. a.** Piano alone, development theme.

        b. Clarinets and bassoons repeat development theme, accompanied by running notes in piano, staccato winds join, piano trill meshes with entrance of

9:19 | 2:49   **5. a.** Full orchestra, *f*, bridge theme; sudden brief pause.

9:32 | 3:02   **b.** Strings and winds, *p*, development theme. Full orchestra, *f*, dotted rhythm, briefly held chord.

Cadenza

11 | 7 | 9:48 | 0:00   **c.** Extended piano solo; long trill closes into

Coda

11:05 | 1:17   **6. a.** Full orchestra, *f*, cadence.

        b. High woodwind phrase, *p*; full orchestra; sudden *p* ending, trills in flutes and violins.

Murray Perahia, Pianist, Playing and Conducting the First Movement of Mozart's Piano Concerto in A Major, K. 488

Murray Perahia, one of the world's leading pianists, was born in New York City in 1947. Though he began to play the piano at age four, his major musical interest during his teens was conducting and composition, which he studied at Mannes College of Music in New York. His career as a piano soloist soared in 1972, when he became the first American to win the Leeds International Piano Competition in England. Starting in the 1980s, Perahia began to conduct from the piano in performances and recordings of works including the piano concertos of Mozart. (His performance of the first movement of Mozart's Piano Concerto in A Major, K. 488, is included in the CD Sets.)

In the early 1990s, a serious thumb injury forced Perahia to stop performing for several years. "You get very depressed when you can't play, because it's your way of communicating," he later recalled. "Bach was a solace to me.... There is something in his music that is life-fulfilling, life-affirming." After recovering from his injury, he made a series of award-winning Bach recordings. In 2004, Perahia was knighted for his musical achievements by Queen Elizabeth II in London, where he now lives.

Perahia feels that great "music has to appeal at many different levels—intellectually, emotionally, metaphysically, spiritually. Every note has to have a reason for being. A masterpiece must be inevitable." He believes that a sense of direction is crucially important in music. Music must not be static: "It should sound spontaneous, so that it never seems mechanical. And at the same time, it must have an inner logic."

Concerning the Piano Concerto in A Major, K. 488, Perahia emphasizes that it is very different from other concertos Mozart composed at that time (1786): "They were all more symphonic in dimension, military-sounding, and they had very virtuosic piano writing—robust and strong." By contrast, in the first movement of the Piano Concerto in A Major, "the piano writing is more melodic, more obviously lyrical." The movement's "passion and ardor" are akin to the world of romantic love depicted in Mozart operas such as *Così fan tutte.* "There is a constant give-and-take with the orchestra, the piano decorating ideas first stated by the orchestra." The movement evokes a world "in perfect concord, an idealized world—soon to be shattered by a slow movement whose depth of pain and despair is matched by its sublimity."

Ludwig van Beethoven

For many people, Ludwig van Beethoven (1770–1827) represents the highest level of musical genius. He opened new realms of musical expression and profoundly influenced composers throughout the nineteenth century.

Beethoven was born in Bonn, Germany, into a family of musicians. By the age of eleven, he was serving as assistant to the court organist, and at age twelve he had several compositions published. When he was sixteen, he played for Mozart, who reportedly said, "Keep your eyes on him; some day he will give the world something to talk about." Shortly before his twenty-second birthday, he left Bonn to study with Haydn in Vienna, where he spent the rest of his life.

Beethoven's first years in Vienna brought hard work, growing confidence, and public praise (although his studies with Haydn were not entirely successful and he went secretly to another teacher). This music-loving city was dazzled by his virtuosity and moved by his improvisations. And although he rebelled against social convention, asserting that an artist deserved as much respect as the nobility, the same aristocrats who had allowed Mozart to die in debt showered Beethoven with gifts. In 1809, three noblemen committed themselves to give him an annual income, their only condition being that he remain in Vienna—an

Beethoven opened new realms of musical expression that profoundly influenced composers throughout the nineteenth century.

arrangement unprecedented in music history. Unlike earlier composers, Beethoven was never actually in the service of the Viennese aristocracy. He earned good fees from piano lessons and concerts, and publishers were quick to buy his compositions.

But during his twenty-ninth year, disaster struck: he felt the first symptoms of deafness, which his doctors could do nothing to halt. On October 6, 1802, Beethoven wrote an agonized letter addressed to his brothers from Heiligenstadt, a village outside Vienna. In the letter (now known as the *Heiligenstadt testament*), he said, "I would have ended my life—it was only my art that held me back." This victory over despair coincided with an important change in his musical style; works that he created after his emotional crisis—perhaps most significantly the gigantic Third Symphony, the *Eroica*, composed from 1803 to 1804—have a new power and heroism. (He planned to name the Third Symphony *Bonaparte*, after Napoleon; but when Napoleon proclaimed himself emperor, Beethoven struck out the dedication and later wrote on the new title page, "Heroic Symphony composed to celebrate the memory of a great man.")

As a man, Beethoven remains something of a mystery. He was self-educated and had read widely, but he was weak in elementary arithmetic. He claimed the highest moral principles but was often unscrupulous in dealing with publishers. He was orderly and methodical when composing but dressed sloppily and lived in incredibly messy apartments. He fell in love with several women but never formed a lasting relationship. The contradictions in his personality are especially evident in his disastrous guardianship of his young nephew Karl, who eventually attempted suicide. Beethoven took consolation from nature for disappointments in his personal life, and ideas came to him as he walked in the countryside. His Sixth Symphony, the *Pastoral*, expresses his recollections of life in the country.

As Beethoven's hearing weakened, this once brilliant pianist was forced to stop performing in public—though he insisted on conducting his orchestral works long after he could do it efficiently. His sense of isolation grew with his deafness. Friends had to communicate with him through an ear trumpet and, during his last years, by writing in notebooks which he carried.

Despite this, and despite mounting personal problems, Beethoven had a creative outburst after 1818 that produced some of his greatest works: the late piano sonatas and string quartets, the *Missa solemnis*, and the Ninth Symphony—out of total deafness, new realms of sound.

Beethoven's Music

For Beethoven, music was not mere entertainment, but a moral force, "a higher revelation than all wisdom and philosophy." His music directly reflects his powerful, tortured personality.

Beethoven's demand for perfection meant long, hard work—sometimes he worked for years on a single symphony while also writing other compositions. He carried musical sketchbooks everywhere, jotting down and revising ideas; the final versions of his works were often hammered out laboriously.

Beethoven mostly used classical forms and techniques, but he gave them new power and intensity. The musical heir of Haydn and Mozart, he bridged the classical and romantic eras; many of his innovations were used by later composers. In his works, tension and excitement are built up through syncopations and dissonances. The range of pitch and dynamics is greater than ever before, so that contrasts of mood are more pronounced. Accents and climaxes seem titanic. Greater tension called for a larger musical framework, and so he expanded his forms; he was a musical architect who could create large-scale structures in which every note seems inevitable. But not all of his music is stormy and powerful; much of it is gentle, humorous, noble, or lyrical.

More than his predecessors, he tried to unify contrasting movements by means of musical continuity. Sometimes one movement leads directly into the next, without the traditional pause; sometimes a musical bond is created by similar themes. He also greatly expanded the development section and coda of sonata-form movements and made them more dramatic. His works often have climactic, triumphant finales toward which the previous movements seem to build—an important departure from the light, relaxed endings of Haydn and Mozart.

Beethoven's most popular works are the nine symphonies, written for larger orchestras than Haydn's or Mozart's. Each of them is unique in character and style, though the odd-numbered symphonies tend to be more forceful and the even-numbered ones calmer and more lyrical. In the finale of the Ninth Symphony *(Choral)*, Beethoven took the unprecedented step of using a chorus and four vocal soloists, who sing the text of Schiller's *Ode to Joy*.

His thirty-two piano sonatas are far more difficult than those of Haydn and Mozart and exploit the improved piano of his time, drawing many new effects from it. In these sonatas, he experimented with compositional techniques which he later expanded in the symphonies and string quartets. The sixteen string quartets are among the greatest music ever composed, and each of the five superb piano concertos is remarkable for its individuality.

While most of Beethoven's important works are for instruments, his sense of drama was also expressed in vocal music, including two masses and his only opera, *Fidelio*.

Beethoven's work is usually divided into three periods: early (up to 1802), middle (1803–1814), and late (1815–1827). Some works of the early period show the influence of Haydn and Mozart, but others clearly show Beethoven's personal style. The works of the middle period tend to be longer and more heroic; the sublime works of the late period often contain fugues as well as passages that sound surprisingly harsh and "modern." When a violinist complained that the music was very difficult to play, Beethoven reportedly replied, "Do you believe that I think of a wretched fiddle when the spirit speaks to me?"

Piano Sonata in C Minor, Op. 13 *(Pathétique;* 1798)

The title *Pathétique,* coined by Beethoven, suggests the tragically passionate character of his famous Piano Sonata in C Minor, Op. 13 (we'll focus on the first of its three movements). Beethoven's impetuous playing and masterful improvisational powers are mirrored in the sonata's extreme dynamic contrasts, explosive accents, and crashing chords. At the age of twenty-seven, during his early period, Beethoven had already created a powerful and original piano style that foreshadowed nineteenth-century romanticism.

First Movement:
Grave (solemn, slow introduction);
Allegro molto e con brio (very fast and brilliant allegro)

Basic Set:
CD 4 **8**

The *Pathétique* begins in C minor with an intense, slow introduction, dominated by an opening motive in dotted rhythm: long-short-long-short-long-long.

8 0:00

This six-note idea seems to pose a series of unresolved questions as it is repeated at higher and higher pitch levels. The tragic mood is intensified by dissonant chords, sudden contrasts of dynamics and register, and pauses filled with expectancy. The slow introduction is integrated into the allegro that follows it in imaginative and dramatic ways.

9 1:41 0:00

The tension of the introduction is maintained in the allegro con brio, a breathless, fast movement in sonata form. The opening theme, in C minor, begins with a staccato idea that rapidly rises up a 2-octave scale. It is accompanied by low broken octaves, the rapid alternation of two tones an octave apart.

1:57 0:16

Growing directly out of the opening theme is a bridge that is also built from a climbing staccato motive.

This bridge motive has an important role later in the movement.

10 2:08 0:00

The contrasting second theme, which enters without a pause, is spun out of a short motive that is repeatedly shifted between low and high registers.

This restless idea begins in E flat minor but then moves through different keys. The exposition is rounded off by several themes, including a high running passage and a return of the opening staccato idea in E flat major.

11 2:53

12 3:11 0:00

The development section begins with a dramatic surprise: Beethoven brings back the opening bars of the slow introduction. This reappearance creates an enormous contrast of tempo, rhythm, and mood. After four bars of slow music, the fast tempo resumes as Beethoven combines two different ideas: the staccato bridge motive and a quickened version of the introduction motive. The introduction motive is presented in a rhythmically altered form: short-short-short-long-long.

3:54 0:43

The bridge motive is then developed in the bass, played by the pianist's left hand while the right hand has high broken octaves. After several high accented notes, the brief development concludes with a running passage that leads down to the recapitulation.

13 4:34

For a while, the recapitulation runs its usual course as themes from the exposition are presented in the tonic key of C minor. But Beethoven has one more surprise for the coda—after a loud dissonant chord and a brief pause, he again brings back the opening of the slow introduction. This time the slow music is even more moving, as it is punctuated by moments of silence. Then the fast tempo resumes, and the opening staccato idea and powerful chords bring the movement to a decisive close.

14 5:51

Symphony No. 5 in C Minor, Op. 67 (1808)

The Fifth Symphony opens with one of the most famous rhythmic ideas in all music, a short-short-short-long motive. Beethoven reportedly explained this four-note motive as "fate knocking at the door." It dominates the first movement and also plays an important role later in the symphony. The entire work can be seen as an emotional progression from the conflict and struggle of the first movement, in C minor, to the exultation and victory of the final movement, in C major. The finale is the climax of the symphony; it is longer than the first movement and more powerful in sound.

Through several different techniques, Beethoven brilliantly welds four contrasting movements into a unified work. The basic rhythmic motive of the first movement (short-short-short-long) is used in a marchlike theme in the third movement. And this third-movement theme is later quoted dramatically within the finale. The last two movements are also connected by a bridge passage.

Beethoven jotted down a few themes for the Fifth Symphony in 1804, but mainly worked on it during 1807 and 1808, an amazingly productive period when he also composed his Mass in C Major; Sonata for Cello and Piano, Op. 69; and Symphony No. 6.

First Movement:
Allegro con brio (allegro with vigor)

Brief Set:

CD 2 45

Basic Set:

CD 4 23

The allegro con brio is an enormously powerful, concentrated movement in sonata form. Its character is determined by a single rhythmic motive, short-short-short-long, from which Beethoven creates an astonishing variety of musical ideas. Tension and expectancy are generated from the very beginning of the movement. Three rapid notes of the same pitch are followed by a downward leap to a held, suspenseful tone. This powerful idea is hammered out twice by all the strings in unison; the second time, it is a step lower in pitch.

As the opening theme continues in C minor, Beethoven maintains excitement by quickly developing his basic idea. He crowds varied repetitions of the motive together and rapidly shifts the motive to different pitches and instruments.

The second theme, in E flat major, dramatically combines different ideas. It begins with an unaccompanied horn call that asserts the basic motive in a varied form (short-short-short-long-long-long).

This horn-call motive announces a new legato melody, which is calm and contrasts with the preceding agitation. Yet even during this lyrical moment, we are not allowed to forget the basic motive; now it is muttered in the background by cellos and double basses.

Beethoven generates tension in the development section by breaking the horn-call motive into smaller and smaller fragments until it is represented by only a single tone. Supported by a chord, this tone is echoed between woodwinds and strings in a breathtaking decrescendo. The recapitulation comes as a tremendous climax as the full orchestra thunders the basic motive. The recapitulation also brings a new expressive oboe solo at the end of the first theme. The heroic closing section of the recapitulation, in C major, moves without a break into a long, exciting coda in C minor. This coda is like a second development section in which the basic motive creates still greater power and energy.

Listening Outline to be read while music is heard

Brief Set: CD 2   Basic Set: CD 4

BEETHOVEN, Symphony No. 5

First Movement: Allegro con brio

Sonata form, duple meter ($\frac{2}{4}$), C minor

2 flutes, 2 oboes, 2 clarinets, 2 bassoons, 2 French horns, 2 trumpets, timpani, 1st violins, 2d violins, violas, cellos, double basses

(Duration, 7:07)

Exposition
First theme

| 45 | 23 | 0:00 | | **1. a.** Basic motive, *ff*, repeated a step lower, strings in unison. |

| | | 0:08 | | **b.** Sudden *p*, strings quickly develop basic motive, minor key, powerful chords, high held tone. |

Bridge

| 46 | 24 | 0:20 | 0:00 | **2. a.** Basic motive, *ff*, orchestra in unison. |
| | | 0:24 | 0:04 | **b.** Sudden *p*, strings quickly develop basic motive, crescendo, *ff*, powerful chords. |

Second theme

| 47 | 25 | 0:44 | 0:00 | **3. a.** Solo French horns, *ff*, horn-call motive. |

| | | 0:47 | 0:03 | **b.** Violins, *p*, lyrical melody in major. Basic motive accompanies in low strings. |

Crescendo to

| 48 | 26 | 1:06 | 0:00 | **4. a.** Triumphant melody, *ff*, violins. |

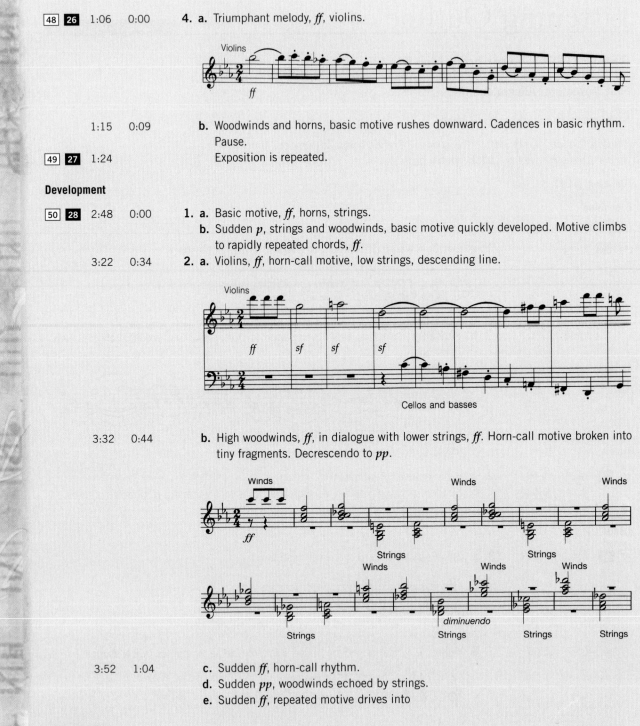

| | | 1:15 | 0:09 | **b.** Woodwinds and horns, basic motive rushes downward. Cadences in basic rhythm. Pause. |
| 49 | 27 | 1:24 | | Exposition is repeated. |

Development

50	28	2:48	0:00	**1. a.** Basic motive, *ff*, horns, strings.
				b. Sudden *p*, strings and woodwinds, basic motive quickly developed. Motive climbs to rapidly repeated chords, *ff*.
		3:22	0:34	**2. a.** Violins, *ff*, horn-call motive, low strings, descending line.

| | | 3:32 | 0:44 | **b.** High woodwinds, *ff*, in dialogue with lower strings, *ff*. Horn-call motive broken into tiny fragments. Decrescendo to *pp*. |

		3:52	1:04	**c.** Sudden *ff*, horn-call rhythm.
				d. Sudden *pp*, woodwinds echoed by strings.
				e. Sudden *ff*, repeated motive drives into

Recapitulation
First theme

51	29	4:05	0:00	**1. a.** Climactic basic motive, full orchestra, *ff*, repeated a step lower.
				b. Sudden *p*, strings quickly develop basic motive, minor key, chords lead to
		4:21	0:16	**c.** Oboe solo.

Bridge

4:38	0:33	**2.** Basic motive quickly developed in strings, crescendo to *ff*, full orchestra.

Second theme

4:58	0:53	**3. a.** Horn-call motive, solo bassoons, *ff*.
		b. Lyrical major melody, *p*, violins and flutes alternate. Basic motive accompanies in timpani, p. Crescendo to
5:25	1:20	**4. a.** Triumphant melody, *ff*, violins.
		b. Woodwinds, basic motive rushes downward. Cadences in basic rhythm.

Coda

52 30	5:41	0:00	**1. a.** Rapidly repeated chords, *ff*.
	5:55	0:14	**b.** Horn-call motive, lower strings, *f*, with higher violin melody, minor.

Descending violin melody, staccato, leads to

6:10	0:29	**2. a.** New, rising theme in strings, legato and staccato.

6:20	0:39	**b.** High woodwinds, *ff*, answered by lower strings in powerful interchange. Rapidly repeated notes lead to
6:42	1:01	**3. a.** Basic motive, *ff*, repeated a step lower, full orchestra.
		b. Sudden *p*, basic motive quickly developed in strings and woodwinds.
		c. Sudden *ff*, powerful concluding chords.

Second Movement:
Andante con moto (moderately slow, with movement)

Brief Set:
CD 2 53

Basic Set:
CD 4 31

The second movement, in A flat major, is mostly relaxed and lyrical, but it includes moments of tension and heroism. It is an extended set of variations based on two themes. The main theme (A), softly introduced by the cellos and violas, is a long, legato melody of great nobility. The second theme (B) begins very gently in the clarinets but soon brings a startling contrast of mood. The full orchestra suddenly bursts in, and the clarinet melody is transformed into a triumphant trumpet fanfare. A hushed transitional passage then leads back to the main theme, presented now in quicker notes.

After several variations, there is a middle section in which fragments of the themes are treated in new ways. Woodwind instruments are featured, and there is a brief episode in minor. The movement concludes with a final variation of the main melody—now majestically proclaimed by the full orchestra—and a coda that poetically recalls what has come before.

Listening Outline to be read while music is heard

Brief Set: CD 2 Basic Set: CD 4

BEETHOVEN, Symphony No. 5

Second Movement: Andante con moto

Theme and variations, triple meter ($\frac{3}{8}$), A flat major

2 flutes, 2 oboes, 2 clarinets, 2 bassoons, 2 French horns, 2 trumpets, timpani,
1st violins, 2d violins, violas, cellos, double basses

(Duration, 9:58)

Theme A

| 53 | 31 | 0:00 |

1. Lyrical melody, violas and cellos, *p*.

Melody continues in higher register, violins alternate with flute.

Theme B

| 54 | 32 | 0:55 | 0:00 |

2. a. Clarinets, *p*, rising phrases.

Violins, *pp*, sudden *ff*, full orchestra.

1:17   0:22   **b.** Trumpets, *ff*, rising phrases.

Violins, *pp*, sustained notes.

Variation A¹

| 55 | 33 | 2:02 | 0:00 |

3. Violas and cellos, *p*, lyrical melody in even-flowing rhythm.

Melody continues in higher register, violins alternate with flute.

Variation B¹

| | 2:54 | 0:52 | **4. a.** Clarinets, *p*, rising phrases. Violins, *pp*, sudden *ff*, full orchestra. |
| | 3:16 | 1:14 | **b.** Trumpets, *ff*, rising phrases. Violins, *pp*, sustained notes, cellos, low repeated notes. |

Variation A²

| 56 34 | 4:01 | 0:00 | **5. a.** Violas and cellos, *p*, lyrical melody decorated by quick, even-flowing notes. |

| | 4:18 | 0:17 | **b.** Violins, *pp*, repeat decorated melody in higher register. |
| | 4:38 | 0:37 | **c.** Loud repeated chords, decorated melody in cellos and double basses. Upward scales lead to high held tone. |

Middle Section

57 35	5:03	0:00	**6.** Sudden *pp*, repeated string chords, clarinet phrase passed to bassoon and flute. High woodwind interlude leads to
	5:58	0:55	**7. a.** Full orchestra, *ff*, rising phrases, timpani rolls.
	6:22	1:19	**b.** Strings, *p*, repeated short figure.
	6:44	1:41	**8. a.** Woodwinds, *p*, staccato variation of lyrical melody, minor key.
	7:05	2:02	**b.** Rising scales in flute, strings. Crescendo.

Variation A³

| 58 36 | 7:25 | 0:00 | **9.** Full orchestra, *ff*, lyrical melody in high register, major key, rising scales. Flute and violins, *p*, continue melody. |

Coda

	8:13	0:48	**10. a.** Più mosso (faster tempo), bassoon, *p*, variation of lyrical phrase. Violins, crescendo.
	8:38	1:13	**b.** Original tempo, flute and strings, *p*, conclusion of lyrical melody.
	9:09	1:44	**c.** Clarinets, *p*, variation of lyrical phrase, low strings, crescendo. Cadence in full orchestra, *ff*.

Third Movement:
Allegro (scherzo)

Brief Set:
CD 2 59

Basic Set:
CD 4 37

Section A
59 37 0:00

The rapid third movement is a scherzo, in C minor, consisting of three sections: A (scherzo) B (trio) A′ (scherzo). The scherzo opens with a hushed, mysterious broken-chord theme played by cellos and double basses in a low register.

Soon, in sharp contrast, a bold repeated-note theme is hammered out loudly by the horns.

This theme is dominated by the rhythmic pattern short-short-short-long and recalls the basic motive of the first movement.

Section B

60 38 1:48

The B section (trio), in major, brings a gruff, hurried theme, played by cellos and double basses.

This theme is imitated, in the style of a fugue, by each of the higher strings. The bustling rhythmic motion of the B section has a feeling of energy and rough humor.

Section A′

61 39 3:15

When the scherzo section (A′) returns, it is hushed and ominous throughout, sounding like a ghost of its former self. The mysterious opening theme is now played pizzicato rather than legato. The repeated note theme is completely transformed in mood; it is no longer proclaimed by horns but is whispered by clarinets, plucked violins, and oboe.

Bridge

62 40 4:27

One of the most extraordinary passages in the symphony follows the scherzo section (A′): a bridge leading from the dark, mysterious world of the scherzo to the bright sunlight of the finale. It opens with a feeling of suspended animation as the timpani softly repeat a single tone against a sustained chord in the strings. Over the timpani pulsation, the violins hesitantly play a fragment of the mysterious scherzo theme. Tension mounts as this fragment is carried higher and higher, until a sudden crescendo climaxes with the heroic opening of the finale.

Fourth Movement:
Allegro

Brief Set:
CD 2 63

Basic Set:
CD 4 41

(continued)
63 41 0:00

The fourth movement, in sonata form, is the climax of the symphony. It brings the victory of C major over C minor, of optimism and exultation over struggle and uncertainty. For greater power and brilliance, Beethoven enlarged the orchestra in the finale to include three trombones, a piccolo, and a contrabassoon. Brass instruments are especially prominent and give a marchlike character to much of the movement.

The exposition is rich in melodic ideas; even the bridge has a theme of its own, and there is also a distinctive closing theme. The triumphant opening theme begins with the three tones of the C major triad, brilliantly proclaimed by the trumpets.

 0:36

A bridge theme, similar in mood to the opening theme, is announced by the horns and continued by the violins.

65 43 1:05

Triplets lend a joyous quality to the second theme, which contrasts loud and soft phrases.

66 44 1:34

Two powerful chords and a brief pause announce the closing theme of the exposition. This melody, made up of descending phrases, is first played by the strings and woodwinds and then forcefully repeated by the entire orchestra.

67 45 2:07
68 46 3:47   0:00

Recapitulation
              4:18   0:31

Coda
69 47 6:26

The development focuses mainly on the second theme and its triplet rhythm. A huge climax at the end of the development is followed by one of the most marvelous surprises in all music. Beethoven dramatically quotes the whispered repeated-note theme (short-short-short-long) of the preceding scherzo movement. This ominous quotation is like a sudden recollection of past anxiety, and it creates a connection between the last two movements. Leading into the powerful recapitulation of the fourth movement, it prepares for the renewal of the victory over uncertainty.

During the long coda of the finale, earlier themes are heard in altered and quickened versions. Several times, the music keeps going, even though the listener thinks it's coming to an end. Over and over, Beethoven affirms the tonic key and resolves the frenzied tensions built up during the symphony. Such control over tension is an essential element of Beethoven's genius.

The Romantic Period

V

"The prevailing qualities of my music are passionate expressiveness, inner fire, rhythmic drive, and unexpectedness."

HECTOR BERLIOZ

The Romantic era put an unprecedented emphasis on individuality of style. Eugène Delacroix's *Paganini* (1831) conveys the intensity of a performance by the most famous violinist of the nineteenth century.

Time-Line Romantic Period (1820–1900)

Dates	Music	Arts and Letters	Historical and Cultural Events
1820–1850	Franz Schubert, *Erlkönig* (1815) Berlioz, *Symphonie fantastique* (1830) Chopin, Nocturne in E Flat major, Op. 9, No. 2 (1831) Chopin, Étude in C Minor, Op. 10, No. 12 (*Revolutionary*) (c. 1831) Robert Schumann, *Carnaval* (1835) Clara Wieck Schumann, *Liebst du um Schönheit* (1841) Chopin, Polonaise in A Flat Major, Op. 53 (1842) Mendelssohn, *Violin Concerto in E Minor*, Op. 64 (1844)	Géricault, *The Raft of the Medusa* (1819) Keats, *Ode to a Nightingale* (1819) Delacroix, *Dante and Virgil in Hell* (1822) Hugo, *The Hunchback of Notre Dame* (1831) Friedrich, *The Evening Star* (1835) Dickens, *Oliver Twist* (1837) Turner, *The Slave Ship* (1840) Dumas, *The Three Musketeers* (1844) Poe, *The Raven* (1845) 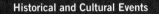	Monroe Doctrine (1823) Revolutions in France, Belgium, Poland (1830) Queen Victoria reigns in England (1837–1901) Revolutions in Europe (1848) Marx and Engels, *The Communist Manifesto* (1848)
1850–1900	Liszt, *Transcendental* Etude in F Minor (1851) Verdi, *Rigoletto* (1851) Wagner, *Die Walküre* (1856) Tchaikovsky, *Romeo and Juliet* (1870) Smetana, *The Moldau* (1874) Brahms, Symphony No. 3 in F Major (1883) Dvořák, Symphony No. 9 in E Minor (*From the New World;* 1893) Puccini, *La Bohème* (1896)	Millet, *The Gleaners* (1857) Dostoevsky, *Crime and Punishment* (1866) Monet, *Impression: Sunrise* (1874) Cézanne, *Still Life with Apples* (1877) Tolstoy, *Anna Karenina* (1877) Twain, *The Adventures of Huckleberry Finn* (1884) Van Gogh, *The Starry Night* (1889) Munch, *The Scream* (1893)	Darwin, *Origin of Species* (1859) American Civil War (1861–65) Franco-Prussian War (1870) Bell invents telephone (1876) Spanish-American War (1898)

208

Romanticism (1820–1900)

The early nineteenth century brought the flowering of romanticism, a cultural movement that stressed emotion, imagination, and individuality. In part, romanticism was a rebellion against the neoclassicism of the eighteenth century and the age of reason. Romantic writers broke away from time-honored conventions and emphasized freedom of expression. Romantic painters used bolder, more brilliant colors and preferred dynamic motion to gracefully balanced poses.

But romanticism was too diverse and complex to be defined by any single formula. It aimed to broaden horizons and encompass the totality of human experience. The romantic movement was international in scope and influenced all the arts.

Emotional subjectivity was a basic quality of romanticism in art. "All good poetry is the spontaneous overflow of powerful feelings," wrote William Wordsworth, the English romantic poet. And "spontaneous overflow" made much romantic literature autobiographical; authors projected their personalities in their work. Walt Whitman, the American poet, expressed this subjective attitude beautifully when he began a poem, "I celebrate myself, and sing myself."

In exploring their inner lives, the romantics were especially drawn to the realm of fantasy: the unconscious, the irrational, the world of dreams. Romantic fiction includes tales of horror and the supernatural, such as *The Cask of Amontillado,* by Edgar Allan Poe; and *Frankenstein,* by Mary Wollstonecraft Shelley. The writer Thomas De Quincey vividly describes his drug-induced dreams in *Confessions of an English Opium-Eater:* "I was buried, for a thousand years, in stone coffins, with mummies and sphinxes. I was kissed, with cancerous kisses, by crocodiles." The visual arts also depict nightmarish visions. In an etching called *The Sleep of Reason Breeds Monsters,* the Spanish painter Francisco

Romantic artists often depicted scenes of extreme violence and suffering. In *The Raft of the Medusa* (1819), French painter Théodore Géricault conveyed the epic tragedy of a contemporary shipwreck. The ship captain—appointed only because of his noble birth—saved himself and other officers, while abandoning many other survivors to their horrible fate on a primitive raft.

Emotional subjectivity was a basic quality of romanticism. The artist's suffering and isolation are depicted in *Portrait of a Young Man in an Artist's Studio,* an anonymous painting of the early nineteenth century.

The Gleaners (1857) by Jean-François Millet. The industrial revolution caused vast social and economic changes and awakened interest in the poor. The French painter Millet portrayed the labor of peasant women picking up leftover grain in the fields.

Eugène Delacroix's painting *Dante and Virgil in Hell* (1822) depicts the agony of the damned. The romantics were also drawn to the realm of the supernatural and drew inspiration from literary works such as Dante's *Inferno.*

The Evening Star
(1830–1835), by the
German painter Caspar
David Friedrich. The
romantics were especially
drawn to the realm of
fantasy: the unconscious,
the irrational, and the
world of dreams.

*Salisbury Cathedral
from the Meadows,* Royal
Academy, 1831, by John
Constable. Of all the inspirations for romantic art,
none was more important
than nature.

Slave Ship (1839) by the English painter J. M. W. Turner. In Turner's seascapes, the sweep of waves expresses not only the power of nature but also human passion.

Goya shows batlike monsters surrounding a sleeping figure. The realm of the unknown and the exotic also interested the French artist Eugène Delacroix, who often depicted violent scenes in far-off lands.

The romantic fascination with fantasy was paired with enthusiasm for the Middle Ages, that time of chivalry and romance. Whereas neoclassicists had thought of the medieval period as the "dark ages," the romantics cherished it. They were inspired by medieval folk ballads and by tales of fantasy and adventure. Romantic novels set in the Middle Ages include *Ivanhoe* (1819), by Walter Scott; and *The Hunchback of Notre Dame* (1831), by the French writer Victor Hugo. Gothic cathedrals, which had long gone unappreciated, now seemed picturesque and mysterious. A "gothic revival" in architecture resulted in the construction of buildings such as the houses of Parliament in London (1836–1852) and Trinity church in New York (1839–1846).

Of all the inspirations for romantic art, none was more important than nature. The physical world was seen as a source of consolation and a mirror of the human heart. Wordsworth, for example, thought of nature as "the nurse,/the guide, the guardian of my heart, and soul." One of his poems begins:

There was a time when meadow,
  grove, and stream,
  The earth, and every common
    sight,
  To me did seem
  Apparelled in celestial light,
The glory and the freshness of a
  dream.

The romantic sensitivity to nature is revealed in landscape painting, which attained new importance. Artists like John Constable and J. M. W. Turner in England were masters at conveying movement in nature: rippling brooks, drifting clouds, stormy seas. In Turner's seascapes, the sweep of waves expresses not only the grandeur of nature, but human passion as well.

Romanticism coincided with the industrial revolution, which caused vast social and economic changes. Many writers and painters recorded the new social realities of their time. The novels of Charles Dickens and the paintings of Honoré Daumier reflect an interest in the working class and the poor.

Subjectivity, fantasy, and enthusiasm for nature and the Middle Ages are only a few aspects of romanticism in literature and painting. We'll now focus on romanticism in music.

Romanticism in Music (1820–1900)

The romantic period in music extended from about 1820 to 1900. Among the most significant romantic musicians were Franz Schubert, Robert Schumann, Clara Wieck Schumann, Frédéric Chopin, Franz Liszt, Felix Mendelssohn, Hector Berlioz, Bedřich Smetana, Antonin Dvořák, Peter Ilyich Tchaikovsky, Johannes Brahms, Giuseppe Verdi, Giacomo Puccini, and Richard Wagner. The length of this list—and some important composers have been omitted from it—testifies to the richness and variety of romantic music and to its continuing impact on today's concert and operatic repertoire.

Composers of the romantic period continued to use the musical forms of the preceding classical era. The emotional intensity associated with romanticism was already present in the work of Mozart and particularly in that of Beethoven, who greatly influenced composers after him. The romantic composers' preference for expressive, songlike melody also grew out of the classical style.

Nonetheless, there are many differences between romantic and classical music. Romantic works tend to have greater ranges of tone color, dynamics, and pitch. Also, the romantic harmonic vocabulary is broader, with more emphasis on colorful, unstable chords. Romantic music is linked more closely to the other arts, particularly to literature. New forms developed, and in all forms there was greater tension and less emphasis on balance and resolution. But romantic music is so diverse that generalizations can be misleading. Some romantic composers, such as Mendelssohn and Brahms, created works that were deeply rooted in classical tradition; other composers, such as Berlioz, Liszt, and Wagner, were more revolutionary.

Characteristics of Romantic Music

Individuality of Style

Romantic music puts unprecedented emphasis on self-expression and individuality of style. There is "not a bar which I have not truly felt and which is not an echo of my innermost feelings," wrote Tchaikovsky of his Fourth Symphony. A "new world of music" was the goal of the young Chopin. Many romantics created music that sounds unique and reflects their personalities. Robert Schumann observed that "Chopin will soon be unable to write anything without people crying out at the seventh or eighth bar, 'That is indeed by him.'" And today, with some listening experience, a music lover can tell within a few minutes—sometimes within a few seconds—whether a piece is by Schumann or Chopin, Tchaikovsky or Brahms.

Expressive Aims and Subjects

The romantics explored a universe of feeling that included flamboyance and intimacy, unpredictability and melancholy, rapture and longing. Countless songs and operas glorify romantic love. Often the lovers are unhappy and face over-whelming obstacles. Fascination with the fantastic and diabolical is expressed in music like the *Dream of a Witches' Sabbath* from Berlioz's *Symphonie fantastique (Fantastic Symphony)*. All aspects of nature attracted romantic musicians. In different sections of Part V we'll study music that depicts a wild horseback ride on a stormy night (Schubert's *Erlkönig*, or *Erlking*) and the flow of a river (Smetana's *Moldau*). Romantic composers also dealt with subjects drawn from the Middle Ages and from Shakespeare's plays.

Nationalism and Exoticism

Nationalism was an important political movement that influenced nineteenth-century music. Musical *nationalism* was expressed when romantic composers deliberately created music with a specific national identity, using the folk songs, dances, legends, and history of their homelands. This national flavor of romantic music—whether Polish, Russian, Bohemian (Czech), or German—contrasts with the more universal character of classical music.

Fascination with national identity also led composers to draw on colorful materials from foreign lands, a trend known as musical *exoticism.* For instance, some composers wrote melodies in an Asian style or used rhythms and instruments associated with distant lands. The French composer Georges Bizet wrote *Carmen,* an opera set in Spain; the Italian Giacomo Puccini evoked Japan in his opera *Madame Butterfly;* and the Russian Rimsky-Korsakov suggested an Arabian atmosphere in his orchestral work *Scheherazade.* Musical exoticism was in keeping with the romantics' attraction to things remote, picturesque, and mysterious.

Program Music

The nineteenth century was the great age of **program music**, instrumental music associated with a story, poem, idea, or scene. The nonmusical element is usually specified by a title or by explanatory comments called a **program.** A programmatic instrumental piece can represent the emotions, characters, and events of a particular story, or it can evoke the sounds and motion of nature. For example, in Tchaikovsky's *Romeo and Juliet,* an orchestral work inspired by Shakespeare's play, agitated music depicts the feud between the rival families, a tender melody conveys young love, and a funeral-march rhythm suggests the lovers' tragic fate. And in *The Moldau,* an orchestral work glorifying the main river of Bohemia, Smetana uses musical effects that call to mind a flowing stream, a hunting scene, a peasant wedding, and the crash of waves.

Program music in some form or another has existed for centuries, but it became particularly prominent in the romantic period, when music was closely associated with literature. Many composers—Berlioz, Schumann, Liszt, and Wagner, for example—were prolific authors as well. Artists in all fields were intoxicated by the concept of a "union of the arts." Poets wanted their poetry to be musical, and musicians wanted their music to be poetic.

Expressive Tone Color

Romantic composers reveled in rich and sensuous sound, using tone color to obtain variety of mood and atmosphere. Never before had timbre been so important.

In both symphonic and operatic works, the romantic orchestra was larger and more varied in tone color than the classical orchestra. Toward the end of the romantic era, an orchestra might include close to 100 musicians. (There were twenty to sixty players in the classical ensemble.) The constant expansion of the orchestra reflected composers' changing needs as well as the growing size of concert halls and opera houses. The brass, woodwind, and percussion sections of the orchestra took on a more active role. Romantic composers increased the power of the brass section to something spectacular, calling for trombones, tubas, and more horns and trumpets. In 1824, Beethoven had broken precedent by asking for nine brasses in the Ninth Symphony; in 1894, the Austrian composer Gustav Mahler (1860–1911) demanded twenty-five brass instruments for his Second Symphony. The addition of valves had made it easier for horns and trumpets to cope with intricate melodies.

The woodwind section took on new tone colors as the contrabassoon, bass clarinet, English horn, and piccolo became regular members of the orchestra. Improvements in the construction of instruments allowed woodwind players to perform more flexibly and accurately. Orchestral sounds became more brilliant and sensuously appealing through increased use of cymbals, the triangle, and the harp.

New sounds were drawn from all instruments of the nineteenth-century orchestra. Flutists were required to play in the breathy low register, and violinists were asked to strike the strings with the wood of their bows. Such demands compelled performers to attain a higher level of technical virtuosity.

Composers sought new ways of blending and combining tone colors to achieve the most poignant and intense sound. In 1844, Hector Berlioz's *Treatise on Modern Instrumentation and Orchestration* signaled the recognition of orchestration as an art in itself.

The piano, the favorite instrument of the romantic age, was vastly improved during the 1820s and 1830s. A cast-iron frame was introduced to hold the strings under greater tension, and the hammers were covered with felt. Thus the piano's tone became more "singing." Its range was also extended. With a stronger instrument, the pianist could produce more sound. And use of the damper ("loud") pedal allowed a sonorous blend of tones from all registers of the piano.

Colorful Harmony

In addition to exploiting new tone colors, the romantics explored new chords and novel ways of using familiar chords. Seeking greater emotional intensity, composers emphasized rich, colorful, and complex harmonies.

There was more prominent use of ***chromatic harmony,*** which uses chords containing tones not found in the prevailing major or minor scale. Such chord tones come from the chromatic scale (which has twelve tones), rather than from the major or minor scales (which have seven tones). Chromatic chords add color and motion to romantic music. Dissonant, or unstable, chords were also used more freely than during the classical era. By deliberately delaying the resolution of dissonance to a consonant, or stable, chord, romantic composers created feelings of yearning, tension, and mystery.

A romantic piece tends to have a wide variety of keys and rapid modulations, or changes from one key to another. Because of the nature and frequency of these key shifts, the tonic key is somewhat less clear than in classical works.

The feeling of tonal gravity tends to be less strong. By the end of the romantic period, even more emphasis was given to harmonic instability and less to stability and resolution.

Expanded Range of Dynamics, Pitch, and Tempo

Romantic music also calls for a wide range of dynamics. It includes sharp contrasts between faint whispers and sonorities of unprecedented power. The classical dynamic extremes—*ff* and *pp*—didn't meet the needs of romantics, who sometimes demanded *ffff* and *pppp*. Seeking more and more expressiveness, nineteenth-century composers used frequent crescendos and decrescendos, as well as sudden dynamic changes.

The range of pitch was expanded, too, as composers reached for extremely high or low sounds. In search of increased brilliance and depth of sound, the romantics exploited instruments like the piccolo and contrabassoon, as well as the expanded keyboard of the piano.

Changes of mood in romantic music are often underlined by accelerandos, ritardandos, and subtle variations of pace: there are many more fluctuations in tempo than there are in classical music. To intensify the expression of the music, romantic performers made use of *rubato,* a slight holding back or pressing forward of tempo.

Forms: Miniature and Monumental

The nineteenth century was very much an age of contradictions. Romantic composers characteristically expressed themselves both in musical miniatures and in monumental compositions. On the one hand are piano pieces by Chopin and songs by Schubert that last but a few minutes. Such short forms were meant to be heard in the intimate surroundings of a home; they met the needs of the growing number of people who owned pianos. The romantic genius for creating an intense mood through a melody, a few chords, or an unusual tone color found a perfect outlet in these miniatures. On the other hand, there are gigantic works by Berlioz and Wagner that call for a huge number of performers, last for several hours, and were designed for large opera houses or concert halls.

Romantic composers continued to write symphonies, sonatas, string quartets, concertos, operas, and choral works, but their individual movements tended to be longer than Haydn's and Mozart's. For example, a typical nineteenth-century symphony might last about 45 minutes, as opposed to 25 minutes for an eighteenth-century symphony. And as the romantic period drew to a close, compositions tended to become ever more extended, more richly orchestrated, and more complex in harmony.

New techniques were used to unify such long works. The same theme or themes might occur in several different movements of a symphony. Here composers followed the pioneering example of Beethoven's Fifth Symphony, where a theme from the scherzo is quoted within the finale. When a melody returns in a later movement or section of a romantic work, its character may be transformed by changes in dynamics, orchestration, or rhythm—a technique known as *thematic transformation.* A striking use of thematic transformation occurs in Berlioz's *Symphonie fantastique* (*Fantastic Symphony,* 1830), where a lyrical melody from the opening movement becomes a grotesque dance tune in the finale.

Different movements or sections of a romantic work can also be linked through transitional passages; one movement of a symphony or concerto may lead directly into the next movement. Here, again, Beethoven was the pioneer. And nineteenth-century operas are unified by melodic ideas that reappear in different acts or scenes, some of which may be tied together by connecting passages.

In dealing with an age that so prized individuality, generalizations are especially difficult. The great diversity found in romantic music can best be appreciated, perhaps, by approaching each piece as its composer did—with an open mind and heart.

2 Romantic Composers and Their Public

The composer's role in society changed radically during Beethoven's lifetime (1770–1827). In earlier periods, part of a musician's job had been to compose works for a specific occasion and audience. Thus Bach wrote cantatas for weekly church services in Leipzig, and Haydn composed symphonies for concerts in the palaces of the Esterházy family. But Beethoven, as we have seen, was one of the first great composers to work as a freelance musician outside the system of aristocratic or church patronage.

The image of Beethoven as a "free artist" inspired romantic musicians, who often composed to fulfill an inner need rather than a commission. Romantic composers were interested not only in pleasing their contemporaries but also in being judged favorably by posterity. The young Berlioz wrote to his father, "I want to leave on this earth some trace of my existence." It became common for romantics to create extended works with no immediate prospects for performance. For example, Wagner wrote *Das Rheingold (The Rhine Gold)*, a 2½-hour opera, and then had to wait fifteen years before seeing its premiere.

Sometimes the romantic composer was a "free artist" by necessity rather than choice. Because of the French Revolution and the Napoleonic Wars (from 1789 to 1815), many aristocrats could no longer afford to maintain private opera houses, orchestras, and "composers in residence." Musicians lost their jobs when many of the tiny princely states of Germany were abolished as political units and merged with neighboring territories. (In Bonn, Germany, the court and its orchestra were disbanded; Beethoven could not have returned to his position there even if he had wanted to.) Many composers who would have had secure, though modest, incomes in the past had to fight for their livelihood and sell their wares in the marketplace.

Romantic composers wrote primarily for a middle-class audience whose size and prosperity had increased because of the industrial revolution. During the nineteenth century, cities expanded dramatically, and a sizable number of people wanted to hear and play music.

The needs of this urban middle class led to the formation of many orchestras and opera groups during the romantic era. Public concerts had developed during

Romantic composers wrote primarily for a middle-class audience. In this picture by Moritz von Schwind, Franz Schubert is shown at the piano accompanying the singer Johann Michael Vogl.

the eighteenth century, but not until the nineteenth century did regular subscription concerts become common. The London Philharmonic Society was founded in 1813, the Paris Société des Concerts du Conservatoire in 1828, and the Vienna Philharmonische Konzerte and the New York Philharmonic in 1842.

The first half of the nineteenth century also witnessed the founding of music conservatories throughout Europe. In the United States, conservatories were founded in Chicago, Cleveland, Boston, Oberlin (Ohio), and Philadelphia during the 1860s. More young men and women than ever before studied to be professional musicians. At first women were accepted only as students of performance, but by the late 1800s they could study musical composition as well.

The nineteenth-century public was captivated by virtuosity. Among the musical heroes of the 1830s were the pianist Franz Liszt and the violinist Niccolò Paganini (1782–1840), who toured Europe and astonished audiences with their feats. Never before had instrumental virtuosity been so acclaimed. After one concert by Liszt in Budapest, Hungarian nobles presented him with a jeweled sword, and a crowd of thousands formed a torchlight parade to escort him to his dwelling. Following Liszt's example, performers like the pianist Clara Wieck Schumann and the violinist Joseph Joachim (1831–1907) began to give solo recitals in addition to their customary appearances with orchestras.

Private music making also increased during the romantic era. The piano became a fixture in every middle-class home, and there was great demand for songs and solo piano pieces. Operas and orchestral works were transcribed, or arranged, so that they could be played on pianos in the home.

Romantic composers came from the social class that was their main audience. Berlioz was the son of a doctor; Robert Schumann was the son of a bookseller; Mendelssohn was the son of a banker. This was a new situation. In earlier periods, music, like cabinetmaking, had been a craft passed from one generation to another. Bach, Mozart, and Beethoven were all children of musicians. But the romantics often had to do a great deal of persuading before their parents permitted them to undertake a musical career. Berlioz wrote to his reluctant father in 1824: "I am voluntarily driven towards a magnificent career (no other term can be applied to the career of an artist) and I am not in the least headed towards damnation. . . . This is the way I think, the way I am, and nothing in the world will change me."

Middle-class parents had reason for concern when their children wanted to be musicians. Few romantic composers were able to support themselves through composition alone. Only a very successful opera composer like Verdi could become wealthy by selling music to opera houses and publishers. Most composers were forced to work in several areas at once. Some were touring virtuosos like Paganini and Liszt. Many taught. Chopin, for instance, charged high fees for giving piano lessons to rich young women in Paris. Music criticism was a source of income for Berlioz and Robert Schumann. (And Berlioz bitterly resented having to waste time reviewing compositions by nonentities.) Some of the finest conductors of the romantic period were composers, among them Mendelssohn and Mahler. Only a few fortunates, such as Tchaikovsky and Wagner, had wealthy patrons to support them while they created.

The Art Song

One of the most distinctive forms in romantic music is the *art song,* a composition for solo voice and piano. Here, the accompaniment is an integral part of the composer's conception, and it serves as an interpretive partner to the voice. Although they are now performed in concert halls, romantic songs were written to be sung and enjoyed at home.

Poetry and music are intimately fused in the art song. It is no accident that this form flowered with the emergence of a rich body of romantic poetry in the early nineteenth century. Many of the finest song composers—Schubert, Robert Schumann, and Brahms, for example—were German or Austrian and set poems in their native language. Among the poets favored by these composers were Johann Wolfgang von Goethe (1749–1832) and Heinrich Heine (1797–1856). The German word *Lied (song)* is commonly used for a song with German text. (*Lied* is pronounced *leet;* its plural, *Lieder,* is pronounced *leader.*)

Yearning—inspired by a lost love, nature, legend, or other times and places—haunted the imagination of romantic poets. Thus art songs are filled with the despair of unrequited love; the beauty of flowers, trees, and brooks; and the supernatural happenings of folktales. There are also songs of joy, wit, and humor. But by and large, romantic song was a reaching out of the soul.

Song composers would interpret a poem, translating its mood, atmosphere, and imagery into music. They created a vocal melody that was musically satisfying and perfectly molded to the text. Important words were emphasized by stressed tones or melodic climaxes.

The voice shares the interpretive task with the piano. Emotions and images of the text take on added dimension from the keyboard commentary. Arpeggios in the piano might suggest the splashing of oars or the motion of a mill wheel. Chords in a low register might depict darkness or a lover's torment. The mood is often set by a brief piano introduction and summed up at the end by a piano section called a *postlude.*

Strophic and Through-Composed Form

When a poem has several stanzas, the musical setting must accommodate their total emotional impact. Composers can use **strophic form,** repeating the same music for each stanza of the poem. Strophic form makes a song easy to remember and is used in almost all folk songs. Or composers might use **through-composed form,** writing new music for each stanza. (*Through-composed* is a translation of the German term *durchkomponiert.*) Through-composed form allows music to reflect a poem's changing moods.

The art song is not restricted to strophic or through-composed form. There are many ways that music can be molded to the structure and feeling of a poem. A three-stanza poem is frequently set as follows: A (stanza 1)—B (stanza 2)—A (stanza 3). This might be called a **modified strophic form,** since two of the three stanzas are set to the same music.

The Song Cycle

Romantic art songs are sometimes grouped in a set, or **song cycle.** A cycle may be unified by a story line that runs through the poems, or by musical ideas linking the songs. Among the great romantic song cycles are *Die Winterreise* (*The Winter Journey,* 1827) by Schubert, and *Dichterliebe* (*Poet's Love,* 1840) by Robert Schumann.

In many of their art songs, romantic composers achieved a perfect union of music and poetry. They created an intensely personal world with a tremendous variety of moods. These miniatures contain some of the most haunting melodies and harmonies in all music.

Franz Schubert

Franz Schubert (1797–1828), the earliest master of the romantic art song, was unlike any great composer before him: he never held an official musical position and was neither a conductor nor a virtuoso; his income came entirely from composition. "I have come into the world for no other purpose than to compose," he said. The full measure of his genius was recognized only years after his tragically early death.

Schubert was born in Vienna, the son of a schoolmaster. Even as a child, he had astounding musical gifts. "If I wanted to instruct him in anything new," recalled his amazed teacher, "he knew it already." At eleven, he became a choirboy in the court chapel and won a scholarship to the Imperial Seminary.

Schubert managed to compose an extraordinary number of masterpieces in his late teens while teaching at his father's school, a job he hated. His love of

Franz Schubert.

poetry led him to the art song; he composed his first great song, *Gretchen am Spinnrade (Gretchen at the Spinning Wheel)*, when he was seventeen, and the next year he composed 143 songs, including *The Erlking*.

When he was nineteen, Schubert's productivity rose to a peak; he composed 179 works, including two symphonies, an opera, and a mass. At twenty-one, he gave up teaching school to devote himself to music. He associated with a group of Viennese poets and artists who led a bohemian existence; often, he lived with friends because he had no money to rent a room of his own. Working incredibly fast, from seven in the morning until early afternoon, he turned out one piece after another. He spent his afternoons in cafés and many of his evenings at "Schubertiads," parties where only his music was played. Most of his works were composed for performances in the homes of Vienna's cultivated middle class; unlike Beethoven, he did not mingle with the aristocracy. The publication and performance of his songs brought him some recognition, but his two most important symphonies—the *Unfinished* and the *Great* C Major—were not performed in public during his lifetime.

Schubert died in 1828, age thirty-one. He was thought of mainly as a fine song composer, until the *Unfinished* Symphony was performed nearly forty years later and the world could recognize his comprehensive greatness.

Schubert's Music

Along with over 600 songs, Schubert composed symphonies, string quartets and other chamber music, sonatas and short pieces for piano, masses, and operas. The songs embrace an enormous variety of moods and types; their melodies range from simple, folklike tunes to complex lines that suggest impassioned speech, and their piano accompaniments are equally rich and evocative. Schubert's imaginative harmonies and dissonances provide some of the most poetic moments in music.

The spirit of song pervades his instrumental music, too, and his longer works often include variation movements based on his own songs; his famous *Trout* Quintet in A Major (1819) is an example. Many of the symphonies and chamber works have long, lyrical melodies, and some—especially the *Unfinished* Symphony (1822) and the *Great* C Major Symphony (1825–1826)—are comparable in power and intensity to Beethoven's. The *Unfinished* was written six years before

Schubert's death; no one knows why it has only two (rather than four) movements. The *Great* C Major Symphony was discovered ten years after his death by Robert Schumann.

Erlkönig (The Erlking; 1815)

Brief Set:
CD 3 [12]

Basic Set:
CD 4 [48]

Schubert's song *Erlkönig (The Erlking)* is one of the earliest and finest examples of musical romanticism. It is a musical setting of a narrative ballad of the supernatural by Goethe. A friend of Schubert's tells how he saw the eighteen-year-old composer reading Goethe's poem. "He paced up and down several times with the book; suddenly he sat down, and in no time at all (just as quickly as he could write) there was the glorious ballad finished on the paper." Goethe's ballad, in dialogue almost throughout, tells of a father riding on horseback through a storm with his sick child in his arms. The delirious boy has visions of the legendary Erlking, the king of the elves who symbolizes death.

Schubert creates a through-composed setting to capture the mounting excitement of the poem. The piano part, with its rapid octaves and menacing bass motive, conveys the tension of the wild ride.

The piano's relentless triplet rhythm unifies the episodes of the song and suggests the horse's gallop.

By imaginatively varying the music, Schubert makes one singer sound like several characters in a miniature drama. The terrified boy sings in a high register in minor. Three times during the poem, he cries out, "My father, my father." Each time, the boy sings a musical outcry that is intensified through dissonant harmonies.

Mein Va - ter, mein Va - ter,

To convey mounting fear, Schubert pitches the boy's outcry higher and higher each time. The reassuring father sings in a low register that contrasts with the high-pitched outcries of his child. The Erlking, who tries to entice the boy, has coy melodies in major keys.

"Du lie - bes Kind,komm,geh mit mir! gar schö - ne Spie-le spiel' - ich mit dir;

The deeply moving climax of *The Erlking* comes when father and son arrive home and the galloping accompaniment gradually comes to a halt. In a bleak, heartbreaking recitative that allows every word to make its impact, the narrator tells us, "In his arms the child was dead!"

Vocal Music Guide to be read while music is heard | Brief Set: CD 3 | Basic Set: CD 4

SCHUBERT, *Erlkönig*

12 **48** 0:00
Piano introduction, rapid octaves, *f*, bass motive, minor key.

	Narrator
Wer reitet so spät durch Nacht und Wind?	Who rides so late through the night and the wind?
Es ist der Vater mit seinem Kind;	It is the father with his child;
Er hat den Knaben wohl in dem Arm,	he holds the boy close in his arms,
Er fasst ihn sicher, er hält ihn warm.	he clasps him securely, he holds him warmly.

13 **49** 0:56
Low register.

	Father
"Mein Sohn, was birgst du so bang dein Gesicht?"	"My son, why do you hide your face so anxiously?"

14 **50** 1:04 0:00
Higher register

	Son
"Siehst, Vater, du den Erlkönig nicht? Den Erlenkönig mit Kron' und Schweif?"	"Father, don't you see the Erlking? The Erlking with his crown and his train?"

1:20 0:16
Low register

	Father
"Mein Sohn, es ist ein Nebelstreif."	"My son, it is a streak of mist."

15 51 1:29			**Erlking**	
Coaxing tune, *pp*, higher register, major.		*"Du liebes Kind, komm, geh mit mir!*	"Dear child, come, go with me!	

Gar schöne Spiele spiel' ich mit dir, Manch bunte Blumen sind an dem Strand, Meine Mutter hat manch gülden Gewand."

I'll play the prettiest games with you. Many colored flowers grow along the shore; My mother has many golden garments."

16 52 1:54 0:00		**Son**
Outcry, *f*, minor.	*"Mein Vater, mein Vater, und hörest du nicht, Was Erlenkönig mir leise verspricht?"*	"My father, my father, and don't you hear the Erlking whispering promises to me?"

2:07 0:13		**Father**
Low register.	*"Sei ruhig, bleibe ruhig, mein Kind: In dürren Blättern säuselt der Wind."*	"Be quiet, stay quiet, my child; the wind is rustling in the dead leaves."

2:17 0:23		**Erlking**
Playful tune, *pp*, major.	*"Willst, feiner Knabe, du mit mir gehn?*	"My handsome boy, will you come with me?

Meine Töchter sollen dich warten schön; Meine Töchter führen den nächtlichen Reihn Und wiegen und tanzen und singen dich ein."

My daughters shall wait upon you; my daughters lead off in the dance every night, and cradle and dance and sing you to sleep."

17 53 2:36 0:00		**Son**
Outcry, *f*, higher than before, minor.	*"Mein Vater, mein Vater, und siehst du nicht dort Erlkönigs Töchter am düstern Ort?"*	"My father, my father, and don't you see there the Erlking's daughters in the shadows?"

2:48 0:12		**Father**
Lower register.	*"Mein Sohn, mein Sohn, ich seh' es genau: Es scheinen die alten Weiden so grau."*	"My son, my son, I see it clearly; the old willows look so gray."

		Erlking
	"Ich liebe dich, mich reizt deine schöne Gestalt; Und bist du nicht willig, so brauch' ich Gewalt."	"I love you, your beautiful figure delights me! And if you are not willing, then I shall use force!"

			Son
3:18	0:42	*"Mein Vater, mein Vater, jetzt fasst er mich an!*	"My father, my father, now he is taking hold of me!
Outcry, *f*, highest yet.		*Erlkönig hat mir ein Leids getan!"*	The Erlking has hurt me!"
			Narrator
3:31	0:55	*Dem Vater grauset's, er reitet geschwind,*	The father shudders, he rides swiftly on;
		Er hält in Armen das ächzende Kind,	he holds in his arms the groaning child,
		Erreicht den Hof mit Mühe und Not;	he reaches the courtyard weary and anxious:
Piano stops. Recitative.		*In seinen Armen das Kind war tot.*	in his arms the child was dead.

5 Robert Schumann

Robert Schumann (1810–1856) in many ways embodied musical romanticism. His works are intensely autobiographical and usually have descriptive titles, texts, or programs. He expressed his essentially lyrical nature in startlingly original piano pieces and songs. And as a writer and critic, he also discovered and made famous some of the leading composers of his day.

Schumann was born in Zwickau, Germany. He studied law at Leipzig University but actually devoted himself to literature and music. At twenty, he decided to become a piano virtuoso, but this goal became impossible when he developed serious problems with his right hand, which were not helped by medical

Robert Schumann.

treatments or by a gadget he used to stretch and strengthen the fingers. "Don't worry about my finger," he wrote to his mother; "I can compose without it"—and in his twenties he did compose many piano works that remain a basic part of the repertoire, although at the time they were often considered too unconventional and personal. During his twenties, too, he founded and edited the influential *New Journal of Music*, which contained his appreciative reviews of young "radical" composers like Chopin and Berlioz.

While studying piano, Schumann met his teacher's daughter and pupil, Clara Wieck, then a nine-year-old prodigy. The two were engaged when Clara was seventeen; but her father was bitterly opposed, and the couple had to fight against him in court before they could be married. Their marriage was a happy one. Clara—herself a composer—was also the ideal interpreter of Robert's works and introduced many of them to the public.

Schumann held some musical positions but was temperamentally unsuited for them, and during his later years, his mental and physical health deteriorated. In 1854 he tried to drown himself and was committed to an asylum, where he died two years later.

Robert Schumann's Music

During his first ten years as a composer, Schumann published only piano pieces, and his musical style seemed to grow out of piano improvisation. His short pieces often express a single mood through a sensitive melody; dance rhythms, dotted rhythms, and syncopations are also prominent.

In 1840, the year of his marriage, he composed many art songs which also reveal his gift for melody. Both the songs and the short piano pieces are usually organized in sets or cycles, whose titles—*Carnaval (Carnival)*, *Kinderscenen (Scenes of Childhood)*, *Nachtstücke (Night Pieces)*, *Dichterliebe (Poet's Love)*, *Fantasiestücke (Fantasy Pieces)*—give insight into his imagination. Schumann thought of music in emotional, literary, and autobiographical terms; his work is full of extramusical references.

After 1840, possibly as a result of Clara's influence, he turned to symphonies and chamber music. His symphonies are romantic in their emphasis on lyrical second themes, use of thematic transformation, and connections between movements.

Carnaval (Carnival; 1834–1835)

Carnaval is a cycle of twenty-one brief pieces with descriptive titles evoking a festive masked ball, with its varied characters, moods, and activities. This "musical picture gallery," as Schumann called it, includes sketches of fellow musicians, young women in the composer's life, stock characters from *commedia dell'arte* (Italian improvised theater), and self-portraits representing the introverted and outgoing sides of his own personality.

Carnaval was inspired partly by Schumann's brief engagement to Ernestine von Fricken, an eighteen-year-old pianist who studied with Clara Wieck's father. In 1834, Schumann wrote that he had "just discovered that the name Asch [Ernestine's birthplace] is very musical and contains letters that also occur in my name [SCHumAnn]. They are musical symbols." In German, B natural is known as H, and so the letters A S C H refer to the four notes A–E flat–C–B natural, if the S is read as Es (German for E flat); or to the three notes A flat–C–B natural, if A and S are compressed to As (German for A flat). Schumann used these four-note or three-note groups to open most of the pieces in *Carnaval*, creating musical links between them. However, these links are quite concealed, because the same notes are presented in continually changing rhythms, melodic shapes, and harmonies. By using musical ideas related to himself and his fiancée, Schumann permeated *Carnaval* with autobiographical references.

We will now focus on two pieces from this best-known of Schumann's extended piano works. The two successive pieces *Estrella* and *Reconnaissance* (Nos. 13 and 14) illustrate the contrasting moods within *Carnaval*. The first of these is in minor, and the second is in major. Each opens with the same three-note group, A flat–C–B natural (see the letters at the beginning of the music examples).

Estrella

Brief Set:
CD 3 `18`

Basic Set:
CD 5 `4`

Estrella, marked *con affecto (with feeling)*, is a sketch of Schumann's fiancée Ernestine von Fricken. The composer thought of Estrella as "the kind of name one would put under a portrait to fix it more clearly in one's memory." *Estrella* is in minor and in triple meter; it includes a variety of rhythmic patterns and has a waltzlike accompaniment.

Section A
`18` `4` 0:00

Section B
`19` `5` 0:15   0:00

Section A'
         0:29   0:14

Estrella is in A B A' (abridged) form. The outer sections, which are consistently forceful, contrast with the middle section, which begins softly. Section B is permeated by syncopations—accents on the second and third beats—a distinctive feature of Schumann's music.

Reconnaissance (Reunion)

Brief Set:
CD 3 `20`

Basic Set:
CD 5 `6`

Reconnaissance is a lyrical piece, which Schumann described as a "scene of reunion." In A B A' form, it is longer than *Estrella*. Schumann's style of piano writing is highly original here. In the outer (A) sections, which are in major, the pianist's right hand simultaneously plays two versions of the same melody an octave apart: the higher melody is legato, whereas the lower one is decorated with fast, staccato, repeated notes.

Section A
`20` `6` 0:00

Perhaps these pulsating repeated notes represent the throbbing hearts of the reunited lovers.

The calmer middle section (B) brings a new major key and a shift from homophonic to polyphonic texture. The original melody is presented in the top part and imitated in the bass. Rhythmic excitement is maintained by a syncopated accompaniment in the middle parts.

Section B

21 7 0:44 0:00

Section A

1:36 0:52

The concluding A' section is a shortened and slightly varied version of the opening A section.

Together, *Estrella* and *Reconnaissance* reveal different facets of Schumann's musical personality.

6 Clara Wieck Schumann

Clara Wieck Schumann (1819–1896), a leading nineteenth-century pianist, premiered many works of her husband Robert and her close friend Johannes Brahms. She was born in Leipzig, Germany, and was an acclaimed child prodigy, taught by her father, the well-known piano pedagogue Friedrich Wieck.

She married Robert Schumann despite her father's opposition and continued to concertize and compose while caring for him and their seven children. In 1853 the twenty-year-old composer Johannes Brahms came to play his works

Clara Wieck Schumann.

for the Schumanns, beginning a friendship with Clara that lasted until her death; that same year, she met the violinist Joseph Joachim, with whom she would often perform. After her husband's death, she also became renowned as a teacher and edited his collected works. She helped refine the tastes of audiences by presenting works of earlier composers like Bach, Mozart, and Beethoven as well as works by Robert Schumann and Brahms.

Clara Wieck Schumann's Music

Clara Schumann considered herself primarily a performing artist ("I feel I have a mission to perform beautiful works. Robert's above all," she once wrote) and stopped composing when she was thirty-six. Her doubts about composing were perhaps influenced by the negative attitude toward women composers that predominated during her lifetime, and by her relationship with overwhelming geniuses like her husband and Brahms. Until recently, she was known primarily as a famous pianist who had been the wife of one great composer and the close friend of another. But her compositions are now being increasingly performed and recorded. They include piano pieces; a piano concerto; a trio for piano, violin, and cello; and songs, one of which will be studied here.

Liebst du um Schönheit (If you love for beauty; 1841)

Brief Set:
CD 3 22

Basic Set:
CD 5 8

A few months after their wedding, Robert and Clara Schumann had the idea of a joint song cycle composed partly by him and partly by her. In January 1841, Robert wrote songs set to love lyrics by the poet Friedrich Rückert (*Liebesfrühling; Spring of Love*). At the beginning of June of the same year, Clara also composed songs on poems by Rückert, writing in their marriage diary that they were "for my dear Robert. If he should enjoy them just a little, my wish would be fulfilled." On June 8, she gave the songs to Robert as a birthday gift. When the cycle of twelve songs—nine by Robert and three by Clara—was published in 1841, the composers of the individual songs were not identified, fulfilling Robert's wish that "posterity shall regard us as one heart and one soul and not find out what is yours and what is mine." Robert presented the published songs to Clara on her twenty-second birthday, thirteen days after the birth of their first child.

Clara Schumann's song *Liebst du um Schönheit (If you love for beauty),* from this joint cycle, reflects the glorification of romantic love by nineteenth-century musicians, artists, and writers. In Rückert's poem, the speaker says that she (or he) should be cherished for pure love itself, not for beauty, youth, or riches. *Liebst du um Schönheit* is in varied strophic form: A (stanza 1)-A' (stanza 2) A (stanza 3)-A" (stanza 4). Stanzas 1 and 3 are set to essentially the same melody. Stanzas 2 and 4 begin like the other stanzas but then take different musical paths. Repeated-note patterns (as on *Liebst du um*) contribute to the melody's folklike quality.

The flowing piano accompaniment sensitively responds to the vocal melody and text; it fills the rests between vocal phrases and sometimes continues melodic ideas initiated by the voice. *Liebst du um Schönheit* reaches an emotional high point at the end of the fourth stanza, when a single word, *immerdar (forever)*, is extended through two measures of music.

dich   lieb ich   im _ _ _   mer _ dar! _____

An expressive piano postlude rounds off the song, perhaps evoking the beloved's response to the thoughts expressed by the voice.

Vocal Music Guide to be read while music is heard   Brief Set: CD 3   Basic Set: CD 5

CLARA WIECK SCHUMANN, *Liebst du um Schönheit*

|22| |8| 0:00
Piano
introduction

A

Liebst du um Schönheit,	If you love for beauty,
O nicht mich liebe!	O love not me!
Liebe die Sonne,	Love the sun,
Sie trägt ein gold'nes Haar.	It has golden hair.

|23| |9| 0:27
A'

Liebst du um Jugend,	If you love for youth,
O nicht mich liebe!	O love not me!
Liebe den Frühling,	Love the spring,
Der Jung ist jedes Jahr!	That's young every year.

|24| |10| 0:48
A

Liebst du um Schätze,	If you love for treasure,
O nicht mich liebe!	O love not me!
Liebe die Meerfrau,	Love the mermaid,
Sie hat vielen Perlen Klar!	Who has many bright pearls.

|25| |11| 1:09
A''

Liebst du um Liebe,	If you love for Love,
O ja mich liebe!	O yes, love me!
Liebe mich immer,	Love me always,
Dich, lieb'ich immerdar.	I love you forever.

Piano
postlude

7 Frédéric Chopin

Frédéric Chopin (1810–1849) was the only great composer who wrote almost exclusively for the piano. The son of a Polish mother and a French father, he was brought up in Warsaw and graduated from the Warsaw Conservatory. At twenty-one, he arrived in Paris, then the center of romanticism and the artistic capital of Europe.

In Paris, he met such writers as Victor Hugo, Balzac, and Heine and became close friends with the painter Delacroix and with Liszt and Berlioz. His playing soon gained him access to aristocratic salons; he was a shy, reserved man who preferred salons to concert halls, and it was for such intimate gatherings that he conceived his short pieces like the nocturnes, waltzes, and preludes. He earned a good living teaching piano to the daughters of the rich and lived in luxury.

Chopin had a well-known love affair with Aurore Dudevant, a novelist whose pen name was George Sand; a frail man, he thrived on her care and composed many of his greatest works during the years they lived together. After they separated, his health declined rapidly and he composed very little. He died of tuberculosis at thirty-nine.

Frédéric Chopin in a portrait by Eugène Delacroix.

Chopin's Music

By the age of eighteen, Chopin had evolved an utterly personal and original style. Most of his pieces are exquisite miniatures; they evoke an infinite variety of moods and are always elegant, graceful, and melodic. Unlike Schumann's works, they do not have literary programs or titles. The mazurkas and polonaises—stylized dances—capture a Polish spirit without actually using folk tunes.

No other composer has made the piano sound as beautiful as Chopin, who creates the illusion that the piano sings. He uses graceful and delicate ornamentation and exploits the pedals sensitively. His colorful treatment of harmony was highly original and influenced later composers.

Nocturne in E Flat Major, Op. 9, No. 2 (1830–1831)

Brief Set:
CD 3 [26]

Basic Set:
CD 5 [12]

Chopin composed his popular Nocturne in E Flat Major, Op. 9, No. 2, when he was about twenty. A *nocturne,* or *night piece,* is a slow, lyrical, intimate composition for piano. Like much of Chopin's music, this nocturne is tinged with melancholy.

Nocturne in E Flat Major opens with a legato melody containing graceful upward leaps, which become wider as the line unfolds. This melody is heard again three times during the piece. With each repetition, it is varied by ever more elaborate decorative tones and trills. The nocturne also includes a subordinate melody, which is played with rubato—slight fluctuations of tempo.

A sonorous foundation for the melodic line is provided by the widely spaced notes in the accompaniment, connected by the damper ("loud") pedal. The waltzlike accompaniment gently emphasizes the $\frac{12}{8}$ meter: 12 beats to the measure subdivided into four groups of 3 beats each.

The nocturne is reflective in mood until it suddenly becomes passionate near the end. The new concluding melody begins softly but then ascends to a high register and is played forcefully in octaves. After a brilliant trill-like passage, the excitement subsides; the nocturne ends calmly.

Listening Outline to be read while music is heard   Brief Set: CD 3   Basic Set: CD 5

CHOPIN, Nocturne in E Flat Major, Op. 9, No. 2

Andante, $\frac{12}{8}$ meter

Piano

(Duration, 4:05)

[26] [12] 0:00   **1. a.** Main melody, dolce, espressivo, waltzlike accompaniment.

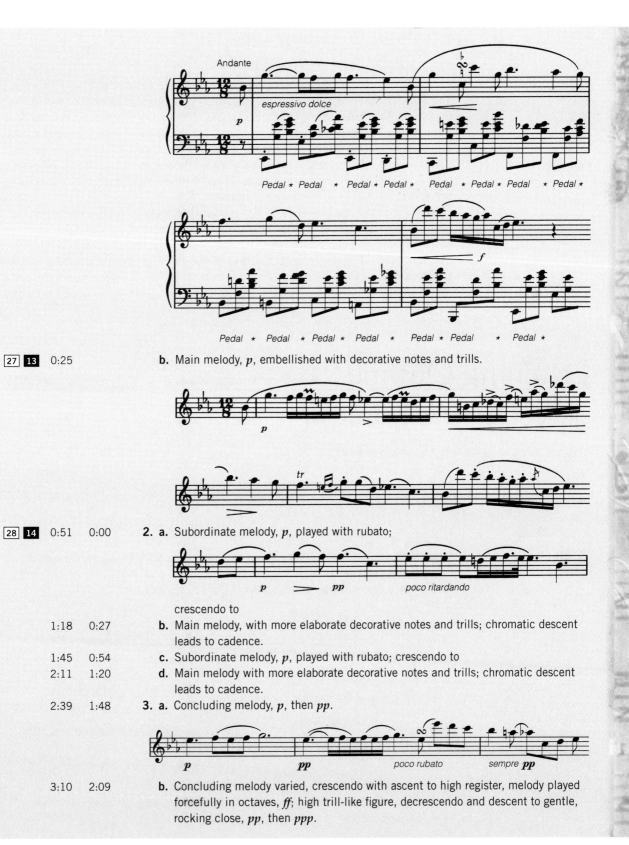

27 13	0:25		**b.** Main melody, *p*, embellished with decorative notes and trills.

28 14	0:51	0:00	**2. a.** Subordinate melody, *p*, played with rubato;

crescendo to

	1:18	0:27	**b.** Main melody, with more elaborate decorative notes and trills; chromatic descent leads to cadence.
	1:45	0:54	**c.** Subordinate melody, *p*, played with rubato; crescendo to
	2:11	1:20	**d.** Main melody with more elaborate decorative notes and trills; chromatic descent leads to cadence.
	2:39	1:48	**3. a.** Concluding melody, *p*, then *pp*.

	3:10	2:09	**b.** Concluding melody varied, crescendo with ascent to high register, melody played forcefully in octaves, *ff*; high trill-like figure, decrescendo and descent to gentle, rocking close, *pp*, then *ppp*.

Étude in C Minor, Op. 10, No. 12 (*Revolutionary*; 1831?)

Brief Set:

CD 3 29

Basic Set:

CD 5 15

The Russian takeover of Warsaw in 1831 may have inspired Chopin to compose the blazing, furious *Revolutionary* Étude in C Minor, Op. 10, No. 12. An *étude* is a study piece designed to help a performer master specific technical difficulties. The *Revolutionary* Étude, for example, develops speed and endurance in a pianist's left hand, which must play rapid passages throughout. Chopin's études reach beyond mere exercises in technique to become masterpieces of music, exciting to hear as well as to master.

The *Revolutionary* Étude, in A A'—coda form, begins with a dramatic outburst. High, dissonant chords and downward rushing passages lead to the main melody, marked *appassionato (impassioned)*, which is played in octaves by the right hand. Tension mounts because of the melody's dotted rhythms and its tempestuous accompaniment. After a climax at the end of section A', the coda momentarily relaxes the tension. Then a torrential passage sweeps down the keyboard to come to rest in powerful closing chords.

Listening Outline to be read while music is heard   Brief Set: CD 3   Basic Set: CD 5

CHOPIN, Étude in C Minor, Op. 10, No. 12 *(Revolutionary)*

Allegro con fuoco (allegro with fire), duple meter ($\frac{2}{2}$)

Piano

(Duration, 2:42)

A

29 15 0:00   **1. a.** High accented chords, *f*, answered by downward rushing passages; low running notes introduce

  0:16   **b.** Passionate main melody in octaves, *f*, dotted rhythm, minor,

decrescendo to

  0:34   **c.** Repetition of main melody, *p*, with different continuation, syncopated chords, crescendo to cadence in major.

  0:49   **d.** Lyrical melody in dotted rhythm, minor, crescendo and downward running notes; very high descending phrases lead to return of

A'

  1:11   **2. a.** High accented chords, *f*, answered by downward rushing passages; low running notes introduce

1:28	**b.** Passionate main melody intensified, *f*, decrescendo; low running notes introduce
1:47	**c.** Repetition of intensified main melody leads to
1:55	**d.** Majestic downward phrases in major, *ff*, decrescendo, *p*, return to minor, low running notes rise and fall, ritardando to

Coda

| 2:22 | **e.** Gentle upward phrase repeated with ritardando. Sudden *ff*, downward rushing passage, powerful closing chords, *fff*. |

Polonaise in A Flat Major, Op. 53 (1842)

Basic Set:
CD 5 **16**

Introduction
16 0:00

Section A
17 0:28

The *polonaise,* a piece in triple meter, originated as a stately processional dance for the Polish nobility. Chopin's heroic polonaises evoke the ancient splendor of the Polish people.

His Polonaise in A Flat Major is majestic and powerful, with moments of lyrical contrast. It may be outlined as follows: introduction—A B A'—coda. Its main theme makes a grand entrance.

Section B
18 2:54

Section A'
19 5:17

The majesty of this theme is enhanced by intervals of thirds in the right hand and by the resonant, wide-ranging accompaniment. After the main theme is repeated twice with an even richer texture, Chopin offers the contrasting middle section (B). This is a marchlike melody accompanied by relentlessly repeated rapid octaves in the left hand. This section tests a pianist's strength and endurance. Powerful crescendos bring mounting excitement. Then Chopin gradually relaxes the mood to prepare for the final return of the heroic main theme (A').

Franz Liszt

Franz Liszt (1811–1886) was handsome, magnetic, irresistible to women, an incredible showman, and a pacesetter in musical history. During the 1840s, he performed superhuman feats at the piano, overwhelming the European public and impressing musicians as much as concertgoers.

Chopin wished that he could play his own piano études the way Liszt did. Schumann wrote that Liszt "enmeshed every member of the audience with his art and did with them as he willed." Brahms later said, "Whoever has not heard Liszt cannot speak of piano playing."

Liszt was born in Hungary; his father was an administrator for the Esterházy family (which Haydn had also served). At age eleven, Liszt studied in Vienna, where he met Schubert and Beethoven; during his teens and twenties, he lived in Paris, a city where romanticism flourished and a mecca for virtuosos. When he was nineteen and already acclaimed, Liszt was awed by the great violinist Paganini, who drove audiences into a frenzy and was half suspected of being in league with the devil. Young Liszt was determined to become the Paganini of the piano. He withdrew from the concert stage for a few years, practiced from eight to twelve hours a day, and emerged as probably the greatest pianist of his time.

Franz Liszt.

To display his incomparable mastery, Liszt composed his *Transcendental Études* and made piano transcriptions of Paganini's violin pieces. "My piano," he wrote, "is my very self. . . . Ten fingers have the power to reproduce the harmonies which are created by hundreds of performers." Once, after an orchestral performance of a movement from Berlioz's *Fantastic Symphony,* Liszt played his own piano arrangement and made a more powerful effect than the entire orchestra. He toured Europe tirelessly between 1839 and 1847, playing mainly his own piano music and receiving unprecedented adulation.

But Liszt also wanted recognition as a serious composer. At thirty-six, he abandoned his career as a traveling virtuoso to become court conductor in Weimar, where he composed many orchestral pieces (developing a new and influential form of program music) and conducted works by such contemporaries as Berlioz, Schumann, and Wagner. Unselfish and generous, he taught hundreds of gifted pianists free of charge and provided musical and financial support crucial to Wagner's success. He also wrote music criticism and books on Chopin and on Gypsy music. His literary efforts were aided by two aristocratic women writers: Countess Marie d'Agoult and, later, the Russian Princess Carolyne Sayn-Wittgenstein. (Marie d'Agoult left her husband to live with Liszt; she and Liszt had three children, one of whom, Cosima, later left her own husband to marry Richard Wagner.)

Liszt went to Rome for religious studies in 1861, and in 1865 he took minor holy orders, becoming Abbé Liszt. This seeming incongruity—a notorious Don Juan and diabolical virtuoso as churchman—stunned his contemporaries. In Rome, he composed oratorios and masses.

During his last years, Liszt traveled between Rome, Weimar, and Budapest, where he was president of the new Academy of Music. Now he began to write curious, experimental piano pieces that foreshadowed some features of twentieth-century music. Though these late works went unappreciated, Liszt had become a living legend. The grand duke of Weimar said, "Liszt *was* what a prince *ought* to be."

Liszt's Music

Liszt's music is controversial. Some consider it vulgar and bombastic; others revel in its extroverted romantic rhetoric. Yet few would deny Liszt's originality, his influence, or his importance as the creator of the symphonic poem.

Liszt found new ways to exploit the piano; his melodies are sometimes surrounded by arpeggios that create the impression of three hands playing; and in the *Hungarian Rhapsodies*, which influenced a generation of nationalist composers, he makes the piano sound at times like an entire Gypsy band. His piano works contain daring leaps, rapid octaves and runs, and an unprecedented range of dynamics. Before the age of recordings and frequent concerts, Liszt's transcriptions made it possible for people to play operas and symphonies on their own pianos.

Breaking away from classical sonata form and the standard four-movement symphony, Liszt created the **symphonic poem,** or **tone poem,** a one-movement orchestral composition based to some extent on literary or pictorial ideas (see Section 10). Among his favorite inspirations were the works of Goethe, on which he based his *Faust* Symphony (1854); and those of Dante, which inspired the

Dante Symphony (1856). Many of his compositions are concerned with the devil or death and bear titles like *Mephisto Waltz*, *Totentanz (Dance of Death)*, and *Funérailles*. Constant changes of tempo and mood and alternations between diabolical fury and semireligious meditation contribute to a feeling of improvisation; but in his symphonic poems and other orchestral works, contrasting moods are often unified through thematic transformations of a single, recurring musical idea.

Liszt's music influenced many composers, including Wagner, who admitted to him: "When I compose and orchestrate, I always think only of you." As a stupendous performer, innovative composer, and charismatic personality, Liszt typified the romantic movement.

Transcendental Étude No. 10 in F Minor (1851)

Basic Set:
CD 5 **20**

As dazzling, passionate, and poetic as Liszt himself, the *Transcendental* Étude No. 10 in F Minor is one of the finest virtuoso pieces of the romantic era. Liszt had written an early, simpler version of this piece in 1824, when he was only thirteen, and included it in a group of twelve studies. Fifteen years later, at the peak of his career as a virtuoso, he published a revised version that demanded transcendent, almost superhuman technical skill from the pianist. (Robert Schumann was so overwhelmed by Liszt's études that he described them as "studies in storm and dread meant to be played by, at most, ten or twelve players in the world.") In 1851, after retiring from the concert stage, Liszt dedicated a third and final version—which we'll study—to his piano teacher Carl Czerny "as a token of esteem, gratitude, and friendship."

The étude taxes the player with left-hand passages that require rapid skips and changes of hand position. Though written in A B A'—coda form, it almost seems like an improvisation, owing to its frequent alternations between brilliant virtuoso passages and more melodic ideas. Section A contains three themes. The first, in minor, is fragmentary and syncopated.

20 0:00

21 0:42

The second, in major, is more lyrical and in a high register, with dotted rhythms, and with rapid notes in the accompaniment.

22 1:14

The third, which has a processional character, is a transformation of the second. A melody that was introduced in major in a high register is now presented in minor, in a low register set against higher arpeggios.

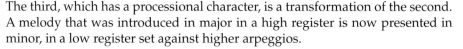

23 1:26
24 2:04
25 4:05

The brief section B develops and transforms the syncopated main theme. All three themes return in section A′, which is introduced by a decrescendo and ritardando. The étude ends with a furious coda based on a speeded-up transformation of the main theme.

Felix Mendelssohn

Felix Mendelssohn (1809–1847), a romantic whose music was rooted in classicism, was born in Hamburg, Germany, to a wealthy and distinguished Jewish family. (He was, however, raised as a Protestant.) By the age of nine, he was a brilliant pianist; by thirteen, he had written symphonies, concertos, sonatas, and vocal works of astounding quality. As a teenager, he performed his works at home with a private orchestra for the intellectual and artistic elite of Berlin, where the Mendelssohns had settled.

In 1829, at age twenty, he conducted Bach's *St. Matthew Passion* in its first performance since the composer's death. This historic concert rekindled interest in Bach and earned Mendelssohn an international reputation. He performed as a pianist, organist, and conductor in Germany and in England, where his music was especially popular. He often visited and played for Queen Victoria, and the high point of his career was the triumphant premiere of his oratorio

Felix Mendelssohn.

Elijah in Birmingham in 1846. When only twenty-six, he became conductor of the Leipzig Gewandhaus Orchestra; and he founded the Leipzig Conservatory at age thirty-three.

Mendelssohn's personal life was more conventional than that of many romantics; he was happily married and had four children. But constant travel and work sapped his strength, and he died, after a stroke, at thirty-eight.

Mendelssohn's Music

Mendelssohn's music radiates the elegance and balance of his personality; it evokes many moods but avoids emotional extremes and typically conveys an elfin quality through rapid movement, lightness, and transparent orchestral texture. He wrote an enormous amount of music in all the forms of his day except opera; today, only a few of his works are in the concert repertoire, but these are very popular. They include the Violin Concerto—which we'll study—the *Midsummer Night's Dream* and *Hebrides* overtures; the *Italian* (1833) and *Scottish* (1842) symphonies; the oratorio *Elijah;* and a number of chamber works.

Concerto for Violin and Orchestra in E Minor, Op. 64 (1844)

The Violin Concerto in E Minor, Op. 64, was inspired by Mendelssohn's friendship with the concertmaster of his orchestra, the famous violinist Ferdinand David. "I should like to make a violin concerto for you next winter," Mendelssohn wrote. "One in E minor runs in my head and its beginning gives me no rest." With David as soloist, Mendelssohn's Violin Concerto met with great success at its premiere in 1845, and its unique fusion of lyricism and virtuosity has made it one of the best-loved concertos.

The concerto's three movements are played without pause, in a characteristic linking technique used by romantic composers. Mendelssohn's love of balance is reflected in the cooperation and interplay between soloist and orchestra. Themes pass from one to the other, producing a beautiful contrast of tone color and expression. At one moment, the violinist plays a melody while the orchestra discreetly accompanies; at another, the woodwinds present thematic fragments while the soloist has dazzling running passages.

First Movement:
Allegro molto appassionato (very impassioned allegro)

Brief Set:
CD 5 ☐1☐

Basic Set:
CD 5 ☐26☐

Though Mendelssohn is usually considered a conservative composer, a "classical romantic," his opening movement departs from classical concerto form. Traditionally, the opening movement of a concerto began with an extended section for orchestra. But Mendelssohn's first movement begins with the soloist, who presents the main theme. This ardent, expansive melody is heard high above a murmuring string accompaniment. The orchestra then expands the violin's theme and introduces a new, flowing melody that begins the bridge section of this sonata-form movement. Toward the end of the bridge, the excitement is gradually relaxed to prepare for the second theme, a tranquil woodwind melody which the soloist accompanies with a single sustained tone. This unusual combination of instruments produces a delicate, intimate sound. Following this, the violin reclaims the spotlight and sings the tranquil theme while the woodwinds support it.

The cadenza has a new function in this movement. In classical concertos, the cadenza was improvised by the soloist and played near the end of the movement. Here, the composer has written it out and placed it at the end of the development section as a transition to the recapitulation. Mendelssohn wanted the cadenza to be an integral part of the movement, not merely something tacked on to display the soloist's virtuosity. Listen for the magical moment when the violinist's rapid arpeggios are joined by the orchestra softly playing the first theme of the recapitulation.

Listening Outline to be read while music is heard

Brief Set: CD 5   Basic Set: CD 5

MENDELSSOHN, Concerto for Violin and Orchestra in E Minor

First Movement: Allegro molto appassionato

Sonata form, duple meter ($\frac{2}{2}$), E minor

Solo violin, 2 flutes, 2 oboes, 2 clarinets, 2 bassoons, 2 French horns, 2 trumpets, timpani, 1st violins, 2d violins, violas, cellos, double basses

(Duration, 12:01)

Exposition

First theme

 1 26 0:00

1. **a.** Strings, *p*, introduce solo violin. Main melody in minor, high register, legato.

0:29	**b.** Running notes in solo violin. Crescendo, climbing phrases.
0:53	**c.** Orchestra, *ff*, main melody. Increased rhythmic motion leads to cadence.

Bridge

 2 27 1:22 0:00

2. **a.** Violins, flowing bridge theme. Solo violin repeats bridge theme an octave higher.

1:35 0:13 **b.** Solo violin phrases sweep downward and upward through wide range. Flute joins. Crescendo. Running passage rises and falls. Decrescendo, mood calms.

Second theme

| 3 | 28 | 2:34 | 0:00 | **3. a.** Clarinets and flutes, *pp*, calm melody in major. Solo violin accompanies with sustained tone. |

Clarinet

pp   tranquillo

		2:49	0:15	**b.** Solo violin, *pp*, calm theme expanded. Woodwinds, then strings accompany.
		3:53	1:19	**4. a.** Main melody in solo violin, major. Brilliant running passages, pizzicato accompaniment. Crescendo.
		4:40	2:06	**b.** Climactic orchestral trills alternate with solo violin, opening of main melody. Decrescendo.

Development

4	29	5:00	0:00	**1. a.** Solo violin, *p*, flowing bridge theme. Violins, *f*.
		5:13	0:13	**b.** Running passage in solo violin and fragments of main melody in orchestra.
		5:38	0:38	**2.** Solo violin, *p*, main melody varied. Decrescendo. Violin melody slowly descends. Orchestral crescendo to *ff*.

Cadenza

| 5 | 30 | 6:27 | | **3.** Unaccompanied solo violin, broken chords. Ascents to high tones, trills, fragment of main melody. Rapid broken chords lead into |

Recapitulation

First theme

| 6 | 31 | 8:01 | 0:00 | **1.** Main melody in orchestra, *p*. Broken chords continue in solo violin. Crescendo. |

Bridge

| | | 8:18 | 0:17 | **2. a.** Orchestra, *ff*, bridge theme. |
| | | | | **b.** Solo violin, *mf*, bridge theme carried downward. Decrescendo. |

Second theme

		8:48	0:47	**3. a.** Woodwinds, *pp*, calm melody in major. Solo violin accompanies with sustained tone.
		9:02	1:01	**b.** Solo violin, *pp*, calm theme expanded. Woodwinds, then strings accompany.
		10:09	2:08	**4. a.** Brilliant running passages in solo violin. Pizzicato accompaniment. Crescendo.
		10:55	2:54	**b.** Climactic orchestral trills alternate with solo violin, opening of main melody. Decrescendo.

Coda

| | | 11:14 | 3:13 | **5.** Solo violin, bridge theme. Tempo becomes faster. Crescendo. Brilliant running passages. Full orchestra, *ff*. |

Second Movement:
Andante

A single bassoon tone links the brilliant opening movement with the hushed introduction to the slow second movement. The C major andante is a songlike, intimate piece in A B A' form. Its opening section (A) features a warm, expansive melody in the solo violin's high register; a string accompaniment gently emphasizes the $\frac{6}{8}$ meter (**1**-2-3-**4**-5-6). The middle section (B) becomes more agitated, and the accompaniment is rhythmically more active. The orchestra plays a more important role as it engages in dialogue with the soloist. Mendelssohn requires the solo violinist to play a melody and a trembling accompaniment figure at the same time. The soloist also presents the melody in full-sounding octaves. The transition to the concluding A' section is very smooth because the trembling accompaniment figure is maintained. The andante ends quietly with a tender epilogue for solo violin and woodwinds.

Third Movement:
Allegretto non troppo (transitional section);
Allegro molto vivace (very lively allegro)

A pensive transitional section for solo violin and strings connects the andante with the concluding movement of the concerto. The very rapid finale, in sonata form, creates the lightness, joy, and brilliance so typical of Mendelssohn's art. Forceful chords in the woodwinds and upward solo figures usher in the playful and mostly staccato opening theme of the exposition; it is presented by the solo violin and high woodwinds.

A dazzling series of running passages and a long upward scale lead directly into the second theme, which is also a carefree one. With great effect, it combines a loud, marchlike phrase by the full orchestra with a softer motive from the opening theme.

In the development, the woodwinds softly present the marchlike phrase while the soloist plays brilliant running passages. A highlight of the development comes when the violinist presents a new legato melody which the strings lightly accompany with fragments of the opening theme.

Hilary Hahn, Violinist, Playing the First Movement of Mendelssohn's Violin Concerto in E Minor, Op. 64

Though still in her twenties, Hilary Hahn is one of the most prominent concert violinists of our time. In 1999, when she was nineteen, *Time* Magazine called her "America's best" young classical musician.

As with most concert artists, Hahn's extraordinary musical talent was recognized at a very early age. When not quite four, she began studying violin, and at age ten she was accepted to the Curtis Institute of Music in Philadelphia. At sixteen, she signed a recording contract, made her debut at Carnegie Hall with the Philadelphia Orchestra, and completed the requirements for her bachelor of music degree. However, she chose to delay her graduation from Curtis for three years: "I loved the school, so I stayed as long as I could. There were a lot of classes that interested me that I hadn't taken yet; for extra electives, I enrolled in poetry- and fiction- writing workshops and several literature classes, in addition to continuing with German."

For Hahn, "communicating music to people is something that I feel very lucky to be able to do." She writes her own liner notes for her recordings and maintains an online journal (on her Web site, HilaryHahn.com) of her experiences in cities where she performs. To expand children's musical horizons, Hahn often plays in grade schools. "I always play solo Bach, a slow and a fast movement. The music casts a spell. They really like it."

Hahn enjoys music in a wide range of styles, from blues and world music to trip-hop and classical. Her prizewinning recordings include works by Mendelssohn, Bach, Beethoven, and Bernstein, and she performs on the sound track of the M. Night Shyamalan film *The Village,* as well as on an album by Austin alt-rockers . . . *And You Will Know Us by the Trail of Dead.*

Hahn learned the Mendelssohn Violin Concerto when she was eleven and performed excerpts with the Curtis Orchestra the following year. (Her performance of the first movement of the concerto is included in the CD Sets.) "Not long after, I performed the entire concerto with a chamber orchestra in Florida, and since then the Mendelssohn concerto has been a staple of my repertoire." For Hahn, the first movement of the concerto is full of "lyricism, fire, drama, and contrast."

Hahn observes that performing a concerto requires close cooperation with the conductor and members of the orchestra. "Sometimes the conductor and I will disagree about something and meet in the middle. There's a system of give-and-take, opinions, and compromise—though as a musician, you try to never be compromised or compromise someone else's interpretation. Musicians inevitably interact with each other, so we have to be aware of what the others are doing. For example, if I share a solo line with the flute, I will pay attention to how the flutist plays the line so that it sounds like a duet. The conductor coordinates some of that, but in a concerto, the minutiae are really decided by the musicians, by listening to each other and reacting to the musical ideas that we hear."

For Hahn, playing before a live audience is very different from recording in a studio. "The audience influences performing to a large extent because the presence of people affects the way the concert hall sounds. The energy in the hall is hard to describe, but there is a different feeling when you know people are there to absorb the music (both acoustically and psychologically). It's quite energizing and inspiring. In recording, you have a limited time and an empty hall—any tiny noise can ruin a take, so no audience is allowed in the studio—and you have to get it right, so that situation takes a different approach. I try to keep the feeling as similar as possible, though, by imagining an audience listening in the hall, or in their car, or to their stereo."

Then there is a reversal of roles: the strings sing the lyrical melody while the soloist gracefully presents the fragment of the opening theme.

At the beginning of the recapitulation, the two themes are combined once again. The French horn and lower strings play the warm legato melody while the soloist brings back the sparkling first theme. After a return of the second theme, the movement builds to an exciting climax in the coda, which is fuller in sound than anything that has come before.

Program Music

Romantic composers were particularly attracted to **program music**—instrumental music associated with a story, poem, idea, or scene. Programmatic works such as Berlioz's *Fantastic Symphony,* Tchaikovsky's *Romeo and Juliet,* and Smetana's *Moldau* depict emotions, characters, and events, or the sounds and motions of nature; these nonmusical ideas are usually specified by the title or by the composer's explanatory comments (the **program**).

Program compositions draw on music's capacity to suggest and evoke. Music can, of course, imitate certain sounds (birdsongs, bells, thunder, wind), and composers sometimes exploit the correspondence between musical rhythm and objects in motion (continuous rapid notes, for example, can evoke waves or a stream). Most important is the ability of music to create mood, emotion, and atmosphere: an agitated theme may represent conflict; a lyrical melody may symbolize love. However, music alone makes no definite reference to ideas, emotions, and objects; it cannot identify anything. What lets us fully grasp a composer's source or inspiration is the title or a verbal explanation.

The aim of most program music is expression more than mere description; Beethoven, for example, referred to his Sixth Symphony (the *Pastoral*) as "an expression of feeling rather than painting." Even the most "realistic" episodes in program music can also serve a purely musical function; and one can generally appreciate a descriptive piece as pure music, without knowing its title or program. (We can enjoy the lyrical theme of Tchaikovsky's *Romeo and Juliet* without associating it with young love.) The forms used for program music are similar to those used for nonprogram music, or **absolute music;** thus a programmatic work can be heard simply as a rondo, fugue, sonata form, or theme and variations. But our pleasure may be greater when we can relate music to literary or pictorial ideas, and romantic composers were well aware of this. Occasionally, they even added programs or titles to finished works; and both musicians and audiences in the romantic era liked to read stories into all music, whether intended by the composer or not.

Most romantic program music was written for piano or orchestra. The main forms of orchestral program music are the program symphony, the concert overture, the symphonic poem (tone poem), and incidental music.

A **program symphony** is a composition in several movements—as its name implies, a symphony with a program. Usually, each movement has a descriptive title. For example, Berlioz's *Fantastic Symphony* has five movements: (1) *Reveries, Passions,* (2) *A Ball,* (3) *Scene in the Country,* (4) *March to the Scaffold,* and (5) *Dream of a Witches' Sabbath.* (This work is discussed in Section 11.)

A *concert overture* has one movement, usually in sonata form. The romantic concert overture was modeled after the opera overture, a one-movement composition that establishes the mood of an opera. But the concert overture is *not* intended to usher in a stage work; it is an independent composition. Well-known concert overtures include Mendelssohn's *Hebrides* Overture and Tchaikovsky's *Romeo and Juliet* Overture-Fantasy (which is studied in Section 14) and *Overture 1812.*

A *symphonic poem,* or *tone poem,* is also in one movement. Symphonic poems take many traditional forms—sonata form, rondo, or theme and variations—as well as irregular forms. This flexibility of form separates the symphonic poem from the concert overture, which is usually in sonata form. Franz Liszt developed the symphonic poem in the late 1840s and 1850s, and it became the most important type of program music after 1860. Well-known tone poems include *Les Préludes* (1854) and *Hamlet* (1858), by Liszt; *Danse macabre* (1874), by Camille Saint-Saëns (1835–1921); and *The Sorcerer's Apprentice* (1897), by Paul Dukas (1865–1935). A leading composer of tone poems at the end of the nineteenth century was Richard Strauss (1864–1949). His tone poems—characterized by brilliant orchestration—inlcude *Don Juan* (1888), *Till Eulenspiegel* (1895), and *Also sprach Zarasthustra* (*So Spoke Zoroaster;* 1896), which was used in the film *2001: A Space Odyssey.* In the late nineteenth century, symphonic poems became an important form for nationalism in music. In Section 12, we'll consider a nationalistic tone poem, Smetana's *Moldau,* which depicts a river of Bohemia (a region which became part of the modern Czech Republic) as it winds through the countryside.

Incidental music is music to be performed before and during a play. It is "incidental" to the staged drama, but it sets the mood for certain scenes. Interludes, background music, marches, and dances are all incidental music (as are today's movie scores). Mendelssohn's incidental music for *A Midsummer Night's Dream* includes his famous *Wedding March.*

11 Hector Berlioz

Hector Berlioz (1803–1869), one of the first French romantic composers and a daring creator of new orchestral sounds, was born in a small town near Grenoble. His father, a physician, sent him to Paris to study medicine, but he was "filled with horror" by the dissecting room and shocked his parents by abandoning medicine to pursue a career in music. He studied at the Paris Conservatory, haunted the opera house, and composed.

When he was twenty-three, Berlioz was overwhelmed by the works of Shakespeare and also fell madly in love with a Shakespearean actress, Harriet Smithson, to whom he wrote such wild, impassioned letters that she considered him a lunatic and refused to see him. To depict his "endless and unquenchable passion," Berlioz wrote the *Symphonie fantastique (Fantastic Symphony)* in 1830, which startled Parisians by its sensationally autobiographical program, its amazingly novel orchestration, and its vivid depiction of the weird and diabolical.

In 1830, too, Berlioz won the Prix de Rome (the Rome Prize), subsidizing two years' study in Rome; when he returned to Paris, he finally met and married Harriet Smithson—after she had attended a performance of the *Fantastic Sym-*

Hector Berlioz.

phony and realized that it depicted her. (They separated, however, after only a few years.)

Berlioz's unconventional music irritated the opera and concert establishment. To get a hearing for his works, he had to arrange concerts at his own expense—an enormous undertaking which drained him financially, physically, and emotionally. Although he had a following of about 1,200 who faithfully bought tickets to his concerts, this was not enough support for a composer of difficult, monumental works requiring hundreds of performers. Berlioz turned to musical journalism, becoming a brilliant and witty music critic who tried to convince the Parisians that music was not merely entertainment but dramatic emotional expression.

Outside France, Berlioz's stock was higher. After 1840, he was in demand throughout Europe, conducting his own and others' music. As one of the first great conductors, he influenced a whole generation of musicians. But his last years were bitter; he was passed over for important positions and honors and composed very little during the six years before his death at sixty-five.

Berlioz's Music

"The prevailing qualities of my music," wrote Berlioz, "are passionate expressiveness, inner fire, rhythmic drive, and unexpectedness." Above all, Berlioz's music sounds unique. It includes abrupt contrasts, fluctuating dynamics, and many changes in tempo.

As an orchestrator, Berlioz was extraordinarily imaginative and innovative. At a time when the average orchestra had about sixty players, he often assembled hundreds of musicians to achieve new power, tone colors, and timbres. His melodies are often long, irregular, and asymmetrical, taking unexpected turns. Most of his works are for orchestra, or orchestra with chorus and vocal soloists; all are dramatic and programmatic. He invented new forms: his "dramatic symphony" *Romeo and Juliet* (1839) is for orchestra, chorus, and vocal soloists; and his "dramatic legend" *The Damnation of Faust* (1846) combines opera and oratorio. He also wrote three operas and a grandiose, monumental Requiem (1837).

Berlioz knew he was a pioneer; he wrote of the Requiem, "I have seen one man listening in terror, shaken to the depths of his soul, while his next neighbor could not catch an idea, though trying with all his might to do so."

Symphonie fantastique (Fantastic Symphony; 1830)

The astonishing *Symphonie fantastique (Fantastic Symphony)*, a five-movement program symphony (we'll study its fourth and fifth movements), is a romantic manifesto. Both the music and Berlioz's program reflect the twenty-six-year-old composer's unrequited passion for the actress Harriet Smithson:

> A young musician of extraordinary sensibility and abundant imagination, in the depths of despair because of hopeless love, has poisoned himself with opium. The drug is too feeble to kill him but plunges him into a heavy sleep accompanied by weird visions. His sensations, emotions, and memories, as they pass through his affected mind, are transformed into musical images and ideas. The beloved one herself becomes to him a melody, a recurrent theme *(idée fixe)* which haunts him continually.

A single melody, which Berlioz called the **idée fixe**, or *fixed idea*, is used to represent the beloved. When introduced in the first movement—*Reveries, Passions*—it sounds, in Berlioz's description, "passionate but at the same time noble and shy."

It appears in all five movements and unifies the contrasting episodes of the symphony. This recurrence of the same theme in every movement of a symphony was a striking novelty in Berlioz's day. The theme changes in character during the work. For example, in the second movement—*A Ball*—it is transformed into a waltz, and in the third movement—*Scene in the Country*—it is played against an agitated countermelody.

Another innovation in the symphony is its use of a very large and colorful orchestra: piccolo, 2 flutes, 2 oboes, English horn, 2 clarinets, 4 bassoons, 4 French horns, 2 cornets, 2 trumpets, 3 trombones, 2 tubas, 4 timpani, bass drum, snare drum, cymbals, bells (chimes), 2 harps, and strings. (Beethoven, for one, had not used the English horn, tuba, bells, cornet, or harp in his symphonies.) Berlioz saves the heaviest orchestration for the last two movements, where he depicts the fantastic and diabolical. Though the macabre and supernatural had long been dealt with in opera (in Mozart's *Don Giovanni*, for example), this is their first expression in an important symphony.

Fourth Movement: *March to the Scaffold*
Allegretto non troppo

He dreams that he has murdered his beloved, that he has been condemned to death and is being led to the scaffold. The procession moves forward to the sounds of a march that is now somber and fierce, now brilliant and solemn, in which the muffled sounds of heavy steps give way without transition to the noisiest outbursts. At the end the *idée fixe* returns for a moment, like a last thought of love interrupted by the death blow.

Brief Set:
CD 3 30

Basic Set:
CD 5 **32**

"The *March to the Scaffold* is fifty times more frightening than I expected," Berlioz gleefully observed after the first rehearsals of the *Fantastic Symphony*. It is not until this fiendish fourth movement that all the brass and percussion instruments enter the action. Berlioz creates a menacing atmosphere with the opening orchestral sound, a unique combination of muted French horns, timpani tuned a third apart, and basses playing pizzicato chords.

Two contrasting themes alternate within *March to the Scaffold*. The first theme, described as "somber and fierce" in Berlioz's program, is introduced by cellos and basses and moves down the scale for two octaves. This scalewise melody appears both in minor and in major, and is combined with countermelodies. It is also inverted, moving upward rather than downward. The second theme, described as "brilliant and solemn" in the program, is a syncopated march tune blared by the brasses and woodwinds. At the end of the march a solo clarinet begins to play the *idée fixe* but is savagely interrupted by a very loud chord representing the fall of the guillotine's blade. The following string pizzicato may well have been intended to suggest the bouncing of the severed head.

Listening Outline to be read while music is heard   **Brief Set: CD 3** Basic Set: CD 5

BERLIOZ, *Symphonie Fantastique*

Fourth Movement: *March to the Scaffold*

Allegretto non troppo

2 flutes, 2 oboes, 2 clarinets, 4 bassoons, 2 trumpets, 2 cornets, 4 French horns, 3 trombones, 2 tubas, timpani, bass drum, snare drum, cymbals, 1st violins, 2d violins, violas, cellos, double basses

(Duration, 4:48)

| 30 | 32 | 0:00 | | **1.** Timpani, pizzicato basses, ***pp***; syncopations in muted French horns, ***p***, crescendo to ***ff*** chord. |
| 31 | 33 | 0:27 | 0:00 | **2. a.** Basses and cellos alone, ***ff***, downward scalewise melody, minor, decrescendo. |

0:41	0:14	b.	Downward melody repeated with countermelody in high bassoons.
0:54	0:27	c.	High violins, *f*, downward melody, major, accompanied by staccato lower strings. Sudden *ff*. Melody repeated by violins, *f*.
1:19	0:52	d.	Staccato bassoons, *p*, together with pizzicato strings, minor, decrescendo to *pp*, quick crescendo to
32 34 1:39	0:00	**3.**	Brasses and woodwinds, *f*, syncopated march tune, major. March tune repeated.

2:04	0:25	**4. a.**	Very loud brass and woodwind fanfare introduces
2:11	0:32	b.	Splintered downward melody, pizzicato and bowed strings, staccato winds, minor. Pizzicato violins and timpani, crescendo to
2:22	0:43	c.	Brasses, woodwinds, *f*, syncopated march tune, major, active string accompaniment. March tune repeated.
2:46	1:07	d.	Very loud brass and woodwind fanfare introduces
2:54	1:15	e.	Splintered downward melody, pizzicato and bowed strings, staccato winds, minor.
3:02	1:23	f.	Brasses, *mf*, shortened downward melody repeated on higher pitches, active string accompaniment, crescendo.
3:16	1:37	**5. a.**	Whole orchestra, downward melody, *ff*, timpani, cymbals, minor, decrescendo to *pp*.
3:27	1:48	b.	Sudden *ff*, whole orchestra, upward scalewise melody, major, timpani, cymbals.

Staccato strings alone, orchestral punctuation, *ff*, excited dotted rhythm in strings, repeated figure in brasses and woodwinds; downward staccato strings, *ff*, lead to

4:01	2:22	c.	Wind and string chords alternate, *f*, decrescendo to *pp*. Sudden *ff*, full orchestra.
33 35 4:14	0:00	d.	Solo clarinet, *idée fixe*,

interrupted by

4:24	0:10	e.	Short orchestral chord, *ff* (fall of guillotine blade) and string pizzicato (bouncing of severed head), powerful timpani roll, *ff*, brasses and woodwinds *f*, repeated major chord, strings, *ff*, cymbals, ending chord by full orchestra, *ff*.

Fifth Movement: *Dream of a Witches' Sabbath*
Larghetto; Allegro

Basic Set:
CD 5 **36**

He sees himself at a witches' sabbath in the midst of a hideous crowd of ghouls, sorcerers, and monsters of every description, united for his funeral. Strange noises, groans, shrieks of laughter, distant cries, which other cries seem to answer. The melody of the loved one is heard, but it has lost its character of nobleness and timidity; it is no more than a dance tune, ignoble, trivial, and grotesque. It is she who comes to the sabbath! . . . A howl of joy greets her arrival.... She participates in the diabolical orgy.... The funeral knell, burlesque of the *Dies irae*. Witches' dance. The dance and the *Dies irae* combined.

Dream of a Witches' Sabbath is the most "fantastic" movement of the symphony; it depicts a series of grotesque events. Its slow, hushed introduction (larghetto) immediately draws the listener into the realm of the macabre and supernatural, evoking "strange noises, groans, shrieks of laughter" and "distant cries." Eerie tremolos in high muted strings and menacing low tones of cellos and basses begin a succession of fragmentary ideas in starkly contrasting tone colors, registers, and dynamics. In the exploratory spirit of his romantic age, Berlioz dared to create sounds that are weird rather than conventionally pleasing.

36 0:00

37 1:39

In the allegro section, the beloved is revealed to be a witch. Her theme, the once "noble and timid" *idée fixe*, is transformed into a dance tune that is "trivial and grotesque." Played shrilly by a high-pitched clarinet, the tune moves in quick notes decorated by trills.

38 3:22

A "funeral knell" of sonorous bells lends an awesome atmosphere to the next part of the movement. Tubas and bassoons intone a solemn low melody in long, even notes.

This melody is the medieval chant *Dies irae (Day of wrath)*, traditionally sung in the mass for the dead. Berlioz quotes it here as a symbol of eternal damnation.

Soon the chant melody is shifted up to a high register and played by woodwinds and pizzicato strings in a quick dancelike rhythm.

39   3:54

Thus Berlioz dared to parody a sacred chant by transforming it into a trivial tune, as he had just done moments earlier with the *idée fixe*.

Berlioz conveys the frenzy of a witches' dance in a fuguelike section. The fugue subject (the witches' dance) is introduced by the lower strings and then imitated by other instruments.

40   5:14

41   7:52

A crescendo builds to a powerful climax in which the rapid witches' dance, played in the strings, is set against the slower-moving *Dies irae*, proclaimed by the brasses and woodwinds. This musical nightmare ends in an orgy of orchestral power.

 # Nationalism in Nineteenth-Century Music

During the nineteenth century, Europeans felt strongly that their homelands merited loyalty and self-sacrifice. These nationalistic feelings were awakened during the upheavals of the French Revolution and the Napoleonic Wars (1789–1815), when French armies invaded much of Europe. In many countries, military resistance to Napoleon aroused the citizens' sense of national identity. Common bonds of language, culture, and history were strengthened, since now battles were fought by soldiers drawn from the general population—not by mercenaries, as in the past. Patriotic feeling was intensified, too, by romanticism, which glorified love for one's national heritage.

As a revolutionary political movement, nationalism led to the unification of lands—like Germany and Italy—that had previously been divided into tiny states. It spurred revolts in countries under foreign rule, such as Poland and Bohemia (later part of the Czech Republic).

Nationalism was a potent cultural movement as well, particularly regarding language. In lands dominated by foreign powers, the national language was used increasingly in textbooks, newspapers, and official documents. For example, in Bohemia there was a revival of the Czech language, which before 1800 had lost ground to the German spoken by Austrian rulers. By the 1830s and 1840s, important textbooks on astronomy and chemistry were written in Czech, and there were many collections of Czech folk poetry. In every land, the "national spirit" was felt to reside in the "folk," the peasantry. The national past became a subject of intense historical investigation, and there was new enthusiasm for folk songs, dances, legends, and fairy tales.

Nationalism influenced romantic music, as composers deliberately gave their works a distinctive national identity. They used folk songs and dances and created original melodies with a folk flavor. Nationalist composers wrote operas and program music inspired by the history, legends, and landscapes of their native lands. Their works bear titles like *Russian Easter* Overture (Rimsky-Korsakov), *Finlandia* (Sibelius), and *Slavonic Dances* (Dvořák). But a genuine feeling of national style does not come merely through the use of folk songs or patriotic subjects. A piece of music will *sound* French, Russian, or Italian when its rhythm, tone color, texture, and melody spring from national tradition. There were regional traits in music before the romantic period, but never had differences of national style been emphasized so strongly or so consciously.

In these revolutionary times, musical compositions could symbolize nationalist yearnings and sometimes stirred audiences to violent political demonstrations. The Italian opera composer Giuseppe Verdi deliberately chose librettos that fanned public hatred for Austrian overlords; censors constantly pressured him to change scenes that might be interpreted as anti-Austrian or antimonarchical. A twentieth-century parallel occurred when the Nazis banned performances of Smetana's symphonic poem *The Moldau* in Prague, the composer's home city.

The strongest impact of nationalism was felt in lands whose own musical heritage had been dominated by the music of Italy, France, Germany, or Austria. During the romantic period, Poland, Russia, Bohemia, the Scandinavian countries, and Spain produced important composers whose music had a national flavor. Early in the nineteenth century, Chopin transformed his native Polish dances into great art. After about 1860, groups or "schools" of composers consciously declared their musical independence and established national styles. Among the leading musical nationalists were Mussorgsky, Rimsky-Korsakov, and Borodin from Russia; Smetana and Dvořák from Bohemia; Edvard Grieg (1843–1907) from Norway; Jean Sibelius (1865–1957) from Finland; and Isaac Albéniz (1860–1909) from Spain.

An important national school is the Russian, which created highly distinctive music. The opera *A Life for the Tsar,* by Mikhail Glinka (1804–1857), laid the groundwork for a national style, and in the 1860s five young men—now known as the *Russian five*—formed a true national school. They were Mily Balakirev

(1837–1910), César Cui (1835–1918), Alexander Borodin (1833–1887), Nikolai Rimsky-Korsakov (1844–1908), and Modest Mussorgsky (1839–1881). Remarkably, all but Balakirev began as amateurs, and most of them held nonmusical jobs. Mussorgsky was the most original of the Russian five, and his opera *Boris Godunov* is a masterpiece of musical nationalism.

Nationalism had an impact on American music as well. Around the middle of the nineteenth century, the leading nationalist composer in the United States was Louis Moreau Gottschalk (1829–1869), the first American concert pianist to gain international recognition. Born in New Orleans and trained in Paris, Gottschalk used African American, Cuban, and Puerto Rican melodies and rhythms in such works as *Bamboula: African-American Dance* and the symphony *A Night in the Tropics* (1858–1859). During the 1890s and the first decade of the twentieth century, Edward MacDowell (1860–1908)—composer, pianist, and teacher—was the outstanding musical figure in America. His best-known compositions incorporating American folk material are the orchestral work *Indian Suite* (1896)—based on Native American melodies—and a set of piano pieces called *Woodland Sketches* (1896). A leading American composer and conductor of band music was John Philip Sousa (1854–1932) whose works include *The Stars and Stripes Forever.*

We'll turn now to a famous nationalistic work, *The Moldau.*

The Moldau (1874), by Bedřich Smetana

Brief Set:
CD 3 34

Basic Set:
CD 6 1

Bedřich Smetana (1824–1884) was the founder of Czech national music. His works are steeped in the folk music and legends of his native Bohemia. But he grew up when Bohemia was under Austrian domination, and in this repressive atmosphere his musical nationalism could make little headway; he emigrated to Sweden in 1856.

In 1862, when Austria had made some liberal concessions, Smetana returned to Prague. He was active as a composer, pianist, conductor, and teacher and wrote *The Bartered Bride,* his most famous opera. At age fifty, he became completely deaf, but some of his finest works followed, including *Má Vlast (My Country,* 1874–1879), a cycle of six symphonic poems. His last years were blighted by syphilis, and he died at sixty in an asylum.

"Today I took an excursion to the St. John Rapids where I sailed in a boat through huge waves. . . . The view of the landscape was both beautiful and grand." Smetana's trip inspired his symphonic poem *The Moldau,* which depicts Bohemia's main river as it flows through the countryside. This orchestral work, part of the cycle *Má Vlast (My Country),* is both a romantic representation of nature and a display of Czech nationalism. It was written in three weeks shortly after Smetana became deaf. *The Moldau's* fresh, optimistic mood gives no hint of the composer's anguish and despair. Smetana wrote the following program to preface his score:

> The composition depicts the course of the river, beginning from its two small sources, one cold the other warm, the joining of both streams into one, then the flow of the Moldau through forests and across meadows, through the countryside where merry feasts are celebrated; water nymphs dance in the moonlight; on nearby rocks can be seen the outline of ruined castles, proudly soaring into the sky. The Moldau swirls

through the St. John Rapids and flows in a broad stream toward Prague. It passes Vyšehrad [where an ancient royal castle once stood], and finally the river disappears in the distance as it flows majestically into the Elbe.

The Moldau has contrasting musical sections that represent scenes and episodes described in the program. Hunting along the riverbank is suggested by horn fanfares, a peasant wedding by a rustic polka—the Bohemian dance—and a moonlit night by shimmering woodwinds and a serene melody in high muted strings. An expansive recurring folklike theme symbolizes the river. Smetana unifies the symphonic poem by running notes evoking the movement of water, sometimes rippling, sometimes turbulent.

Listening Outline to be read while music is heard | Brief Set: CD 3   Basic Set: CD 6

3 9

SMETANA, *The Moldau*

Allegro commodo non agitato (unhurried allegro, not agitated), sextuple meter ($\frac{6}{8}$), E minor

Piccolo, 2 flutes, 2 oboes, 2 clarinets, 2 bassoons, 4 French horns, 2 trumpets, 3 trombones, tuba, timpani, bass drum, triangle, cymbals, harp, 1st violins, 2d violins, violas, cellos, double basses

(Duration, 11:35)

Two springs

34 **1** 0:00

1. a. Flutes, *p*, running notes. Harp, pizzicato violins.

Clarinets, *p*, join, running notes.

b. Lower strings, *p*, running notes lead to

The river

35 **2** 1:10   0:00

2. Violins, songlike river theme, minor key. Running-note accompaniment in strings.

1:39   0:29   River theme extended.

Forest hunt

36 **3** 3:00

3. a. French horns and trumpets, *f*, hunting calls. Strings, running notes. Crescendo to *ff*.

b. Decrescendo to *ppp*.

Peasant wedding

37 4 3:57 **4. a.** Strings, *p*, polka.

Crescendo to *f*, triangle strokes.
b. Decrescendo to *ppp*, melody descends.

Moonlight dance of water nymphs

38 5 5:19 0:00 **5. a.** Woodwinds, *pp*, sustained tones. Flutes, *p*, running notes lead to
    5:42 0:23 **b.** High muted violins, *pp*, serene legato melody, flutes and harp accompany, *p*.
    6:58 1:39 **c.** Brasses, *pp*. Gentle staccato chords join accompaniment to violin melody.
    7:36 2:17 **d.** Crescendo. Woodwinds, running notes lead to

The river

    7:59 2:40 **6.** Violins, river theme. Running-note accompaniment in strings.

The rapids

39 6 8:40 **7. a.** Full orchestra, *ff*. Brasses, timpani roll, piccolo, cymbal crashes.
    b. Strings, *pp*. Quick crescendo.

The river at its widest point

40 7 9:53 0:00 **8.** Full orchestra, *ff*, river theme in major key. Faster tempo.

Vyšehrad, the ancient castle

    10:21 0:28 **9. a.** Brasses and woodwinds, *ff*, hymnlike melody. Cymbal crashes.
    b. Decrescendo. Violins, *ppp*. Full orchestra, *ff*, closing chords.

13 Antonin Dvořák

Antonin Dvořák (1841–1904) followed Smetana as the leading composer of Czech national music. He infused his symphonies and chamber music with the spirit of Bohemian folk song and dance.

Dvořák's father was a poor innkeeper and butcher in a small town near Prague. After working in his father's butcher shop, Dvořák left home at the age of sixteen to study music in Prague. For years he earned a meager living by playing in an opera orchestra under Smetana's direction. He was little known as a composer until his works came to the attention of the German master Brahms, who recommended Dvořák to his own publisher: "I took much pleasure in the works of Dvořák of Prague. If you play them through, you will enjoy them as much as I have done. Decidedly he is a very talented man."

From this time on—Dvořák was then about thirty-six—his fame spread rapidly. He was invited several times to England, where the melodiousness of his symphonies, chamber music, Slavonic dances, and choral works appealed to the English love for folk music and the countryside. Although Dvořák rarely quoted actual folk tunes, his works breathe a folk quality and express a cheerful, direct personality.

In 1892, Dvořák went to New York, where he was to spend almost three years as director of the National Conservatory of Music. He received a salary of $15,000, about twenty times what he was earning as a professor at the Prague Conservatory. Besides his urban impressions, Dvořák learned about the American heartland by spending a summer in Spillville, Iowa, where there was a colony of Czechs.

Dvořák encouraged American composers to write nationalistic music. He had become interested in Native American melodies and African American spirituals, which he learned about from his student Harry T. Burleigh, a black composer and baritone. Dvořák told a reporter from the New York *Herald* that in the spirituals he had "found a secure basis for a new national musical school. America can have her own music, a fine music growing up from her own soil and having its own character—the natural voice of a free and great nation."

In 1895 Dvořák returned to his homeland and rejoined the faculty of the Prague Conservatory, becoming its director six years later.

Symphony No. 9 in E Minor (*From the New World;* 1893)

Dvořák wrote his *New World* Symphony, Symphony No. 9 in E Minor, during his first year in the United States. One of the best known of all symphonies, it glorifies the American and the Czech folk spirit. Its popular character grows out of Dvořák's use of syncopations, ***pentatonic*** (five-note) *scales,* and modal scales often found in folk music. Colorful orchestration and melodious thematic material add to the attractiveness of the *New World* Symphony. Its four contrasting movements are unified through quotation of thematic material: themes from the first movement are recalled in the second and third movements, and the finale brings back themes from all three preceding movements. We'll examine the first movement.

First Movement: Adagio (slow introduction); Allegro molto

Brief Set:
CD 3 41

The slow introduction to the first movement builds great tension and contains an ominous low motive foreshadowing the opening theme of the energetic allegro that follows. In the exposition of this sonata-form movement, there are three distinctive themes. The first begins in minor with a syncopated arpeggio motive that dominates the entire symphony. The dancelike second theme, also in minor, is gentler than the first and narrower in range. Dvořák shifts to a major key for the third theme, a gracious melody which resembles the spiritual *Swing Low, Sweet Chariot*. (In the listening outline this is called the *Swing Low theme,* but with no implication that Dvořák meant it to recall the spiritual.) Between these themes come beautiful bridge passages that rise to a climax and then calm down to usher in new melodic material. In his development, Dvořák concentrates on the first and third themes, which he varies and combines. The recapitulation of all three themes is followed by a coda, which brings the first movement to a climactic close.

Listening Outline *to be read while music is heard*   Brief Set: CD 3   Basic Set: CD 6

DVOŘÁK, Symphony No. 9 in E Minor *(From the New World)*

First Movement: Adagio (slow introduction); Allegro molto

Sonata form, duple meter ($\frac{2}{4}$), E minor

Piccolo, 2 flutes, 2 oboes, 2 clarinets, 2 bassoons, 4 French horns, 2 trumpets, 3 trombones, timpani, 1st violins, 2d violins, violas, cellos, double basses

(Duration: 9:00)

Adagio (slow introduction)

41 8 0:00   **1. a.** Cellos, *pp*, downward phrases. French horns.

0:32   **b.** Flute, *p*, downward phrases.
0:55   **2. a.** Strings, *ff*, alternate with timpani, woodwinds, horns, *ff*.
       b. Cellos and basses, *pp*.
       c. High woodwinds alternate with low strings, bass motive.
       d. Full orchestra, crescendo, timpani roll, violin tremolo, *pp*.

**Allegro molto
EXPOSITION
First theme**

42 9 1:53   **1. a.** Horns, arpeggio motive. Woodwinds, *p*, playful rhythm, minor key.

       b. Oboes, arpeggio motive. Woodwinds, playful rhythm.
       c. Strings, *ff*, arpeggio motive developed. Crescendo.

Bridge

43 **10** 2:25		**2. Brasses,** *ff*, arpeggio motive. Strings, playful rhythm developed. Decrescendo.

Second theme

| 44 **11** 2:57 | **3. a.** Flute and oboe, *p*, dancelike tune. |

b. Violins, *ppp*, dancelike tune developed, crescendo to *f*. Decrescendo.

Third theme

| 45 **12** 4:03 | **4. a.** Flute, *p*, *Swing Low* theme, major. |

b. Violins, *Swing Low* theme. Crescendo to *ff*, full orchestra.

DEVELOPMENT

46 **13** 4:32	0:00	**1.** Strings, decrescendo.
4:45	0:13	**2. a.** Horn, *p*, *Swing Low* motive, piccolo. Crescendo.
		b. Trumpets, *f*, *Swing Low* motive. Trombones, *f*, arpeggio motive. Horns, *ff*. Strings, *ff*.
		c. Trombones, *ff*, arpeggio motive. High violins, *ff*. Rhythm quickens.
5:52	1:20	**3.** Oboes, *p*, arpeggio motive, flute. Crescendo.

RECAPITULATION
First theme

47 **14** 6:08	0:00	**1. a.** Horns, *mf*, arpeggio motive. Woodwinds, *p*, playful rhythm, minor.
		b. Oboes, arpeggio motive. Woodwinds, *p*, playful rhythm.
		c. Strings, *ff*, arpeggio motive developed. Descrescendo.

Second theme

6:48	0:40	**2. a.** Flute, *p*, dancelike tune.
		b. Woodwinds, *p*, dancelike tune. Strings, dancelike tune developed, crescendo to *ff*. Descrescendo.

Third theme

7:50	1:42	**3. a.** Flute, *p*, *Swing Low* theme, major.
		b. Violins, *Swing Low* theme. Crescendo.

Coda

8:18	2:10	**1.** Full orchestra, *fff*. *Swing Low* and arpeggio motives, minor.
		2. Repeated chords, *ff*, at end.

14 Peter Ilyich Tchaikovsky

Peter Ilyich Tchaikovsky (1840–1893), the most famous Russian composer, started his career as a government clerk and began to study music theory at the relatively late age of twenty-one. His progress in music was rapid, however. After graduating from the St. Petersburg Conservatory, he became a professor of harmony at the Moscow Conservatory and composed furiously: a symphony, an opera, a tone poem, and—by the age of thirty—his first great orchestral work, *Romeo and Juliet.*

The year 1877 was dramatic for Tchaikovsky. He married, disastrously and apparently only to conceal his homosexuality; attempted suicide two weeks after the wedding; and had a nervous collapse. (He and his wife separated and never saw each other again.) But in 1877 he also acquired a wealthy benefactress, Nadezhda von Meck, with whom he had a curious but intimate friendship—they corresponded but did not meet. Madame von Meck gave him an annuity that allowed him to leave the conservatory and devote himself to composition; fourteen years later, he was deeply hurt when she cut off the annuity and stopped writing to him.

During these years, Tchaikovsky achieved success conducting his own works throughout Europe (and, in 1891, in the United States), but he always remained a spiritually troubled man. In 1893, nine days after conducting the premiere of his Symphony No. 6 *(Pathétique)*—which ends unconventionally with a slow, despairing finale—he died at the age of fifty-three.

Tchaikovsky's Music

Tchaikovsky thought of himself as "*Russian* in the fullest sense of the word," but his style was influenced by French, Italian, and German music as well as Russian folk song. His works are much more in the western tradition than those of his contemporaries, the Russian five. He fused national and international elements to produce intensely subjective and passionate music.

Peter Ilyich Tchaikovsky.

Among his most popular orchestral compositions are Symphonies No. 4 (1877), No. 5 (1888), and No. 6 (*Pathétique*, 1893); Piano Concerto No. 1 in B Flat Minor (1875); the Violin Concerto (1878); and the overture-fantasy *Romeo and Juliet*, which we'll study. He wrote some of the best scores for ballet—*Swan Lake* (1876), *The Sleeping Beauty* (1889), and *The Nutcracker* (1892)—and the spirit of ballet permeates much of his music. He also wrote eight operas and the orchestral show-pieces *Marche slave* and *Overture 1812*.

Romeo and Juliet, Overture-Fantasy

Basic Set:

CD 5 **46**

Romantic composers felt an artistic kinship to Shakespeare because of his passionate poetry, dramatic contrasts, and profound knowledge of the human heart. Some of Shakespeare's plays inspired many of the finest nineteenth-century compositions. Among these were *Macbeth* and *Othello*, set as operas by Verdi; and *A Midsummer Night's Dream*, depicted in incidental music by Mendelssohn. *Romeo and Juliet* inspired both a "dramatic symphony" by Berlioz and a concert overture by Tchaikovsky.

Tchaikovsky composed *Romeo and Juliet* at twenty-nine, near the beginning of his musical career. Now one of the best-loved orchestral works, *Romeo and Juliet* was a dismal failure at its premiere in 1870. "After the concert we dined. . . . No one said a single word to me about the overture the whole evening. And yet I yearned so for appreciation and kindness." Tchaikovsky decided to revise the overture. He composed a new theme to represent Friar Laurence, adopting a suggestion of his friend Balakirev. Despite this, the work remained unappreciated. Only about twenty years later, after further revisions, did *Romeo and Juliet* achieve worldwide popularity.

Like Shakespeare's play, Tchaikovsky's *Romeo and Juliet* glorifies a romantic love powerful enough to triumph over death. Tchaikovsky captures the essential emotions of Shakespeare's play without defining each character or the exact course of events. Highly contrasted themes are used to express the conflict between family hatred and youthful love. Tchaikovsky also depicts the gentle, philosophical Friar Laurence, intermediary between the lovers and the harsh outside world.

Romeo and Juliet is a concert overture consisting of a slow introduction and a fast movement in sonata form. (Tchaikovsky's title—*Overture-Fantasy*—implies that he treated the musical material in a free and imaginative way.) We can enjoy *Romeo and Juliet* as an exciting orchestral piece without knowing the play. However, a new dimension is added to our listening experience when we associate the music with the drama.

Tchaikovsky opens the overture with the Friar Laurence theme, a solemn, hymnlike melody.

Introduction

46 0:00

First theme

47 5:16

As the slow introduction unfolds, brooding strings set an atmosphere of impending tragedy. The clash of swords and the anger of the feud between the Montagues and the Capulets are suggested by the violent first theme of the allegro.

Bridge
48 6:38

Syncopations, rushing strings, and massive sounds create enormous excitement. The exposition continues with a bridge section that brings a sudden *p*, a calmer mood, and a slower rhythm.

Second theme
49 7:28

The second theme of the exposition, a tender love theme, is expressively scored for English horn and muted violas.

Pulsating Melody
50 7:48

It is followed by a gently pulsating melody in the muted violins.

Development
51 10:32

Recapitulation
52 12:35

The development section focuses mainly on the feud theme and the Friar Laurence theme. In the recapitulation, the gently pulsating melody precedes the love theme, which now has a new exultant character as Tchaikovsky envelops the listener in opulent sound. There are long crescendos as the melody is led higher and higher to ever more passionate orchestral climaxes.

Pulsating Melody
53 12:57

In the coda, Tchaikovsky transforms the love theme into a song of mourning, while timpani softly beat the rhythm of a funeral march.

Love theme
54 13:34

Coda
55 16:24

Then, a new hymn and a tender reminiscence of the love theme suggest that Romeo and Juliet are reunited in death.

15 Johannes Brahms

Johannes Brahms (1833–1897) was a romantic who breathed new life into classical forms. He was born in Hamburg, Germany, where his father made a precarious living as a bass player. At thirteen, Brahms led a double life: during the day he studied piano, music theory, and composition; at night he played dance music in cafés.

On his first concert tour, when he was twenty, Brahms met Robert Schumann and Schumann's wife Clara, who were to shape the course of his artistic and personal life. The Schumanns listened enthusiastically to Brahms's music, and Robert published an article hailing young Brahms as a musical messiah.

As Brahms was preparing new works for an eager publisher, Robert Schumann had a nervous collapse and tried to drown himself. When Robert Schumann was committed to an asylum, leaving Clara with seven children to support, Brahms came to live in the Schumann home. He stayed for two years, helping to care for the children when Clara was on tour and becoming increasingly involved with Clara, who was fourteen years older than he. It is not known what passed between them (they destroyed many of their letters). Afterward, they remained lifelong friends, and Brahms never married.

Brahms desperately wanted to become conductor of the Philharmonic Orchestra in Hamburg. When he was passed over for the post in 1862, he left Hamburg for Vienna, where he spent the rest of his life. He conducted a Viennese musical society and introduced many forgotten works of Bach, Handel, and Mozart. He had a wide knowledge of older music (which made him extremely critical of his own work), edited baroque and classical compositions, and collected music manuscripts.

Brahms always lived frugally, though he earned a good income from publishers and from playing and conducting his works. He hid a shy, sensitive nature behind a mask of sarcasm and rudeness; yet he could be very generous to talented young musicians (Dvořák was one).

When Clara Schumann lay dying in 1896, his grief found expression in the haunting *Four Serious Songs;* not long after, it was discovered that he had cancer.

Johannes Brahms.

On March 7, 1897, he dragged himself to hear a performance of his Fourth Symphony; the audience and orchestra gave him a tremendous ovation. Less than a month later, at age sixty-four, he died.

Brahms's Music

Brahms created masterpieces in all the traditional forms (except opera): four symphonies; two concertos for piano, one for violin, and one for violin and cello; piano pieces; over 200 songs; some magnificent choral music, such as the *German Requiem*; and numerous chamber pieces. His work is personal in style but rooted in the music of Haydn, Mozart, and Beethoven. Brahms reinterpreted classical forms using the harmonic and instrumental resources of his own time.

Brahms's music has a range of moods, but particularly an autumnal feeling and lyrical warmth. Lyricism pervades even the rich polyphonic textures he was so fond of, and he was always able to make them sound natural and spontaneous. One scholar has observed, "It is possible to sing every Brahms movement from beginning to end as though it were a single, uninterrupted melody." His music is rhythmically exciting, with contrasting patterns and syncopations (the use of "2 against 3"—one instrument playing two even notes to a beat while another plays three—is one of his trademarks). It also has a special quality of sound: rich, dark tone colors and, in the orchestral works, a blending of the instrumental choirs that favor mellow instruments like the viola, clarinet, and French horn.

All his music radiates the security and solidity of a complete master who fully justified Robert Schumann's prediction of greatness.

Symphony No. 3 in F Major, Op. 90

Shortly after completing his Third Symphony during the summer of 1883, Brahms was visited in Vienna by the younger composer Antonin Dvořák, whose *New World* Symphony was studied in Section 13. "At my request to hear something of his new symphony," Dvořák reported later, Brahms "was immediately forthcoming" and played two movements on the piano. Dvořák's reaction was ecstatic: "What magnificent melodies are to be found! It is full of love, and it makes one's heart melt."

The briefest of Brahms's symphonies, the Third Symphony is characterized by thematic connections among its four movements and pervasive contrasts between major and minor. At the very end of the last movement, for example, the impassioned opening of the symphony, which combines F major and F minor harmonies, is gently recalled in F major. We'll focus on the third movement, a short interlude between the slow movement and the climactic finale.

Third Movement: Poco Allegretto

Brief Set:
CD 3 48

Instead of using a rapid scherzo, standard in nineteenth-century symphonies, Brahms created a unique kind of third movement that is moderate in tempo (poco allegretto) and intensely lyrical in character. Brahms enhanced the intimate mood

Basic Set:

CD 6 **15**

of the poco allegretto by reducing the size of its orchestra, which does not include the trumpets, trombones, contrabassoon, and timpani heard in the outer movements. Though romantic in style, the poco allegretto reflects Brahms's strong feeling for musical tradition: it has the triple meter, ternary form, and relaxed middle section typical of third movements in classical symphonies.

The poco allegretto contains one of Brahms's most haunting melodies. (Recently, this melody was used by Carlos Santana and Dave Matthews in their song "Love of My Life," from the album *Supernatural*.) The melody's yearning mood is created by its minor key and by its three-note dotted-rhythmic motive (long-short-long) that rises on the upbeat and falls on the downbeat.

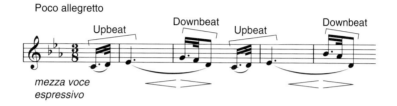

In the poco allegretto, Brahms creates variety by presenting the main melody in different tone colors and in successively higher octaves. In the opening section (A), the melody is introduced by the cellos, playing expressively (*espressivo*) and softly in an intimate "half voice" (*mezza voce*). Then it is heard in the violins, and—after an interlude—in the flute. When the opening section returns (A'), Brahms reorchestrates the main melody, which now is presented first by the French horn, then by the oboe, and finally by the high violins, as the climax of the movement.

The middle section (B) brings a shift from minor to major, from yearning to graciousness. Section B opens with a lilting waltzlike melody in the winds, accompanied by a staccato syncopated figure in the cellos. Later, Brahms creates a contrast of mood and tone color by introducing a new expressive melody in the strings alone. A hushed transition smoothly links the middle section (B) to the concluding A' section. Brahms prepares beautifully for the return of the main melody with an upward sequence in the woodwinds of the melody's initial dotted-rhythm motive (long-short-long). After the reorchestrated repetition of the opening section (A'), we hear a coda in which the dotted-rhythm motive flowers into an eloquent phrase that epitomizes the movement's intense lyricism.

Listening Outline to be read while music is heard · Brief Set: CD 3 · Basic Set: CD 6

BRAHMS, Symphony No. 3 in F Major

Third Movement: Poco allegretto

A B A' Coda form, triple meter (3/8), C minor

2 flutes, 2 oboes, 2 clarinets, 2 bassoons, 2 French horns, 1st violins, 2d violins, violas, cellos, double basses

(Duration, 5:45)

A (minor)

48 15 0:00

1. a. Cellos, **p**, yearning main melody in minor, middle register, strings and pizzicato basses accompany; ends with incomplete cadence.

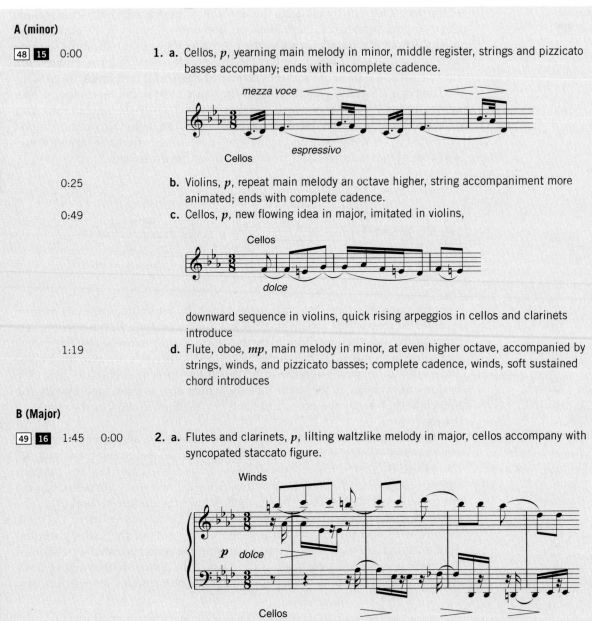

0:25

b. Violins, **p**, repeat main melody an octave higher, string accompaniment more animated; ends with complete cadence.

0:49

c. Cellos, **p**, new flowing idea in major, imitated in violins,

downward sequence in violins, quick rising arpeggios in cellos and clarinets introduce

1:19

d. Flute, oboe, **mp**, main melody in minor, at even higher octave, accompanied by strings, winds, and pizzicato basses; complete cadence, winds, soft sustained chord introduces

B (Major)

49 16 1:45   0:00

2. a. Flutes and clarinets, **p**, lilting waltzlike melody in major, cellos accompany with syncopated staccato figure.

1:59   0:14

b. Winds, **p**, repeat waltzlike melody, violins and cellos accompany with syncopated staccato arpeggios.

2:13   0:28

c. Strings alone, **pp**, new expressive legato melody, crescendo to **f**, decrescendo to **p**.

2:32   0:47

d. Winds, soft waltzlike melody, accompanied by syncopated staccato arpeggios in violins and cellos.

2:46   1:01   **e.** Strings alone, *p*, expressive legato melody, decrescendo to *pp*, woodwinds, *p*, upward sequence of opening dotted-rhythm motive from main melody, sustained chord.

A′ (Minor)

50 17   3:23   0:00   **3. a.** French horn, *p*, main melody in minor, middle register, strings and pizzicato basses accompany, ends with incomplete cadence.

3:50   0:27   **b.** Oboe, *p*, repeats main melody an octave higher, strings accompany, ends with complete cadence.

4:12   0:49   **c.** High bassoon, *p*, flowing idea in major, imitated in clarinet, downward sequence in winds; clarinets and bassoons alone, quick rising arpeggios in strings and flute introduce

4:43   1:20   **d.** Violins, *mp*, main melody in minor at even higher octave, accompanied by strings, winds, pizzicato basses; complete cadence.

Coda

5:08   1:45   **4. a.** Winds, soft sustained chords.
5:17   1:54   **b.** Strings and winds, *pp*, repeat soft chords, eloquent rising and falling phrase in dotted rhythm, cadence;

soft sustained wind chord, pizzicato strings close movement.

Giuseppe Verdi

Giuseppe Verdi (1813–1901), the most popular of all opera composers, was born in a tiny Italian village. He began studying music in a nearby town, Busseto, where he was taken into the home of a wealthy patron who later also supported his education in Milan. When he completed his studies, he became municipal music director in Busseto and married his patron's daughter; three years later he returned to Milan with the score of his first opera, *Oberto*.

Oberto was produced at La Scala (Milan's opera house) in 1839, had a modest success, and brought Verdi a contract for more operas. Then disaster struck: his wife and their two children died. Verdi managed to complete his next opera, but it was a failure and, in despair, he vowed to compose no more.

What changed his mind was a libretto about the ancient Jews exiled from their homeland. Verdi was an ardent nationalist who yearned for a free and united Italy and saw the Jews as a symbol of the oppressed Italians. He quickly composed *Nabucco* (*Nebuchadnezzar,* king of Babylon, 1842), which was a huge success. From then on, Verdi and his operas came to symbolize Italian independence. (The cry *Viva Verdi* also stood for the patriotic slogan "*Vittorio Emmanuele, Re D'Italia*"—*Victor Emmanuel, king of Italy.*)

In his late thirties, Verdi composed *Rigoletto* (1851), *Il Trovatore* (1853), and *La Traviata* (1853). Although the public loved them, critics were often scandalized by their subject matter—they seemed to condone rape, suicide, and free love. But Verdi was fiercely independent and himself lived openly with his second wife for ten years before marrying her.

After these successes had made him wealthy, Verdi bought an estate in Busseto; and in 1861 he was elected to the first parliament that convened after Italy had become a nation. In his later years he wrote *Aïda* (1871), *Otello* (1887), and—at the age of seventy-nine—his final opera, *Falstaff* (1893).

Verdi's Music

Verdi composed not for the musical elite but for a mass public whose main entertainment was opera. He wanted subjects that were "original, interesting, . . . and passionate; passions above all!" Almost all his mature works are serious and end unhappily; they move quickly and involve extremes of hatred, love, jealousy, and fear, and his powerful music underlines the dramatic situations.

Expressive vocal melody is the soul of a Verdi opera. There are many duets, trios, and quartets; and the chorus plays an important role. Verdi's style became

Giuseppe Verdi.

less conventional as he grew older; his later works have greater musical continuity, less difference between aria and recitative, more imaginative orchestration, and richer accompaniments. His last three operas—*Aïda, Otello,* and *Falstaff*—are perhaps his greatest. *Falstaff,* his final work, is a comic masterpiece which ends with a carefree fugue to the words *All the world's a joke!*

Rigoletto (1851)

Verdi dared to create an operatic hero out of a hunchback, a court jester named Rigoletto, whose only redeeming quality is an intense love for his daughter Gilda. Rigoletto's master, the licentious Duke of Mantua, has won Gilda's love while posing as a poor student. He seduces the innocent girl, causing Rigoletto to plot his death. Gilda loves the Duke even after learning about his dissolute character, and she ultimately sacrifices her own life to save his. Vice triumphs in this powerful drama.

Act III:
La donna è mobile   *(Woman is fickle)*

Basic Set:
CD 6 **19**

Act III of *Rigoletto* contains one of the most famous and popular pieces in opera, the Duke's aria *La donna è mobile.* The scene is an inn where the Duke has come to meet Maddalena, the voluptuous sister of Sparafucile, a cutthroat whom Rigoletto has hired to kill the Duke. *La donna è mobile (Woman is fickle)*, carefree and tuneful, expresses the Duke's pleasure-loving personality. Even before the premiere of *Rigoletto,* which was to take place in Venice, Verdi knew this aria would be a hit; so that it would not leak out during rehearsals and be sung by every Venetian gondolier, he waited until the last possible moment before giving the manuscript to the tenor who was to sing it.

19 0:00
Aria. Orchestra introduces Duke's melody.

La donna è mobile	Woman is fickle
Qual piuma al vento,	Like a feather in the wind,
Muta d'accento	She changed her words
E di pensiero.	And her thoughts.
Sempre un amabile	Always a lovable
Leggiadro viso,	And lovely face,
In pianto o in riso,	Weeping or laughing,
È menzognero.	Is lying.
La donna è mobile, ecc.	Woman is fickle, etc.

1:05
Orchestra. Duke's melody repeated with different words.

È sempre misero	The man's always wretched
Chi a lei s'affida,	Who believes in her,
Chi le confida	Who recklessly entrusts
Mal cauto il core!	His heart to her!
Pur mai non sentesi	And yet one who never
Felice appieno	Drinks love on that breast
Chi su quel seno	Never feels
Non liba amore!	Entirely happy!
La donna è mobile, ecc.	Woman is fickle, etc.

17 Giacomo Puccini

Giacomo Puccini (1858–1924), who created some of the best-loved operas, came from a long line of composers and church organists. During his student years at Milan University, he lived a hand-to-mouth existence; but the success of his first opera, shortly after his graduation, brought him commissions and an annual income from Italy's leading music publisher. In 1893, he became known throughout Italy for his opera *Manon Lescaut;* after 1896, he was wealthy and world-famous from the enormous success of *La Bohème. Tosca* (1900) and *Madama Butterfly* (1904) were also very popular; he died before finishing his last opera, *Turandot,* which was completed by a friend.

Puccini's marvelous sense of theater has given his operas lasting appeal. His melodies have short, memorable phrases and are intensely emotional; he used the orchestra to reinforce the vocal melody and to suggest mood. To achieve unity and continuity, he minimized the difference between aria and recitative and used the same material in different acts. Puccini was very much concerned with the literary and dramatic qualities of his librettos; he spent as much time polishing them as composing the music and often demanded endless changes from the librettists. Some of his operas (notably *Tosca*) reflect an artistic trend of the 1890s known as *verismo*—that is, *realism,* or the quality of being "true to life." But they also feature exoticism: *Madama Butterfly* is set in Japan and *Turandot* in China, and both have melodic and rhythmic elements derived from the music of those countries.

La Bohème (1896)

La Bohème (Bohemian Life) takes place in the Latin Quarter of Paris around 1830. Its hero is Rodolfo, a young poet who shares a garret with Marcello, a painter; Colline, a philosopher; and Schaunard, a musician. Mimi, the heroine, is a poor, tubercular seamstress who lives in the same building. The simple, touching plot has been aptly summarized as "boy meets girl, boy loses girl, boy and girl are reunited as girl dies of consumption in boy's arms and curtain falls." Everyone can relate to the characters and emotions of this enchanting opera. Though there are many realistic touches in this picture of bohemian life, it is seen through a romantic haze.

Brief Set:
CD 3 [51]
CD 5 video clip

Basic Set:
CD 6 [22]
CD 9 Video clip

Act I:
Scene between Rodolfo and Mimi through Rodolfo's aria
Che gelida manina (How cold your little hand is!)

Brief Set:
CD 3 [51]

Basic Set:
CD 6 [22]

Mimi and Rodolfo meet and fall in love toward the end of Act I, which takes place on a cold Christmas eve. Her candle has blown out, and she knocks on his door asking for a light. At Rodolfo's insistence, Mimi enters, but she suddenly has a coughing fit and faints in his arms. She revives after Rodolfo sprinkles water on her face. She then leaves, her candle alight, but she returns immediately, for she has lost her key. They must search for the key in the dark—a gust of wind has extinguished their candles. When their hands touch, Rodolfo sings the aria *Che gelida manina (How cold your little hand is!)*.

Puccini's sensuous melody casts a glow over the entire scene. His music has an improvisatory quality, with many fluctuations of tempo that reflect changes of mood and dramatic action. In the musical dialogue between Mimi and Rodolfo, Puccini easily alternates between speechlike and melodic phrases. When Mimi enters, the orchestra murmurs a touching phrase—Mimi's theme—which suggests her fragility and tenderness. Mimi's coughing fit is evoked by agitated music and her fainting by a poignant oboe solo. When Mimi returns to get her key, she introduces a new melody in a faster tempo.

Rodolfo's aria begins simply, in conversational repeated tones for the words *Che gelida manina*. Then the melody becomes warmer and higher as he offers to tell her about himself *(chi son, e che faccio)*. The climactic phrase of the aria, sung to the words *Talor dal mio forziere (My hoard of treasure is stolen by two thieves: a pair of beautiful eyes)*, is the love theme of the opera. Following the excerpt studied here, Mimi responds to Rodolfo with a poetic description of herself in the aria *Mi chiamano Mimi (They call me Mimi)* and the two join in a love duet that closes Act I.

Veronica Villaroel as Mimi and Roberto Aronica as Rodolfo in a performance of *La Bohème* at the San Francisco Opera.

Giacomo Puccini.

Vocal Music Guide to be read while music is heard   `Brief Set: CD 3`   `Basic Set: CD 6`

PUCCINI, *La Bohème*

Excerpt from Act I

`51` `22`   0:00

Flute melody.	(Rodolfo closes the door, sets his light on the table, and tries to write. But he tears up the paper and throws the pen down.)	

		Rodolfo
	Non sono in vena.	I'm not in the mood.
	(A timid knock at the door.)	
Speechlike.	*Chi è la?*	Who's there?
		Mimi
	Scusi.	Excuse me.
		Rodolfo
	Una donna!	A woman!
		Mimi
Mimi's theme,	*Di grazia, me si è spento*	I'm sorry . . . my light
pp, in	*Il lume.*	Has gone out.
orchestra.		
		Rodolfo
		(opens the door)
	Ecco.	Here.
		Mimi
	(in the doorway, with a candlestick and a key)	
	Vorrebbe . . . ?	Would you . . . ?
		Rodolfo
	S'accomodi un momento.	Come in for a moment.
		Mimi
	Non occorre.	There's no need.
		Rodolfo
	La prego, entri.	Please . . . come in.
	(Mimi enters, has a fit of coughing.)	
		Rodolfo
	Si sente male?	You're not well?
		Mimi
	No . . . nulla.	No . . . it's nothing.
		Rodolfo
	Impallidisce!	You're pale!

<table>
<tbody>
<tr><td></td><td colspan="2" align="center">**Mimi**</td></tr>
<tr><td></td><td>*È il respir . . . quelle scale . . .*</td><td>I'm out of breath . . . the stairs . . .</td></tr>
</tbody>
</table>

1:04
Oboe.

(She faints, and Rodolfo is just in time to support her and help her to a chair. The key and the candlestick fall from her hands.)

Rodolfo
Ed ora come faccio? — Now what shall I do?

Pizzicato
violins.

(He gets some water and sprinkles her face.)

Così. — So.
Che viso d'ammalata! — How ill she looks!

1:28
Staccato
muted strings.

(Mimi comes to.)

Si sente meglio? — Are you better now?

Mimi
Sì. — Yes.

Rodolfo
Qui c'è tanto freddo. — It's so cold here.
Segga vicino al fuoco. — Come and sit by the fire.
(He helps her to a chair by the stove.)
Aspetti . . . un po' di vino. — Wait . . . some wine.

Mimi
Grazie. — Thank you.

Rodolfo
A lei. — Here.

Mimi
Poco, poco. — Just a little.

Rodolfo
Così. — There.

Mimi
Grazie. — Thank you.

Rodolfo
(Che bella bambina!) — (What a lovely creature!)

Mimi
(rising)
Ora permetta — Now, please,
Che accenda il lume. — Relight my candle.
E tutto passato. — I'm better now.

Rodolfo
Tanta fretta. — Such a hurry!

Mimi

Sì
(Rodolfo lights her candle for her.)

Yes.

Mimi

Grazie. Buona sera.

Thank you. Good evening.

Rodolfo

Buona sera.
(Mimi goes out, then reappears at the door.)

Good evening.

2:28
A little faster.
Tuneful vocal
melody.

Mimi

Oh! sventata, sventata,
La chiave della stanza
Dove l'ho lasciata?

Oh! foolish me! . . .
Where have I left
The key to my room?

Rodolfo

Non stia sull'uscio:
Il lume vacilla ai vento.
(Her candle goes out.)

Don't stand in the door:
The wind makes your light flicker.

Mimi

O Dio! Torni ad accenderlo.
(Rodolfo rushes to her with his light, but when he reaches the door, his candle goes out, too. The room is dark.)

Heavens! Will you relight it?

Rodolfo

Oh Dio! Anche il mio s'è spento.

There . . . Now mine's out, too.

Mimi

Ah! E la chiave ove sarà?

Ah! And where can my key be?

Rodolfo

Buio pesto!

Pitch dark!

Mimi

Disgraziata!

Unlucky me!

Rodolfo

Ove sarà?

Where can it be?

Mimi

Importuna è la vicina . . .

You've a bothersome neighbor . . .

Rodolfo

Ma le pare!

Not at all.

Mimi

Importuna è la vicina . . .

You've a bothersome neighbor . . .

Rodolfo

Cosa dice, ma le pare!   What do you mean? Not at all!

Mimi

Cerchi.   Search.

Rodolfo

Cerco.   I'm searching.
(They both grope on the floor for the key.)

Mimi

Ove sarà?   Where can it be?

Rodolfo

(finds the key, pockets it)
Ah!   Ah!

Mimi

L'ha trovata?   Did you find it?

Rodolfo

No.   No.

Mimi

Mi parve . . .   I thought . . .

Rodolfo

In verità!   Truthfully!

Mimi

Cerca?   Are you hunting?

Rodolfo

Cerco.   I'm hunting for it.

3:50
Orchestra
alone, tempo
slows.

(Guided by her voice, Rodolfo pretends to search as he draws closer to her.
Then his hand meets hers, and he holds it.)

Mimi
(surprised)
Ah!   Ah!
(They rise. Rodolfo continues to hold Mimi's hand.)

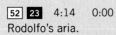 4:14   0:00
Rodolfo's aria.

Rodolfo

Che gelida manina,   How cold your little hand is!
Se la lasci riscaldar.   Let me warm it for you.

Che ge - li - da ma - ni - na, se la la - sci ri - scal - dar.

Harp.

Cercar che giova? Al buio	What's the use of searching?
Non si trova. Ma per fortuna	We'll never find it in the dark.
È una notte di luna,	But luckily there's a moon,
E qui la luna l'abbiamo vicina.	And she's our neighbor here.
Aspetti, signorina,	Just wait, my dear young lady,
Le dirò con due parole chi son,	And meanwhile I'll tell you
Chi son, e che faccio, come vivo.	In a word who and what I am.
Vuole?	Shall I?
(Mimi is silent)	
Chi son? Chi son? Son un poeta.	Who am I? I'm a poet.
Che cosa faccio? Scrivo.	My business? Writing.
E come vivo? Vivo.	How do I live? I live.
In povertà mia lieta	In my happy poverty
Scialo da gran signore	I squander like a prince
Rime ed inni d'amore.	My poems and songs of love.
Per sogni e per chimere	In hopes and dreams
E per castelli in aria	And castles in air,
L'anima ho milionaria.	I'm a millionaire in spirit.

6:42   2:28

Love theme

Talor dal mio forziere	My hoard of treasure
Ruban tutti i gioielli	Is stolen by two thieves:
Due ladri: gli occhi belli.	A pair of beautiful eyes.

Ta - lor dal mio for - zie - re ____ ru-ban tut-ti i gio-

iel - li due la - dri: gli oc - chi bel - li.

V'entrar con voi pur ora	They came in now with you.
Ed i miei sogni usati,	And all my lovely dreams,
Ed i bei sogni miei	My dreams of the past,
Tosto si dileguar!	Were soon stolen away.
Ma il furto non m'accora	But the theft doesn't upset me,
Poichè, poichè v'ha preso stanza	Since the empty place was filled
La speranza.	With hope.
Or che mi conoscete	Now that you know me,
Parlate voi, deh! parlate.	It's your turn to speak.
Chi siete? Vi piaccia dir?	Who are you? Will you tell me?

Luciano Pavarotti, Tenor, Singing the Part of Rodolfo in Puccini's La Bohème

The operatic tenor Luciano Pavarotti is probably the world's best-known classical performer. During the late twentieth century, he appeared frequently not only on operatic and concert stages, but in stadiums, on television, and in movies. In June 1993, more than 500,000 fans attended his performance in New York's Central Park and millions more watched on television. In July 1994, he participated in the second of several "Three Tenors" concerts—together with Placido Domingo and José Carreras——in Dodger Stadium, Los Angeles; it was seen on television by an estimated billion people in 107 countries.

Pavarotti was born in Modena, Italy, in 1935. As a boy, he listened avidly to recordings of tenors brought home by his father, an amateur singer. At nineteen Pavarotti began serious vocal study, and at twenty-five he won a singing competition that led to his operatic debut as Rodolfo in Puccini's *La Bohème.* Pavarotti later recalled the thrill of "singing for the first time with a full orchestra. All those years of studying and thinking of yourself as a singer—there is always an orchestra there, in your mind. But the first time it is *really* there—it is an experience, impossible to describe to someone who hasn't dreamed for years of becoming an opera singer." From then on his career rose rapidly: he made his debut at Milan's La Scala—Italy's most important opera house—in 1965, and his debut at New York's Metropolitan Opera in 1968.

Pavarotti has written insightfully on his approach to Rodolfo's aria *Che gelida manina* from Puccini's *La Bohème* (included in the video clip found on the CD sets). "For me the most difficult notes for the tenor in *La Bohème* are in Act I when Rodolfo sings to Mimi, '*Che gelida manina.*' . . . Those quiet low notes must have a big rich sound—a steady, pure sound that floods the opera house. They may be soft notes, but they must have behind them all your power as a singer. They must have the same amount of support from your diaphragm that you give the big notes."

Pavarotti is inspired by the great conductors with whom he works: they reveal deeper aspects of the drama, and they influence him to try new approaches "to passages I had sung many times in a different way." When the conductor Carlos Kleiber directed a performance of *La Bohème* at La Scala, "difficult places in the score that had caused me problems before, I found myself singing without effort. As an example, it is traditional to transpose '*Che gelida manina*' down a half tone to spare the tenor the difficult high C at the end. Although few people were aware of it, most of the great tenors of the past had done this. But Kleiber made me sing the aria in the original key. Somehow I soared up to the high C with no strain. It may seem like superstition, but I am sure that was due to the inspiration of working with him and the way he conducted." No one has done more than Pavarotti to introduce listeners to the magic of opera.

18 Richard Wagner

Few composers have had so powerful an impact on their time as Richard Wagner (1813–1883). His operas and artistic philosophy influenced not only musicians but also poets, painters, and playwrights. Such was his preeminence that an opera house of his own design was built in Bayreuth, Germany, solely for performances of his music dramas.

Wagner was born in Leipzig into a theatrical family. His boyhood dream was to be a poet and playwright, but at fifteen he was overwhelmed by Beethoven's music and decided to become a composer. He taught himself by studying scores and had almost three years of formal training in music theory, but he never mastered an instrument. As a student at Leipzig University he dueled, drank, and gambled; and a similar pattern persisted later—he always lived shamelessly off other people and ran up debts he could not repay.

During his early twenties, Wagner conducted in small German theaters and wrote several operas. In 1839, he decided to try his luck in Paris, then the center of grand opera; he and his wife spent two miserable years there, during which he was unable to get an opera performed and was reduced to musical hackwork. But he returned to Germany in 1842 for the production of his opera *Rienzi* in Dresden; the work was immensely successful, and he was appointed conductor of the Dresden Opera. Wagner spent six years at this post, becoming famous as both an opera composer and a conductor.

When the revolutions of 1848 were sweeping across Europe, Wagner's life in Dresden had become difficult because of accumulated debts. Hoping that a new society would wipe these out and produce conditions favorable to his art, he participated in an insurrection and then had to flee to Switzerland. For several years he did no composing; instead, he worked out his theories of art in several essays and completed the librettos to *Der Ring des Nibelungen (The Ring of the Nibelung)*, a set of four operas based on Nordic myth, which would occupy him for twenty-five years. He interrupted his work on the music for *The Ring* to compose *Tristan and Isolde* (1857–1859).

Richard Wagner.

Wagner had several bad years after finishing *Tristan*. His opera *Tannhäuser* was a failure at the Paris Opera; *Tristan* was abandoned by the Vienna Opera; and he was hounded by creditors. In 1864, however, he was rescued by King Ludwig of Bavaria, an eighteen-year-old fanatical Wagnerite who put all the resources of the Munich Opera at his disposal. At this time, Wagner fell in love with Cosima von Bülow, who was Liszt's daughter and the wife of Hans von Bülow, Wagner's close friend and favorite conductor; she gave birth to two of Wagner's children while still married to von Bülow. Shortly after Wagner's first wife died, he married Cosima.

In Wagner, musical genius was allied with selfishness, ruthlessness, rabid German nationalism, and absolute self-conviction. He forged an audience for his complex music dramas from a public accustomed to conventional opera. The performance of the *Ring* cycle at Bayreuth in 1876 was perhaps the single most important musical event of the century; and—though some critics still found his music too dissonant, heavily orchestrated, and long-winded—he was generally acclaimed the greatest composer of his time. A year after completing *Parsifal* (1877–1882), his last opera, he died in Venice at age sixty-nine.

Wagner's Music

For Wagner, an opera house was a temple in which the spectator was to be overwhelmed by music and drama. He wrote his own librettos, based on medieval Germanic legends and myths and with characters that are usually larger than life—heroes, gods, demigods. He called his works *music dramas* rather than operas, but today many people find his music more exciting than his rather static drama.

Within each act, there is a continuous musical flow (Wagner called this "unending melody") instead of traditional arias, recitatives, and ensembles; and there are no breaks where applause can interrupt. His vocal line, which he conceived as "speech song," is inspired by the rhythms and pitches of the German text. Wagner revolutionized opera by shifting the focus from voice to orchestra and treating the orchestra symphonically. His expanded and colorful orchestration expresses the drama and constantly develops, transforms, and intertwines musical ideas. (And the orchestral sound is so full that only very powerful voices can cut through it.) In the orchestra—and sometimes in the vocal parts—he uses brief, recurrent musical themes called *leitmotifs (leading motives)*. A **leitmotif** is a short musical idea associated with a person, an object, or a thought in the drama.

The tension of Wagner's music is heightened by chromatic and dissonant harmonies—ultimately, these led to the breakdown of tonality and to the new musical language of the twentieth century.

Die Walküre (The Valkyrie; 1856)

Die Walküre (The Valkyrie) is the second and most widely performed of the four music dramas in Wagner's gigantic cycle *Der Ring des Nibelungen (The Ring of the Nibelung)*. Despite its gods, giants, dwarfs, and magic fire, the *Ring* is really about Wagner's view of nineteenth-century society. He uses Nordic mythology to warn that society destroys itself through lust for money and power. It is fitting that Wagner first sketched the plot of the *Ring* in 1848, the year that brought Marx's *Communist Manifesto* and revolutions throughout Europe.

Act I:
Love scene (conclusion)

Brief Set:
CD 4 ☐1☐

Basic Set:
CD 6 26

Wagner builds the first act of *Die Walküre* to an overwhelming climax in the passionate love scene that concludes it. To grasp this scene fully, it's helpful to know what has happened earlier in the *Ring*.

A Nibelung dwarf, Alberich, has stolen gold belonging to the Rhinemaidens, mermaids in the Rhine River. From this gold, the dwarf fashions a ring that can bestow immense power on anyone who wears it and is willing to renounce love. The dwarf, in turn, is robbed of his prize by Wotan, king of the gods. (*Wednesday* comes from *Wotan's day*.) Soon Wotan himself is forced to give up the ring; he then lives in fear that Alberich will get it back and use it to destroy him. Hoping to protect himself, he surrounds his castle, Valhalla, with a bodyguard of heroes. His daughters, goddesses called *Valkyries,* swoop over battlefields on horseback and bear away the dead bodies of the bravest warriors. The Valkyrie of the opera's title is Brünnhilde, Wotan's favorite daughter.

Johanna Meier as Sieglinde and Jon Vickers as Siegmund in the love scene from Act I of *Die Walküre.*

Seeking to create a hero who can help him regain the ring, Wotan takes a human wife and fathers the Volsung twins—a son, Siegmund; and a daughter, Sieglinde. The twins know their father as Wälse, unaware that he is the god Wotan. They are separated as children when a hostile clan kidnaps Sieglinde and kills their mother. Siegmund becomes an outlaw and Sieglinde is eventually forced to marry the warrior-chief Hunding, whom she hates. During the wedding feast in Hunding's home, Wotan appears, disguised as an old man dressed in gray. He thrusts a magic sword into the tree around which the house is built, and proclaims that the weapon belongs to the one who can draw it out. Hunding and his followers try but are unable to withdraw the sword.

The first act of *Die Walküre* begins as Siegmund, weaponless and pursued by enemies, unwittingly takes refuge in the house of Hunding, who is away hunting. Sieglinde and Siegmund almost immediately fall in love, unaware that they are brother and sister. Hunding returns and soon realizes that the stranger—who identifies himself as *Wehwalt (Woeful)*—is an enemy of his clan. He says that Siegmund is his guest for the night, but the next day they must do battle. Sieglinde gives her husband a sleeping potion and tells Siegmund that her shame and misery will be avenged by the hero who can withdraw the sword from the tree. As they embrace passionately, the door of the hut suddenly opens, allowing the moonlight of a beautiful spring night to shine on them.

The following excerpt occurs at the end of the love scene, when Siegmund and Sieglinde gradually become aware of their amazing resemblance to each other and finally realize that they are brother and sister. Since her beloved no longer wants to be called *Wehwalt*, Sieglinde renames him *Siegmund (Victor)*. With a powerful effort, Siegmund withdraws the sword from the tree and the lovers rapturously embrace. (The offspring of this unlawful union will be Siegfried, the human hero of the *Ring* cycle. In the mythology and folklore of many lands, heroes are often born of incestuous love.)

In the excerpt which we'll study, Wagner creates a continuous musical flow that depicts the surging passions of the lovers through frequent changes of tempo, dynamics, and orchestral color. Typically, the vocal lines range from speechlike to highly melodic and closely reflect the inflections and meaning of the text. For example, the word *Notung (Needful)*—the name of the sword—is powerfully emphasized when it is sung to the downward leap of an octave.

Several leitmotifs are heard, sometimes together. In this excerpt, the leitmotif *Valhalla*—Wotan's castle—is first presented when Sieglinde looks at Siegmund and later returns when she recalls how their father (Wotan disguised as the old man) gazed at her during her marriage feast. The very important *sword* leitmotif is barely noticeable when it first appears, as Sieglinde refers to the fire in Siegmund's eyes. It is presented *pp*, in combination with the leitmotif *Volsung* (the people to which Siegmund and Sieglinde belong). Later, the sword motive is very prominent when it is proclaimed by the brasses as Siegmund draws the sword out of the tree and as the lovers embrace during the orchestral conclusion of the act. Other leitmotifs heard in our excerpt are *love* and *spring*.

Vocal Music Guide to be read while music is heard   Brief Set: CD 4   Basic Set: CD 6

WAGNER, *Die Walküre*

Act I, Love Scene, Conclusion

(Sieglinde pushes Siegmund's hair back from his brow and looks at him with astonishment.)

Sieglinde

1 26 0:00

Wie dir die Stirn so offen steht,
der Adern Geäst in den Schläfen sich
schlingt!
Mir zagt es vor der Wonne, die mich
entzückt!

Look how your forehead broadens out,
and the network of veins winds into
your temples!
I tremble with the delight that
enchants me.

2 27 0:23
Valhalla,
French horns,
p.

Ein Wunder will mich gemahnen:
den heut zuerst ich erschaut,
mein Auge sah dich schon!

It brings something strange to my mind:
though I first saw you today,
I've set eyes on you before.

Siegmund

Ein Minnetraum gemahnt auch mich:
in heissem Sehnen sah ich dich schon!

A dream of love comes to my mind as well:
burning with longing I have seen you
before.

Sieglinde

Im Bach erblickt' ich mein eigen Bild
und jetzt gewahr ich es wieder:
wie einst dem Teich es enttaucht,
bietest mein Bild mir nun du!

In the stream I've seen my own likeness;
and now I see it again.
As once it appeared in the water
so now you show me my likeness.

Siegmund

3 28 1:26
Love, voice.

Du bist das Bild, das ich in mir barg.

You are the likeness that I hid in myself.

Sieglinde

Love, French
horn, *p.*

O still! Lass mich der Stimme lauschen:
mich dünkt, ihren Klang hört' ich als Kind.
Doch nein! Ich hörte sie neulich,
als meiner Stimme Schall
mir widerhallte der Wald.

Hush! let me listen to your voice.
Its sound, I fancy, I heard as a child,
but no! I heard it recently—
when the echo of my voice sounded
back through the forest.

Siegmund

O lieblichste Laute, denen ich lausche!   O loveliest sound for me to hear!

4 | 29 | 2:19 | 0:00
Volsung, low strings, *pp*, together with *Sword*, bass trumpet, *pp*.

Sieglinde

Deines Auges Glut erglänzte mir schon: The fire in your eyes has blazed at me before:
so blickte der Greis grüssend auf mich, als der Traurigen Trost er gab.   So the old man gazed at me in greeting when to my sadness he brought comfort.

2:28 | 0:09
Valhalla, French horns, *pp*, then strings, *pp*.

Pause

An dem Blick erkannt' ihn sein Kind, schon wollt' ich beim Namen ihn nennen!   By his look his child recognized him, I even wanted to call him by name.

Wehwalt heisst du fürwahr?   Are you really called Woeful?

Siegmund

Nicht heiss ich so, seit du mich liebst: nun walt ich der hehrsten Wonnen!   I am not called that since you love me: Now I am full of purest rapture.

Sieglinde

Und Friedmund darfst du froh dich nicht nennen?   And "Peaceful" may you not, being happy, be named?

Siegmund

Nenne mich du, wie du liebst, dass ich heisse: Name me what you love to call me.
den Namen nehm ich von dir!   I take my name from you.

Sieglinde

Doch nanntest du Wolfe den Vater?   But did you name Wolf as your father?

Siegmund

Ein Wolf war er feigen Füchsen!   A Wolf he was to craven foxes!
Doch dem so stolz strahlte das Auge, wie, Herrliche, hehr dir es strahlt, der war: Wälse genannt.   But he whose proud eyes shone as grandly as yours, you marvel, his name was "Volsa."

Sieglinde

War Wälse dein Vater, und bist du ein Wälsung,   If "Volsa" was your father and you are a "Volsung,"
stiess er für dich sein Schwert in den Stamm,   it was for you he thrust his sword into the tree—

| | | so lass mich dich heissen, wie ich dich liebe: | so let me call you by the name I love: |
| | | Siegmund: so nenn ich dich! | Siegmund (Victor)—so I name you. |

Siegmund

		Siegmund heiss ich und Siegmund bin ich!	Siegmund I am called and Siegmund I am,
		Bezeug es dies Schwert, das zaglos ich halte!	let this sword, which I fearlessly hold, bear witness.
		Wälse verhiess mir, in höchster Not	Volsa promised me that in deepest distress
4:47	2:28	fänd' ich es einst: ich fass es nun!	I should one day find it. Now I grasp it.
		Heiligster Minne höchste Not,	Holiest love's deepest distress,
		sehnender Liebe sehrende Not	yearning love's scorching desire,
		brennt mir hell in der Brust,	burn bright in my breast,
		drängt zu Tat und Tod:	urge me to deeds and death.

5 **30** 5:11
Voice,
downward
octave leaps.

		Notung! Notung! so nenn ich dich, Schwert.	"Needy," "Needy," I name you, sword.
		Notung, Notung! neidlicher Stahl!	"Needy," "Needy," precious blade,
		Zeig deiner Schärfe schneidenden Zahn:	show your sharpness and cutting edge:
		heraus aus der Scheide zu mir!	come from your scabbard to me!

6 **31** 5:42 0:00
Sword,
trumpets, ff.

(With a powerful effort, Siegmund pulls the sword from the tree, showing it to the astonished and delighted Sieglinde.)

6:00	0:18		
Volsung,		Siegmund, den Wälsung, siehst du, Weib!	You see Siegmund, the Volsung, woman!
trumpets, pp.		Als Brautgabe bringt er dies Schwert:	As wedding gift he brings this sword;
		so freit er sich	so he weds
		die seligste Frau;	the fairest of women;
		dem Feindeshaus entführt er dich so.	he takes you away from the enemy's house.
		Fern von hier folge mir nun,	Now follow me far from here,

7 **32** 6:29
Spring, voice.

| | | fort in des Lenzes lachendes Haus: | out into springtime's smiling house. |

dort schützt dich Notung, das Schwert,
wenn Siegmund dir liebend erlag!

For protection you'll have "Needy" the sword,
even if Siegmund expires with love.

Sieglinde

Bist du Siegmund, den ich hier sehe,
Sieglinde bin ich, die dich ersehnt:
die eig'ne Schwester
gewannst du zu eins mit dem Schwert!

Are you Siegmund whom I see here?
I am Sieglinde who longed for you:
your own sister
you have won and the sword as well.

Siegmund

Braut und Schwester bist du dem Bruder,
so blühe denn Wälsungen-Blut!

Wife and sister you'll be to your brother.

So let the Volsung blood increase!

8 | 33 | 7:29
Sword,
brasses, *ff.*
Passionate
orchestral
conclusion.

(He draws her to him with passionate fervor.)

In Pablo Picasso's *Three Musicians* (1921), two characters from Italian *commedia dell'arte*, Pierrot and Harlequin, are combined with a monklike figure in a two-dimensional space. A year before Picasso painted *Three Musicians* he designed the costumes for *Pulcinella* (1920), a ballet with music by Igor Stravinsky.

The Twentieth Century and Beyond

VI

"We find ourselves confronted with a new logic of music that would have appeared unthinkable to the masters of the past. This new logic has opened our eyes to riches whose existence we never suspected."

IGOR STRAVINSKY

Time-Line Twentieth Century and Beyond

(1900–2006)

Dates	Music	Arts and Letters	Historical and Cultural Events
1900–1945	Debussy, *Prelude to the Afternoon of a Faun* (1894) Webern, *Five Pieces for Orchestra* (1911–13) Schoenberg, *Pierrot lunaire* (1912) Stravinsky, *The Rite of Spring* (1913) Berg, *Wozzeck* (1917–22) Gershwin, *Rhapsody in Blue* (1924) Bessie Smith, *Lost Your Head Blues* (1926) Armstrong, *Hotter Than That* (1927) Stravinsky, *Symphony of Psalms* (1930) Still, *Afro-American Symphony* (1931) Ellington, *C-Jam Blues* (1942) Bartók, Concerto for Orchestra (1943) Copland, *Appalachian Spring* (1943–44)	Picasso, *Les Demoiselles d'Avignon* (1907) Kirchner, *Street, Berlin* (1913) Kandinsky, *Panels for Edward R. Campbell* (1914) Kafka, *The Metamorphosis* (1915) Eliot, *The Waste Land* (1922) Joyce, *Ulysses* (1922) Faulkner, *The Sound and The Fury* (1929) Picasso, *Girl before a Mirror* (1932) Lawrence, *The Migration Series* (1940–41) Camus, *The Stranger* (1942)	Freud, *Interpretation of Dreams* (1900) Einstein, special theory of relativity (1905) First World War (1914–1918) Russian Revolution begins (1917) Great Depression begins (1929) Stalin dictator of Soviet Union (1929–1953) Franklin D. Roosevelt inaugurated (1933) Hitler appointed chancellor of Germany (1933) Second World War (1939–1945) Atomic Bomb destroys Hiroshima (1945)
1945–2006	Benjamin Britten, *Young Person's Guide to the Orchestra* (1946) Cage, *Sonatas and Interludes* (1946–48) Schoenberg, *A Survivor from Warsaw* (1947) Parker, *Bloomdido* (1950) Babbitt, *Semi-Simple Variations* (1956) Bernstein, *West Side Story* (1957) Varèse, *Poème électronique* (1958) Penderecki, *Threnody: To the Victims of Hiroshima* (1960) Carter, Double Concerto (1961) The Beatles, *Sgt. Pepper's Lonely Hearts Club Band* (1967) Piazzolla, *Fugata* (1969) Crumb, *Ancient Voices of Children* (1970) Philip Glass, *Einstein on the Beach* (1976) Zwilich, *Concerto Grosso 1985* Adams, *Short Ride in a Fast Machine* (1986) Walker, *Lilacs* (1996) Reich, *You Are* (Variations; 2004) Adams, *Dr. Atomic* (2005)	Sartre, *Existentialism and Humanism* (1946) Mailer, *The Naked and the Dead* (1948) Pollock, *One* (1950) Salinger, *Catcher in the Rye* (1951) Baldwin, *Notes of a Native Son* (1955) Riley, *Hesitate* (1964) Warhol, *Campbell's Soup Cans* (1962) Frankenthaler, *Flood* (1967) Solzhenitsyn, *The Gulag Archipelago* (1974) Morrison, *Beloved* (1988) Hockney, *Thrusting Rocks* (1990) Larson, *Rent* (1996) Kiefer, *The Sky Palace* (2002) Parks, *Topdog/Underdog* (2002) Gehry, Walt Disney Concert Hall (2003) Rowling, *Harry Potter and the Half-Blood Prince* (2005)	Korean War (1950–53) Crick and Watson discover the structure of DNA (1953) Vietnam War (1955–1975) Fidel Castro becomes premier of Cuba (1959) President Kennedy assassinated (1963) American astronauts land on the moon (1969) President Nixon resigns (1974) Ronald Reagan inaugurated (1981) George Bush inaugurated (1989) Reunification of Germany (1990) Dissolution of the Soviet Union (1991) Bill Clinton inaugurated (1993) Mandela elected president of South Africa (1994) George W. Bush inaugurated (2001) Terrorist attacks in United States on September 11, 2001 War in Iraq begins (2003) George W. Bush reelected (2004) Hurricane Katrina causes flooding of New Orleans (2005)

Twentieth-Century Developments

Extremes of violence and progress marked the twentieth century. During the first half of the century, two world wars—in 1914–1918 and 1939–1945—unleashed new weapons of unprecedented destructive force. Between the wars, dictatorships and a global depression caused massive hardship. The second half of the century saw the breakup of colonial empires, an extended cold war between the United States and the Soviet Union (a nation that later dissolved), and armed conflicts around the world. At the same time, rapid economic growth propelled prosperity for many. The principle of equal rights gained ground after protracted struggles by women, African Americans, and others.

Extraordinarily accelerated developments in technology and science transformed politics and society. The Wright brothers made the first powered flight in 1903; sixty-six years later, humans walked on the moon. A flood of new technologies like sound recordings, movies, radio, satellites, computers, and the Internet triggered a continuous revolution in communications. Albert Einstein reshaped our understanding of the universe with his theory of relativity, Sigmund Freud probed the unconscious, and Francis Crick and James Watson discovered the structure of DNA, the basic material of heredity.

Rapid changes and radical breaks with earlier traditions characterized the arts. Shock as a goal was a twentieth-century phenomenon. In the decade before World War I, Isadora Duncan's modern dance clashed with conventions of classical ballet; Pablo Picasso's cubist paintings distorted figures and objects, showing them from several angles at one time; and Wassily Kandinsky's abstract paintings no longer tried to represent the visual world at all.

In the arts, as in other aspects of life, there was an increased emphasis on pluralism and diversity. Contradictory styles and tendencies coexisted, as conservative and avant-garde works appeared at the same time. Moreover, individual artists, such as Picasso and the composer Igor Stravinsky, often alternated between radical and more traditional styles.

In *Dance* (1909), by Henri Matisse, there is little sense of perspective or realistic detail. The five dancers are flattened to silhouettes, and colors are mainly limited to large areas of green, blue, and flesh tones.

In the cubist painting *Violin and Grapes* by Pablo Picasso, the violin is flattened into fragmented planes.

Girl Before a Mirror (1932) by Pablo Picasso. The young girl on the left looks at an older, troubled reflection of herself. Here, Picasso reinterprets a traditional theme: a woman seeing a death's-head in her mirror. Twentieth-century composers such as Stravinsky have also reinterpreted earlier musical forms and styles.

Summarizing such an incredibly diverse cultural landscape is difficult, yet any overview must include the following developments:

1. The United States powerfully shaped world culture and entertainment, as well as politics and economics. Cities like Paris and Vienna that had so dominated nineteenth and early twentieth-century culture were supplanted by New York and Hollywood.
2. Nonwestern cultures and thought had wide and profound effects on all the arts. Examples include the impact of African sculpture on Picasso, of Japanese design on the architect Frank Lloyd Wright, and of Indian philosophy on the composer John Cage.
3. New technologies stimulated many artists. Sculptors used such materials as plastic, fluorescent lights, and television monitors; architects called for reinforced concrete and steel girders; and musicians exploited audiotape, electric guitars, and computers.
4. Artists explored the varieties of human sexuality with extraordinary frankness.
5. The concerns of women, African Americans, and other minorities were more powerfully represented in the arts than ever before.
6. Many artists expressed alienation, antirationality, nihilism, and dehumanization in their works, partly in reaction to catastrophic wars and massacres. The antihero became a prominent feature of novels, plays, and musical compositions.

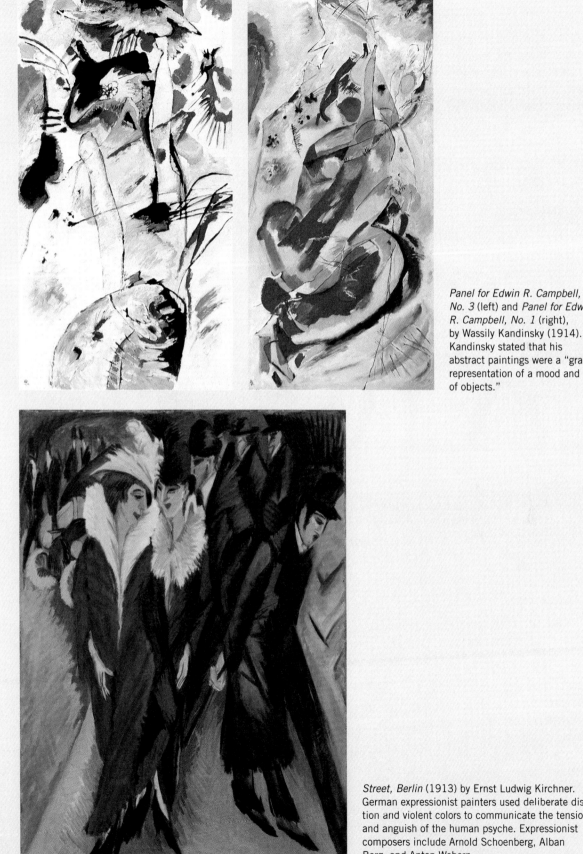

Panel for Edwin R. Campbell, No. 3 (left) and *Panel for Edwin R. Campbell, No. 1* (right), by Wassily Kandinsky (1914). Kandinsky stated that his abstract paintings were a "graphic representation of a mood and not of objects."

Street, Berlin (1913) by Ernst Ludwig Kirchner. German expressionist painters used deliberate distortion and violent colors to communicate the tension and anguish of the human psyche. Expressionist composers include Arnold Schoenberg, Alban Berg, and Anton Webern.

291

7. Since the 1960s, many painters, architects, writers, and musicians have rejected the seriousness of modernism in favor of more pluralistic approaches. "Postmodern" artists have combined different styles, blurred the boundaries between elite and popular culture, and used pre-existing images and texts from history, advertising, and the media. The pop artist Andy Warhol, for example, painted multiple Campbell's soup cans and heads of Marilyn Monroe.

Panel 58, "In the North the African American had more educational opportunities," from *The Migration Series* (1940–1941) by the history painter Jacob Lawrence. In his depictions of black experiences in the United States, Lawrence was influenced by the Harlem Renaissance, a cultural movement of the 1920s and 1930s that included African American writers, artists, and musicians. An important musical voice of this movement was William Grant Still, who often made use of spirituals, ragtime, and blues.

Musical Styles: 1900–1945

In music, as in the other arts, the early twentieth century was a time of revolt. The years following 1900 saw more fundamental changes in the language of music than any time since the beginning of the baroque era. There were entirely new approaches to the organization of pitch and rhythm and a vast expansion in the vocabulary of sounds, especially percussive sounds. Some compositions broke with tradition so sharply that they were met with violent hostility. The most famous riot in music history occurred in Paris on May 29, 1913, at the premiere of Igor Stravinsky's ballet *Le Sacre du printemps (The Rite of Spring).* Police had to be called in as hecklers booed, laughed, made animal noises, and actually fought with those in the audience who wanted to hear Stravinsky's evocation of primitive rites. One music critic complained that *The Rite of Spring* produced a "sensation of acute and almost cruel dissonance" and that "from the first measure to the last, whatever note one expects is never the one that comes. . . ." Another wrote, "To say that much of it is hideous in sound is a mild description. . . . It has no relation to music at all as most of us understand the word."

Today, we are amused by the initial failure of some music critics to understand this composition, now recognized as a masterpiece. Chords, rhythms, and percussive sounds that were baffling in 1913 are now commonly heard in jazz, rock, and music for movies and television. But the hostile critics of the early 1900s were right in seeing that a great transformation in musical language was taking place.

From the late 1600s to about 1900, musical structure was governed by certain general principles. As different as the works of Bach, Beethoven, and Brahms may be, they share fundamental techniques of organizing pitches around a central tone. Since 1900, however, no single system has governed the organization of pitch in all musical compositions. Each piece is more likely to have its own unique system of pitch relationships.

In the past, composers depended on the listener's awareness—conscious or unconscious—of the general principles underlying the interrelationship of tones and chords. For example, they relied on the listener's expectation that a dominant chord would normally be followed by a tonic chord. By substituting another chord for the expected one, a composer could create a feeling of suspense, drama, or surprise. Twentieth-century music relies less on preestablished relationships and expectations. Listeners are guided primarily by musical cues within an individual composition. This new approach to the organization of sound makes twentieth-century music fascinating. When we listen openly, with no assumptions about how tones "should" relate, this music is an adventure.

1900–1945: An Age of Musical Diversity

The range of musical styles during the first half of the twentieth century was vast. The stylistic diversity in the works of Claude Debussy, Igor Stravinsky, Arnold Schoenberg, Alban Berg, Anton Webern, Béla Bartók, Charles Ives, George Gershwin, William Grant Still, and Aaron Copland—to name only composers studied here—is a continuation and intensification of the diversity we've seen in romantic music. During the twentieth century, differences among styles were so great that composers seemed to be using different musical languages, not merely different dialects of the same language. Radical changes of style occurred even within the works of individual composers.

This great variety of musical styles reflected the diversity of life during the early twentieth century. More people were free to choose where to live, how to earn a living, and how to spend their time. The automobile, airplane, telephone, phonograph, movies, and radio all made the world more accessible and expanded the range of experiences.

Through the work of scholars and performers, a wider range of music became available. Composers drew inspiration from an enormous variety of sources, including folk and popular music, the music of Asia, Latin America, and Africa, and European art music from the Middle Ages through the nineteenth century.

Elements of folk and popular music were often incorporated within personal styles. Composers were especially attracted to unconventional rhythms, sounds, and melodic patterns that deviated from the common practice of western music. Folk music was studied more systematically than before, partly because scholars could now record the actual sounds of peasant songs. One of the greatest twentieth-century composers, Béla Bartók, was also a leading scholar of the peasant music of his native Hungary and other parts of eastern Europe. "Studies of folk music in the countryside," he wrote, "are as necessary to me as fresh air is to other people." Bartók's imagination was fired by Hungarian, Bulgarian, and Romanian folk songs, and he believed that peasant music provided "the ideal starting point for a musical renaissance." Other composers stimulated by folklore were Stravinsky, who drew on the folk songs of his native Russia; and Charles Ives, who used American revival hymns, ragtime, and patriotic songs.

During the early twentieth century, non-European music had a deep influence on the music of the west. Western composers and painters were more receptive and sympathetic to Asian and African cultures than they had been earlier. For example, in 1862, Hector Berlioz could say that "the Chinese sing like dogs howling, like a cat screeching when it has swallowed a toad." But in 1889, Debussy was delighted by the Javanese music he heard at the Paris International Exhibition. "If we listen without European prejudice to the charm of their percussion," he wrote later, "we must confess that our percussion is like primitive noises at a country fair." Echoes of the gamelan (Indonesian orchestra) can be heard in the bell-like sounds and five-tone melodic patterns of Debussy's piano piece *Pagodes* (*Pagodas*, 1903). Another French composer influenced by Asian culture was Olivier Messiaen (1908–1992); Messiaen's novel rhythmic procedures grew out of his study of Indian music.

American jazz was another non-European influence on twentieth-century composers. Musicians were fascinated by its syncopated rhythms and improvisational quality, as well as by the unique tone colors of jazz bands. Unlike a string-dominated symphony orchestra, a jazz band emphasizes woodwinds, brasses, and percussion.

Jazz elements were used in works as early as Debussy's *Golliwog's Cake-Walk* (from the suite *Children's Corner*, 1908) and Stravinsky's *Ragtime* (from *The Soldier's Tale*, 1918). But the peak of jazz influence came during the 1920s and 1930s, with works such as the ballet *La Création du monde* (*The Creation of the World*, 1923) by Darius Milhaud, the Piano Concerto (1926) by Aaron Copland, and the *Afro-American Symphony* 1931 by William Grant Still. For Americans, jazz idioms represented a kind of musical nationalism, a search for an "American sound." For European composers, the incorporation of jazz rhythms and tone colors represented a kind of musical exoticism. During the 1920s and 1930s, popular composers such as George Gershwin used jazz and popular elements within "classical" forms. Gershwin's *Rhapsody in Blue* (1924) and his opera *Porgy and Bess* (1934–1935) are well known.

Modern composers can also draw inspiration from a wider historical range of music. During the twentieth century, music from remote times was unearthed by scholars and then published, performed, and recorded. There was a rediscovery of earlier masters such as Perotin and Machaut from the medieval period, Josquin Desprez and Gesualdo from the Renaissance, and Purcell and Vivaldi from the baroque. Some important twentieth-century composers were music historians, like Anton Webern; or experts in the performance of "old" music, like Paul Hindemith.

Music from the past has been a fruitful source of forms, rhythms, tone colors, textures, and compositional techniques. Baroque dances like the gavotte and gigue and forms like the passacaglia and concerto grosso are being used again. The long-forgotten harpsichord has been put to new use in compositions such as Elliott Carter's Sonata for Flute, Oboe, Cello, and Harpsichord (1952). In the *Classical Symphony* (1917) by the Russian composer Sergei Prokofiev (1891–1953), a classical orchestra is used, and the texture is light and transparent like much late eighteenth-century music. Occasionally twentieth-century composers use themes of earlier composers, as Benjamin Britten did in *The Young Person's Guide to the Orchestra*, which is based on a theme by Henry Purcell (about 1659–1695).

Modern compositions were and still are inspired by older music, but this does not mean that they simply imitate past styles. Instead, a traditional form might be used with harmonies, rhythms, melodies, and tone colors that would have been inconceivable before the twentieth century.

Modern composers were also influenced by the music of the immediate past. Nineteenth-century composers such as Wagner, Brahms, Gustav Mahler, Richard Strauss, and Modest Mussorgsky were musical points of departure for composers of the early twentieth century. Wagner's music, in particular, was as potent an influence as Beethoven's was for romantic musicians. Composers took Wagner's style as a point of departure, or else they reacted violently against all he stood for.

Characteristics of Twentieth-Century Music

Having reviewed some of the sources of inspiration for twentieth-century music, let's now examine some of its characteristics.

Tone Color

During the twentieth century, tone color became a more important element of music than it ever was before. It often took a major role, creating variety, continuity, and mood. In Webern's Orchestral Piece, Op. 10, No. 3 (1913), for example, the use of eerie, bell-like sounds at the beginning and end is vital to the form. If this composition were altered in tone color—say, by being played on a piano—it would lose much. An orchestral work from an earlier period, like Beethoven's Fifth Symphony, suffers less in a piano arrangement.

In modern music, noiselike and percussive sounds are often used, and instruments are played at the very top or bottom of their ranges. Uncommon playing techniques have become normal. For example, the *glissando,* a rapid slide up or down a scale, is more widely used. Woodwind and brass players are often asked to produce a fluttery sound by rapidly rolling the tongue while playing. And string players frequently strike the strings with the stick of the bow, rather than draw the bow across the strings.

Percussion instruments have become prominent and numerous, reflecting the twentieth-century interest in unusual rhythms and tone colors. Instruments that became standard during the 1900s include the xylophone, celesta, and wood block, to name a few. Composers occasionally called for noisemakers—typewriters, sirens, automobile brake drums. A piano was often used to add a percussive edge to the sound of an orchestra. Composers often drew hard, drumlike sounds from the piano, in contrast to the romantics, who wanted the instrument to "sing." Besides expanding the percussion section of the orchestra, early twentieth-century composers wrote works for unconventional performing groups in which percussion plays a major role. Well-known examples are Stravinsky's *Les Noces* (*The Wedding,* 1914–1923), for vocal soloists, chorus, four pianos, and percussion; Bartók's Music for Strings, Percussion, and Celesta (1936); and Varèse's *Ionisation* (1931), which was one of the first works for percussion ensemble.

Modern orchestral and chamber works often sound transparent; individual tone colors are heard clearly. To bring out the individuality of different melodic lines that are played simultaneously, a composer would often assign each line to a different timbre. In general, there is less emphasis on blended sound than there was during the romantic period. Many twentieth-century works are written for nonstandard chamber groups made up of instruments with sharply contrasting tone colors. Stravinsky's *L'Histoire du soldat* (*The Soldier's Tale,* 1918), for example, is scored for violin, double bass, clarinet, bassoon, cornet, trombone, and percussion. Even orchestral works often sound as though they are scored for a group of soloists.

Harmony

Consonance and dissonance

The twentieth century brought fundamental changes in the way chords are treated. Up to about 1900, chords were divided into two opposing types: consonant and dissonant. A consonant chord was stable; it functioned as a point of rest or arrival. A dissonant chord was unstable; its tension demanded onward motion, or resolution to a stable, consonant chord. Traditionally, only the triad, a three-tone chord, could be consonant. All others were considered dissonant. In the nineteenth century, composers came to use ever more dissonant chords, and they treated dissonances with increasing freedom. By the early twentieth century, the traditional distinction between consonance and dissonance was abandoned in much music. A combination of tones that earlier would have been used to generate instability and expectation might now be treated as a stable chord, a point of arrival. In Stravinsky's words, dissonance "is no longer tied down to its former function" but has become an entity in itself. Thus "it frequently happens that dissonance neither prepares nor anticipates anything. Dissonance is thus no more an agent of disorder than consonance is a guarantee of security."

This "emancipation of dissonance" does not prevent composers from differentiating between chords of greater or lesser tension. Relatively mild-sounding chords may be goals of motion, while harsher chords are used for transitional sounds. But no longer is there a general principle that determines whether a chord is stable or not. It is now entirely up to the composer's discretion. "We find ourselves confronted with a new logic of music that would have appeared unthinkable to the masters of the past," wrote Stravinsky. "This new logic has opened our eyes to riches whose existence we never suspected."

New chord structures

Before 1900, there were general principles governing chord construction: certain combinations of tones were considered chords, while others were not. At the core of traditional harmony is the triad. A triad might be made up of alternate tones of a major scale, such as the first *(do)*, third *(mi)*, and fifth *(sol)*. Within a triad, there are two intervals of a third:

Although the triad often appears in twentieth-century music, it is no longer so fundamental.

Some twentieth-century composers created fresh harmonies by placing one traditional chord against another. Such a combination of two chords heard at the same time is called a *polychord.*

Copland, *Appalachian Spring*

A polychord can be heard either as a single block of sound or as two distinct layers, depending on whether the two combined chords contrast in tone color and register.

Another development in twentieth-century music was the use of chordal structures *not* based on triads. One used commonly is the *fourth chord,* in which the tones are a fourth apart, instead of a third. (From *do* to *fa,* or from *re* to *sol,* is an interval of a fourth.)

Ives, *The Cage*

Harmonic resources were also extended through the *tone cluster,* a chord made up of tones only a half step or a whole step apart. A tone cluster can be produced on a piano by striking a group of adjacent keys with the fist or forearm.

Ives, *The Majority*

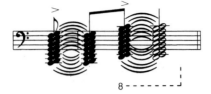

Alternatives to the Traditional Tonal System

In addition to creating new chord structures, twentieth-century composers explored alternatives to the traditional tonal system. This system of tonal gravity, known as *tonality* or *key,* governed the organization of pitch from the 1600s to about 1900. By the late nineteenth century, the gravitational pull of a central tonality had been weakened by rapid and frequent key shifts. After 1900, some composers continued to use the traditional system, but others modified it greatly and still others discarded it entirely.

Before looking at new approaches to pitch organization, recall the basic principles of the traditional tonal system. As we saw in Part I (Elements), *tonality,* or *key,* refers to the use of a central tone, scale, and chord within a composition. The central tone, called the *tonic* or *keynote (do),* is the composition's resting point. The tonic major or minor scale and the tonic triad are built on this tone. Since the tonic triad is stable and restful, compositions almost always ended with it. Next in importance to the tonic triad is the *dominant chord,* which is built on the fifth tone *(sol)* of the tonic scale. There is a special gravitational pull from the dominant chord toward the tonic chord, and the motion from dominant to tonic is the essential chord progression of the tonal system. This cadence provides a strong sense of conclusion, and traditionally it was used to round off melodies, sections, and entire pieces. In summary, the tonal system is based on a central tone, a major or minor scale, and a triad; and there is a special relationship between the tonic and dominant chords.

After 1900, this system was modified in many different ways. The new techniques of pitch organization are so varied as to resist easy generalization. Some compositions have a central tone but are missing other traditional elements, such as the tonic triad, the central major or minor scale, or the dominant-tonic relationship.

This modified approach to tonality is reflected even in the titles of compositions, which are less likely to include the terms *major* or *minor.* For example, one piano piece by Stravinsky is entitled *Serenade in A* to show that it revolves around the tone A but is not in a major or minor key.

To create fresh sounds, composers used scales other than major or minor. For example, they breathed new life into the church modes—scales that had been used widely before 1600 as well as in folk songs of every period. Other scales were borrowed from the musical tradition of lands outside western Europe, and still others were invented by composers.

Twentieth-century compositions are often organized around a central chord other than the triad. Thus, the basic chord may well be one that was considered a dissonance earlier. In some works, the traditional relationship between dominant and tonic triads is replaced by other chord relationships. Melodies, sections, or entire pieces are rounded off not by the usual dominant-tonic cadence but by other chord progressions.

Another twentieth-century approach to pitch organization is the use of two or more keys at one time: this is known as ***polytonality.*** When only two different keys are used at once—as is actually most common—the technique is called ***bitonality.*** A famous bitonal passage occurs in Stravinsky's ballet *Petrushka,* when one clarinet plays in C major and another plays in F sharp major:

In general, the greater the contrast of tone color, register, and rhythm between the different layers of sound, the more we can hear the different keys.

A further departure from tradition is ***atonality,*** the absence of tonality or key. Atonality was foreshadowed in nineteenth-century works such as Wagner's *Tristan and Isolde,* where the pull of a central key is weakened by frequent modulations and by liberal use of all twelve tones in the chromatic scale. Arnold Schoenberg wrote the first significant atonal pieces around 1908. He avoided traditional chord progressions in these works and used all twelve tones without regard to their traditional relationship to major or minor scales. But atonality is not a specific technique of composition; each atonal work is structured according to its own needs. (Though the word *atonality* is imprecise and negative, no other term has yet come into general use.)

Before long, Schoenberg felt the need for a more systematic approach to atonal composition, and during the early 1920s he developed the *twelve-tone system,* a new technique of pitch organization. This system gives equal prominence to each of the twelve chromatic tones, rather than singling out one pitch, as the tonal system does. For about twenty years, only Schoenberg and a few disciples used the twelve-tone system, but during the 1950s it came to be used by composers all over the world.

Rhythm

The new techniques of organizing pitch were accompanied by new ways of organizing rhythm. The rhythmic vocabulary of music was expanded, with increased emphasis on irregularity and unpredictability. Rhythm is one of the most striking elements of twentieth-century music; it is used to generate power, drive, and excitement.

New rhythmic procedures were drawn from many sources, including jazz, folk music from all over the world, and European art music from the Middle Ages through the nineteenth century. The syncopations and complex rhythmic combinations of jazz fired the imagination of Stravinsky and Copland. Béla Bartók used the "free and varied rhythmic structures" of east European peasant music. And irregular phrase structures in Brahms's music inspired rhythmic innovations in Schoenberg's works.

Rapidly changing meters are characteristic of twentieth-century music, whereas baroque, classical, and romantic music maintain a single meter throughout a movement or section. Before the twentieth century, beats were organized into regularly recurring groups; the accented beat came at equal time intervals. Rhythmic irregularities such as syncopations or accents on weak beats were heard against a pervasive meter. But in many twentieth-century compositions, beats are grouped irregularly, and the accented beat comes at unequal time intervals. In some modern music the meter changes with almost every bar, so that we might count *1–2–3, 1–2–3–4–5, 1–2–3–4–5, 1–2–3, 1–2–3–4, 1–2–3–4–5, 1–2–3–4–5–6, 1–2–3–4–5, 1–2, 1–2–3–4–5–6:*

Brief Set:

CD 4 23

Basic Set:

CD 7 22

Stravinsky, *Ritual of Abduction* from *The Rite of Spring*

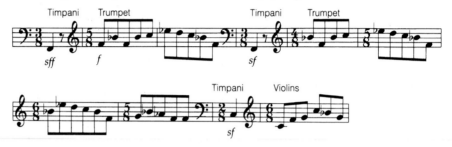

Count this again quickly and experience some of the rhythmic excitement of twentieth-century music, which often has a rapid and vigorous beat with jolting accents at unexpected times.

The rhythmic resources of twentieth-century music were also expanded through unconventional meters. Along with traditional meters such as duple and triple, twentieth-century composers used meters with five or seven beats to the measure. The pulses within a measure of any length might be grouped in irregular, asymmetrical ways. For example, eight quick pulses in a measure might be subdivided 3 + 3 + 2, or **1**–2–3–**4**–5–6–**7**–8, **1**–2–3–**4**–5–6–**7**–8. This meter, common in east European folk music, is used by Bartók in one of his *Six Dances in Bulgarian Rhythm:*

Twentieth-century music often has two or more contrasting, independent rhythms at the same time; this is called *polyrhythm.* Each part of the musical texture goes its own rhythmic way, often creating accents that are out of phase with accents in the other parts. Different meters are used at the same time. For example, one instrument may play in duple meter (*1–2, 1–2*) while another plays in triple meter (*1–2–3, 1–2–3*). Although polyrhythm occurs in classical and romantic music, it became more common and more complex after 1900. The polyrhythms of jazz strongly influenced composers in the 1920s and 1930s.

Rhythmic repetition of a group of pitches is a widely used unifying technique in twentieth-century music. Many modern compositions contain an *ostinato,* a motive or phrase that is repeated persistently at the same pitch throughout a section. The ostinato may occur in the melody or in the accompaniment. (The accompaniment for the example from Bartók's *Six Dances* has an eight-note ostinato: **1**–2–3–4–5–6–7–8.) Ostinatos can be found in music from various periods and cultures. In twentieth-century music, they usually serve to stabilize particular groups of pitches.

Melody

The new techniques of pitch and rhythmic organization that we've surveyed had a strong impact on twentieth-century melody. Melody was no longer necessarily tied to traditional chords or to major and minor keys. It could be based on a wide variety of scales, or it could freely use all twelve chromatic tones and have no tonal center. Melody today often contains wide leaps that are difficult to sing. Rhythmic irregularity and changing meters tend to make twentieth-century melodies unpredictable. They often consist of a series of phrases that are irregular in length. In general, twentieth-century music relies less than classical and romantic music on melodies that are easy to sing and remember. Melody is as rich and varied as twentieth-century music itself; neither can be classified easily.

Music and Musicians in Society

The twentieth century saw dramatic changes in how music reaches its listeners. The living room became the new "concert hall" through recordings, radio, and television. These technological advances brought music to a larger audience than ever before, besides vastly increasing the range of music available. By the end of the century, the repertoire of recorded music included not only familiar classics, but also Renaissance, early baroque, nonwestern, and unconventional twentieth-century works—music not often played in concert. Recordings of such lesser-known music multiplied with the appearance of long-playing discs in 1948. But as early as 1904, composers' interpretations of their own works were recorded, giving composers an unprecedented opportunity to communicate precisely their intentions about phrasing, dynamics, and tempo.

Radio broadcasts of live or recorded music began to reach a large audience during the 1920s. In the 1930s, radio networks in several countries formed orchestras specifically to broadcast live music. The best-known American ensemble of this kind was the NBC Symphony Orchestra, directed by Arturo Toscanini. In addition to such radio-sponsored groups, regular broadcasts of the Saturday matinee performances of the Metropolitan Opera made opera available to millions of people.

With television, broadcast music performances could be seen as well as heard. Christmas Eve, 1951, brought the premiere of the first opera created for television, *Amahl and the Night Visitors,* by the Italian-American composer Gian-Carlo

Menotti (b. 1911). Other television highlights included appearances of Leonard Bernstein conducting the New York Philharmonic orchestra. Apart from such notable exceptions, commercial television has devoted little time to opera and symphonic music. Public television, however, brought a wide range of music to home viewers; successful music programming included *Live from Lincoln Center* and *Live from the Met*. In addition, music videos of operas, symphonies, and solo performances became popular.

In the first half of the twentieth century, the concert and operatic repertoire was dominated by music from earlier periods rather than by contemporary works. This was a new situation in music history. In Mozart's time, for instance, audiences demanded and got the latest music, not operas by Handel or cantatas by Bach. Even during the romantic period, when interest in past music was high, concert programs consisted mainly of recent works.

After 1900, however, listeners and performers were often baffled by the dissonances, percussive sounds, and irregular rhythms in some of the new music. (Remember the riot at the first performance of Stravinsky's *Rite of Spring*.) To avoid alienating audiences, many conductors chose not to perform "difficult" contemporary works, but favored works that were relatively accessible in style. One result was that some of the most innovative twentieth-century composers— Ives, Webern, and Varèse, for example—were neglected.

After World War I, organizations were formed for the specific purpose of giving the public a greater opportunity to hear new music. The International Society for Contemporary Music was the most influential, with branches in many countries.

Starting in the 1950s, major orchestras and opera companies began to program more twentieth-century music. Long-playing recordings gave listeners access to works that had seemed incomprehensible; these works could now be played repeatedly until they were understood and enjoyed. Musicians themselves grew more accustomed to intricate modern rhythms and thus were better able to perform them.

Many modern compositions were commissioned by ballet and opera companies, foundations, orchestras, performers, film studios, and wealthy music lovers. Developments in dance had an especially strong impact on twentieth-century music. A single company, Sergei Diaghilev's Russian Ballet, provided the impetus for masterpieces such as Stravinsky's *Petrushka* (1911), Ravel's *Daphnis et Chloé* (1912), and Debussy's *Jeux* (1913). Films provided a new stimulus for music, too. Though many film scores were merely background music, some, like Prokofiev's *Lieutenant Kijé* (1934), were enjoyed apart from the movie. Philanthropic foundations have become significant music patrons in our time. One, most active in the field of chamber music, was established by Elizabeth Sprague Coolidge in 1925 at the Library of Congress in Washington. Her generosity spurred the creation of many fine compositions, including Bartók's Fifth String Quartet (1934) and Schoenberg's Fourth String Quartet (1936). Yet, however important commissions were in the twentieth century, few serious musicians could live on them alone. Most composers were, and still are, also teachers, conductors, or performers. Recently, some have become "composers in residence" with symphony orchestras. They advise music directors on the contemporary repertoire and compose works for performance by the host orchestra.

The twentieth century saw the emergence of important composers from Latin America. The earliest to achieve international recognition was the Brazilian

Heitor Villa-Lobos (1887–1959), a nationalist who fused contemporary musical techniques with the rhythms and tone colors of folk and popular music from his homeland. Villa-Lobos's best known work is *Bachianas brasileiras No. 5,* for soprano solo and eight cellos. Other prominent Latin American composers include the Mexicans Silvestre Revueltas (1898–1940) and Carlos Chávez (1899–1978), and the Argentinians Alberto Ginastera (1916–1983) and Astor Piazzolla (1921–1992). Piazzolla's tango-like composition *Fugata* will be studied in Section 19.

In the twentieth century, more women than ever before became active as composers, virtuoso soloists, and music educators. Among the most noted American women composers are Amy Beach (1867–1944), Ruth Crawford-Seeger (1901–1953), Miriam Gideon (1906–1996), Vivian Fine (1913–2000), Pauline Oliveros (b. 1932), Joan Tower (b. 1938), Ellen Taaffe Zwilich (b. 1939), Barbara Kolb (b. 1940), and Shulamit Ran (b. 1949), to name only a few. The French musician Nadia Boulanger (1887–1979) was among the most important teachers of musical composition in the twentieth century. And in the years after World War II (1939–1945), women joined professional orchestras as instrumentalists and conductors.

African American composers and performers—both women and men—have become increasingly prominent during the twentieth century. One of the pioneer black composers was William Grant Still (1895–1978), who often made use of spirituals, ragtime, and blues. Other leading African American composers include Howard Swanson (1907–1978), Ulysses Kay (1917–1995), Olly Wilson (b. 1937), Tania León (b. 1943), and George Walker (b. 1922), who won a Pulitzer Prize in 1996 for *Lilacs,* a work for soprano and orchestra based on a poem by Walt Whitman.

For many years, African American musicians were admitted as students in music schools but were barred as performers and conductors in established opera companies and symphony orchestras. Color barriers in major American opera companies were not broken until the baritone Todd Duncan performed at the New York City Opera company in 1945 and the contralto Marian Anderson sang at the Metropolitan Opera in 1955. During the 1950s and 1960s black conductors like Dean Dixon and Everett Lee had to go to Europe to find permanent positions; but starting in the 1970s, important conducting posts were occupied by such musicians as Henry Lewis, who directed the New Jersey Symphony; and James DePriest, who led the Quebec Symphony.

Like all people, musicians were affected by the political, economic, and social upheavals of the twentieth century. The violence and chaos of the Russian Revolution (1917) caused many musicians—including the composer Sergei Rachmaninoff (1873–1943)—to leave Russia. Under Stalin's totalitarian regime in the Soviet Union—later renamed the Commonwealth of Independent States (including Russia)—musicians' lives and careers were strictly controlled. Starting in the 1930s, the Communist Party demanded that Soviet composers reject modernism and write optimistic, accessible music that praised the regime. Dmitri Shostakovich (1906–1975), for example, wrote an oratorio, *Song of the Forests* (1949), glorifying the government's reforestation plan.

Hitler's rise to power in Germany in 1933 had an especially dramatic impact on musicians. Avant-garde, socialist, and Jewish musicians were abruptly ousted from their jobs, and their works were no longer performed. Dictatorship, persecution, and the onset of World War II led to the largest migration of artists and intellectuals in history. Many composers, including Stravinsky, Bartók, Schoenberg, and Hindemith, left Europe for the United States. Such distinguished refugees made enormous contributions to American musical culture. Schoenberg and Hindemith, for example, taught in universities and helped train some of the finest composers in the United States.

During the twentieth century, the United States became a potent force in music. American jazz and popular music swept the world. After 1920 the country produced a large group of composers representing a wide spectrum of contemporary styles. In addition, the United States now has more first-rank symphony orchestras than any other country.

American colleges and universities have played an unusually vital role in our musical culture. They have trained and employed many of our leading composers, performers, and scholars. Music courses have expanded the horizons and interests of countless students. And since the 1950s, many universities have sponsored performing groups specializing in twentieth-century music. In addition, they have housed most of the electronic music studios. Thus, American colleges and universities have indirectly become patrons of music, much as the church and nobility were in earlier times.

 3 Impressionism and Symbolism

Many different musical styles coexisted around the beginning of the twentieth century. Among the most important was impressionism, best represented by the music of the French composer Claude Debussy (1862–1918). We'll look closely at musical impressionism in Section 4; first, two related, but slightly earlier, artistic movements in France demand our attention: impressionist painting and symbolist poetry.

French Impressionist Painting

In 1874, a group of French painters including Claude Monet (1840–1926), Auguste Renoir (1841–1919), and Camille Pissarro (1830–1903) had an exhibition in Paris. One Monet painting entitled *Impression: Sunrise*—a misty scene of boats in port—particularly annoyed an art critic, who wrote, "Wallpaper in its embryonic state is more finished than that seascape." Using Monet's title, the critic mockingly called the entire show "the exhibition of the impressionists." The term *impressionist* stuck, but it eventually lost its derisive implication.

Today most of us appreciate impressionist paintings, which colorfully depict the joys of life and the beauties of nature. But during the 1870s, they were seen as formless collections of tiny colored patches—which they are when viewed closely. From a distance, however, the brushstrokes blend and merge into recognizable forms and shimmering colors. Impressionist painters were concerned primarily with effects of light, color, and atmosphere—with impermanence, change, and fluidity. Monet created a series of twenty paintings (1892–1894)

Impression, Sunrise (1874) by Claude Monet. At an exhibition in Paris in 1874, this painting annoyed a critic who saw it as a formless collection of tiny colored patches. Using Monet's own title, he mockingly called the entire show the "exhibition of the impressionists." Like the impressionist painters, the French composer Claude Debussy was a master at evoking a fleeting mood and misty atmosphere.

showing Rouen Cathedral at different times of the day, from dawn to dusk. In this series, the cathedral's stone facade is desolidified and looks like colored mist. Many impressionist painters preferred to work in the open air rather than in a studio. They were fascinated by outdoor scenes from contemporary life, picnics in the woods, and crowds on Parisian boulevards. But most of all, the impressionists were obsessed with water. Using light pastel colors, they depicted the ripples and waves of the ocean and sailboats on the river Seine.

French Symbolist Poetry

As impressionist painters broke from traditional depictions of reality, writers called *symbolists* rebelled against the conventions of French poetry. Like the painters, poets such as Stéphane Mallarmé (1842–1898), Paul Verlaine (1844–1896), and Arthur Rimbaud (1854–1891) emphasized fluidity, suggestion, and the purely musical, or sonorous, effects of words. "To *name* an object," insisted Mallarmé, "is to suppress three-quarters of the enjoyment of a poem, which is made up of gradually guessing; the dream is to *suggest* it."

Claude Debussy was a close friend of many symbolist poets, especially Mallarmé, whose poem *L'Après-midi d'un faune (The Afternoon of a Faun)* inspired Debussy's most famous orchestral work. Many poems by Verlaine became texts for Debussy's songs. (And, more personally, Verlaine's mother-in-law was Debussy's first piano teacher.) Both impressionist painting and symbolist poetry were catalysts for many developments during the twentieth century. Section 4 describes their effect on music.

Claude Debussy

The French impressionist composer Claude Debussy (1862–1918) linked the romantic era with the twentieth century. From the early age of ten until he was twenty-two he studied at the Paris Conservatory, where his teachers regarded him as a talented rebel. In 1884 he won the prestigious Prix de Rome, which subsidized three years of study in Rome; but he left after two years because he lacked musical inspiration away from his beloved Paris.

Influences on Debussy's work included several visits to Russia, where he worked as a pianist for Tchaikovsky's patroness, Nadezhda von Meck, and formed a lifelong interest in Russian music. He was also influenced by the Asian music performed at the Paris International Exposition of 1889, and by the ideas and music of Richard Wagner, which were having a profound effect in France and both attracted and repelled him.

For years, Debussy led an unsettled life, earning a small income by teaching piano. His friends were mostly writers, like Stéphane Mallarmé, whose literary gatherings he attended regularly. He was little known to the musical public and

Claude Debussy.

not completely sure of himself, though he composed important works, including his String Quartet (1893) and the tone poem *Prelude to The Afternoon of a Faun* (1894). But his opera *Pelléas and Mélisande* (1902) marked a turning point in his career: although the critics were sharply divided over it, it soon caught on, and he was recognized as the most important living French composer.

Debussy led a life filled with financial and emotional crises, constantly borrowing money (he had a craving for luxury) and having tempestuous love affairs. He was not gifted as a conductor and hated appearing in public, but to maintain his high standard of living he undertook concert tours and presented his music throughout Europe. He died in Paris in 1918.

Debussy's Music

Like the impressionist painters and symbolist poets, Debussy evoked fleeting moods and misty atmosphere, as the titles of his works suggest: *Reflets dans l'eau (Reflections in the Water), Nuages (Clouds),* and *Les sons et les parfums tournent dans l'air du soir (Sounds and Perfumes Swirl in the Evening Air).*

Debussy was often inspired by literary and pictorial ideas, and his music sounds free and spontaneous, almost improvised. His stress on tone color, atmosphere, and fluidity is characteristic of *impressionism* in music.

Tone color truly gets unprecedented attention in his works; they have a sensuous, beautiful sound and subtle but crucial changes of timbre. The entire orchestra seldom plays together to produce massive sound; instead, there are brief but frequent solos. Woodwinds are prominent; strings and brasses are often muted. In his music for piano—which includes some of the finest piano works of the twentieth century—he creates hazy sonorities and uses a rich variety of bell- and gonglike sounds.

Debussy's treatment of harmony was a revolutionary aspect of musical impressionism. He tends to use a chord more for its special color and sensuous quality than for its function in a standard harmonic progression. He uses successions of dissonant chords that do not resolve. (As a young man, Debussy was asked which harmonic rules he followed; he replied, simply, "My pleasure.") He freely shifts a dissonant chord up or down the scale; the resulting parallel chords characterize his style.

Debussy, *La Cathédrale engloutie (The Sunken Cathedral)*

Debussy's harmonic vocabulary is large. Along with traditional three- and four-note chords, he uses five-note chords with a lush, rich sound. Chord progressions that were highly unorthodox when Debussy wrote them soon came to seem mild and natural.

"One must drown the sense of tonality," he wrote. Although he never actually abandoned tonality, he weakened it by avoiding progressions that would strongly affirm a key and by using scales in which the main tone is not emphasized. He turned to the medieval church modes and the pentatonic scales heard in Javanese music. A *pentatonic* scale is a five-tone scale, such as that produced by the five black keys of the piano in succession: F♯–G♯–A♯–C♯–D♯.

Debussy's most unusual and tonally vague scale is the *whole-tone scale,* made up of six different notes each a whole step away from the next (C–D–E–F♯–G♯–A♯–C). Unlike major and minor, the whole-tone scale has no special pull from *ti* to *do,* since its tones are all the same distance apart. And because no single tone stands out, the scale creates a blurred, indistinct effect.

Debussy, *Voiles (Sails)*

The pulse in Debussy's music is sometimes as vague as the tonality. This rhythmic flexibility reflects the fluid, unaccented quality of the French language, and in fact he set French to music very sensitively. He composed fifty-nine art songs, many of which are set to symbolist poems. His only opera, *Pelléas and Mélisande,* is an almost word-for-word setting of a symbolist play by Maurice Maeterlinck. It is the essence of musical impressionism: nebulous, mysterious, dreamlike, with a discreet, understated orchestral accompaniment.

Although not large, Debussy's output is remarkably varied; in addition to his opera and art songs it includes works for piano, orchestra, and chamber ensembles. Echoes of his music can be heard in the works of many composers of the years 1900–1920; but no other musician can so fairly be described as an impressionist. Even the composer most similar to him, his younger French contemporary Maurice Ravel (1875–1937), wrote music with greater clarity of form. Debussy's style was both a final expression of romanticism and the beginning of a new era.

Prélude à L'Après-midi d'un Faune (Prelude to The Afternoon of a Faun; 1894)

Brief Set:
CD 4 9

Basic Set:
CD 7 1

"The music of this Prelude," wrote Debussy of his *Prelude to The Afternoon of a Faun,* "is a very free illustration of the beautiful poem by Stéphane Mallarmé, *The Afternoon of a Faun.*" This poem evokes the dreams and erotic fantasies of a pagan forest creature who is half man, half goat. While playing a "long solo" on his flute, the intoxicated faun tries to recall whether he actually carried off two beautiful nymphs or only dreamed of doing so. Exhausted by the effort, he falls back to sleep in the sunshine.

Debussy intended his music to suggest "the successive scenes through which pass the desires and dreams of the faun in the heat of this afternoon." The subtle, sensuous timbres of this miniature tone poem were new in Debussy's day. Woodwind solos, muted horn calls, and harp glissandos create a rich variety of delicate sounds. The dynamics are usually subdued, and only rarely does the entire orchestra—from which trombones, trumpets, and timpani are excluded— play at one time. The music often swells sensuously and then subsides in voluptuous exhaustion.

The prelude begins with an unaccompanied flute melody; its vague pulse and tonality make it dreamlike and improvisatory. This flute melody is heard again and again, faster, slower, and against a variety of lush chords. Though the form of the prelude may be thought of as A B A', one section blends with the next. It has a continuous ebb and flow. The fluidity and weightlessness typical of impressionism are found in this music. We are never tempted to beat time to its subtle rhythms. The prelude ends magically with the main melody, played by muted horns, seeming to come from far off. The bell-like tones of antique cymbals finally evaporate into silence. With all its new sounds and musical techniques, the piece has aptly been described as a "quiet revolution" in the history of music.

Listening Outline to be read while music is heard   Brief Set: CD 4   Basic Set: CD 7

DEBUSSY, *Prélude à L'Après-midi d'un Faune*

At a very moderate tempo, A B A' form, E major

3 flutes, 2 oboes, 1 English horn, 2 clarinets, 2 bassoons, 4 French horns, 2 harps, antique cymbals, 1st violins, 2d violins, violas, cellos, double basses

(Duration, 9:40)

A

9 **1** 0:00   **1. a.** Solo flute, *p*, main melody.

Harp glissando; soft horn calls. Short pause. Harp glissando; soft horn calls.

10 **2** 0:43   **b.** Flute, *p*, main melody; tremolo strings in background. Oboe, *p*, continues melody. Orchestra swells to *f*. Solo clarinet fades into

11 **3** 1:35   0:00   **c.** Flute, *p*, main melody varied and expanded; harp and muted strings accompany. Flute melody comes to quiet close.

| | 2:48 | 1:13 | **2. a.** Clarinet; harp and cellos in background. |
| 12 | 4 | 3:16 | **b.** New oboe melody. |

Violins take up melody, crescendo and accelerando to climax. Excitement subsides. Ritardando. Clarinet, *p*, leads into

B

| | 13 | 5 | 4:33 | 0:00 | **3. a.** Woodwinds, *p*, legato melody in long notes. Crescendo. |

| | 5:16 | 0:43 | **b.** Strings repeat melody; harps and pulsating woodwinds in background, crescendo. Decrescendo. Horns, *p*, solo violin, *p*, clarinet, oboe. |

A′

14	6	6:21		**4. a.** Harp accompanies flute, *p*, main melody in longer notes. Oboe, staccato woodwinds.
	6:56	0:35	**b.** Harp accompanies oboe, *p*, main melody in longer notes. English horn, harp glissando.
15	7	7:39	0:00	**5. a.** Antique cymbals, bell-like tones. Flutes, *p*, main melody. Solo violins, *pp*, in high register.
	8:16	0:37	**b.** Flute and solo cello, main melody; harp in background.
	8:45	1:06	**c.** Oboe, *p*, brings melody to close. Harps, *p*.
	9:10	1:31	**d.** Muted horns and violins, *ppp*, beginning of main melody sounding far off. Flute, antique cymbals, and harp; delicate tones fade into silence.

5 Neoclassicism

From about 1920 to 1950, the music of many composers, including Igor Stravinsky and Paul Hindemith, reflected an artistic movement known as *neoclassicism*. Neoclassicism is marked by emotional restraint, balance, and clarity; neoclassical compositions use musical forms and stylistic features of earlier periods, particularly of the eighteenth century. Stravinsky summed it up: "I attempted to build a new music on eighteenth-century classicism." Neoclassical music is not merely a revival of old forms and styles; it uses earlier techniques to organize twentieth-century harmonies and rhythms.

"Back to Bach" was the slogan of this movement, which reacted against romanticism and impressionism. (Since many neoclassical compositions were modeled after Bach's music, the term *neobaroque* might have been more appropriate.) Neoclassical composers turned away from program music and the gigantic orchestras favored at the turn of the century. They preferred absolute (nonprogrammatic) music for chamber groups. This preference for smaller performing groups partly reflected economic necessity: during the post–World War I period, economic conditions were so bad in parts of Europe that there was little money to hire large orchestras. Favoring clear polyphonic textures, composers wrote fugues, concerti grossi, and baroque dance suites. Most neoclassical music was tonal and used major and minor scales. Still, neoclassicism was more an attitude than a style. Schoenberg wrote minuets and gigues using his twelve-tone system. And though neoclassical composers referred to many past styles, their works sound completely modern. They play on a delightful tension between our expectations about old forms and styles and the novel harmonies and rhythms.

Neoclassicism was an important trend in other arts, too. The poet T. S. Eliot often quoted and alluded to earlier writers. Picasso, who designed sets for Stravinsky's first neoclassical work, *Pulcinella* (1920), went through a phase during which he created paintings that show the influence of ancient Greek art. Picasso described the neoclassical attitude by saying that artists "must pick out what is good for us where we find it. When I am shown a portfolio of old drawings, for instance, I have no qualms about taking anything I want from them."

Igor Stravinsky

Even during his lifetime, Igor Stravinsky (1882–1971) was a legendary figure. His once revolutionary works had already become modern classics, and he influenced three generations of composers and other artists. Cultural giants like Picasso and T. S. Eliot were his friends. President John F. Kennedy honored him at a White House dinner in his eightieth year.

Stravinsky was born in Russia, near St. Petersburg, grew up in a musical atmosphere, and studied with Nikolai Rimsky-Korsakov. He had his first important opportunity in 1909, when the great impresario Sergei Diaghilev heard his music.

Diaghilev was the director of the Russian Ballet, an extremely influential troupe which employed great painters as well as dancers, choreographers, and composers. Diaghilev first asked Stravinsky to orchestrate some piano pieces by Chopin as ballet music and then, in 1910, commissioned an original ballet, *The Firebird*, which was immensely successful. A year later (1911), Stravinsky's second ballet, *Petrushka*, was performed, and Stravinsky was hailed as a modern master. When his third ballet, *The Rite of Spring*, had its premiere in Paris in 1913, a riot erupted in the audience—spectators were shocked and outraged by its pagan primitivism, harsh dissonance, percussiveness, and pounding rhythms—but it too was recognized as a masterpiece and influenced composers all over the world.

During World War I, Stravinsky sought refuge in Switzerland; after the armistice, he moved to France, his home until the onset of World War II, when

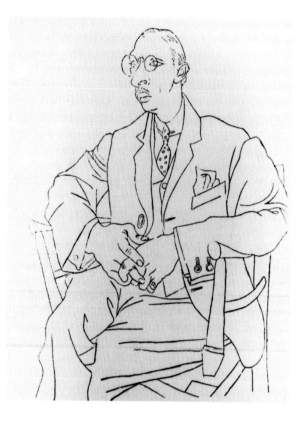

Sketch of Igor Stravinsky
by Pablo Picasso.

he came to the United States. In the 1920s and 1930s he was an international celebrity, constantly touring in Europe and the United States; and his compositions—which had originally been inspired by Russian folk music—became cooler and more objective. During his years in the United States (he lived outside Los Angeles), his young musical assistant, Robert Craft, familiarized him with the works of Schoenberg, Berg, and Webern, and in the 1950s Stravinsky astonished his followers by adopting Schoenberg's twelve-tone system.

Unlike Schoenberg and Bartók, Stravinsky got well-paying commissions for his work and was an astute businessman; he also loved order and discipline and said that he composed "every day, regularly, like a man with banking hours." In his seventies and eighties he was still touring, conducting his rich, intense late works.

Stravinsky's Music

Stravinsky's extensive output includes compositions of almost every kind, for voices, instruments, and the stage; and his innovations in rhythm, harmony, and tone color had an enormous influence.

His development shows dramatic changes of style. The three early ballets—*The Firebird* (1910), *Petrushka* (1911), and *The Rite of Spring* (1913)—call for very large orchestras and draw on Russian folklore and folk tunes. During World War I, he wrote for chamber groups, using unconventional combinations of instruments and incorporating ragtime rhythms and popular dances (an example is *The Soldier's Tale,* 1918). From about 1920 to 1951 (his "neoclassical" period), he was inspired largely by eighteenth-century music; his ballet *Pulcinella* (1920) was based partly on the music of Giovanni Battista Pergolesi (1710–1736), and his opera *The Rake's Progress* (1951) was modeled on Mozart. Stravinsky's neoclassical works emphasize restraint, balance, and wit and are far removed from the violence of *The Rite of Spring.* But his shift to the twelve-tone system in the 1950s was an even more dramatic change of approach, since until then all his music had a clear tonal center. Inspired by Anton Webern (1883–1945), Stravinsky now wrote brief works in which melodic lines were "atomized" into short fragments in constantly changing tone colors and registers.

Despite such stylistic changes, however, all his music has an unmistakable "Stravinsky sound." Tone colors are dry and clear; the beat is strong. His work abounds in changing and irregular meters, and sometimes several meters are heard at once. Ostinatos—repeated rhythmic or melodic patterns—often unify sections of a piece. His treatment of musical form is also unique: rather than connecting themes with bridge passages, he makes abrupt shifts, but his music nevertheless sounds unified and continuous. The effectiveness of his rhythms, chords, and melodies often depends largely on his orchestration, in which highly contrasting tone colors are frequently combined. And his music has rich, novel harmonies—he makes even conventional chords sound unusual.

Stravinsky drew on a wide range of styles, from Russian folk songs to baroque melodies, from Renaissance madrigals to tango rhythms. He sometimes used existing music to create original compositions, but more often the music is entirely his own, while vaguely suggesting a past style.

Le Sacre du printemps (The Rite of Spring, 1913)

Few compositions have had so powerful an impact on twentieth-century music as *Le Sacre du printemps (The Rite of Spring),* Stravinsky's third score for the Russian Ballet. Its harsh dissonances, percussive orchestration, rapidly changing meters, violent offbeat accents, and ostinatos fired the imagination of many composers. The idea for *The Rite of Spring* came to Stravinsky as a "fleeting vision," while he was completing *The Firebird* in St. Petersburg in 1910. "I saw in imagination a solemn pagan rite: wise elders, seated in a circle, watching a young girl dance herself to death. They were sacrificing her to propitiate the god of spring." Later in life, Stravinsky remarked that the "most wonderful event" of every year of his childhood was the "violent Russian spring that seemed to begin in an hour and was like the whole earth cracking."

Stravinsky's interest in so-called primitive or preliterate culture was shared by many artists and scholars in the early 1900s. In 1907, Picasso's violent, pathbreaking painting *Les Demoiselles d'Avignon* reflected the influence of African sculpture. In 1913—the same year as *The Rite of Spring*—Freud published *Totem and Taboo,* a study of "resemblances between the psychic lives of savages and neurotics." But ***primitivism***—the deliberate evocation of primitive power through insistent rhythms and percussive sounds—did not have a lasting impact on early twentieth-century music. Stravinsky never again wrote anything like *The Rite of Spring;* and with the exception of works like *Allegro barbaro* (1911), a piano piece by Bartók, few primitivistic compositions have entered the repertoire.

The Rite of Spring has two large parts, subdivided into sections that move at varying speeds and follow each other without pause. The titles of the dances suggest their primitive subject matter. Part I, *The Adoration of the Earth,* consists of (1) *Introduction;* (2) *Omens of Spring: Dances of the Youths and Maidens;* (3) *Ritual of Abduction;* (4) *Spring Rounds;* (5) *Games of the Rival Tribes;* (6) *Procession of the Wise Elder;* (7) *Adoration of the Earth;* (8) *Dance of the Earth.* Part II, *The Sacrifice,* consists of (1) *Introduction;* (2) *Mysterious Circles of the Young Girls;* (3) *Glorification of the Chosen Maiden;* (4) *Evocation of the Ancestors;* (5) *Ritual of the Ancestors;* (6) *Sacrificial Dance.* Each of the two large parts has a slow introduction and ends with a frenzied, climactic dance.

The Rite of Spring is written for an enormous orchestra including eight horns, four tubas, and a very important percussion section made up of five timpani, bass drum, tambourine, tam-tam, triangle, antique cymbals, and a guiro (a notched gourd scraped with a stick). The melodies of *The Rite of Spring* are

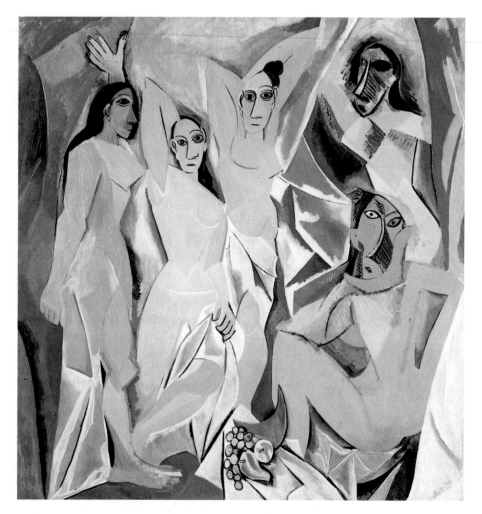

Les Demoiselles d'Avignon (1907) by Picasso reflects the influence of African sculpture.

folklike. Like ancient Russian folk tunes, they have narrow ranges, and they are made up of fragments that are repeated with slight changes in rhythm and pitch. Many individual chords are repeated, and each change of harmony produces a great impact. This melodic and harmonic repetition gives the music a ritualistic, hypnotic quality. Rhythm is a vital structural element in *The Rite of Spring*; it has a life of its own, almost independent of melody and harmony. Today, *The Rite of Spring* is performed more frequently as a concert piece than as a ballet.

We'll now take a closer look at four sections of *The Rite of Spring: Introduction, Omens of Spring—Dances of the Youths and Maidens,* and *Ritual of Abduction,* which open Part I; and *Sacrificial Dance,* which concludes Part II.

Part I:
Introduction

Brief Set:
CD 4 16

Basic Set:
CD 7 15

For Stravinsky, the *Introduction* to Part I represented "the awakening of nature, the scratching, gnawing, wiggling of birds and beasts." It begins with the strangely penetrating sound of a solo bassoon straining at the top of its register. As though improvising, the bassoon repeats a fragment of a Lithuanian folk tune in irregular ways.

Soon other woodwind instruments join the bassoon with repeated fragments of their own. The impression of improvisation is strengthened by the absence of a clearly defined pulse or meter. Dissonant, unconventional chord structures are used. Toward the end of the *Introduction,* different layers of sounds—coming mostly from woodwinds and brasses—are piled on top of each other, and the music builds to a piercing climax. But suddenly, all sound is cut off; only the solo bassoon forlornly repeats its opening melody. Then the violins, playing pizzicato, introduce a repeated four-note "ticking" figure. This figure later serves as an ostinato in *Omens of Spring—Dances of the Youths and Maidens,* which immediately follows the *Introduction.*

Part I:
Omens of Spring—Dances of the Youths and Maidens

Brief Set:
CD 4 18

Basic Set:
CD 7 17

Sounding almost like drums, the strings pound out a dissonant chord. There are unexpected and irregular accents whose violence is heightened by jabbing sounds from the eight horns. The passage might be counted (with a rapid pulse): 1–2–3–4, 1–2–3–4, 1–2–3–**4**, 1–2–3–4, 1–**2**–3–4, **1**–2–3–4, **1**–2–3–4, 1–**2**–3–4. The unchanging dissonant harmony is a polychord that combines two different traditional chords. Successive melodic fragments soon join the pounding chord and other repeated figures. The melodic fragments, played by brasses and woodwinds, are narrow in range and are repeated over and over with slight variations. The rhythmic activity is constant and exciting, and gradually more and more instruments are added.

It's interesting to contrast Stravinsky's musical techniques in *Dances of the Youths and Maidens* with those of a classical movement in sonata form. A classical movement grows out of conflicts between different keys; this section of *The Rite of Spring* is based almost entirely on repetition of a few chords. Themes in a classical movement are developed through different keys, varied, and broken into fragments that take on new emotional meanings. In *Dances of the Youths and*

Maidens, Stravinsky simply repeats melodic fragments with relatively slight variation. To create movement and growth, he relies instead on variations of rhythm and tone color—a technique that can be traced back to nineteenth-century Russian musical tradition.

Part I:
Ritual of Abduction

Brief Set:
CD 4 22

Basic Set:
CD 7 21

The frenzied *Ritual of Abduction* grows out of the preceding section and is marked by violent strokes on the timpani and bass drum. Enormous tension is generated by powerful accents and rapid changes of meter (see the music example on page 300). This section of *The Rite of Spring* closes with high trills in the strings and flutes.

Listening Outline to be read while music is heard | Brief Set: CD 4   Basic Set: CD 7 |

STRAVINSKY, *Le Sacre du Printemps*

Part I: *Introduction, Omens of Spring—Dances of the Youths and Maidens, Ritual of Abduction*

2 piccolos, 3 flutes, alto flute, 4 oboes, English horn, E flat clarinet, 3 clarinets, 2 bass clarinets, 4 bassoons, 2 contrabassoons, 8 French horns, small trumpet in D, 4 trumpets, 3 trombones, 3 tubas, timpani, bass drum, triangle, antique cymbals, 1st violins, 2d violins, violas, cellos, double basses

(Duration, 7:24)

Introduction

16 15 0:00

1. **a.** High solo bassoon, repeated folk song fragment in changing meters, joined by French horn, *mp,* then clarinets and bass clarinets, *p.*

0:43	**b.** English horn, new melodic fragment; high bassoon; English horn, melodic fragment, bassoons accompany in faster rhythm.
1:12	**c.** Pizzicato strings, oboe, repeated notes introduce high clarinet melody.
1:24	**d.** Oboe phrase, *f,* high flutes accompany; English horn phrase, *mf,* bass clarinets accompany; flutes and English horn move in even rhythm; violin trill joins.
1:53	**e.** Pizzicato cello pulsations, rhythmic activity quickens, rapid shifts between large and small wind groups; clarinet, repeated descending phrase.
2:18	**f.** Oboe with rapid alto flute accompaniment; piercing high clarinet, *ff,* joins; music builds to *ff* climax, different layers of woodwind and brass sound piled on each other.

2:52   **2. a.** Sudden *p*, solo high bassoon, opening fragment; clarinet trill, joined by

`17` `16` 3:03   **b.** Pizzicato violins, "ticking" ostinato figure.

Low held tones in bass clarinet; high tones in violins; pizzicato violins, "ticking" ostinato figure.

Omens of Spring—Dances of the Youths and Maidens

`18` `17` 3:22   0:00   **3. a.** Sudden *f*, strings, repeated dissonant polychord with punctuations in French horns, irregular accents, moderate tempo, duple meter.

3:29   0:07   **b.** English horn, *mf*, "ticking" ostinato figure.
3:39   0:17   **c.** Strings, *f*, repeated dissonant polychord with punctuations in French horns; piccolos, trumpets, oboes join.
3:49   0:27   **d.** Pizzicato basses and cellos introduce loud, rapid interjections in high trumpet and piccolos;
3:54   0:32   **e.** Strings, *f*, repeated dissonant polychord with punctuations in French horns.

`19` `18` 4:02   0:00   **f.** Bassoons join with melodic fragment played staccato, string pulsations; trombone joins;

Bassoons repeat staccato melodic fragment; oboes, flute, and trombone imitate;

4:28   0:26   **g.** Sudden break in pulse, French horns, *f*, sustained tone, timpani strokes, tubas, *ff*, low sustained tone;
4:33   0:31   **h.** High "ticking" ostinato figure descends to English horn, *mf*, trills in winds and strings; loud "ticking" ostinato in violins and trumpet.

`20` `19` 4:49   0:00   **i.** French horn, *mp*, joins with legato melody; flute answers;

descending figure in oboes and trumpet.

5:07   0:18   **j.** Legato melody in alto flute; legato melody in high flutes, pizzicato strings accompany.

21 20 5:20 0:00 **k.** Trumpets join with repeated-note melody; triangle joins.

5:34 0:14 **l.** Sudden *p*, strings and syncopated accents introduce piccolo, high legato melodic fragment; full orchestra, melodic figures repeated with long crescendo to

Ritual of Abduction

22 21 6:10 0:00 **4. a.** Sustained brass chord, violent strokes on timpani and bass drum; high trumpet, rapid-note fanfare, very fast tempo, changing meters.

6:23 0:13 **b.** Horn calls, *f*, alternate with piccolo and flutes, rapid-note fanfare; timpani, bass drum join; crescendo to

6:43 0:33 **c.** High woodwinds and brasses, *ff*, staccato passage in changing meters; horn calls; full orchestra, *ff*.

23 22 6:59 0:00 **d.** Timpani accents punctuate staccato phrases with changing meters in trumpets and high winds; timpani accents punctuate repeated rapid figure in strings.

7:18 0:19 **e.** Trill in violins, *ff*, accented chords; trill in flutes, *p*.

Part II:
Sacrificial Dance

Basic Set:
CD 7 23

Section A
23 0:00

Section B
24 0:27

Section C
25 2:17

Sacrificial Dance is the overwhelming climax of the work. It consists of sections that can be outlined as follows: A B A' C A" (very brief) C A"'. In the opening section (A), explosive, percussive chords fight brutal blows on the timpani. The time signature changes with almost every bar: $\frac{3}{16}$ $\frac{2}{16}$ $\frac{3}{16}$ $\frac{2}{8}$ $\frac{2}{16}$ $\frac{3}{16}$. The rapid pulse and irregular, jolting accents create intense excitement.

The second section (B) begins with a sudden drop in dynamic level as a single chord is repeated obsessively. Brief silences between these repeated chords urge the listener to supply accents.

Section C features brasses and percussive sounds from five timpani, a tam-tam (gong), and a bass drum. *Sacrificial Dance* glorifies the power of rhythm, as does the entire *Rite of Spring*.

7 Expressionism

Much music of the twentieth century reflects an artistic movement called *expressionism,* which stressed intense, subjective emotion. It was largely centered in Germany and Austria from 1905 to 1925. Expressionist painters, writers, and composers explored inner feelings rather than depicting outward appearances. They used deliberate distortions to assault and shock their audience, to communicate the tensions and anguish of the human psyche. Expressionism grew out of the same intellectual climate as Freud's studies of hysteria and the

The Scream (1893), by the Norwegian expressionist Edvard Munch. Expressionist painters reacted against French impressionism; they often used jarring colors and grotesquely distorted shapes to explore the subconscious.

unconscious. German expressionist painting was in part a reaction against French impressionism, with its pleasant subjects, delicate pastel colors, and shimmering surfaces.

The expressionists rejected conventional prettiness. Their works may seem "ugly" in their preoccupation with madness and death. Expressionist painters such as Ernst Ludwig Kirchner, Emil Nolde, Edvard Munch, and Oskar Kokoschka often use jarring colors and grotesquely distorted shapes. Expressionist art tends to be fragmentary; the scenes of an expressionist play may be episodic and discontinuous. Expressionism is also an art concerned with social protest. It movingly conveyed the anguish felt by the poor and oppressed. Many expressionists opposed World War I and used art to depict their horror of bloodshed.

There was close communication among expressionist writers, painters, and musicians. Many of these were creative in more than one art form. The painter Wassily Kandinsky wrote essays, poetry, and plays; the composer Schoenberg painted and even participated in the shows of expressionist artists.

Twentieth-century musical expressionism grows out of the emotional turbulence in the works of romantics like Wagner and Mahler. Immediate precedents for expressionism are the operas *Salome* (1905) and *Elektra* (1908) by Richard Strauss, in which extremely chromatic and dissonant music depicts perversion and murder. In Sections 8, 9, and 10, we'll study four expressionistic compositions: *Pierrot lunaire*, Op. 21 (*Moonstruck Pierrot*, 1912), and *A Survivor from Warsaw*, Op. 46 (1947), by Schoenberg; the opera *Wozzeck* (1917–1922), by Alban Berg; and Five Pieces for Orchestra, Op. 10 (1911–1913), by Anton Webern. These works all stress harsh dissonance and fragmentation and exploit extreme registers and unusual instrumental effects. All four avoid tonality and traditional chord progressions. Both *A Survivor from Warsaw* and *Wozzeck* depict a nightmarish world and express a profound empathy with the poor and tormented.

8 Arnold Schoenberg

Arnold Schoenberg (1874–1951), who was born in Vienna, was an almost entirely self-taught musician; he acquired his profound knowledge of music by studying scores, playing in amateur chamber groups, and going to concerts. After he lost his job as a bank clerk at age twenty-one, he devoted himself to music, earning a poor living conducting a choir of industrial workers and orchestrating popular operettas. Performances of his own early works met with hostility; but in 1904 he began to teach music theory and composition in Vienna, and he inspired love and loyalty in his students, two of whom—Alban Berg and Anton Webern—themselves became leading composers.

Around 1908 Schoenberg took the revolutionary step of abandoning the traditional tonal system. He was a man possessed ("I have a mission," he said; "I am but the loudspeaker of an idea"), and his productivity between 1908 and 1915 was incredible. For the next eight years, however, he searched for a way to organize his musical discoveries and published nothing. Then, in 1921, he told a student, "I have made a discovery which will ensure the supremacy of German music for the next hundred years," and shortly thereafter (1923–1925) he began publishing compositions using his new twelve-tone system. Although his music did not find a large audience, many important musicians respected it, and he received an important appointment at the Prussian Academy of Arts in Berlin.

After the Nazis seized power in Germany, Schoenberg, who was Jewish, was dismissed from his post; the same year—1933—he and his family came to the

Arnold Schoenberg.

United States, where he joined the music faculty at the University of California in Los Angeles. Schoenberg felt neglected in America: his music was rarely performed and he was financially unsuccessful. But after his death, the twelve-tone system was used increasingly by composers throughout the world. It remains an important influence to this day.

Schoenberg's Music

"I claim the distinction of having written a truly new music which, based upon tradition as it is, is destined to become tradition." This assertion by Schoenberg contains a great deal of truth: his musical language was indeed new, but it had evolved from the past and was eventually widely adopted.

His early works, like the string sextet *Verklarte Nacht* (*Transfigured Night*, 1899), show many features of the late romantic style. Some of them—such as the immense cantata *Gurrelieder* (*Songs of Gurre*, 1901)—use very large orchestras; dissonances and angular melodies create a feeling of subjectivity; chromatic harmony is prominent; and the central tonality is weakened as the music moves through remote keys. But from 1903 to 1907, he departed farther from romanticism, and in the *Chamber Symphony*, Op. 9 (1906), he uses whole-tone scales and fourth chords.

Atonality

Around 1908, Schoenberg began to write atonal music. *Atonality*—the absence of key—evolved from his earlier use of chromatic harmony and the chromatic scale; but in his atonal works, all twelve tones are used without regard for their traditional relationship to major and minor scales. Dissonances are "emancipated" from the necessity of resolving to consonances. Atonality does not imply a single system of composition: each atonal work has its own means of achieving unity, and a piece usually grows out of a few short motives transformed in many different ways.

Schoenberg's atonal compositions include Five Pieces for Orchestra, Op. 16 (1909), and *Pierrot lunaire*, Op. 21 (*Moonstruck Pierrot*, 1912); they are characterized by jagged melodies, novel instrumental effects, extreme contrasts of dynamics and register, and irregular phrases. *Pierrot lunaire* and some other works require an unusual style of vocal performance—*Sprechstimme* (literally, *speech-voice*)—halfway between speaking and singing. Schoenberg's atonal style was soon adopted by his students Berg and Webern; but their early atonal works tended to be short: without a musical system like tonality, extended compositions were possible only when there was a long text to serve as an organizing force.

The Twelve-Tone System

In the early 1920s, Schoenberg developed a more systematic method of organizing atonal music; he called it the "method of composing with twelve tones." It is partly applied in Five Piano Pieces, Op. 23, and Serenade, Op. 24, and fully elaborated in Suite for Piano, Op. 25 (all composed from 1920 to 1923); and it enabled him to write more extended compositions, such as the monumental Variations for Orchestra (1928) and the unfinished opera *Moses und Aron* (*Moses and Aaron,* 1930–1932). From 1933 to 1951, in the United States, he used it in many rich and varied works.

The ***twelve-tone system*** is a twentieth-century alternative to tonality, a new way of organizing pitch in a composition. It is a systematized form of atonality which gives equal importance to each of the twelve chromatic tones. In a twelve-tone composition, the ordering or unifying idea is called a ***tone row, set,*** or ***series*** (for this reason, the method is also referred to as *serial technique* or *serialism*). The composer creates a unique tone row for each piece (the choice of rows is practically limitless, since there are 479,001,600 possible arrangements of the twelve tones), and the row is the source of every melody and chord in it. No pitch occurs more than once in the row; this prevents any tone from receiving too much emphasis.

A composition is built by manipulating the tone row, which may be presented in four basic forms: (1) forward (original form), (2) backward (retrograde), (3) upside down (inversion), and (4) backward and upside down (retrograde inversion). (See the illustrations below, which show the row used in Suite for Piano, Op. 25.) Any of the four forms of a row may be shifted to any pitch level—that is, it can begin on any of the twelve tones while keeping the original pattern of intervals. Thus there are forty-eight (twelve times four) possible versions of a row. Each tone of a row may also be placed in any register; this enhances the flexibility of the system and may partially explain why so many twelve-tone melodies have very wide leaps. Finally, the tones of a row

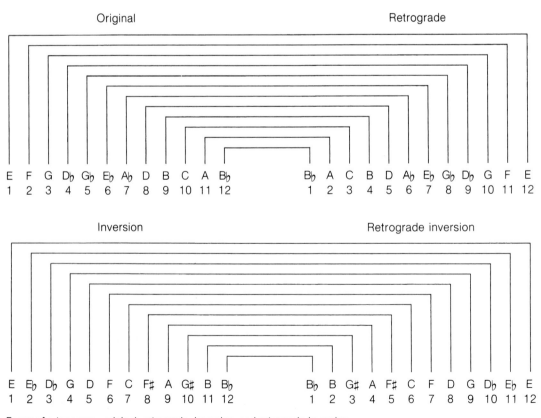

Forms of a tone row—original, retrograde, inversion, and retrograde inversion.

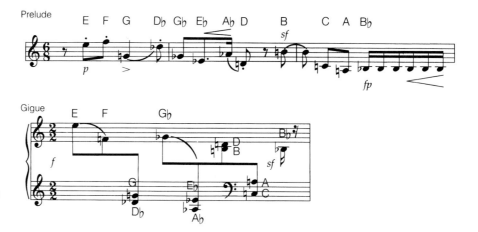

Two treatments of the tone row in Schoenberg's Suite for Piano, Op. 25.

may be presented one after another (as a melodic line) or simultaneously (as chords). Shown above is the row from the Suite for Piano treated in two different ways.

We'll now study two works by Schoenberg: the "freely" atonal *Pierrot lunaire*, Op. 21 (*Moonstruck Pierrot*; 1912); and the twelve-tone cantata *A Survivor from Warsaw*, Op. 46 (1947), composed almost thirty-five years later.

Pierrot lunaire, **Op. 21** (*Moonstruck Pierrot;* 1912)

Like Stravinsky's *The Rite of Spring*, composed around the same time, Schoenberg's *Pierrot lunaire*, or *Moonstruck Pierrot*, is a revolutionary masterpiece that profoundly influenced twentieth-century music. It is a cycle of twenty-one songs for female voice and an ensemble of five musicians who play eight instruments: piano, cello, violin-viola, flute-piccolo, clarinet-bass clarinet. The instrumental ensemble varies with each piece. For example, *The Sick Moon* (No. 7) uses only the flute; *Prayer to Pierrot* (No. 9) uses the piano and clarinet; and *O Ancient Scent* (No. 21) uses all eight instruments. A song cycle accompanied by a chamber-music ensemble—rather than by piano alone—represented a departure from convention. Another novelty was the pervasive use of *Sprechstimme*, the technique of half speaking, half singing developed by Schoenberg. The rhythms and pitches of the words are precisely notated, but the voice touches the notated pitch only momentarily and then departs from it.

Pierrot lunaire is based on weird poems written in 1884 by the Belgian poet Albert Giraud and later translated into German by Schoenberg's friend Otto Erich Hartleben. Many of the poems deal with the puppet Pierrot, a tragic clown character derived from the centuries-old *commedia dell'arte* (Italian improvised theater). Pierrot, who represented the isolated modern artist, was a favorite subject for artists, writers, and musicians of the late nineteenth century and the early twentieth century.

The cycle divides into three groups of seven songs that evoke a surrealistic night vision. In the first group, Pierrot, a poet, drunk on moonlight, becomes increasingly deranged. The second group is a nightmare filled with images of death and martyrdom. In the third group, Pierrot seeks refuge from the nightmare through clowning, sentimentality, and nostalgia. *Pierrot lunaire* is expressionist in its weird text, eerie *Sprechstimme*, unique instrumental effects, and atonal musical language. We'll focus on the opening piece of the cycle, *Mondestrunken (Moondrunk)*.

Mondestrunken (Moondrunk)

Brief Set:
CD 4 24

Basic Set:
CD 7 27

Scored for voice, piano, flute, violin, and cello, *Mondestrunken (Moondrunk)* begins the fantastic nocturnal journey. Its text depicts moonlight as a sacramental "wine we drink through the eyes." The poet (Pierrot) becomes intoxicated as moonlight floods the still horizon with desires that are "horrible and sweet." Like the other poems in *Pierrot lunaire*, *Mondestrunken* is a rondeau—a verse form—of thirteen lines in which lines 1–2 reappear as lines 7–8 and line 1 repeats as line 13.

Mondestrunken is mostly soft and light in texture. It opens with a high seven-note motive that hypnotically repeats in the piano and evokes a feeling of moonlight.

The pervasive varied recurrence of this ostinato motive in different instruments unifies the piece. Schoenberg's music parallels the changing images of the text. The wine that "the moon pours down in torrents," for example, is depicted by a descending sequence of the motive in the piano and flute.

The poet's intoxication from "the holy drink" is suggested by a sudden *forte*, thick piano chords, and the first appearance of the cello. *Mondestrunken* rounds off with a final appearance of the motive at a slower tempo in the piano and flute.

Vocal Music Guide to be read while music is heard | Brief Set: CD 4 | Basic Set: CD 7

SCHOENBERG, *Pierrot lunaire (Moonstruck Pierrot)*

No. 1, *Mondestrunken (Moondrunk)*

24 27
Piano,
pp, high
repeated motive.

Flute	*Den Wein, den man mit Augen trinkt,*	The wine that with eyes is drunk,
	Giesst Nachts der Mond in Wogen nieder,	at night the moon pours down in waves,
	Und eine Springflut überschwemmt	and a spring-flood overflows
	Den stillen Horizont.	the silent horizon.
Long flute melody, high piano		
	Gelüste, schauerlich und süss.	Desires shuddering and sweet
	Durchschwimmen ohne Zahl die Fluten!	swim countless through the floods!
	Den Wein, den man mit Augen trinkt,	The wine that with eyes is drunk
Piano, flute, motive descends	*Giesst Nachts der Mond in Woge nieder.*	at night the moon pours down in waves.
Sudden *f*, cello enters.	*Der Dichter, die den Andacht treibt*	The poet, whom devotion inspires
	Berauscht sich an dem heiligen Tranke,	made drunk by the sacred drink,
High violin.	*Gen Himmel wendet er verzückt*	toward heaven he turns
	Das Haupt und taumelnd saugt und schlürft er	his entranced head and, reeling, sucks and slurps
	Den Wein, den man mit Augen trinkt.	the wine that with eyes is drunk.
Piano motive, flute imitates.		

A Survivor from Warsaw, Op. 46 (1947)

Brief Set:
CD 4 25

Basic Set:
CD 7 28

A Survivor from Warsaw, a dramatic cantata for narrator, male chorus, and orchestra, deals with a single episode in the murder of 6 million Jews by the Nazis during World War II. Schoenberg wrote the text himself, basing it partly on a direct report by one of the few survivors of the Warsaw ghetto. Over 400,000 Jews from this ghetto died in extermination camps or of starvation; many others perished during a heroic revolt against the Nazis in 1943.

The narrator's text is spoken in English, except for some terrifying Nazi commands, which are shouted in German. The narrator's part is a kind of *Sprechstimme,* the novel speech-singing developed by Schoenberg. The rhythms of the spoken words are precisely notated, but their pitch fluctuations are indicated only approximately.

Besides English and German, the text includes Hebrew. These were the three languages of Schoenberg's life: German, his native tongue; English, his adopted language in the United States; and Hebrew, the language of the faith to which he returned. The 6-minute cantata builds to an overwhelming conclusion when the male chorus sings in unison the Hebrew words of the prayer *Shema Yisroel*

(Hear, O Israel). For centuries this has been the prayer of Jewish martyrs in their last agonized moments.

A Survivor from Warsaw is a twelve-tone composition written in 1947, when Schoenberg was seventy-two. The music vividly sets off every detail in the text.

A Survivor from Warsaw opens with a brief orchestral introduction that captures the nightmarish atmosphere which prevailed as Nazi soldiers awakened the Warsaw Jews for transport to death camps. We hear a weirdly shrill reveille in the trumpet and fragmentary sounds in the military drum and high xylophone.

During the narrator's opening lines, Schoenberg already prepares for the concluding Hebrew prayer. As the narrator speaks of "the old prayer they had neglected for so many years," a French horn softly intones the beginning of the melody that is later proclaimed by the chorus.

An especially vivid musical description comes when the narrator describes how the Nazis counted their victims: "They began again, first slowly: One, two, three, four, became faster and faster. . . ." The music itself becomes faster and louder, building to the powerful entrance of the chorus.

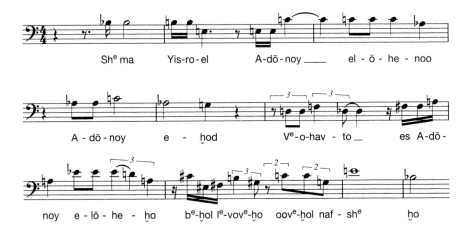

The sung Hebrew contrasts dramatically with the spoken English and German that comes before, and it is the first extended melody in the work.

Vocal Music Guide to be read while music is heard | Brief Set: CD 4 Basic Set: CD 7

SCHOENBERG, *A Survivor from Warsaw*

[25] [28]

Orchestral introduction

French
horn, *pp*.

I cannot remember everything. I must have been unconscious most of the time; I remember only the grandiose moment when they all started to sing, as if prearranged, the old prayer they had neglected for so many years—the forgotten creed!

But I have no recollection how I got underground to live in the sewers of Warsaw so long a time.

The day began as usual. Reveille when it still was dark—get out whether you slept or whether worries kept you awake the whole night: you had been separated from your children, from your wife, from your parents, you don't know what happened to them; how could you sleep?

They shouted again: "Get out! The sergeant will be furious!" They came out; some very slow, the old ones, the sick men, some with nervous agility. They fear the sergeant. They hurry as much as they can. In vain! Much too much noise, much too much commotion and not fast enough!

The Feldwebel shouts: *"Achtung! Still gestanden! Na wird's mal, oder soll ich mit dem Gewehrkolben nachhelfen? Na jut; wenn Ihr's durchaus haben wollt!"* ("Attention! Stand still! How about it, or should I help you along with the butt of my rifle? Oh well, if you really want to have it!")

The sergeant and his subordinates hit everyone: young or old, strong or sick, guilty or innocent—it was painful to hear the groaning and moaning.

I heard it though I had been hit very hard, so hard that I could not help falling down. We all on the ground who could not stand up were then beaten over the head.

I must have been unconscious. The next thing I knew was a soldier saying, "They are all dead!" Whereupon the sergeant ordered to do away with us.

There I lay aside half conscious. It had become very still—fear and pain—Then I heard the sergeant shouting: *"Abzählen!"* ("Count off!")

They started slowly, and irregularly: One, two, three, four, *"Achtung."* The sergeant shouted again: *"Rascher! Nochmals von vorn anfangen! In einer Minute will ich wissen wieviele ich zur Gaskammer abliefere! Abzählen!"* ("Faster! Once more, start from the beginning! In one minute I want to know how many I am going to send off to the gas chamber! Count off!")

Accelerando,
crescendo.

They began again, first slowly: one, two, three, four, became faster and faster, so fast that it finally sounded like a stampede of wild horses, and all of a sudden, in the middle of it, they began singing the *Shema Yisroel*.

27 30 Chorus.

Shema Yisroel Adonoy elohenoo Adonoy eḥod. Veohavto es Adonoy eloheḥo beḥol levoveḥo ooveḥol nafsheḥo ooveḥol meodeḥo. Vehoyoo haddevoreem hoelleh asher onoḥee metsavveḥo hayyom al levoveḥo. Veshinnantom levoneḥo vedibbarto bom beshivteḥo beveteḥo oovelehteḥo baddereh ooveshohbeḥo oovekoomeḥo. ("Hear, O Israel, the Lord our God, the Lord is One! And thou shalt love the Lord thy God with all thy heart, and with all thy soul, and with all thy might. And these words, which I command thee this day, shall be in thy heart. And thou shalt teach them diligently unto thy children, and speak of them when thou sittest in thy house, and when thou goest on the way, and when thou liest down, and when thou risest up." [Deuteronomy 6:4–9])

 # Alban Berg

Alban Berg (1885–1935), a student of Schoenberg, wrote music that is a unique synthesis of traditional and twentieth-century elements. Berg, who was born in Vienna, first attracted international attention in 1925, when his opera *Wozzeck* was premiered in Berlin; its atonality baffled many critics, but it made a powerful impression on the public and was soon performed throughout Europe and in the United States. Perhaps because of chronic ill health, Berg did not perform or conduct, and he composed relatively few works—these include the *Chamber Concerto,* for piano, violin, and thirteen winds (1925); the *Lyric Suite,* for string quartet (1926); the opera *Lulu* (1929–1935), orchestration not completed; and the Violin Concerto (1935).

Wozzeck (1917–1922)

Wozzeck is the tragic story of a soldier who is driven to murder and madness by a hostile society. An antihero obsessed by strange visions, Wozzeck is persecuted by his sadistic captain, used as a guinea pig by a half-demented doctor, and betrayed by the woman with whom he lives, Marie. Wozzeck stabs Marie to death and drowns while trying to wash her blood from his hands.

Berg's musical imagination was fired in 1914 when he saw *Woyzeck,* a play by the German dramatist and revolutionary Georg Büchner (1813–1837). Though written in the early 1830s, the play is amazingly modern in its starkly realistic dialogue and disconnected scenes. Berg adapted the play into an opera while in the Austrian army in World War I. His own traumatic army experiences may well have deepened his sympathy for Wozzeck.

The opera's nightmarish atmosphere makes it a musical counterpart of expressionist painting and literature. Berg conveys the tensions and torments of the unconscious through harsh dissonances and grotesque distortions. The range of emotions and styles in the music is tremendous. Though most of *Wozzeck* is freely atonal—it does not use the twelve-tone system—major and minor keys occasionally add contrast. The vocal line includes speaking, shrieking, *Sprechstimme,* distorted folk songs, and melodies with wide leaps that are difficult to sing. The gigantic orchestra closely parallels the dialogue and stage action. Descriptive effects include vivid orchestral depiction of the moon rising, frogs croaking, and water engulfing the drowning Wozzeck. Berg's music rapidly shifts between very high and very low registers, between *ffff* and *pppp*.

Wozzeck has three acts, each with five scenes. Connecting the scenes are short orchestral interludes that comment musically on the preceding action and serve as preparation for what is to come. As in Wagner's music dramas, there is a continuous musical flow within each act, and characters are associated with specific musical ideas. A novel feature of *Wozzeck* is that the music for each scene is a self-contained composition with a particular form (passacaglia, sonata form, etc.) or of a definite type (military march, lullaby). The five scenes of the last act—we'll study scenes 4 and 5—are organized as (1) variations on a theme, (2) variations on a single tone, (3) variations on a rhythmic pattern, (4) variations on a chord, and (5) variations on continuous running notes. But

Doctor

(Stands still and listens.)

Das stöhnt . . . als stürbe ein Mensch.	It groans . . . It sounds like a dying man . . .
Da ertrinkt Jemand!	Someone's drowning there.

3:59   0:56
Celesta.

Captain

Unheimlich! Der Mond rot und die	It's eerie . . .The moon is red and the
Nebel grau. Hören Sie? . . . Jetzt	mist is . . . grey. Did you hear?
wieder das Ächzen.	It's groaning again.

Doctor

Stiller, . . . jetzt ganz still.	It's fainter. . . . and now quite silent.

Captain

Kommen Sie! Kommen Sie schnell.	Come away! Hurry!

(Drags the Doctor off with him.)

34   4:40
Extended
orchestral
interlude.

Scene 5

(Street before Marie's door. Bright morning. Sunshine. Children are playing and shouting. Marie's child is riding a hobbyhorse.)

Children

35   7:40

Ringel, Ringel, Rosenkranz, Ringel-	Ring around the rosie
reih'n! Ringel, Ringel, Rosenkranz,	Ring around the rosie
Rin . . .	

(They stop, and other children come rushing on.)

One of them

Du Käthel! . . . Die Marie . . .	Hey. Katie! You know about Marie?

Second Child

Was is?	What?

First Child

Weisst' es nit? Sie sind schon	I don't know, they've all gone
Alle'naus.	there.

Third Child

(To Marie's child.)

Du! Dein Mutter ist tot!	Hey, you! Your mother's dead.

Marie's Child

(Still riding his horse.)

Hopp, hopp! Hopp, hopp! Hopp, hopp!	Hop, hop! Hop, hop! Hop, hop!

Second Child

Wo is sie denn?	So where is she?

First Child

Draus' leigt sie, am Weg, neben dem Teich.

She's over there, by the pond, lying on the path.

Third Child

Kommt, anschaun!

Come, let's have a look!

(All the children run off.)

Marie's Child

(Continues to ride.)

Hopp, hopp! Hopp, hopp! Hopp, hopp!   Hop, hop! Hop, hop! Hop, hop!

Music breaks off.   (He hesitates for a moment, then rides off after the other children.)

Anton Webern

Anton Webern (1883–1945) was neglected during his lifetime, though his music influenced composers throughout the world during the 1950s and 1960s. He was born in Vienna; studied piano, cello, and music theory as a young man; and earned a doctorate in music from the University of Vienna. While at the university, he studied composition privately with Schoenberg. His career was solid but unspectacular: he made a modest income conducting various choruses and orchestras, though the rare performances of his own works were usually met with ridicule. He was a shy man, devoted to his family, and a Christian mystic who loved to commune with nature.

Although his life seems ordinary enough, his death was a bizarre tragedy—he was shot by mistake by an American soldier toward the end of World War II.

Webern's Music

Poetic lyricism pervades Webern's music, which is amazingly original in its brevity, quietness, and concentration. Most of his works are miniatures lasting only 2 or 3 minutes, and virtually all of his mature output can be played in less than $3\frac{1}{2}$ hours—rarely has a composer exerted such worldwide influence on the basis of so little music.

About half of Webern's music is for solo voice or chorus; the rest is for chamber orchestra and small chamber groups. He wrote atonal works at about the same time as Schoenberg (starting in 1908–1909) and adopted the twelve-tone system soon after Schoenberg developed it. He also exploited Schoenberg's idea of a "melody built of tone colors." Webern's melodic lines are "atomized" into two-note or three-note fragments which may at first seem isolated but add up to a unified whole. He forces us to focus on the tone color, dynamic level, and register of each note. His textures are delicate and transparent; usually, not more than a few solo instruments play at once. In his twelve-tone works, there is often strict polyphonic imitation.

Composers in the 1950s and 1960s were fascinated by Webern's techniques and often imitated his deceptively "cool" sound. Works that appealed to very few during his lifetime became a source of inspiration after his death.

Five Pieces for Orchestra, Op. 10 (1911–1913)

Webern's unique style is fully revealed in his early, atonal Five Pieces for Orchestra, Op. 10, composed before he adopted the twelve-tone system. These five "expressions of musical lyricism," as Webern called them, are among the shortest orchestral compositions ever written. The fourth piece is only $6\frac{1}{3}$ measures long and lasts less than 30 seconds. Webern's chamber orchestra of eighteen soloists includes unconventional instruments like the mandolin, guitar, cowbells, and harmonium (a small organ with metal reeds). Each piece (we'll consider the third) is scored for a different number and combination of instruments.

Melodic fragments are whispered by ever-changing solo instruments and framed by poetic silences. Tone-color melodies replace "tunes" in this music. There are few notes, but each is crucial. The tempo constantly fluctuates. Brasses and strings are usually muted.

Third Piece:
Very slow and extremely calm

Brief Set:
CD 4 28

Basic Set:
CD 7 36

With its bell sounds coming as though from far off, the third piece has a feeling of solitude and eerie stillness. The dynamics never rise above *pp*. The sustained bell-like sounds—produced by mandolin, celesta, guitar, harp, glockenspiel, cowbells, chimes, and harmonium—are heard both at the beginning and at the end. This creates a vague A B A' effect. Melodic fragments in ever-changing solo instruments are set apart from one another by brief moments of near silence.

Listening Outline to be read while music is heard

Brief Set: CD 4 Basic Set: CD 7

WEBERN, Third Piece from Five Pieces for Orchestra

Clarinet, muted French horn, muted trombone, harmonium, mandolin, guitar, celesta, harp, bass drum, snare drum, chimes, cowbells, violin, muted viola, muted cello

Very slow and extremely calm

(Duration, 1:28)

28 36	0:00	**1. a.** Pulsating bell-like sounds, *ppp*.
		b. Violin, *pp*, pulsating bell-like sounds, *ppp*.
		c. Muted horn, *pp*, chimes, *ppp*.
	0:38	**2.** Quicker notes in clarinet. Muted viola.
	0:47	**3. a.** Pulsating bell-like sounds, *ppp*.
		b. Muted trombone, *ppp*; pulsating bell-like sounds, *ppp*. Snare-drum roll, extremely soft.

Béla Bartók

Béla Bartók (1881–1945), whose music is infused with the spirit of east European folk song, was born in Hungary. His mother gave him his first lessons on the piano, an instrument which was important in his career; he taught piano at his alma mater, the Budapest Academy of Music, from 1907 to 1934, and gave recitals throughout Europe. During the early 1900s, Bartók was influenced by the Hungarian nationalist movement and spent most of his free time in small villages recording peasant folk songs. He became an authority on peasant music, and his own music was profoundly influenced by it.

Though he was neglected in Hungary until the Budapest premiere of his ballet *The Wooden Prince* in 1917, Bartók was recognized early as an important composer abroad and had a successful career during the 1920s and 1930s. But he was vehemently anti-Nazi, and in 1940 he emigrated to the United States, where he was to spend the last five years of his life. This was a bleak period for him: he had little money, was in poor health, and felt isolated and neglected.

In 1943, while in a hospital in New York, he received an unexpected commission for the Concerto for Orchestra, now his best-known work; and its success resulted in several other commissions. Tragically, however, Bartók had only a year to live and could complete just two more compositions, his Sonata for Solo Violin (1944) and Third Piano Concerto (1945). Soon after his death in New York in 1945, he became one of the most popular twentieth-century composers.

Bartók's Music

"I do not reject any influence," wrote Bartók, "provided it be pure, fresh, and healthy"; but he emphasized that the "Hungarian influence is the strongest." He evolved a completely individual style that fused folk elements, classical

Béla Bartók.

Caught up in the nationalist movement that swept Hungary, Bartók spent most of his free time in tiny villages recording folk songs on a cylinder phonograph.

forms, and twentieth-century sounds. He did arrange many folk tunes (often with highly dissonant accompaniments), but in most of his works he does not quote folk melodies—he uses original themes that have a folk flavor.

Bartók's genius found its most characteristic expression in instrumental music; he wrote many works for piano solo, six string quartets (which are among the finest since Beethoven's) and other chamber music, three piano concertos, two violin concertos, and several pieces for orchestra. His music embraces a wide range of emotions and is deeply expressive; and he revitalized and reinterpreted traditional forms such as the rondo, fugue, and sonata form.

He always organized his works around a tonal center; but within this framework he often used harsh dissonances, polychords, and tone clusters (though some of his late works have a more traditional, less dissonant vocabulary). Rhythmically, his music is characterized by a powerful beat, unexpected accents, and changing meters. He was imaginative in his use of tone colors, particularly of percussion instruments—in Music for Strings, Percussion, and Celesta (1936), for example, he drew unusual sounds from the xylophone and timpani. Like many twentieth-century composers, he also drew percussive, drumlike sounds from the piano.

Concerto for Orchestra (1943)

The commission that led to Bartók's Concerto for Orchestra was offered to him in 1943, while he was hospitalized in New York City. Serge Koussevitzky, the conductor of the Boston Symphony Orchestra, offered him $1,000 for a new work. While recuperating at Saranac Lake, New York, Bartók was able to work "practically day and night" on his new composition. He finished it in six weeks. Concerto for Orchestra was an enormous success at its premiere in Boston in 1944 and has since become Bartók's most popular work.

"The general mood of the work," wrote Bartók, "represents, apart from the jesting second movement, a gradual transition from the sternness of the first movement and the lugubrious death-song of the third, to the life-assertion of the last one." Bartók explained that the unusual title reflects the work's "tendency to treat the single orchestral instruments in a *concertant* or soloistic manner."

Indeed, Concerto for Orchestra is a showpiece for an orchestra of virtuosos. It is romantic in spirit because of its emotional intensity, memorable themes, and vivid contrasts of mood. Though its melodies were created by Bartók, they have a distinct folk flavor. The concerto is an example of Bartók's mellow "late" style, which is characterized by more frequent use of traditional chords. In all five movements, time-honored procedures like A B A form, sonata form, and fugue are fused with twentieth-century rhythms and tone colors. We'll focus on the second movement.

Second Movement: *Game of Pairs*
Allegretto scherzando

Brief Set:
CD 4 [29]

Basic Set:
CD 7 [46]

The jesting second movement, *Game of Pairs*, which is in A B A' form, is a "game" involving different pairs of woodwind and brass instruments. The melodic lines of each pair are in parallel motion and are separated by a distinctive pitch interval.

In the opening section (A), pairs of bassoons, oboes, clarinets, flutes, and muted trumpets play a chain of five melodies consecutively. The contrasting middle section (B) is a hymnlike melody played softly by brass instruments. When the opening section returns (A'), it has a more active accompaniment. The incisive sound of a snare drum (without snares) is prominent throughout the movement. It plays syncopated solos at the beginning and the end, as well as in the hymnlike middle section.

Listening Outline to be read while music is heard   Brief Set: CD 4   Basic Set: CD 7

BARTÓK, Concerto for Orchestra

Second Movement: *Game of Pairs* (Allegretto scherzando)

A B A' form, duple meter ($\frac{2}{4}$)

2 flutes, 2 oboes, 2 clarinets, 3 bassoons, 4 French horns, 2 trumpets, 2 trombones, tuba, timpani, snare drum, 2 harps, 1st violins, 2d violins, violas, cellos, double basses

(Duration, 6:40)

A

[29] [46] 0:00   **1.** Solo snare drum (without snares), *mf.*
        0:12   **2.** Two bassoons, *p*, accompanied by pizzicato strings.
[30] [47] 0:36   **3. a.** Two oboes, *p*, in higher register. Pizzicato strings accompany.
               b. Low strings, pizzicato, while oboes sustain tones.

31 **48** 1:05   **4. a.** Two clarinets.
                   b. Low strings, accented notes.

32 **49** 1:27   **5. a.** Two flutes, *mf*, in higher register.
                   b. Low strings, pizzicato, while flutes sustain tones.

33 **50** 2:14   **6.** Two muted trumpets, *p*. Muted string tremolos, *pp*, in background.

B

34 **51** 3:02   **1. a.** Brasses, *mf*, hymnlike legato melody. Snare drum accompanies.
                   b. French horns, *p*, conclude hymnlike melody and sustain chord.
                   2. Oboe, flute, and clarinet, *p*, lead to

A'

35 **52** 4:09 0:00   **1.** Two bassoons, *p*, opening melody. Staccato third bassoon in background.
         4:33 0:24   **2. a.** Two oboes, *p*, in higher register. Clarinets and strings in background.
                       b. Low strings, pizzicato, while oboes sustain tones.
         4:50 0:41   **3. a.** Two clarinets. Flutes and strings in background.
                       b. Low strings, accented notes.
         5:19 1:10   **4. a.** Two flutes, *mf*, in higher register. Woodwinds and strings in background.
                       b. Low strings, pizzicato, while flutes sustain tones.
         5:44 1:35   **5.** Two muted trumpets, *mf*. Harp glissandos and muted string tremolos in background.
         6:20 2:11   **6.** Woodwinds, *p*, repeated chord; solo snare drum, decrescendo, ends *Game of Pairs*.

Charles Ives

The American composer Charles Ives (1874–1954) wrote startlingly original music that was far ahead of its time. He was born in Danbury, Connecticut, the son of a bandmaster who loved to experiment with unusual sounds ("Pa taught me what I know," he later recalled), and he studied composition at Yale University. But when he graduated, he entered the insurance business, having decided that he could keep his music "stronger, cleaner, bigger, and freer" if he did not try to make a living out of it. (He also said that he did not want to raise a family who would "starve on his dissonances.") Eventually he founded a successful insurance agency and became very wealthy.

Ives composed furiously after business hours, on weekends, and on holidays, in isolation from the musical world; he was completely unknown, none of his major works was publicly performed, and his scores accumulated in the barn of his Connecticut farm. World War I dampened his creative urge, however, and in 1918 he had a heart attack from which he never completely recovered; after 1921 he composed almost nothing but instead began to make his work known to the public.

Charles Ives.

From 1920 to 1922, he privately printed and distributed his monumental *Concord* Sonata (1909–1915) for piano and his collection *114 Songs;* at first, they aroused little more than ridicule, but gradually a few young composers and performers recognized that Ives was enormously original. In 1939, the *Concord* Sonata received an ovation at its first complete New York performance; and by the 1940s, many considered Ives the first great composer from the United States. In 1947 he won a Pulitzer Prize for his Third Symphony (1904–1911), written some forty years earlier.

Ives's Music

Though experimental, Ives's compositions are rooted deeply in the folk and popular music he knew as a boy: revival hymns, ragtime, village bands, church choirs, patriotic songs, and barn dances. He was inspired by the "unconventional" features of the American tradition—the village fiddler playing slightly out of tune, the cornetist a fraction ahead of the rest of the band, the church organist accidentally holding one chord while the choir sings another. His polyrhythms, polytonality, and tone clusters grew out of the music he knew. One boyhood experience in particular seems to have had an important influence: two bands playing different music passed each other as they marched by him in opposite directions. In later works Ives simultaneously presents musical events that seem unrelated: two bands play in different keys; consonant chords are set against dissonant chords; conflicting meters and rhythmic patterns are intertwined. To evoke memories, he often quotes snatches of familiar tunes, develops them, and integrates them within his music. Even the titles of his works suggest his New England heritage—for example, the movements of the *Concord* Sonata are *Emerson, Hawthorne, The Alcotts,* and *Thoreau;* and we'll study one movement from a set of orchestral pieces called *Three Places in New England.*

Ives's music has a wide range of emotions, styles, and techniques; it includes mild, consonant chords and earsplitting dissonances. (He scorned those who couldn't take dissonance: "Beauty in music," he wrote, "is too often confused with something that lets the ears lie back in an easy chair.") Much of his music is extraordinarily difficult to perform. His large and varied output includes five symphonies and other orchestral music; works for piano, chorus, and chamber ensembles; and over 200 songs.

Putnam's Camp, Redding, Connecticut (1912), from Three Places in New England (1908?–1914)

Basic Set:
CD 8 **7**

Putnam's Camp, Redding, Connecticut (1912), is part of *Three Places in New England,* a set of three pieces for orchestra evoking American history, life, and landscape. Though completed around 1914, *Three Places in New England* was not performed until 1930. Today it is one of Ives's most popular works and is considered a landmark in American music.

The daring, brilliant second movement, *Putnam's Camp,* is a child's impression of a Fourth of July picnic. Ives recaptures his boyhood memory of two marching bands clashing dissonantly as they play different tunes. His quotations of snatches of marches and patriotic songs contribute to the piece's popular flavor. Like much of his music, *Putnam's Camp* shifts abruptly between conventional harmonies and harsh "modern" dissonances.

Ives prefaced his score with a literary program for the movement. "Near Redding Center, Conn., is a small park preserved as a Revolutionary Memorial; for here General Israel Putnam's soldiers had their winter quarters in 1778–1779." One Fourth of July, "a child went there on a picnic held under the auspices of the First Church and the Village Cornet Band." The child wanders "away from the rest of the children past the camp ground into the woods. As he rests on the hillside of laurel and hickories, the tunes of the band and the songs of the children grow fainter. . . ." He falls asleep and dreams of "a tall woman standing . . . the Goddess of Liberty . . . pleading with the soldiers not to forget their 'cause'. . . . But they march out of the camp with fife and drum to a popular tune of the day. Suddenly a new national note is heard. Putnam is coming over the hills from the center—the soldiers turn back and cheer. The little boy awakes, he hears the children's songs and runs down past the monument to 'listen to the band' and join in the games and dances."

Putnam's Camp is in three sections (A B A') that parallel the composer's descriptive program. The first section, which is marked *quick step time,* captures the gaiety and confusion of a picnic. After a raucous, highly dissonant introduction, the strings play the main theme, a vigorous march that begins with conventional harmonies.

Introduction
7 0:00

Main theme
0:10

Such abrupt shifts between harsh dissonances and mild consonances are typical of Ives and are heard throughout *Putnam's Camp.* The piano, woodwinds, and brasses begin to compete for the listener's attention, and soon it sounds as though two bands are playing against each other. The mood becomes even

8 1:05

more comic when a parody of the opening phrase of *Yankee Doodle* is quickly played by trumpet, flute, and violins.

A sentimental violin melody probably represents the child, whose falling asleep is suggested when the music becomes softer and slows to a halt.

9 2:14

The middle section (B) represents the child's dream. The goddess of liberty pleading with the soldiers is suggested by the impression of two bands playing in different tempos. One band begins with a sad oboe melody accompanied by strings, the other with a march rhythm in the piano and snare drum. A quota-

10 3:11

tion of *The British Grenadiers,* a favorite tune of the Revolutionary army, represents the army marching out of the camp.

11 4:20

In the riotous concluding section (A'), Ives creates deliberate melodic and rhythmic confusion as the main march theme is combined with *The British Grenadiers* and other fragments.

George Gershwin

Popular songs and musical comedies as well as jazz-flavored orchestral works and opera won international fame for the American composer George Gershwin (1898–1937). His parents were Russian-Jewish immigrants, and he grew up on the lower east side of Manhattan. As a boy, he taught himself to play hit tunes on a neighbor's piano; when he was thirteen, he began studying with a teacher who recognized his talent and introduced him to piano works ranging from Bach to Liszt to Debussy.

At fifteen, he left school to become a pianist demonstrating new songs in the salesrooms of a music publisher; three years later, he started his own career as a songwriter, and in 1919 (at the age of twenty) he wrote *La, La, Lucille,* his first complete Broadway musical. The next year, his song *Swanee* was a tremendous hit; during the 1920s and 1930s he wrote one brilliant musical after another—including *Lady, Be Good* (1924), *Funny Face* (1927), and *Of Thee I Sing* (1931)—usually with his brother Ira as lyricist.

Gershwin was not only a creator of the golden age of American musical theater but also a successful composer of music for the concert hall, beginning with the triumphant premiere of *Rhapsody in Blue* in 1924. He gave the first performance of his Concerto in F at Carnegie Hall in 1925 and traveled to Europe in the 1920s (meeting Berg in Vienna and Ravel and Stravinsky in Paris); part of his symphonic poem *An American in Paris* (1928) was composed on one of these visits. His most extended work is the opera *Porgy and Bess* (1935), which deals with the lives of poor black people in Charleston, South Carolina; it has been performed all over the world.

George Gershwin.

Gershwin was outgoing, a sportsman, an art collector and amateur painter, and irresistible to women; he was also wealthy, from royalties, concert fees, and his weekly radio show. During the last year of his life, he lived in Hollywood, where he wrote the music for several movies (and played tennis with Arnold Schoenberg in his spare time). He died of a brain tumor at the age of thirty-eight.

Rhapsody in Blue (1924)

Rhapsody in Blue, Gershwin's most famous composition, is a one-movement work for piano and orchestra. The title reflects its free, rhapsodic form and blues flavor (see pages 372–374 for a description of blues). But it is not true jazz, though it employs jazzlike rhythms and melodies and the orchestration suggests the distinctive sounds of jazz. There are three main sections and a coda; the extended piano solos in the main sections reflect Gershwin's own dazzling pianism and his genius as an improviser.

Rhapsody in Blue opens with a now-famous clarinet solo that starts from a low trill, climbs the scale, and then slides up to a high "wailing" tone. The blues-like opening theme, which grows out of the clarinet slide, is marked by the syncopations so typical of Gershwin's style.

It is followed by a repeated-note theme, presented by French horns, which reappears many times.

The opening section continues with an extended piano solo, a return of the blues theme, and a marchlike trumpet theme.

A new jazzlike theme, introduced in the low register, begins the lively second section, marked *con moto.*

The moderately slow third section is based on a lyrical, romantic melody first presented by the violins. This memorable tune is combined with a countermelody played by the French horns.

Rhapsody in Blue concludes with a rapid coda, which is ushered in by an accelerated transformation of the romantic melody.

William Grant Still

The flowering of African American culture during the years 1917–1935—sometimes called the "Harlem Renaissance"—found musical expression in the works of the composer William Grant Still (1895–1978). His *Afro-American Symphony* (1931), which we'll study, was the first composition by a black composer to be performed by a major American symphony orchestra.

Still was born in Woodville, Mississippi, but grew up in Little Rock, Arkansas, where he began to study violin. At the age of sixteen, Still enrolled at Wilberforce University (Ohio) as a premedical student; but he devoted himself to musical activities, such as playing violin in the university string quartet, and decided to abandon medicine for music. He left college before graduating to enter the world of popular music as an arranger and performer. Still worked for the composer and publisher W. C. Handy in Memphis and arranged Handy's *St. Louis Blues* for military band (1916). In 1917, he enrolled at Oberlin College Conservatory to continue his formal music training, but he soon left to serve in the navy in World War I.

William Grant Still.

After his navy service and a brief return to studies at Oberlin College, Still moved to New York, where he lived a double life as a popular musician and as a composer of concert works. He made band arrangements and played in the orchestras of such all-black musical shows as *Shuffle Along* (1921). He also studied privately with two important composers in opposing musical camps: the conservative George Whitefield Chadwick and the modernist Edgard Varèse. After composing a few highly dissonant works under Varèse's influence, Still turned away from avant-garde styles and wrote compositions with a uniquely African American flavor that were performed to critical acclaim in New York.

A turning point in Still's career came in 1931, with the highly successful premiere of his *Afro-American Symphony* by the Rochester Philharmonic. Within the next two decades, this symphony was performed by thirty-eight orchestras in the United States and Europe. In 1934, Still was awarded a Guggenheim Fellowship, and the next year he moved to Los Angeles, where he wrote film scores, concert works, and operas. Still was the first African American to conduct a major symphony orchestra—the Los Angeles Philharmonic, in 1936. He was also the first to have an opera performed by a major opera company—*Troubled Island*, about the Haitian slave rebellion, in 1949. In 1981, three years after Still's death, his opera *A Bayou Legend*, written in 1941, was broadcast on national television.

Afro-American Symphony (1931)

Afro-American Symphony, Still's best-known work, was composed in 1930, shortly after the onset of the great depression. "It was not until the depression struck," he later observed, "that I was jobless long enough to let the symphony take shape. In 1930, I rented a room in a quiet building not far from my home in New York, and began to work." Still devised his own blues theme and explained that he "wanted to demonstrate that the blues, so often considered a lowly expression, could be elevated to the highest musical level." The blues theme is introduced in the first movement and then reappears in various transformations in the three later movements as a unifying thread. Still also gave an African American character to the symphony by using a tenor banjo as part of the orchestra and by inventing themes that recall spirituals and jazz tunes. Each of the symphony's four movements has a subtitle and is prefaced by lines from a poem by the African American poet Paul Laurence Dunbar (1872–1906). We'll focus on the third movement.

Third Movement: Animato

Brief Set:

CD 4 36

Basic Set:

CD 7 53

Still gave this joyful, scherzo-like movement the subtitle *Humor* and prefaced it with the following quotation from Dunbar's poem: "An' we'll shout ouah hallelujahs/On dat mighty reck'nin' day." After a brief introduction, Still presents two melodies that reappear in varied guises within the movement. The lively, syncopated opening melody is made up of short motives, each ending with a repeated note and pause. Still called this the *hallelujah* melody, perhaps because its opening four notes fit the word "hallelujah." The *hallelujah* melody is accompanied by a syncopated countermelody. This jubilant second melody, more fully orchestrated than the first, is reminiscent of a spiritual. It includes two "blue" notes, the lowered third and seventh of the scale. The movement falls into three sections (1, 2, 3 in the listening outline), of which the last is an abridged return of the first. Varied orchestral colors and lively countermelodies contribute to the movement's high spirits.

Listening Outline to be read while music is heard

Brief Set: CD 4   Basic Set: CD 7

STILL, *Afro-American Symphony*

Third Movement: Animato

Quadruple meter ($\frac{4}{4}$), A flat major

Piccolo, 2 flutes, 2 oboes, English horn, 2 clarinets, bass clarinet, 4 French horns, 3 trumpets, 3 trombones, tuba, timpani, small cymbal, large suspended cymbal, tenor banjo, 1st violins, 2d violins, violas, cellos, double basses

(Duration, 3:00)

36 53

1. **a.** Timpani roll, syncopated motive in French horns, *f*, syncopated motive in brasses, cymbal crash, introduce

37 54 0:15

   b. Syncopated *hallelujah* melody in major, violins, *f*, off-beat accompaniment in banjo and French horns, *mf*,

      0:24

   c. Syncopated countermelody in high wooodwinds introduces

38 55 0:31 0:00

   d. Full orchestra, *f*, second melody.

0:49	0:18	**e.**	Suddenly softer, *hallelujah* melody in oboe, then flutes, running notes in bass clarinet.
1:04	0:33	**f.**	Sudden *ff*, trombones and French horns in unison, minor; suddenly softer, violins lead upward, violins, *f*, cymbals, answered by brasses, dotted rhythm, decrescendo to

39 **56** 1:34 0:00 **2. a.** Staccato flutes, *mp*, *hallelujah* melody varied, continuation in oboes,

legato flutes, English horn, violins, *p*, descend.

1:59	0:25	**b.**	Muted trumpets answered by French horns, *p*, new variation of *hallelujah* melody,
2:07	0:33	**c.**	Sudden *f*, trombones and tuba in unison, minor, full orchestra, cymbal crashes.
2:19	0:45	**3. a.**	Violins, *mf*, *hallelujah* melody, with high flute and piccolo countermelody, banjo accompanies, oboes and flutes, *hallelujah* melody embellished.
2:35	1:01	**b.**	Violins, *mf*, second melody, sudden *f*, low strings and woodwinds in unison, minor.

40 **57** 2:57 **c.** Full orchestra, *ff*, jubilant variant of *hallelujah* melody,

quick brass countermelody, rising strings, cymbal crash, and staccato ending chord.

15 Aaron Copland

Aaron Copland (1900–1990), a leading American composer, was born in Brooklyn; his parents (like Gershwin's) were Russian-Jewish immigrants. "No one ever talked music to me or took me to a concert," he recalled; but he discovered music on his own and at fifteen decided to become a composer. He was drawn to "modern" music, although his first teacher discouraged it; and in 1921 he went to France to study with Nadia Boulanger, an extraordinary woman who taught several generations of American composers and was sympathetic to contemporary trends.

Copland's music went through several phases. When he first returned to New York, he wanted to write works that would be "American in character"—and to him, *American* meant jazz. An example is his *Music for the Theater* (1925), a piece for small orchestra with elements of blues and ragtime; but this "jazz period" lasted only a few years. During the early 1930s he composed serious, very dissonant, sophisticated works (such as the highly regarded *Piano Variations*, 1930) that convey starkness, power, percussiveness, and intense concentration.

In the late 1930s, he modified his style again, writing more accessible works for a larger audience. These were the depression years, when many composers rejected the idea of writing for an elite, and Copland now drew on American folklore—as in his ballets *Billy the Kid* (1938), *Rodeo* (1942), and *Appalachian Spring* (1944)—and on jazz, revival hymns, cowboy songs, and other folk tunes. His scores for films and his patriotic works (such as *A Lincoln Portrait*, 1942) also reached a mass public, and his name became synonymous with American music.

Copland accomplished the difficult feat of writing simple yet highly professional music. His textures are clear; his slow-moving harmonies—often almost motionless—seem to evoke the openness of the American landscape; and, though strongly tonal, his works embody twentieth-century techniques such as polychords, polyrhythms, changing meters, and percussive orchestration. He also used serial technique (that is, the manipulation of a tone row, or series) in such works as *Connotations* for orchestra (1962).

Aaron Copland.

Scene from a production of *Appalachian Spring*.

Aside from his numerous compositions, Copland made many other contributions to American music by directing composers' groups, organizing concerts, lecturing, writing books and articles, teaching, and conducting.

Appalachian Spring (1943–1944)

Appalachian Spring originated as a ballet score for Martha Graham, the great modern dancer and choreographer. It took Copland about a year (1943–1944) to finish the music. While composing *Appalachian Spring,* he thought, "How foolhardy it is to be spending all this time writing a thirty-five-minute score for a modern-dance company, knowing how short-lived most ballets *and* their scores are." But in 1945 Copland arranged parts of the ballet as a suite for full orchestra (originally, the ballet used only thirteen instrumentalists); this suite won important prizes and brought his name to a large public. Today, *Appalachian Spring* is widely performed both as a ballet and as a concert piece.

The ballet concerns a "pioneer celebration in spring around a newly built farmhouse in the Pennsylvania hills" in the early 1800s. Its characters include a bride and groom, a neighbor, and a revivalist preacher with his followers. The rhythms and melodies are American-sounding and suggest barn dances, fiddle tunes, and revival hymns. But Copland uses only one actual folk tune in the score—a Shaker melody entitled *Simple Gifts.* (The Shakers were a religious sect established in America around the time of the Revolution. They expressed religious fervor through shaking, leaping, dancing, and singing.) *Appalachian Spring* is bright and transparent, has a clear tonality, and is basically tender and calm in mood. The score's rhythmic excitement comes from delightful syncopations and rapid changes of meter. As in many twentieth-century works, the orchestra includes a piano and a large percussion section.

The ballet suite has eight sections, including a duo for the bride and groom, a fast dance for the revivalist preacher and his followers with "suggestions of square dances and country fiddlers," and a finale in which the couple are left "quiet and strong in their new house." We'll focus on Section 7, which originally accompanied "Scenes of daily activity for the Bride and her Farmer-husband."

Section 7:
Theme and Variations on *Simple Gifts*

Brief Set:
CD 4 [41]

Basic Set:
CD 8 [12]

Section 7 is a theme and five variations on the Shaker tune *Simple Gifts.* The melody's folklike simplicity reflects the Shaker text, which opens as follows:

'Tis the gift to be simple, 'tis the gift to be free,
'Tis the gift to come down where we ought to be.

In each variation, Copland brings the tune back unadorned, creating variety and contrast through changes of tempo, tone color, dynamics, register, accompaniment, and key. Variation 2 sounds thoughtful and lyrical, as the tune is played more slowly, in a lower register, with polyphonic imitations. Variation 3 brings a brilliant contrast, as *Simple Gifts* is presented faster and staccato by trumpets and trombones. In each of the last two variations, Copland uses only part of the tune: its second part in the pastoral variation 4, and its first part in the majestic closing variation.

Listening Outline to be read while music is heard

Brief Set: CD 4   Basic Set: CD 8

COPLAND, *Appalachian Spring*

Section 7: Theme and Variations on *Simple Gifts*

Theme and variations, duple meter ($\frac{2}{4}$), A flat major

2 flutes, 2 oboes, 2 clarinets, 2 bassoons, 2 French horns, 2 trumpets, 2 trombones, timpani, triangle, glockenspiel, harp, piano, 1st violins, 2d violins, violas, cellos, double basses

(Duration, 3:09)

Theme

41 12 0:00   Clarinet, *p*, *Simple Gifts*, legato.

Variation 1

42 13 0:33   Oboe, *mp*, and bassoon, *mp*, *Simple Gifts*, slightly faster, in higher register.

Variation 2

43 14 1:00   High harp, piano, glockenspiel, *p*, introduce *Simple Gifts*, violas and trombone, *mf*, played half as fast, in lower register. *Simple Gifts* imitated in violins, *f*, then in cellos and basses, *f*. Woodwinds, *p*, brief transition to

Variation 3

44 15 1:52   Trumpets and trombones, *f*, *Simple Gifts*, twice as fast, staccato.

Variation 4

45 16 2:16   Woodwinds, *mf*, second part of *Simple Gifts*, slightly slower than variation 3, gentle and legato.

Variation 5

46 17 2:34   Full orchestra, *fff*, first part of *Simple Gifts*, played slowly and majestically, in high register.

Musical Styles since 1945

Since World War II, we have lived with instant communication—television, computers, and space satellites provide access to a virtually unlimited flow of information. Not only have we been bombarded by an incredible variety of stimuli, but there has also been a constant demand for novelty. New styles in fashion and the visual arts spread rapidly and then disappear.

In music as well, the emphasis has been on novelty and change. Musical innovations since 1945 have been even more far-reaching than those of the first half of the twentieth century. There have been many new directions, and the range of musical styles and systems is wider than ever. As the American composer Milton Babbitt (b. 1916) observed in 1984, "the world of music never before has been so pluralistic, so fragmented."

Particularly since the 1970s, many composers have advocated stylistic pluralism or eclecticism. Their works include sections in a variety of styles ranging from baroque to rock. In 1999, the American composer John Adams (b. 1947) told an interviewer, "We're in a kind of post-style era. Composers of my age and younger, we are not writing in one, highly defined, overarching expression." Adams believes that the contemporary composer can follow the examples of Bach, Mahler, and Stravinsky, and be "somebody who just reached out and grabbed everything" and through musical technique and spiritual vision "turned it into something great." In Section 17, we will study *Fugata* (1969) by Astor Piazzolla, who created a highly individual style by fusing the tango of his homeland, Argentina, with procedures drawn from jazz and music by Bach, Bartók, and Stravinsky.

Characteristics of Music since 1945

Accurately describing the relatively recent past is difficult. Yet any overview of music since 1945 must include the following major developments:

1. Increased use of the *twelve-tone system.*
2. *Serialism*—use of the techniques of the twelve-tone system to organize rhythm, dynamics, and tone color.
3. *Chance music,* in which a composer chooses pitches, tone colors, and rhythms by random methods, or allows a performer to choose much of the musical material.
4. *Minimalist music,* characterized by a steady pulse, clear tonality, and insistent repetition of short melodic patterns.
5. *Musical quotation,* works containing deliberate quotations from earlier music.
6. *Tonal music and a return to tonality* by some composers.
7. *Electronic music.*
8. *"Liberation of sound"*—greater exploitation of noiselike sounds.
9. *Mixed media.*
10. New concepts of *rhythm* and *form.*

Since 1945, long-playing records, audiotape, compact discs, DVDs, and the Internet have spread these new musical ideas far and wide. In Asia, for example,

Flood (1967) by Helen Frankenthaler. Working without a brush, Frankenthaler allows paint to soak and stain an unprimed canvas stretched on the floor.

interest in western music has increased dramatically. Many young musicians from Japan, China, Taiwan, and South Korea study in American music schools and universities, and Asian performers are prominent on the international concert scene.

Increased Use of the Twelve-Tone System

A striking development after World War II (1945) was the gradual abandonment of tonality in favor of the twelve-tone system. From the early 1920s—when Schoenberg invented the system—to about 1950, most composers still wrote music with a tonal center. Few were attracted to the new method, because it was associated with Schoenberg's expressionist style, which had gone out of fashion. During the 1950s, however, the twelve-tone system was adopted by many composers, including Stravinsky, who had been the leading composer of tonal music.

What contributed to this dramatic shift? In Europe, the end of the war brought a strong desire for new musical beginnings. During the Nazi years, composers had been denied access to the twelve-tone works of Schoenberg and Webern; when peace came, they were eager to explore unfamiliar musical territory. In the United States, twelve-tone music was now available on long-playing records, and complex scores became easier to study.

Since 1950, there have been many new styles in the visual arts. Bridget Riley's *Nataraja* (1993) is *op*—or *optical*—art, which exploits visual effects and illusions.

But the most important reasons for the shift to the twelve-tone system were the resources of the system itself. Composers discovered that it was a compositional technique rather than a special musical style. Musicians as different as Bach, Mozart, and Chopin had all used the tonal system; a comparable diversity of style was possible within the twelve-tone system. The new method also had the advantage of stimulating unconventional approaches to melody, harmony, and form. As Aaron Copland once expressed it, "I began to hear chords that I wouldn't have heard otherwise. Heretofore I had been thinking tonally, but this was a new way of moving tones about. It freshened up one's technique and one's approach."

Many composers of the 1950s and 1960s chose to write music that was stylistically reminiscent of Anton Webern, Schoenberg's disciple. They created "pointillist" music in which melodic lines are "atomized" into tiny fragments that are heard in widely separated registers and framed by moments of silence. Webern's style answered the needs of the post-World War II generation: his music had a lean, "modern" sound, whereas Schoenberg's was considered too "romantic" and traditional in form. The French composer Pierre Boulez (b. 1925) spoke for many of his generation in 1952 when he unfavorably compared Schoenberg's alliance with the "decadence of the great German romantic tradition" and Webern's reaction "against all inherited rhetoric."

Extensions of the Twelve-Tone System: Serialism

During the late 1940s and early 1950s, the techniques of the twelve-tone system came to be used to organize dimensions of music other than pitch, such as rhythm, dynamics, and tone color. Recall that in early twelve-tone music the system was used primarily to order *pitch* relationships. All the pitches of a twelve-tone composition would be derived from a single tone row, or series. After 1950, a series of durations (rhythmic values), dynamic levels, or tone colors also could serve as a unifying idea. A rhythmic or dynamic series might be manipulated like the series of twelve tones. The use of a series, or ordered group of musical elements, to organize several dimensions of a composition is called *serialism.* Proponents of serialism include Milton Babbitt (b. 1916) in the United States, Karlheinz Stockhausen (b. 1928) in Germany, and Pierre Boulez in France. Their methods lead to a totally controlled and organized music, but the actual sound—in certain cases—might seem random and chaotic. The complex relationships in the music are often difficult to perceive.

Chance Music

The 1950s witnessed not only serialism but an opposite approach known as *chance,* or *aleatory, music* (from Latin *alea,* or *game of chance*). In chance music, composers choose pitches, tone colors, and rhythms by random methods such as throwing coins. They may also ask performers to choose the ordering of the musical material, or even to choose much of the material itself. For example, a composer might write out brief passages of a composition but ask the performer to play them in any desired order. Or a composer might indicate a group of pitches but direct the performer to invent rhythmic patterns.

The most famous and influential creator of chance music was the American John Cage (1912–1992). At the very beginning of this book, a reference was made to Cage's silent "composition" entitled *4′33″* (1952), which requires the performer *not* to make a sound for 4 minutes and 33 seconds. The "music" is made up of the unintentional sounds that an audience might produce in this time span. "I try to arrange my composing means," Cage once explained, "so that I won't have any knowledge of what might happen. . . . My purpose is to eliminate purpose." For Cage, "The purpose of this purposeless music would be achieved if people learned to listen. Then when they listened they might discover that they preferred the sounds of everyday life to the ones they would presently hear in the musical program. . . . That was all right as far as I was concerned." Cage's approach is also illustrated by his *Imaginary Landscape* No. 4 (1951), for twelve radios. The score gives precise directions to the performers—two at each radio—for manipulating the dials affecting wavelength and volume. Yet all the indications in the score were chosen by chance means. They show no regard for local station wavelengths or the time of performance. "At the actual performance of *Imaginary Landscape,*" reported one member of the audience, "the hour was later than anticipated before the work's turn came on the program, so that the instruments were unable to capture programs diversified enough to present a really interesting result." This is not surprising, since Cage had chosen the wavelengths and dynamics by throwing dice.

With Cage's work as an example, serial composers such as Pierre Boulez and Karlheinz Stockhausen introduced elements of chance into their compositions during the mid-1950s. Stockhausen's Piano Piece No. 11 (1956) has nineteen short segments of music printed on a large roll of paper that measures 37 by 21 inches. The segments can be played in any order, and the performer is instructed to begin with the fragment that first catches the eye. The piece is likely to be different each time it is played.

Chance effects are incorporated into *One (Number 31, 1950)* by the abstract expressionist painter Jackson Pollock. The artist dripped, poured, and flung paint onto an enormous canvas tacked to the floor.

Chance music makes a complete break with traditional values in music. It asserts, in effect, that one sound or ordering of sounds is as meaningful as another. To most listeners, a piece of chance music is more often significant as an idea than as a collection of actual sounds. Some composers may be attracted by the sheer novelty of chance music, by its ability to shock and attract attention. Others are influenced by Asian philosophies such as Zen Buddhism, which stresses the harmony of beauty and nature. Finally, some composers may want to give performers a major part in the creative process.

Minimalist Music

The mid-1960s saw the development of an artistic movement called *minimalism*, which was partly a reaction against the complexity of serialism and the randomness of chance music. **Minimalist music** is characterized by steady pulse, clear tonality, and insistent repetition of short melodic patterns. Its dynamic level, texture, and harmony tend to stay constant for fairly long stretches of time, creating a trancelike or hypnotic effect. Leading minimalist composers, such as Terry Riley (b. 1935), Steve Reich (b. 1936), Philip Glass (b. 1937), and John Adams (b. 1947) have been profoundly influenced by nonwestern thought; many have studied African, Indian, or Balinese music. Minimalist music grew out of the same intellectual climate as minimalist art, which features simple forms, clarity, and understatement. Indeed, in the 1960s, minimalist musicians were appreciated more by painters and sculptors than by their fellow composers. "I gravitated towards artists because they were always more open than musicians, and I liked looking at what they did," Philip Glass has said.

Minimalist composers have generally tried to bring their music to the widest possible audience. "One mode of feedback I rely on most," writes Steve Reich,

Untitled (1984) by Donald Judd (1928–1994) is a minimalist sculpture in four identical parts.
Art © Judd Foundation. Licensed by VAGA, New York, NY.

"is the popular naive reactions. . . . My work, and that of Glass and Riley, comes as a breath of fresh air to the new music world. . . . This feeling is very healthy. It's a feeling of moving back away from a recondite and isolated position, toward a more mainstream approach." Both Reich and Glass have ensembles that perform their music in auditoriums and rock clubs. A turning point in public acceptance of minimalist music came in 1976, when Reich's *Music for 18 Musicians* received an ovation in Town Hall in New York and—also in New York—Glass's opera *Einstein on the Beach* sold out the Metropolitan Opera House. After the early 1970s, minimalist music became progressively richer in harmony, tone color, and texture, as is exemplified in Adams's opera *Nixon in China* (1987).

Musical Quotation

Since the mid-1960s, many composers have written works in which they deliberately make extensive use of quotations from earlier music, usually fairly familiar works of the eighteenth, nineteenth, and twentieth centuries. Like minimalist music, *quotation music* often represents a conscious break with serialism, as well as an attempt to improve communication between composer and listener. The quoted material usually either conveys a symbolic meaning or is varied, transformed, and juxtaposed with other music. For example, in the outer movements of *Concerto Grosso 1985*, which we'll study, Ellen Taaffe Zwilich juxtaposes parts of a Handel sonata with original passages. In *Sinfonia* (1968), a composition for voices and orchestra by the Italian composer Luciano Berio (1925–2003), the third section is based on the scherzo from Mahler's Second Symphony; on this quoted material from Mahler, Berio superimposes fragments of music by Bach, Debussy, Ravel, Berlioz, Schoenberg, and other composers, creating a musical collage. Like Charles Ives early in the twentieth century, composers since the 1960s have often juxtaposed heterogeneous material. The

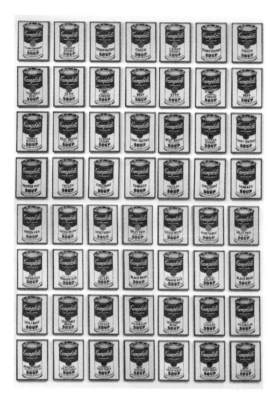

Campbell's Soup Cans (1962) by Andy Warhol. Pop artists like Warhol use ordinary subjects from everyday life and the mass media.

American composer George Crumb (b. 1929) explained that in writing his song cycle *Ancient Voices of Children* (1970), he "was conscious of an urge to fuse various unrelated stylistic elements, . . . a suggestion of Flamenco with a Baroque quotation . . . or a reminiscence of Mahler with a breath of the orient."

Occasionally, modern composers will not only quote earlier composers but also imitate earlier styles. In String Quartet No. 3 (1972) by the American composer George Rochberg (b. 1918), there are sections of atonal music and passages in the styles of Beethoven and Mahler.

Tonal Music and a Return to Tonality

As in the early twentieth century, many composers since 1945 have written tonal music, as opposed to atonal or twelve-tone music. (It may be helpful to review the discussion of alternatives to the traditional tonal system on pages 298–299.) Such tonal music spans a vast range of styles and compositional methods, and includes works by composers as diverse as Benjamin Britten, Dmitri Shostakovich, Leonard Bernstein (1918–1990), and John Adams. Tonal compositions may include central tones or chords as well as consonant sonorities. Some works are entirely tonal, while others are basically atonal but contain chord progressions that provide a fleeting sensation of tonality.

Starting in the late 1960s, some composers, such as the Americans George Rochberg (b. 1918) and David Del Tredici (b. 1937), returned to tonality after having written atonal or twelve-tone music. These composers are sometimes referred to as "new romantics," to emphasize the emotional intensity of their works.

Tonality could be a fascinating "novel" option for musicians trained in the twelve-tone system. "For me," explained Del Tredici, "tonality was actually a daring discovery. I grew up in a climate in which, for a composer, only dissonance and atonality were acceptable. Right now, tonality is exciting for me."

Electronic Music

Since the development of tape studios, synthesizers, and computers in the 1950s and 1960s, composers have had potentially unlimited resources for the production and control of sound. Electronic music is as diverse as nonelectronic music. Its spectrum includes rock, chance music, and serial compositions.

Electronic instruments let composers control tone color, duration, dynamics, and pitch with unprecedented precision. Composers are no longer limited by human performers. For the first time, they can work *directly* in their own medium—sound. There is no more need for intermediaries, that is, performers. The audiotape of a composition *is* the composition. Thus, a composer alone is now responsible for putting into music the subtle variations of rhythm, tone color, and dynamics that once rested with the performer.

Many composers have felt a need to "humanize" their electronic music by combining it with live performers. This humanization can be accomplished in several ways. Some pieces use one or more live performers in conjunction with taped sounds. The taped sounds may be electronic pitches or noises, or they may be previously recorded sounds of live performers. In some cases, performers may be involved in a duet with themselves, or a duet with electronically manipulated versions of their own performances. In combining live performers with taped sounds, composers face the problem of synchronizing sounds that change from performance to performance—those of the live musicians—and the taped sounds, which don't vary. Recently, some composers have dealt with this problem by creating interactive works for performers and computer. In such compositions, the computer is programmed by the composer to respond in musically meaningful ways to the live performance.

There are also works for traditional instruments and digital synthesizers and samplers that are performed "live." In addition, traditional instruments may also be "electrified" through amplification. Composers use "electric" pianos and violins, for instance.

Electronic music is important not only in itself but also in its influence on musical thought in general. Electronic instruments have suggested new sounds and new forms of rhythmic organization. "These limitless electronic media," said Milton Babbitt,

> have shown us new boundaries and new limits that are not yet understood—the very mysterious limits, for example, of the human capacity to hear, to conceptualize, and to perceive. Very often we will specify something and discover that the ear can't take in what we have specified. . . . The human organism simply cannot respond quickly enough, cannot perceive and differentiate as rapidly and precisely as the synthesizer can produce it and as the loudspeaker can reproduce it.

"Liberation of Sound"

Composers today use a wider variety of sounds than ever before, including many that were once considered undesirable noises. Composers have achieved what Edgard Varèse called "the liberation of sound . . . the right to make music with any and all sounds." Electronic music may include environmental sounds, such as thunder, or electronically generated hisses and blips. But composers may also draw novel sounds from voices and nonelectronic instruments. Singers are asked to scream, whisper, laugh, groan, sneeze, cough, whistle, and click their tongues. They may sing phonetic sounds rather than words. Composers may treat their vocal text merely as a collection of sounds and not attempt to make the meaning of the words clear to the audience.

Wind and string players tap, scrape, and rub the bodies of their instruments. A brass or woodwind player may hum while playing, thus creating two pitches at once. A flutist may click the keys of the instrument without producing a tone; a pianist may reach inside the piano to pluck a string and then run a chisel along it, creating a sliding sound. To communicate their intentions to performers, composers may devise new systems of music notation, because standard notation makes no provision for many noiselike sounds. Recent music scores contain graphlike diagrams, new note shapes and symbols, and novel ways of arranging notation on the page (see the illustration on page 358). But composers are not the only ones to invent unusual sounds. Often the players themselves discover new possibilities for their instruments. Many modern works have been inspired by the discoveries of inventive performers.

The greatest expansion and experimentation have involved percussion instruments. In many recent compositions, percussion instruments outnumber strings, woodwinds, and brasses. Traditional percussion instruments are struck with new types of beaters made of glass, metal, wood, and cloth. Unconventional instruments now widely used include tom-toms, bongos, slapstick, maracas, guiro, and vibraphone.

In the search for novel sounds, increased use has been made of **microtones,** intervals smaller than the half step. Small intervals like quarter tones have long been used in nonwestern music, but they have only recently become an important resource for western composers. Electronic instruments have stimulated this development, since they are not restricted to conventional scales and do not force players to unlearn performance habits.

Composers like Krzysztof Penderecki (b. 1933) create sounds bordering on electronic noise through tone clusters—closely spaced tones played together. Clusters are unlike traditional chords in that one usually hears not individual tones but a mass, block, or band of sound. Composers may achieve a sense of growth or change by widening or narrowing such a band, or by making it more or less dense.

The directional aspect of sounds—how they are projected in space—has taken on new importance. Loudspeakers or groups of instruments may be placed at opposite ends of the stage, in the balcony, or at the back and sides of the auditorium. In electronic compositions like Edgard Varèse's *Poème électronique* (1958) and nonelectronic works like Elliott Carter's Double Concerto for harpsichord and piano with two chamber orchestras (1961), sounds are made to travel gradually in space, passing from one loudspeaker or player to another.

Mixed Media

Electronic music is often presented together with visual counterparts such as slide projections, films, light shows, gestures, and theatrical action. One such

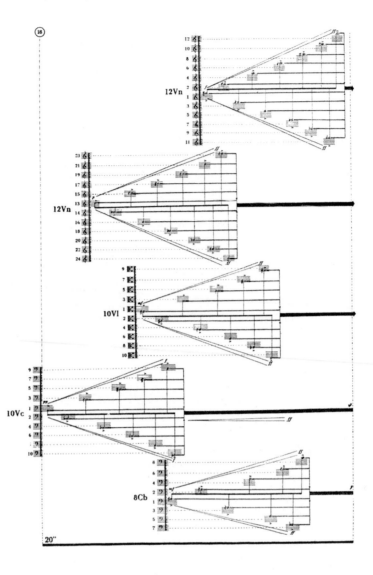

Scores for recent music often include notes in new shapes, new symbols, and novel ways of arranging notation on the page. Here is a page from the score *Threnody to the Victims of Hiroshima* by Krzysztof Penderecki.

mixed-media presentation was Varèse's *Poème électronique*, which combined electronic sounds with images projected on walls. But multimedia works are not confined to electronic music. Chance music and other types of recent music sometimes require performers to function as both actors and sound producers, as in Crumb's *Ancient Voices of Children*. Mixed-media presentations are generally intended to break down the ritual surrounding traditional concerts and to increase communication between composer and audience.

Rhythm and Form

Rhythm and form have undergone some of the most striking changes in music since 1950. Earlier in the century, composers often changed meters or used unconventional meters such as $\frac{7}{8}$ and $\frac{5}{8}$. After 1945, some composers abandoned the concepts of beat and meter altogether. This is a natural outcome of electronic

Percussion instruments are imaginatively exploited in much recent music. The percussionist Evelyn Glennie rehearsing with the New York Philharmonic conducted by Leonard Slatkin. Glennie is profoundly deaf.

Frank Gehry (b. 1930), Walt Disney Concert Hall, Los Angeles, California, completed 2003. Gehry designs his buildings as a series of separate but interdependent units with curved contours.

music, which needs no beat to keep performers together. In nonelectronic music, too, the composer may specify duration in absolute units such as seconds rather than in beats, which are relative units. In some recent music, there may be several different speeds at the same time.

More than ever, each piece of music follows its own laws, and its form grows out of its material. Some composers no longer write music in traditional forms, such as A B A, sonata form, or rondo. Indeed, form may unfold with little or no obvious repetition of material.

17 Music since 1945: Five Representative Pieces

Sonatas and Interludes for Prepared Piano (1946–1948), by John Cage

The American composer John Cage (1912–1992) was the highly influential creator of chance music—as discussed in Section 16—and a major figure in the development of percussion music. He invented the prepared piano, a grand piano whose sound is altered by objects such as bolts, screws, rubber bands, pieces of felt, paper, and plastic inserted between the strings of some of the keys. "In practice, the preparation takes about three hours," Cage explained. Such preparation results in a wide variety of sounds that resemble those of drums, cymbals, xylophones, tambourines, and gongs. When the pianist's finger strikes a key, sometimes more than one sound is produced.

Cage invented the prepared piano around 1940 when he was asked to write music for a modern dance on an African theme. The dance was to be performed in a small auditorium with enough space for a small grand piano, but not for a group of percussionists. "In effect," Cage wrote, "the prepared piano is a percussion ensemble under the control of a single player."

The large-scale *Sonatas and Interludes* (1946–1948), lasting around 66 minutes, is Cage's best-known work for prepared piano and one of his most widely performed and recorded compositions. It includes twenty short pieces—sixteen one-movement sonatas and four interludes—ranging in length from 1½ minutes to 5 minutes. *Sonatas and Interludes* reflects the composer's study of eastern philosophy. Cage explained that the cycle aims to express the range of stylized emotional states described in Indian aesthetic theory: "the heroic, erotic, wondrous, mirthful, odious, sorrowful, fearful, angry, and their common tendency toward tranquillity." We'll focus on the second sonata of the cycle.

Brief Set:
CD 4 47

Sonata II

Basic Set:
CD 8 18

The two-minute Sonata II, in A A B B form, is characterized by a gradual thickening of texture and an increase in rhythmic momentum. Part A moves from a

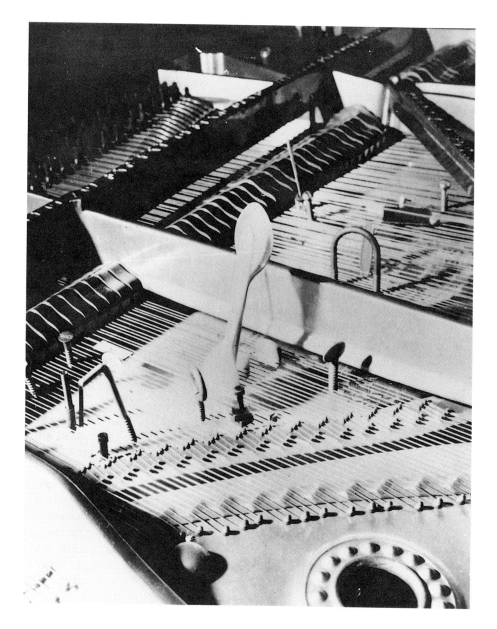

The inside of a prepared piano.

Part A
47 19

single melodic line—sometimes accompanied by percussive sounds—to a two-voice texture. This part is predominantly soft, in a fairly high register. Short phrases, arranged in question-and-answer pairs, are framed by silences. In two phrases, a melodic fragment immediately repeats.

Part B
48 20

Part B is almost twice as long as A and has more extended phrases and a richer texture. It begins abruptly with a loud, dense sonority that contrasts with the gentle, lingering sounds and pause ending part A. The concluding phrase of part B is the most extended, climactic, and rhythmically active. It begins with a torrent of high running notes and ends with a high trill-like figure and an upward swoop to a single accented tone.

Poème électronique (Electronic Poem; 1958), by Edgard Varèse

Brief Set:
(Opening section)
CD 4 49

Basic Set:
CD 8 26

Edgard Varèse (1883–1965), one of the great innovators of twentieth-century music, was born in France but spent most of his life in the United States. As early as 1916, he dreamed of freeing music from the limitations of traditional instruments and expanding the vocabulary of sounds. During the 1920s and 1930s, Varèse pioneered in the exploration of percussive and noiselike sounds, and he wrote the first important work for percussion ensemble (*Ionisation*, 1931).

But it was the new electronic developments of the 1950s that enabled Varèse to realize his vision of a "liberation of sound." In 1958, at the age of seventy-five, he composed *Poème électronique,* one of the earliest masterpieces of electronic music created in a tape studio. The 8-minute work was designed to be heard within the pavilion of the Philips Radio Corporation at the 1958 Brussels World's Fair. Varèse obtained unique spatial effects by projecting sound from 425 loudspeakers placed all over the interior surfaces of the pavilion. The composer worked in collaboration with the architect Le Corbusier, who selected a series of images—photographs, paintings, and writing—that were projected on the walls as the music was heard. However, Varèse did not make any attempt to synchronize the sounds with the images chosen by Le Corbusier, which included "birds and beasts, fish and reptiles, . . . masks and skeletons, idols, girls clad and unclad, cities in normal appearance and then suddenly askew," as well as atomic mushroom clouds.

Because it was created in a tape studio, *Poème électronique* exists in only a single "performance" whose duration (8 minutes) is fixed on audiotape. Varèse's raw sound material—tones and noises—came from a wide variety of sources, including electronic generators, church bells, sirens, organs, human voices, and machines. The sounds are often electronically processed in such a way that they cannot be precisely identified. In the listening outline, the effect of such sounds is conveyed by words placed in quotation marks; for example, "wood blocks" or "chirps." Varèse unifies *Poème électronique* through a distinctive group of three rising tones heard several times. Tension is created by suspenseful pauses lasting from 2 to 7 seconds. Varèse organizes his sounds into an electronic poem that seems weird, yet is amazingly logical and compelling. The listening outline describes the opening 2 minutes and 43 seconds of this work, a segment which begins and ends with low bell tolls.

Listening Outline to be read while music is heard   Brief Set: CD 4   Basic Set: CD 8

VARÈSE, *Poème électronique (Electronic Poem)*

Excerpt: Opening Segment

Tape studio

(Duration, Brief Set, 2:43; Basic Set, 8:00)

<table>
<tr><td>49 26</td><td>0:00</td><td>**1.** Low bell tolls. "Wood blocks." Sirens. Fast taps lead into high, piercing sounds. 2-second pause.</td></tr>
<tr><td></td><td>0:43</td><td>**2.** "Bongo" tones and higher grating noises. Short "squawks." Three-tone group stated three times.</td></tr>
<tr><td></td><td>1:11</td><td>**3.** Low sustained tones with grating noises. Sirens. Short "squawks." Three-tone group. 2-second pause.</td></tr>
<tr><td></td><td>1:40</td><td>**4.** Short "squawks." High "chirps." Variety of "shots," "honks," "machine noises." Sirens. Taps lead to</td></tr>
<tr><td>50 27</td><td>2:36</td><td>**5.** Low bell tolls.</td></tr>
</table>

Fugata (1969), by Astor Piazzolla

Brief Set:

CD 5 7

Basic Set:

CD 8 **30**

The *tango* is a sensuous dance in quadruple meter for couples in close embrace. A musical symbol of Argentina, the tango originated around 1890 in the slums and brothels of Buenos Aires and became a dance craze in Europe and the United States during the early twentieth century.

The Argentinian composer Astor Piazzolla (1921–1992) created a unique style of concert tango music that fuses the traditional dance with elements from classical music and jazz. At first the dissonant harmonies and polyphonic textures of Piazzolla's "new tango" (*tango nuevo*) angered traditionalists, but since the 1980s his compositions have been performed worldwide by such leading musicians and ensembles as the cellist Yo-Yo Ma and the Kronos Quartet. Today, Piazzolla's albums may be found in the classical, jazz, and world music sections of record stores.

Piazzolla was born in Argentina but grew up in New York City, where his parents immigrated when he was four. At age eight, he began to play the *bandoneon,* a square accordion used in tango bands, operated entirely with buttons. Piazzolla soon became a virtuoso on this instrument, playing Bach and Chopin as well as tangos, folk music, and jazz. At thirteen, he accompanied the Argentinian superstar tango singer and composer Carlos Gardel during the year Gardel spent in New York.

In 1937, Piazzolla returned to Argentina, where he studied musical composition from age twenty to twenty-five with Alberto Ginastera, an important Argentinian composer, and played in tango bands in nightclubs. "I did my homework in dressing rooms," Piazzolla later recalled. His homework included analysis of musical scores by Stravinsky and Bartók, composers who had an impact on his own style.

When Piazzolla was thirty-two, his *Buenos Aires* Symphony won a prize that subsidized a year (1954–1955) of study in Paris with Nadia Boulanger, the teacher of Aaron Copland and many other leading composers. After examining his musical scores, Boulanger told Piazzolla that his "classical" pieces were well-written but lacked expressivity. However, after she heard him play his tangos, she exclaimed, "Astor, this is beautiful. I like it a lot. This is the true Piazzolla—do not ever leave him." For Piazzolla, his teacher's comment "was the great revelation of my musical life."

In 1955 Piazzolla returned to Argentina. During the 1960s he became one of the leaders of the avant-garde, admired by intellectuals and university students. He performed in nightclubs with his New Tango Quintet (*Quinteto Nuevo Tango*), and wrote the "little opera" (*operita*) *Maria de Buenos Aires* and the hit song *Balada para un loco* (*Ballad for a Madman*), as well as much film music. In 1974, at age fifty-three, Piazzolla left Argentina for Europe, first settling in Rome and then in Paris. During his late fifties and sixties, Piazzolla toured the world with his second Quintet, and composed many works including *Le Grand Tango* (1981) for the cellist Mstislav Rostropovich and *Five Tango Sensations* (1989) for the Kronos Quartet. In 1990, he had a stroke and asked to be flown from Paris to Argentina, where he died on July 4, 1992. An obituary in *The New York Times* hailed him as the "modern master of tango music."

Piazzolla once said, "If I do a fugue in the manner of Bach, it will always be 'tanguificated'"—that is, tango-like. The title *Fugata* derives from the Italian term *fugato*, a fuguelike section in a movement that is not a fugue. *Fugata* opens like a fugue but soon becomes a passionate, modernistic tango, with an ostinato, dissonant harmonies, percussive sounds, string glissandi (slides), and irregular rhythmic patterns. In our recording, *Fugata* is performed by a sextet including cello—played by Yo-Yo Ma—piano, bandoneon, violin, electric guitar, and double bass.

The opening fuguelike section is polyphonic in texture: a long, syncopated fugue subject is presented unaccompanied by the cello, and then imitated in turn by the violin, bandoneon, and double bass. After about a minute, the bandoneon presents melodies with a tango flavor as the texture becomes homophonic and contrasts with the polyphony of the fuguelike opening. Later, the bandoneon alternates with the piano as the main solo instrument. During a solo for bandoneon and piano, Piazzolla creates enormous momentum by introducing an accented four-note ostinato in the bass:

Near the end, the ostinato stops and the mood suddenly becomes eerie, as we hear a moaning cello solo together with upward and downward string slides. A long, low note in unison provides a somber conclusion to *Fugata*.

Listening Outline to be read while music is heard   Brief Set: CD 5   Basic Set: CD 8

Piazzolla, *Fugata*

Quadruple meter ($\frac{4}{4}$)

Cello, piano, bandoneon, violin, electric guitar, double bass

(Duration: 3:47)

**Fuguelike
section**

7 30	0:00		**1. a.** Cello alone, *f*, long, syncopated fugue subject in running notes, minor key.
	0:15		**b.** Violin, fugue subject, cello, countersubject
	0:31		**c.** Bandoneon, *f*, fugue subject, syncopated cello accompaniment.
	0:46		**d.** Bass, *f*, fugue subject, violin, high countermelody, upward leaps in violin.

Tango

8 31	1:03	0:00	**2. a.** Bandoneon and strings, *ff*, syncopated tango melody, bass accompaniment marks the beat.
	1:18	0:15	**b.** Bandoneon and strings, running-note melody with syncopations, bass accompaniment continues to mark the beat, high tremolo leads to
	1:34	0:31	**3.** Bandoneon and violin, melody with downward leaps, piano, irregular accents, violin, upward slide to
	1:49	0:46	**4. a.** Piano, *ff*. running-note melody, cello, pizzicato accompaniment.
	2:03	1:00	**b.** Bandoneon and guitar melody descends chromatically, syncopated bass solo, pizzicato, slow guitar slides, *p*.
	2:22	1:19	**5. a.** Bandoneon and piano, *ff*, accented syncopated chords, four-note ostinato in bass, pizzicato.
	2:30	1:27	**b.** Piano solo, fast syncopated melody in octaves, bass ostinato continues, piano melody descends, ascends to syncopated chords.
	3:01	1:58	**6. a.** Repeated phrase in bandoneon and piano with percussive interjections, bass ostinato continues.
	3:16	2:13	**b.** Ostinato stops, legato cello solo and eerie string slides, decrescendo to long, low ending note in unison, *p*.

Concerto Grosso 1985
(To Handel's Sonata in D Major
for Violin and Continuo, First Movement),
by Ellen Taaffe Zwilich

The American composer Ellen Taaffe Zwilich (b. 1939) won the 1983 Pulitzer Prize for Music for her Symphony No. 1. Zwilich was born in Miami, Florida; her father was an airline pilot. She studied at Florida State University and at the Juilliard School and played for several years as a professional violinist in the American Symphony Orchestra under the direction of Leopold Stokowski. She has composed an impressive series of widely performed instrumental works, including her String Quartet (1974), Symphony No. 2 (1985), Concerto for Piano and Orchestra (1986), Symphony No. 3 (1992), and *Rituals* (2004), for percussion ensemble and chamber orchestra. From 1995 to 1999 she occupied Carnegie Hall's first Composer's Chair, and in 1999 she was named *Musical America's* Composer of the Year. A professor at her alma mater, Florida State University, she was elected to the American Academy of Arts and Sciences in 2004.

Yo-Yo Ma, Cellist, Playing Piazzolla's Fugata

Yo-Yo Ma, one of the world's most famous living cellists, plays not only the classical cello repertoire but a wide range of music including Argentinian tangos, Brazilian sambas, and traditional Asian pieces.

Ma was born in Paris in 1955 to Chinese parents who had come there to study music. He began to play the cello when he was four and at age five gave his first public concert at the University of Paris. At seven, Ma and his family left Paris for the United States. There, the seven-year old played in Washington's Cultural Center (now the Kennedy Center) at a fund-raising event hosted and conducted by Leonard Bernstein and attended by President and Mrs. Kennedy.

When he was almost seventeen, Ma entered Harvard College, which had a major impact on his life. During his freshman year, he played about thirty concerts around the world while taking a full schedule of courses. After graduating from Harvard in 1976, Ma began a full-time career as a concert cellist, playing solos with leading orchestras, making award-winning recordings, giving master classes for talented young musicians, and commissioning many new works for cello by contemporary composers.

Since the 1990s, Ma has intensively explored many different kinds of music outside the western classical tradition. He attributes this stretching of boundaries to his experience at Harvard, where he "was systematically introduced to different worlds and ways of thinking." Inspired by a professor of anthropology, Ma traveled to Africa to learn about the music of a people known as the Bushmen of the Kalahari Desert. He played Bach for Kalahari musicians, listened to their music, and tried to play their homemade instruments. Ma was also attracted to Appalachian fiddle music and collaborated with the fiddler Mark O'Connor and the bass player Edgar Meyer to produce two albums, *The Appalachian Waltz* and *Appalachian Journey*.

His most ambitious enterprise is the Silk Road Project, designed to explore the exchange of ideas among the cultures located along the Silk Road, the ancient trade route connecting Asia and Europe. An important part of this project is the Silk Road Ensemble, consisting of Asian and American musicians who perform on eastern and western instruments. The Ensemble's CD, *Silk Road Journeys: When Strangers Meet,* includes traditional music from Mongolia, China, Persia, Azerbaijan, and Finland, as well as music used in the soundtrack of the film *Crouching Tiger, Hidden Dragon* (2000), performed by Ma and composed by a Chinese-American, Tan Dun (b. 1957).

In 1997, Ma went to Buenos Aires to record the album *Soul of the Tango* with leading tango musicians who had performed with Astor Piazzolla. (Ma's performance of Piazzolla's *Fugata* is included in the CD sets.) Yo-Yo Ma feels that "Piazzolla's music is endlessly passionate—full of yearning—and at the same time endlessly contemporary." For Ma, Piazzolla "is a great musician who influenced dance, jazz, and modernism, and developed a new style of tango music." Piazzolla "had an amazing ear for musical style, and he combined chosen styles—jazz, Bartók, Stravinsky—into a seamless fusion, a very personal and passionate voice." According to Ma, the combination of the tango, a national music, with "foreign" influences is the reason why Piazzolla's music "has that incredibly tight rhythmic sense, but also the Italian rubato and the erotic tensions. . . . That's what makes you go nuts!"

Ellen Taaffe Zwilich.

Concerto Grosso 1985 was commissioned by the Washington Friends of Handel to commemorate Handel's three-hundredth birthday. Each of its five movements uses thematic material drawn from the opening movement of Handel's Sonata for Violin and Continuo in D Major. Zwilich has said: "I performed the [Handel] many years ago, and I especially love the opening theme of the first movement. . . . Throughout *[Concerto Grosso 1985],* I found myself using compositional techniques typical of the baroque period, including terraced dynamics, repeated phrases . . . techniques I would not normally use, but I felt inspired to do so because of the fact that this piece was based on Handel." Like the concerti grossi of Handel and Bach, Zwilich's *Concerto Grosso 1985* is written for a small orchestra including a harpsichord and gives solo instruments prominent roles. Its five movements are arranged symmetrically: the finale is similar to the opening movement, and the fourth movement parallels the second. The two outer movements include entire passages from the Handel sonata, whereas the three inner movements use no quotations but freely develop its opening melodic motive. We'll focus on the first movement, a clear example of "quotation music."

First Movement:
Maestoso (majestic)

Brief Set:
CD 4 [51]

Basic Set:
CD 8 [35]

The maestoso repeatedly alternates quotations from Handel with passages that could have been written only in the twentieth century. Though abrupt, these contrasts somehow add up to a unified whole. Partly, this is because the newly composed sections are often based on a speeded-up variation of Handel's opening four-note motive.

In addition, Zwilich's own music uses compositional techniques associated with the baroque. Long pedal points in the bass give a firm definition of key to melodic lines that use dissonances freely in a twentieth-century manner. And these melodic lines include the repeated rhythmic pattern short-short-long, short-short-long found in music by Bach and Handel.

Listening Outline to be read while music is heard

Brief Set: CD 4   Basic Set: CD 8

ZWILICH, *Concerto Grosso 1985*

First Movement

Maestoso (majestic), quadruple meter ($\frac{4}{4}$), D major

Flute, 2 oboes, bassoon, 2 French horns, harpsichord, 1st violins, 2d violins, violas, cellos, double basses

(Duration, 2:45)

51 35   0:00   **1. a.** Orchestra in unison, *f*, single sustained tone presented three times.
           b. Violins, *f*, vigorous phrase, short-short-long rhythm, sustained tone in bass;

vigorous phrase repeated softly.

51 35   0:34   0:00   **c.** Handel quotation, strings and harpsichord, *mp*,

interrupted by

          0:55   0:21   **2. a.** Vigorous phrase developed in strings and woodwinds; crescendo to *f*; short string phrases with abrupt pauses.
                        b. Handel quotation continued, oboe *mf*, accompanied by harpsichord and strings.

          1:31   0:57   **3. a.** Vigorous phrase in violins, *f*, imitated in flute, *f*; vigorous phrase in violins, *f*.
                        b. Handel quotation continued, *f*; trills in strings and woodwinds; harpsichord; melody closes.

          2:03   1:29   **4. a.** Vigorous phrase in violins, flute, and oboes; crescendo to *ff*.
          2:13   1:39   **b.** Woodwinds, high sustained dissonant chords; low strings, fragments of vigorous string phrase, *ff*. Ends on sustained dissonant chord, *f*.

Short Ride in a Fast Machine (1986), by John Adams

Brief Set:
CD 4 53

John Adams (b. 1947) is a leading American composer who has been aptly described as a postminimalist. His music combines the driving pulse, constant

John Adams.

Basic Set:
CD 8 **37**

repetition, and clear tonality of minimalism with lyrical, expressive melodies and varied orchestral colors. "I grew up in a household where Benny Goodman and Mozart were not separated," Adams once recalled. Indeed, his works reflect the influence of American popular music as well as composers such as Stravinsky and Reich.

A conductor as well as a composer, Adams taught and directed the New Music Ensemble at the San Francisco Conservatory of Music from 1972 to 1982 and was composer in residence with the San Francisco Symphony Orchestra during 1982–1985. His works include *Harmonium* (1980), for chorus and orchestra; the orchestral works *Harmonielehre* (1985) and *Short Ride in a Fast Machine* (1986); and the operas *Nixon in China* (1987), *The Death of Klinghoffer* (1991), and *Dr. Atomic* (2005), dealing with J. Robert Oppenheimer, the physicist known as "the father of the atomic bomb." In 2003, Adams won the Pulitzer Prize in music for *On the Transmigration of Souls* (2002), a work for chorus and orchestra commissioned by the New York Philharmonic in commemoration of those who died in the terrorist attacks on the Pentagon and the World Trade Center on September 11, 2001.

Short Ride in a Fast Machine, a 4-minute fanfare, is one of the most widely performed orchestral works by a living American composer. The work was commissioned by the Great Woods Festival to celebrate its inaugural concert at Great Woods, Mansfield, Massachusetts. *Short Ride in a Fast Machine* generates enormous excitement because of its rapid tempo, rhythmic drive, and powerful, colorful sonorities. The large orchestra includes two synthesizers and a variety of percussion instruments played by four musicians. These percussion instruments include a sizzle cymbal (a large cymbal with loose rivets placed in a ring of holes) and crotales (small cymbals of definite pitch). *Short Ride in a Fast Machine* is pervaded by steady beats in the wood block, rapid-note ostinatos in synthesizers and clarinets, and repeated orchestral chords that alternate between regular pulsations and irregular rhythms. The climax comes toward the end, when Adams introduces a stirring, fanfare-like melody in the trumpets.

Listening Outline to be read while music is heard

Brief Set: CD 4   Basic Set: CD 8

ADAMS, *Short Ride in a Fast Machine*

Delirando (deliriously)

2 piccolos, 2 flutes, 2 oboes, English horn, 4 clarinets, 3 bassoons, contrabassoon, 4 French horns, 4 trumpets, 3 trombones, tuba, timpani, wood blocks, pedal bass drum, large bass drum, suspended cymbal, sizzle cymbal, large gong (tam-tam), tambourine, triangle, glockenspiel, xylophone, crotales, 2 synthesizers, 1st violins, 2d violins, violas, cellos, double basses

(Duration 4:11)

53 37	0:00		**1. a.**		Wood bock pulsations followed by ostinatos in clarinets and synthesizer, staccato repeated chords in trumpets, *f*, trombones and French horns join on faster repeated chords; piccolo fragments and snare drum strokes punctuate.
	0:36			**b.**	Pulsating brass chords, piccolo fragments, brass chords in irregular rhythms, quick snare drum strokes and suspended cymbal announce
54 38	1:06			**c.**	String entrance, chords in irregular rhythms, bass drum strokes, chords rise in pitch, cymbal, bass drum and snare drum strokes, crescendo to *fff*.
55 39	1:46	0:00		**d.**	Suddenly softer, "walking" figure in cellos and basses below pulsating, rising orchestral chords, irregular rhythms in percussion, brass, and woodwinds, crescendo to *fff*.
	2:39	0:53		**e.**	Trombones and tubas, *fff*, low downward skip, repeated chords in brasses and woodwinds; bass drum, gong, cymbals, crescendo to *fff*.
	2:53	1:07		**f.**	Suddenly softer orchestral pulsations, clarinet ostinato.
56 40	3:00	0:00	**2. a.**		Trumpets, *ff*, extended melody, accompanied by pulsating chords and countermelody in French horns, crescendo to *fff*.
	4:03	1:03		**b.**	Repeated major chords in trumpets and trombones, *fff*, percussive concluding chord.

18 Jazz

About the time Schoenberg and Stravinsky were changing the language of music in Europe, a new musical style called *jazz* was being developed in the United States.* It was created by musicians—predominantly African Americans—performing in the streets, bars, brothels, and dance halls of New Orleans and other southern cities.

Jazz can be described generally as music rooted in improvisation and characterized by syncopated rhythm, a steady beat, and unique tone colors and performance techniques. Although the term *jazz* became current in 1917, the music

---

*An excellent recorded anthology of jazz is the *Smithsonian Collection of Classic Jazz,* a set of five compact discs (no. 1848).

itself was probably heard as early as 1900. We do not know exactly when jazz started or how it sounded at first, because this new music existed only in performance, not musical notation. Moreover, very little jazz was captured on recordings before 1923, and none at all before the Original Dixieland Jazz Band recorded in 1917.

Since its beginnings, jazz has developed a rich variety of substyles such as New Orleans style (including Dixieland), swing, bebop, cool, free jazz, and jazz rock. It has produced such outstanding figures as Louis Armstrong, Duke Ellington, Benny Goodman, Charlie Parker, and Miles Davis. Its impact has been enormous and worldwide, affecting not only many kinds of popular music, but the music of such composers as Maurice Ravel, Darius Milhaud, George Gershwin, and Aaron Copland.

Jazz in Society

The world of jazz has witnessed many changes since its beginnings at the turn of the century. Geographically, its center has shifted from New Orleans to Chicago, Kansas City, and New York. Today, it is hard to speak of *a* jazz center, since jazz, in its many substyles, is heard worldwide, from Los Angeles to Tokyo. Jazz has changed in function, too. For a long time, it was basically music for dancing; but since the 1940s, many newer jazz styles have been intended for listening. Now we are as likely to hear jazz in a concert hall or college classroom as in a bar or nightclub. The image of jazz has also changed. Like the blues and rock music, it was originally condemned for its emphasis on sexuality, but it has long since become respected as an American art form.

In recent years, jazz has been sponsored by a number of major American cultural institutions. Both Lincoln Center and Carnegie Hall in New York City have regular jazz series, and a Jazz Masterworks Orchestra has been founded at the Smithsonian National Museum of American History in Washington, D.C. Many colleges and universities now offer courses in jazz as part of the music curriculum.

Roots of Jazz

Early jazz blended elements from many musical cultures, particularly west African, American, and European. West African influences included an emphasis on improvisation, drumming, percussive sounds, and complex rhythms, as well as a feature known as *call and response*. In much west African vocal music, a soloist's phrases are repeatedly answered by a chorus; similarly, in jazz, **call and response** occurs when a voice is answered by an instrument, or when one instrument or group of instruments is answered by another instrument or group.

Actually, the call-and-response pattern of jazz was derived more directly from African American church services in which the congregation vocally responds to the preacher's "call." Other American influences on jazz were the rich body of music that blacks developed here—including work songs, spirituals, gospel hymns, and dances like the cakewalk—and the music of white America. Nineteenth-century American and European musical traditions became

One major source of jazz was the American band tradition.

elements in the background of jazz. In addition to hymns, popular songs, folk tunes, dances, and piano pieces, the American band tradition was a major influence. Many marching band instruments were used in early jazz bands, and band music helped shape the forms and rhythms of early jazz. Along with band music, the immediate sources of jazz were ragtime and the blues.

Ragtime

Maple Leaf Rag
Basic Set:
CD 8 **41**

Ragtime (1890s to about 1915) is a style of composed piano music developed primarily by black pianists who played in southern and midwestern saloons and dance halls. It is generally in duple meter ($\frac{2}{4}$) and performed at a moderate march tempo; the pianist's right hand plays a highly syncopated melody while the left hand steadily maintains the beat with an "oom-pah" accompaniment. The "king of ragtime" was Scott Joplin (1868–1917), whose most famous pieces include *Maple Leaf Rag* and *The Entertainer*.

Blues

Blues refers to a form of vocal and instrumental music and to a style of performance. Blues grew out of African American folk music, such as work songs, spirituals, and the field hollers of slaves. It is uncertain exactly when blues originated, but by around the 1890s it was sung in rural areas of the south. The original "country blues," usually performed with a guitar accompaniment, was unstandardized in form or style.

The poetic and musical form of blues crystallized around 1910 and gained popularity through the publication of *Memphis Blues* (1912) and *St. Louis Blues* (1914), by W. C. Handy (1873–1958). During the 1920s, blues became a national craze among African Americans. Records by such "classic blues" singers as Bessie

Scott Joplin was the leading ragtime composer.

Smith sold in the millions. The 1920s also saw the 12-bar blues (see the bottom of this page) become a musical form widely used by jazz instrumentalists as well as blues singers. Since then, the evolution of jazz and blues has been intertwined. In the 1930s, the singer-guitarist Robert Johnson (1898–1937) combined the sound of country blues—vocal melody accompanied by acoustic guitar—with the formal structure of blues to create music that has influenced many jazz and rock guitarists up to the present.

From the 1920s to the 1950s, Chicago became a blues center because many African American blues singers and instrumentalists had migrated there from the south in the decades after World War I. The 1940s saw the emergence in Chicago of a new, highly energetic blues style—sometimes called "urban blues"—that derived from earlier blues but used electric guitar and amplification. One of the best-known performers of urban blues was Muddy Waters (1915–1983), who had a distinctive style of moaning and shouting. The continuing impact of the blues is apparent in such popular contemporary styles as rhythm and blues, rock and roll, and soul.

Vocal blues is intensely personal, often containing sexual references and dealing with the pain of betrayal, desertion, and unrequited love. The lyrics consist of several 3-line stanzas, each in the same poetic and musical form. The first line is sung and then repeated to roughly the same melodic phrase (a a'); the third line has a different melodic phrase (b). Here is stanza 4 of Bessie Smith's *Lost Your Head Blues,* which we'll study:

a : I'm going to leave baby, ain't going to say goodbye.
a': I'm going to leave baby, ain't going to say goodbye.
b : But I'll write you and tell you the reason why.

A blues stanza is set to a harmonic framework that is usually 12 bars in length. This harmonic pattern, known as *12-bar blues,* involves only three basic chords: tonic (I), subdominant (IV), and dominant (V). (The *subdominant* is the triad based on the fourth note—*fa*—of the scale.) The specific ordering of these chords can be outlined as follows: tonic (4 bars)—subdominant (2 bars)—tonic

(2 bars)—dominant (2 bars)—tonic (2 bars). Here is how the 3-line stanza is set to this chord progression:

	Line 1 (a)				Line 2 (a')				Line 3 (b)			
Bars	1	2	3	4	5	6	7	8	9	10	11	12
Chords	I				IV		I		V		I	

Each stanza of the text is sung to the same series of chords, although other chords may be inserted between the primary chords of the 12-bar blues form outlined above. Singers either repeat the same basic melody for each stanza or improvise new melodies to reflect the changing moods of the lyrics. The music is almost always in quadruple meter ($\frac{4}{4}$), and so each bar contains 4 beats.

Blues singers and instrumentalists have a special style of performance involving "bent" notes and vocal scoops and slides. Their melodies—both composed and improvised—contain many "blue" notes, which provide a highly expressive means of pitch alteration. "Blue" notes are produced by slightly lowering the pitch of the third, fifth, and seventh tones of a major scale. However, "blue" notes often do not precisely match the intonation of any of the tones found on the piano. In C major, for example, they lie somewhere between E and E flat, G and G flat, and B and B flat. Many instruments can produce "blue" notes very similar to those of vocalists.

Blues rhythm is also very flexible. Like other performers of popular music, blues singers and instrumentalists often sing or play "around" the beat, either just before or just after it. This rhythmic freedom gives the music a relaxed feel and creates a sense of urgency and anticipation.

Jazz instrumentalists imitate the performing style of blues singers and use the harmonic pattern of 12-bar blues as a basis for improvisation. This 12-bar pattern is repeated over and over while new melodies are improvised above it. As with the baroque ground bass, the repeated chord progression provides unity while the free flow of improvised melodic lines contributes variety. Music in this 12-bar form can be happy or sad, fast or slow, and in a wide range of styles. Later, we'll consider *Bloomdido*, an instrumental piece based on the harmonic structure of 12-bar blues. Now we'll study a vocal blues by Bessie Smith.

Lost Your Head Blues (1926), by Bessie Smith

Brief Set:

CD 4 [57]

Basic Set:

CD 8 **45**

Bessie Smith (1894–1937), known as the "empress of the blues," was the most famous blues singer of the 1920s. Her *Lost Your Head Blues* is a well-known example of blues form and performance style. The lyrics express the feelings of a woman who plans to leave her man because she's "been treated wrong." Each of the poem's five stanzas is set to the 12-bar blues pattern. Typically, a cornet response follows each line that is sung.

Lost Your Head Blues begins with a 4-bar introduction by the accompanying cornet (Joe Smith) and piano (Fletcher Henderson). Bessie Smith then sings a melody that she'll repeat—with extensive variations of pitch and rhythm—in each stanza. Her "blue" notes, microtonal shadings, and slides between pitches are essential to the effect of the song. Notice the eloquent slides up to *I* in her singing of *I was with you baby,* as well as the ornamental quiver on *down* when she sings the words *throw'd your good gal down.* There are many syncopated

Bessie Smith was one of the most influential blues singers.

rhythms, since words are often sung just before or after the beat. Bessie Smith's vocal melody is highly sensitive to the words. For example, the long high notes at the beginning of the last stanza ("*Days* are lonesome, *nights* are long") produce a wonderful climax. Throughout the song, Bessie Smith's vocal inflections are perfectly matched by the cornet's improvised responses and echoes.

Vocal Music Guide to be read while music is heard   Brief Set: CD 4   Basic Set: CD 8

SMITH, *Lost Your Head Blues*

`57` `45`
Cornet and
piano
introduction.

> I was with you baby when you did not have a dime.
> I was with you baby when you did not have a dime.
> Now since you got plenty money you have throw'd your good gal down.

Once ain't for always, two ain't for twice.
Once ain't for always, two ain't for twice.
When you get a good gal you better treat her nice.

When you were lonesome I tried to treat you kind.
When you were lonesome I tried to treat you kind.
But since you've got money, it's done changed your mind.

I'm going to leave baby, ain't going to say goodbye.
I'm going to leave baby, ain't going to say goodbye.
But I'll write you and tell you the reason why.

Long high notes on Days and nights.

Days are lonesome, nights are long.
Days are lonesome, nights are so long.
I'm a good old gal, but I've just been treated wrong.

Elements of Jazz

Tone Color

Jazz is generally played by a small group (or *combo*) of three to eight players, or by a "big band" of ten to fifteen. The backbone of a jazz ensemble is its *rhythm section,* usually made up of piano, plucked double bass (bass), percussion, and—sometimes—banjo or guitar, which maintains the beat, adds rhythmic interest, and provides supporting harmonies. In a sense, the function of the rhythm section in jazz is comparable to the supporting role of the basso continuo in baroque music.

The rhythm section of a jazz ensemble usually includes piano, bass, and percussion. Pictured is the Dave Brubeck Quartet.

Bessie Smith Singing Lost Your Head Blues

Since Bessie Smith's tragic death in 1937, her recordings not only have delighted listeners worldwide but have had a powerful impact on several generations of singers. The rock star Janis Joplin (1943–1970) said of her: "No one ever hit me so hard. Bessie made me want to sing."

Bessie Smith was born in 1894 to poor African American parents in a one-room shack in Chattanooga, Tennessee. Her professional career began at eighteen, when she joined an entertainment troupe that included Gertrude "Ma" Rainey, a leading blues singer. Over the next decade Smith gradually achieved stardom as she performed in theaters, tents, dance halls, and cabarets, primarily before black audiences in the south and northeast.

A turning point in Bessie Smith's career came in 1923, when her first commercial 78-rpm record—*Down Hearted Blues*—sold 780,000 copies in less than six months. Her powerful voice, emotional intensity, clear diction, and expressive "bent" notes won for her the uncontested title "empress of the blues." She became the highest-paid African-American performer and in 1925 was able to buy her own bright yellow railroad car to transport her troupe of about forty, along with equipment and a large tent. She continued to record blues—including about two dozen of her own compositions—with leading jazz musicians such as Louis Armstrong.

The story of Bessie Smith illustrates how the advent of recording technology changed the position of the performer in musical life. Up until the twentieth century, performers had an impact only on those who heard them in person. Unlike composers, whose notated compositions could be enjoyed by later generations, performers created for the moment, their work surviving only in written descriptions or visual representations. This situation changed dramatically with the invention of recording. Beginning with phonograph records, and later through radio, film, television, compact discs, and digital media, artists like Bessie Smith found a much wider audience and exerted lasting influence.

Many singers have described the impact of Bessie Smith's recordings. The gospel singer Mahalia Jackson (1911–1972), for example, recalled how, as a youngster in New Orleans, she would imitate Bessie Smith: "I'd play that record over and over again, and Bessie's voice would come out so full and round. . . . I'd make my mouth do the same thing."

In 1989 Bessie Smith was inducted into the Rock and Roll Hall of Fame in Cleveland; and in 2001 a play featuring the songs she made famous, *The Devil's Music: The Life and Blues of Bessie Smith,* was performed in New York City. Thanks to her recordings, the epitaph on her tombstone has proved prophetic. "The greatest blues singer in the world will never stop singing."

Bessie Smith's performance of *Lost Your Head Blues* is included in the CD Sets.

The main solo instruments of jazz include the cornet, trumpet, saxophone (soprano, alto, tenor, baritone), piano, clarinet, vibraphone, and trombone. Jazz emphasizes brasses, woodwinds, and percussion rather than the bowed strings that dominate symphonic music. A jazz performance usually involves both solo and ensemble sections. For example, a full ensemble might be followed by a trumpet solo and then by a clarinet solo or a duet for saxophone and trumpet.

The distinctive sounds of jazz are easy to recognize but hard to describe. These sounds result from the specific tones that are chosen, and from the particular way these tones are performed within the melody or accompaniment. For example, melodic tones are often attacked more aggressively in jazz than in other musical styles. Jazz performers sometimes "bend" tones to heighten expressivity or use a distinctive type of vibrato. Transitions between consecutive tones often include a variety of other pitch inflections often referred to as "smears" (gliding from one pitch to another), "scoops" (starting at a pitch lower than the intended pitch and swooping up to it), "falloffs" (performing a descending glissando from the final pitch of a phrase), and "shakes" (a very deliberate and exaggerated vibrato).

Improvisation

At the heart of jazz lies improvisation. Jazz musicians create a special electricity as they simultaneously create and perform, making decisions at lightning speed. The creativity of great improvisers is staggering. Their recorded performances represent only a tiny fraction of the music they create almost nightly. Of course, not all jazz is improvised, and most contains both improvised and composed sections. Yet it is improvisation that contributes most to the freshness and spontaneity of jazz.

A jazz improvisation is usually in theme-and-variations form. The theme is often a popular song melody in A A B A form made up of 32 bars. The improviser varies this original melody by adding embellishments and changing its pitches and rhythms. Some jazz improvisations are based on a harmonic pattern, or series of chords. This harmonic pattern will be repeated over and over while the improviser creates melodies above it. In jazz, each statement of the basic harmonic pattern or melody is called a *chorus.*

A jazz performance usually includes improvised solos by various members of the ensemble. In addition, there may be sections of *collective* improvisation, during which several musicians make up different melodies simultaneously. Their music is held together by the underlying series of chords, which is repeated throughout the performance. Collective improvisation was typical of Dixieland jazz in New Orleans.

Rhythm, Melody, and Harmony

Syncopation and rhythmic swing are two of the most distinctive features of jazz. We say that jazz performers "swing" when they combine a steady beat with a feeling of lilt, precision, and relaxed vitality. In most jazz styles, the beat is provided by the percussionist (on drums or cymbals) and by the bass player. There are usually four beats to the bar. Accents often come on the weak beats: 1–**2**–3–**4.** Many kinds of syncopated rhythms result when accented notes come *between* the beats. Jazz musicians also create a feeling of swing by playing a series of notes slightly unevenly. For example, the second note of a pair of eighth notes is typically shorter than the first. Performers differ in their ways of subdividing the beat for this pair of "swing eighths." Most often, the rhythm falls somewhere between two equal eighth notes ♫ and a triplet pattern in which a quarter note is followed by an eighth note ♩♪. The performed rhythms of jazz are so irregular that it is difficult to notate them accurately. A performer must deviate appropriately from the notated rhythms to get a true jazz feeling. As jazz has evolved, performers have developed the ability to play rhythms that are highly irregular and complex.

Jazz melodies are as flexible in pitch as in rhythm. These melodies—whether improvised or composed—often use a major scale in which the third, fifth, and seventh notes are lowered, or flatted, as in vocal blues. Jazz uses chord progressions like those of the traditional tonal system. But over the years, the harmonic vocabulary of jazz has become increasingly complex, sophisticated, and chromatic. Along with traditional three- and four-note chords, jazz often uses five- or six-note chords that sound rich and lush.

Jazz Styles

New Orleans Style

Jazz in *New Orleans style,* as its name suggests, was developed in New Orleans, which was the major center of jazz during the first two decades of the twentieth century. *Dixieland jazz,* one of the most popular musical styles to develop in New Orleans during this period, was typically played by five to eight performers: a *front line* of melodic instruments (cornet or trumpet; clarinet; and trombone) and a supporting rhythm section (drums; chordal instruments such as piano, banjo, and guitar; and a single-line low instrument such as a tuba or plucked bass). The front-line players improvised several contrasting melodic lines at once, producing a kind of polyphonic texture; and their syncopations and rhythmic independence created a marvelous sense of excitement. This collective improvisation, in which each instrument had a special role, was the most

New Orleans style (or Dixieland) was typically played by five to eight performers. King Oliver (standing at left rear) is shown here with his Creole Jazz Band in 1923. The band included Louis Armstrong (seated, center) and Lil Hardin (at the piano).

distinctive feature of New Orleans jazz, though as the style evolved during the 1920s (mainly in Chicago), solo playing was emphasized.

New Orleans jazz was usually based on a march or church melody, a ragtime piece, a popular song, or 12-bar blues. Some well-known tunes associated with this style are *When the Saints Go Marching In* and *Oh, Didn't He Ramble?* One or more choruses of collective improvisation generally occurred at the beginning and end of a piece. In between, individual players were featured in improvised solos, accompanied by the rhythm section or by the whole band. Sometimes there were brief unaccompanied solos, called **breaks.** The band's performance might begin with an introduction and end with a brief coda.

Dippermouth Blues
Basic Set:
CD 8 46

Notable figures of New Orleans jazz include Ferdinand "Jelly Roll" Morton and Joseph "King" Oliver; Oliver's *Dippermouth Blues* (1923) is a fine example of instrumental blues and New Orleans style. Especially important is the trumpeter and singer Louis "Satchmo" Armstrong (1900-1971), who was one of the greatest jazz improvisers. He revealed new dimensions of the trumpet, showing that it could be played in a higher register than had been thought possible. Armstrong also popularized *scat singing,* vocalization of a melodic line with nonsense syllables like *dat-a bat-a dip-da.* Starting in 1925, he made a series of recordings with bands known as Louis Armstrong's Hot Five and Louis Armstrong's Hot Seven. These recordings established his reputation as the leading jazz trumpeter.

Hotter Than That (1927), by Louis Armstrong and His Hot Five

Brief Set:
CD 4 58

Basic Set:
CD 8 47

Hotter Than That, an outstanding performance by Louis Armstrong and His Hot Five, is based on a tune written by Lillian Hardin Armstrong (1898–1971), who was Armstrong's wife and the pianist of the band. This performance shows how New Orleans style developed in Chicago during the 1920s. The emphasis is on improvisatory solos, based on the harmonic structure of the 32-bar tune *Hotter Than That.* Collective improvisation—so important in earlier New Orleans style—is restricted to the introduction and the last of four choruses. Louis Armstrong performs as both trumpeter and vocalist. His vocal solo, an example of scat singing, is like his trumpet playing in sound and style. Other solos are by the clarinetist Johnny Dodds and the trombonist Kid Ory. At the middle and end of each chorus there is a brief unaccompanied solo, a break. Listen for the syncopations of Armstrong's vocal melody (chorus 3), the call and response between voice and guitar in the interlude following chorus 3, and the dissonant guitar chord that gives *Hotter Than That* an unusual, inconclusive ending.

Listening Outline to be read while music is heard   Brief Set: CD 4   Basic Set: CD 8

LOUIS ARMSTRONG AND HIS HOT FIVE, *Hotter Than That*

Cornet, voice (Louis Armstrong), piano (Lillian Hardin Armstrong), clarinet (Johnny Dodds), trombone (Kid Ory), guitar (Lonnie Johnson)

Rapid tempo, quadruple meter ($\frac{4}{4}$)

Introduction—four choruses of 32 bars—coda

(Duration, 2:59)

Introduction
(8 bars)
`58` `47` 0:00 **1.** All instruments, trumpet predominates, collective improvisation.

Chorus 1
(32 bars)
0:09 **2.** Trumpet solo, accompanied by piano and guitar. Trumpet briefly alone, piano and guitar rejoin.

Chorus 2
(32 bars)
`59` `48` 0:43 **3.** Clarinet solo, piano and guitar accompany.

Chorus 3
(32 bars)
`60` `49` 1:19 **4.** Vocal solo, scat singing, guitar accompanies.

Interlude
(20 bars)
`61` `50` 1:54 **5.** Voice imitated by guitar. Piano leads into

Chorus 4
(32 bars)
`62` `51` 2:17 **6. a.** Muted trombone solo, piano and guitar accompany.
`63` `52` 2:33 **b.** Trumpet, other instruments join, collective improvisation.
Tag (4 bars) **c.** Trumpet, guitar, dissonant chord at end.

Swing

A new jazz style called *swing* developed in the 1920s and flourished from 1935 to 1945 (the "swing era"). It was played mostly by big bands; the typical **swing band** had about fifteen players in three sections—saxophones, brasses (trumpet and trombone), and rhythm (piano, percussion, guitar, and bass). A band of that size needed music which was more composed than improvised and also *arranged,* that is, notated in written-out parts for the musicians. With swing, the arranger became an important figure in jazz.

Melodies were often performed by entire sections of a swing band, either in unison or in harmony. The main melody was frequently accompanied by saxophones and brasses playing short, repeated phrases called **riffs.** The saxophone became one of the most important solo instruments, and percussionists also had a more prominent and spectacular role.

The swing era produced hundreds of "name" bands—both black and white—for example, those of Count Basie, Glenn Miller, Tommy Dorsey, and Benny Goodman (the "king of swing"). Some of the swing bands included leading musicians like the saxophonists Coleman Hawkins and Lester Young and featured singers like Billie Holiday, Ella Fitzgerald, and Frank Sinatra.

Duke Ellington (1899–1974) was perhaps the most important composer, arranger, and conductor of the swing era. Ellington's works are richer in harmony and more varied in form than those of his contemporaries. Their variety of

Duke Ellington and his orchestra in 1943. Ellington was perhaps the most important swing composer, arranger, and conductor.

mood may be sampled in such works as *Ko-Ko, Harlem Air Shaft, In a Melotone,* and *Blue Serge,* all included in *The Smithsonian Collection of Classic Jazz.*

C-Jam Blues (1942), in a rendition by Duke Ellington and his Famous Orchestra, was used as an example in Part I, Section 1 (see the listening outline on page 9). It illustrates how Ellington showcases the remarkable musicianship of his band members. Most of the performance is a series of improvised solos on the harmonic structure of 12-bar blues, each solo introduced by a 4-bar break (items 3, 4, 5, 6, 7). Therefore, every solo constitutes a 4-bar + 12-bar chorus. This pattern is unusual because breaks normally appear during the first four bars of a 12-bar blues structure. The first four solos (violin, muted cornet, tenor saxophone, trombone with plunger mute) are lightly accompanied by the rhythm section. Only during the clarinet solo (item 7) do other instruments join with sustained chords. This buildup leads to a climactic ending chorus (12 bars) played by the full ensemble.

Brief Set:

CD 1 [3]

Basic Set:

CD 1 [10]

Bebop

Bebop, or *bop* (developed in the early 1940s), was a complex style, usually for small jazz groups consisting of four to six players, and meant for attentive listening rather than dancing. It had sophisticated harmonies and unpredictable rhythms, and its performers were a special "in" group. A typical bebop ensemble might have a saxophone and a trumpet supported by a rhythm section of piano, bass, and percussion. The role of the rhythm instruments was different from that in earlier jazz. The beat, often extremely fast, was marked not by the snare drum or bass drum, but mainly by the pizzicato bass and ride cymbal (a large suspended cymbal). The drummer also supplied irregular accents, sometimes played with such power that they are called "bombs." Similarly, the pianist's left hand no longer helped emphasize the basic pulse but joined with the right hand to play complex chords at irregular intervals. Melodic phrases were often varied in length, and chords might have six or seven notes rather than the four or five characteristic of earlier jazz. A bop performance generally began and ended with a statement of the main theme (often derived from a popular song or 12-bar blues) by a soloist, or by two soloists in unison; the remainder of the piece was made up of solo improvisations based on the melody or harmonic structure.

Notable bebop performers included the trumpeter Dizzy Gillespie (1917–1993) and the pianist Thelonious Monk (1917–1982). The alto saxophonist Charlie "Bird" Parker (1920–1955) was a towering figure among bebop musicians and an important influence on instrumentalists.

Bloomdido (1950), by Charlie Parker

Basic Set:
CD 8 **53**

Bebop style and Parker's improvisatory genius are both illustrated in *Bloomdido*, which is performed here by a group of five outstanding musicians: Charlie Parker (alto saxophone), Dizzy Gillespie (trumpet), Curly Russell (bass), Thelonious Monk (piano), and Buddy Rich (percussion).

Bloomdido is typical of many bebop performances. It consists of an introduction by the rhythm section (piano, bass, percussion); a twofold presentation of the melody by the saxophone and trumpet in unison; improvised solos by the saxophone, muted trumpet, piano, and drums; and a repetition of the melody. Parker's high-spirited melody is based on the harmonic structure of 12-bar blues. The following improvised solos by the saxophone, trumpet, and piano are also based on the 12-bar series of chords, not on the melody. The tempo of *Bloomdido* is fast, and the beat is usually marked by the pizzicato bass and the *ride*, or suspended, cymbal.

Cool Jazz

Cool jazz (which emerged in the late 1940s and early 1950s) was related to bop, but far calmer and more relaxed. Cool jazz pieces also tended to be longer than bebop and relied more on arrangements; and they sometimes used instruments new to jazz, including the French horn, flute, and cello. The tenor saxophonists

Bepop was a complex style of music usually for small jazz groups. Charlie Parker (alto saxophone) is shown here with Tommy Potter (bass), Miles Davis (trumpet), and Duke Jordan (piano).

Lester Young (1909–1959) and Stan Getz (b. 1927), the pianist Lennie Tristano (1919–1978), and the trumpeter and bandleader Miles Davis (1926– 1991) were important figures.

Free Jazz

Until about 1960, improvised jazz variations tended to keep the length and chord structure of the original theme, if not its melody. But during the 1960s, some musicians created *free jazz,* a style that was not based on regular forms and established chord patterns. *Free Jazz,* recorded in 1960 by Ornette Coleman (b. 1930) with several other musicians improvising individually and collectively, is an example: it can be compared to the chance music of John Cage and his followers. Another musician who played an important role in the development of free jazz was John Coltrane (1926–1967), who was influential as an improviser, tenor and soprano saxophonist, and composer.

Jazz Rock (Fusion)

Rock became a potent influence on jazz starting in the late 1960s. This influence led to *jazz rock,* or *fusion,* a new style integrating the jazz musician's improvisatory approach into a style employing rock musical forms, rhythms, and tone colors. Instruments used by a jazz rock group were either electronic or acoustic, and often included synthesizers and electric piano, guitar, and bass. In jazz rock and fusion, the bass player assumes a more melodic role in addition to the more traditional functions of providing the beat and emphasizing the harmonic foundation. The percussion section was sometimes larger than that in earlier jazz groups and included a percussionist—or sometimes multiple percussionists—often performing on instruments from Africa, Latin America, or India.

Miles Davis, a leading musician in cool jazz, was also important in jazz rock. Herbie Hancock, Chick Corea, Joe Zawinul, and Wayne Shorter—who made recordings with both Zawinul and Davis—became pacesetters of jazz rock in the 1970s, 1980s, and 1990s. In addition to these jazz musicians who began to incorporate rock elements, a number of rock musicians began to incorporate jazz improvisation and other elements of the style into their recordings and performances. Two of the most successful of these jazz rock groups during the late 1960s and early 1970s were Chicago and Blood, Sweat & Tears.

Miles Runs the Voodoo Down (1969), by Miles Davis

Basic Set:
CD 8 **54**

Miles Runs the Voodoo Down is from the Miles Davis album *Bitches Brew,* one of the early milestones of jazz rock (fusion). It is performed by a large ensemble of twelve musicians including only three brass and woodwind instruments—trumpet (Miles Davis), soprano saxophone (Wayne Shorter), bass clarinet (Bennie Maupin)—but a very large rhythm section: drums (Lenny White, Jack De Johnette, Charles Alias), percussion (Jim Riley), electric pianos (Chick Corea, Larry Young), electric bass (Harvey Brooks), string bass (Dave Holland), and electric guitar (John McLaughlin). *Miles Runs the Voodoo Down* evokes the feeling of a ritual dance through its slow beat, unchanging harmony, and constant

Miles Davis.

background of rock ostinatos in the electric bass and repeated rhythmic figures in African and South American percussion instruments. We'll focus on the opening 4 minutes of this extended piece (lasting 14 minutes), which features a spectacular improvised solo by Miles Davis.

Miles Runs the Voodoo Down opens softly and ominously with repeated rhythmic and melodic figures in the percussion and electric bass. Other instruments gradually join, creating a hypnotic rhythmic background that becomes increasingly prominent during Miles Davis's solo, which begins half a minute into the piece. The solo conveys a blues feeling because Davis often slides from one pitch to another. It is a free and imaginative flow of musical ideas, not based on a regular form or an established chord pattern. The trumpet opens in a middle to low register. Later, Davis's improvisation moves through a very wide range and includes a variety of brief and extended phrases, screaming high held tones, rapid passages in bebop style, and many inflections that sound vocal. *Miles Runs the Voodoo Down* beautifully integrates jazz improvisation with the rhythms and electronic resources of rock.

Jazz rock was only one of the substyles that could be heard from the 1970s up to today. Every kind of jazz we've studied—New Orleans, swing, bebop, cool jazz, and free jazz—had its fans and devoted performers. As they have done since the early days, jazz musicians continue to explore new resources to further the development of their art.

 # Music for Stage and Screen

Musical Theater

Along with jazz and rock, the *musical* was one of the most important American contributions to twentieth-century popular culture. Shows like *Oklahoma! South Pacific, West Side Story,* and *My Fair Lady* are performed and enjoyed all over the world.

Elements of the Musical

A *musical,* or *musical comedy,* is a type of theater that fuses script, acting, and spoken dialogue with music, singing, and dancing and with scenery, costumes, and spectacle. Most musicals are in fact comedies, though some are serious. Many have been produced in theaters around Broadway in New York (hence the term *Broadway musical*), but successful musicals reach nationwide and even worldwide audiences, and some are made into movies (such as *The Sound of Music, Hair, Evita, Chicago, Rent* and *The Producers.*

Generally, a musical is in two acts, of which the second is shorter and brings back some of the melodies heard earlier. Traditionally, the songs consisted of an introductory section (the *verse*) and a main section (the *chorus*) in A A B A form (32 bars). Hit songs like *Ol' Man River* (from *Show Boat,* 1927) and *Some Enchanted Evening* (from *South Pacific,* 1949) often have lasting appeal, independent of their original theatrical context.

The American musical embraces a variety of styles, yet it is a distinct type of musical theater, separate from opera. In contrast to opera, it tends to use simpler harmonies, melodies, and structures; it has more spoken dialogue; and its songs have a narrower pitch range. Also, the musical is an even more collaborative effort: one composer may create the songs, but other musicians are responsible for orchestration, the overture, connective musical passages, and music accompanying dances; and the spoken dialogue and lyrics are usually written by several people. Still, certain works, such as Stephen Sondheim's *Sweeney Todd* (1979), fall somewhere between musicals and operas; and some, like Sondheim's *A Little Night Music* (1973), are eventually performed by opera companies.

Development of the Musical

Sources of the American musical include various musical and dramatic forms of the late nineteenth century and the early twentieth century, such as operetta, vaudeville, and the revue. *Operetta,* or *comic opera,* combines song, spoken dialogue, and dance with sophisticated musical techniques. Examples are the operettas of the Englishmen W. S. Gilbert and Arthur Sullivan, such as *The Mikado* (1885); and those of the American Victor Herbert, such as *Babes in Toyland* (1903) and *Naughty Marietta* (1910). A more popular antecedent was *vaudeville,* a variety show with songs, comedy, juggling, acrobats, and animal acts, but no plot. The *revue,* a variety show without a plot but with a unifying idea, was often satirical; it featured chorus girls and comedians.

A scene from the musical *Wicked* (2003), music and lyrics by Stephen Schwartz; book by Winnie Holzman, based on a novel by Gregory Maguire.

The years from about 1920 to 1960 saw a golden era of the American musical, created by songwriters and composers like Irving Berlin (1888–1989), Jerome Kern (1885–1945), George Gershwin (1898–1937), Cole Porter (1893–1964), Richard Rodgers (1902–1979), Frank Loesser (1910–1969), and Leonard Bernstein (1918–1990). Plots became more believable and wider in range; song and dance were better integrated with the story, and musical techniques became more sophisticated.

During the 1920s and 1930s, despite unrealistic "boy-meets-girl" stories, lyrics were clever and witty, as in Cole Porter's song "You're the Top" (1934):

> You're the top! You're the Colosseum.
> You're the top! You're the Louvre Museum.
> You're a melody from a symphony by Strauss.
> You're a Bendel bonnet, a Shakespeare sonnet, you're Mickey Mouse. . . .

A pathbreaking musical with a serious plot was *Show Boat* (1927, music by Jerome Kern and lyrics by Oscar Hammerstein II), which treated interracial romance. Its songs—including *Ol' Man River* and *Why Do I Love You?*—revealed character and were smoothly woven into the action. In the 1930s, some musicals satirized social and political institutions; one example is George and Ira Gershwin's *Of Thee I Sing* (1931), which poked fun at American presidential elections.

In the late 1930s, ballet became more significant and was used to carry the action forward. For example, the climax of the musical *On Your Toes* (1936) was a ballet choreographed by George Balanchine (1904–1989) called *Slaughter on Tenth Avenue*. *Oklahoma!* (1943)—by Richard Rodgers and the lyricist Oscar Hammerstein II—was a landmark in the integration of dance, songs, and plot; its ballets, created by Agnes De Mille and inspired by square dances, were important for the progress of the story. After World War II, more and more musicals were set in foreign lands, such as Siam (*The King and I*; 1951), France (*Fanny*; 1954), England (*My Fair Lady*; 1956), and Russia (*Fiddler on the Roof*; 1964). Postwar musicals also began to explore new kinds of serious subjects, such as teenage gang warfare in *West Side Story* (1957).

After 1960, some composers of Broadway shows continued to write traditional songs—a conservative trend that was also seen in many revivals of classic musicals. However, other composers departed from the traditional A A B A form; and often their songs were so much a part of the context that they were unlikely to become hits on their own. Like jazz, the musical was affected by the "rock revolution" of the 1960s. One of the rock musicals was *Hair* (1967), which reflected the hippie movement and had a scene of total nudity. Rock elements were also incorporated into *Jesus Christ Superstar* (1971), by the British musician Andrew Lloyd Webber (b. 1948), who also created *Cats* (1982) and *Phantom of the Opera* (1987). The unusual prominence of European composers on the American musical scene was also reflected in *Les Misérables* (1986) and *Miss Saigon* (1989), written by the Frenchmen Claude-Michel Schönberg and Alain Boublil.

Perhaps the most original contributor to American musical theater since the 1960s is the composer-lyricist Stephen Sondheim (b. 1930), who first became known as the lyricist for *West Side Story*. Many of his works are "concept musicals," based more on an idea than on a traditional plot; they include *Company* (1970); *Sunday in the Park with George* (1984); and his most ambitious work, *Sweeney Todd, the Demon Barber of Fleet Street* (1979), which blurs the boundary between musicals and opera. His musical style fuses elements of the traditional Broadway song with elements of Stravinsky, Copland, and Bernstein.

Leonard Bernstein

The extraordinarily versatile Leonard Bernstein (1918–1990), was a twentieth-century culture hero—conductor, pianist, author, lecturer, and composer of orchestral and vocal works, including *West Side Story*. Bernstein was born in Lawrence, Massachusetts; graduated from Harvard University; and studied piano and conducting at the Curtis Institute in Philadelphia. In 1943, he was appointed assistant conductor of the New York Philharmonic orchestra and his spectacular career was launched when a guest conductor became ill: Bernstein took the podium on a few hours' notice with no rehearsal; the concert, which was broadcast on nationwide radio, was hailed as a "dramatic musical event" on the front page of *The New York Times*.

"I have a deep suspicion that every work I write, for whatever medium, is really theater music in some way." Bernstein's words apply not only to his musicals, operas, and ballets and his theater piece *Mass* (1971), but also to his choral work *Chichester Psalms* (1965) and his three programmatic symphonies—*Jeremiah* (1942), *The Age of Anxiety* (1949), and *Kaddish* (1963). His music is clearly

Leonard Bernstein.

tonal, enlivened by syncopations, irregular meters, and jazz and dance rhythms. Like Stravinsky and Copland, both of whom influenced him, Bernstein wrote successful ballets, including *Fancy Free* (1944) and *Facsimile* (1946). Dance is very important and dramatic in his musicals *On the Town* (1944), *Wonderful Town,* (1953), and *West Side Story* (1957). Bernstein accomplished the difficult feat of bridging the worlds of "serious" and popular music. He died in 1990, mourned by people all over the world.

West Side Story (1957)

On January 6, 1949, the choreographer Jerome Robbins first suggested to Leonard Bernstein that they collaborate on a modern version of Shakespeare's *Romeo and Juliet* set in the slums of New York. Bernstein was very enthusiastic about the "idea of making a musical that tells a tragic story in musical-comedy terms, using only musical-comedy techniques, never falling into the 'operatic' trap. Can it succeed? . . . I'm excited. If it can work—it's the first." *West Side Story*—with music by Bernstein, spoken dialogue by Arthur Laurents, and lyrics by Stephen Sondheim—was completed seven years later.

West Side Story deals with a conflict between gang rivalry and youthful love. The feud between the lovers' families in Shakespeare's *Romeo and Juliet* is transformed into warfare between two teenage street gangs: the Jets, native-born Americans led by Riff; and the Sharks, Puerto Ricans led by Bernardo. The plot revolves around a fight ("rumble") between the gangs and the doomed love of Tony (the Romeo character), a former member of the Jets; and Maria (the Juliet character), Bernardo's sister. Tony kills Bernardo after a vain attempt to break up the fight. Later he is shot by one of the Sharks and dies in Maria's arms.

Though it included rough street language and ended unhappily, *West Side Story* was a tremendous popular success and became an Oscar-winning musical

Tony and Maria meet on a fire escape in a scene from the film version of *West Side Story*.

film (1961). It was an unprecedented fusion of song and drama with electrifyingly violent choreography (by Jerome Robbins and Peter Gennaro). Compared with the average Broadway show, *West Side Story* had more music; more complex and unconventional music; and a wider range of styles, from vaudeville (*Gee, Officer Krupke*) and Latin rhythms (*America*) to bebop fugue (*Cool*) and quasi-operatic ensemble (*Tonight*).

Tonight Ensemble

Brief Set:
CD 4 64

Basic Set:
CD 8 56

In the *Tonight* ensemble, Bernstein projects several different emotions at the same time: Riff, Bernardo, and their gangs excitedly planning for the upcoming fight; Anita—Bernardo's girlfriend—looking forward to the "kicks" she's "gonna get"; and Tony and Maria anticipating the joy of being together. Riff, Bernardo, and Anita sing quick, staccato tones in a narrow range, whereas Tony and Maria sing the legato, soaringly lyrical *Tonight* melody, heard in an earlier "balcony scene" on Maria's fire escape. As Verdi did in the Quartet from *Rigoletto,* Bernstein lets us hear the voices separately before combining them in an ensemble. Such dramatic ensembles were uncommon in musicals, which tended to feature solo songs with "hit" potential.

Listening Outline to be read while music is heard

Brief Set: CD 4   Basic Set: CD 8

BERNSTEIN, *Tonight* Ensemble from *West Side Story*

Riff, Bernardo, Anita, Tony, Maria, gang members, orchestra

Fast and rhythmic.

(Duration, 3:38)

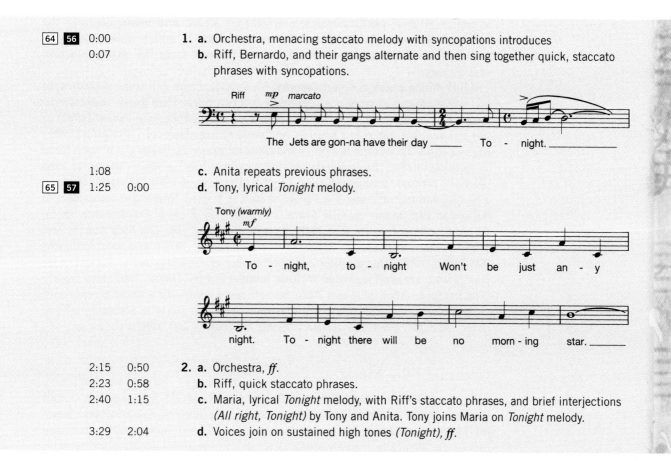

64	56	0:00	**1. a.**	Orchestra, menacing staccato melody with syncopations introduces
		0:07	**b.**	Riff, Bernardo, and their gangs alternate and then sing together quick, staccato phrases with syncopations.

The Jets are gon-na have their day _____ To - night. _____

		1:08	**c.**	Anita repeats previous phrases.
65	57	1:25	0:00	**d.**	Tony, lyrical *Tonight* melody.

To - night, to - night Won't be just an - y

night. To - night there will be no morn - ing star. _____

2:15	0:50	**2. a.**	Orchestra, *ff*.
2:23	0:58	**b.**	Riff, quick staccato phrases.
2:40	1:15	**c.**	Maria, lyrical *Tonight* melody, with Riff's staccato phrases, and brief interjections *(All right, Tonight)* by Tony and Anita. Tony joins Maria on *Tonight* melody.
3:29	2:04	**d.**	Voices join on sustained high tones *(Tonight)*, *ff*.

Music in Film

Early Film Music

Music for film began in the 1890s and emerged as an important musical genre during the twentieth century. During the silent-film era (c. 1890–1926), live pianists, organists, and orchestras accompanied films, both to heighten the emotional effect and to drown out the noise of the movie projector. In the first "talking movie," *The Jazz Singer* (1927), starring Al Jolson, the sound was recorded on vinyl disks. By 1929, new technology enabled sound to be recorded directly on the celluloid filmstrip.

Functions and Styles of Film Music

Synchronized with images on a screen, *film music* provides momentum and continuity, and suggests mood, atmosphere, character, and dramatic action. As in opera and ballet, music in film can convey unspoken thoughts and the emotional implications of a setting. It can clarify the meaning of a scene and enhance the excitement of the action. Movies range widely in the amount and function of the music they contain. At one extreme are musicals and films about musicians, in which musical performer-actors appear on screen and music captures the viewers' attention. At the other extreme are films in which music discreetly accompanies the drama, without diverting viewers from the onscreen action and dialogue.

Most movie music is commissioned for specific films, but some soundtracks include segments of previously existing compositions. Film music is extraordinarily diverse in style, ranging from the rock and roll of *Pulp Fiction* (1994) to the minimalism, electronic sounds, and eerie string effects of *The Matrix* (1999). Many people have come to appreciate classical music by hearing it in such films as *Fantasia* of 1940 (Bach, Beethoven Stravinsky); *2001: A Space Odyssey* of 1968 (Richard Strauss, Johann Strauss, Ligeti); *Amadeus* of 1984 (Mozart); *Shine* of 1996 (Rachmaninoff); and *The Pianist* of 2002 (Chopin). Important composers of American film music include Franz Waxman (*The Bride of Frankenstein*, 1935), Aaron Copland (*The Heiress*, 1948), Dimitri Tiomkin (*The Old Man and the Sea*, 1958) Bernard Herrmann (*Psycho*, 1960; *Taxi Driver*, 1975), and John Williams (*Star Wars*, 1977; *Harry Potter and the Prisoner of Azkaban*, 2003). Recent composers who are well regarded include James Horner (*Titanic*, 1997) and Danny Elfman (*Spider-Man*, 2002 and 2004). Sometimes, a composer will collaborate with a particular director on many films, as John Williams did with Steven Spielberg (*Jaws*, 1975; *E.T. The Extra-Terrestrial*, 1982; *Schindler's List*, 1993).

Creating Film Music

Up to the 1950s, a major Hollywood film studio, like MGM or Paramount, would have a resident orchestra and staff composers, conductors, and arrangers. Since the 1960s, most film music is composed, arranged, and performed by freelance musicians. Typically, the composer views the movie and—in collaboration with the director, producer, editor, and music editor—decides exactly where music will appear in the film, and how long the musical passage, known as a *cue*, will last. Composition, orchestration—usually by one or more orchestrators—and recording are often completed within a few months or less. John Williams has vividly described his preferred method of composing for film: "I'll get a sense of the film's kinetic ebb and flow . . . a sense of where the film may be slowing down, or where it's accelerating, and where I can pick up on the rhythms of the film." For Williams, the "most important issue in scoring films is tempo. Anyone who takes a home movie and puts records to it knows this: if you put one piece of music to it, the film will be one kind of musical experience, and another piece of music will change the experience totally." While composing, Williams will view the scene "many times and have a timing cue sheet that's been prepared for the scene and then I'll write three or four bars and go back and look at it and then write four bars more and look at it again. And it's a constant process of writing, looking, checking, running it in my mind's ear against the film, even conducting with a stopwatch against the action of the film."

Music and Image

In movie scores, musical themes—or leitmotifs—often become associated with specific characters, objects, emotions, or ideas in the film, a technique derived from the music dramas of Richard Wagner. The "shark theme" in *Jaws* (1975), the "007 theme" in the James Bond movies, and the Imperial March (Darth Vader) theme in the *Star Wars* movies are well-known examples. As in Wagner's music dramas, these musical themes are varied and transformed to convey evolving dramatic situations and changes of character. They can remind the audience of the associated character, whether or not he or she appears onscreen.

The mood of movie music does not always match that of the synchronized visual image. In such instances, the music is meant to produce a distancing or ironic effect. Well-known instances are *Goodfellas* (1990) and *Kill Bill* (2003), in which scenes of horrific violence are accompanied by gentle or happy music, making the action seem almost unreal.

During the last few decades, the importance of music in film has become widely recognized. Interest in film music continues to grow, as many movie-goers have come to appreciate the significant contributions of this musical genre. Today, soundtrack albums and concert performances bring film music to millions of people outside the movie theater.

Rock

The mid-1950s saw the growth of a new kind of popular music that was first called *rock and roll* and then simply *rock.* Though it includes diverse styles, **rock** tends to be vocal music with a hard, driving beat, often featuring electric guitar accompaniment and heavily amplified sound.

Early rock grew mainly out of *rhythm and blues,* a dance music of African Americans that fused blues, jazz, and gospel styles. Rock also drew upon *country and western,* a folklike, guitar-based style associated with rural white Americans, and on pop music, a smooth, highly-polished style exemplified by such performers as Frank Sinatra and Perry Como. In little more than a decade, rock evolved from a simple, dance-oriented style to music that was highly varied in its tone colors, lyrics, musical forms, and electronic technology.

Development of Rock

In the late 1940s, rhythm and blues became the dominant style among African Americans. The rhythm and blues of the 1950s differed from earlier blues in its more powerful beat and its use of the saxophone and electric guitar. Among the leading performers were Little Richard, Chuck Berry, and vocal groups such as the Platters. During the 1950s many rhythm-and-blues hits were issued by white performers in versions ("covers") with less sexually explicit lyrics. Little Richard's *Tutti Fruiti* and *Long Tall Sally,* for example, were issued in "cover" versions by Pat Boone one month after the release of the originals.

One of the earliest important rock and roll groups was Bill Haley and His Comets, whose *Rock Around the Clock* is often identified as the first big hit of the

During the 1950s Chuck Berry was a leading performer of rhythm and blues.

new style, though this distinction could just as appropriately be awarded to any number of singles from the period. The song was recorded in 1954, but did not become a number-one hit until a year later, when it was prominently featured in *The Blackboard Jungle,* a provocative movie about teenage delinquency in a contemporary setting: a New York City high school. To many people, the new music seemed rebellious in its loudness, pounding beat, and sexual directness; and the image of youthful rebellion was also projected by Elvis Presley, who reigned as "king" of rock and roll.

During the 1960s, much of the rock music by black performers was called *soul,* a term that emphasized its emotionality, its gospel roots, and its relationship to the black community. Soul musicians included James Brown, Ray Charles, and Aretha Franklin. *Motown*—derived from "Motor Town USA," a nickname for Detroit, the city from which the style emerged—was a type of music that blended rhythm and blues with elements of popular music; among its stars were Diana Ross and the Supremes and Stevie Wonder. With motown, African American composers and performers entered the mainstream of popular music.

A new era of British influence began in 1964 with the American tour of the Beatles, an English rock group whose members probably have been the most influential performers in the history of rock. The Beatles—the singer-guitarists Paul McCartney, John Lennon, and George Harrison; and the drummer Ringo Starr (all born in the early 1940s)—dominated the popular music scene in the United States, along with the Rolling Stones and other British groups. As a result of the Beatles' influence, especially the music of their experimental period during the mid-1960s, rock musicians explored a wider range of musical sources and sounds, including electronic effects, "classical" and nonwestern instruments, and unconventional chord progressions. Apart from the influence of the British invasion, rock in the 1960s also absorbed elements of folk music and expressed contemporary social issues; *Blowin' in the Wind,* by the songwriter and singer Bob Dylan, is a well-known example. At rock festivals, like the 3-day Woodstock Music and Art Fair in August 1969, over 300,000 people listened in open fields to the music of Joan Baez, Janis Joplin, Jimi Hendrix, Jefferson Airplane, and Santana, among many others. The diversity of rock styles of this

Carlos Santana

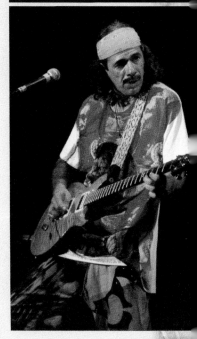

The guitarist and songwriter Carlos Santana fuses rock with Latin and African rhythms as well as elements of jazz and the blues. A major figure in Spanish-language rock, and leader of the band *Santana,* he was inducted into the Rock & Roll Hall of Fame in 1998.

Santana, a fourth-generation musician, was born in 1947 in the town of Autlán de Novarra in Mexico. When he was five his father—a violinist and bandleader—began teaching him the violin and at eight he switched to the guitar. In 1955, Santana moved with his family to Tijuana, Mexico, where he sang and played guitar on the streets for tourists. At age fourteen, he moved to San Francisco and five years later formed the Santana Blues Band. A turning point in Santana's career came in 1969, when his band created a sensation at the Woodstock rock festival and its first album, *Santana,* was hailed by *Rolling Stone* magazine as "an explosive fusion of Hispanic-edged rock, Afro-Cuban rhythms, and interstellar improvisation."

During the 1970s, Santana's band became one of the most famous in the world due to its best-selling recordings and concert tours in the United States, Europe and Africa. Some of his band's albums of the early 1970s, including *Caravanserai* (1972), were close in style to jazz-rock fusion. Besides recording with his band, Santana has also made solo albums that have had a powerful impact on the rock scene. He often records with star performers in other fields like Bob Dylan (folk rock), Herbie Hancock (jazz), Wayne Shorter (jazz), and John McLaughlin (jazz-rock fusion). Remarkably for a rock performer, at age fifty-two Santana created his biggest hit so far, the album *Supernatural* (1999), which was voted Best Rock Album of the Year and has sold over twenty-one million copies worldwide.

Santana usually begins to create a song by recording his guitar improvisation for two or three hours. Then he selects the best segments, and works on them with a collaborator. Santana has vividly described the way he created the song "Love of my Life," together with the singer and guitarist Dave Matthews. "I was picking up my son from school and I thought, okay, time to listen to some radio. I turned on a classical station and the first thing I heard was this melody. . . . They didn't say who the composer was." Santana went into a record store and sang the melody for a salesperson, who told him that it came from Brahms's Third Symphony (studied in Part V, Section 15). He bought the recording and later played Brahms's melody—with slightly changed rhythm—for Dave Matthews and recited the beginning of the lyrics. "Dave sat down and—bam— wrote the song lyrics right there on the spot, and we recorded it."

"Playing the guitar is both a physical and metaphysical experience," Santana once wrote. "When you can play from your heart, you are being open and honest . . . the instrument becomes the vehicle by which you can reach others with the music." Santana's guitar sound has a vocal quality. "When you listen to vocalists like Aretha Franklin and Dionne Warwick, you learn to phrase differently," Santana has said. "I love musicians who make you want to cry and laugh at the same time. . . . You want to bend notes, you want to be able to express joy . . . anger and a cry."

Bruce Springsteen is shown at a concert in New York's Madison Square Garden during his summer 2000 tour.

period—which produced the first rock musical (*Hair*, 1967) and the first rock opera (*Tommy*, 1969)—is reflected in the terms *folk rock, jazz rock, art rock, psychedelic rock,* and *acid rock.*

The 1970s saw a continuation of many 1960s styles, the revival of early rock and roll, and the rise of a dance music called *disco.* In addition to veteran performers, new stars emerged, such as Linda Ronstadt, Billy Joel, Bruce Springsteen, and Donna Summer. A blend of country music and rock called *country rock* became popular; other musical styles included *reggae* (from the West Indies), *funk* (featuring electrification and syncopated rhythms), and *punk,* a raucous style of rock in which the musical material was typically ultrasimple and performers were not expected to be expert on their instruments. Some groups performed *art rock,* rock arrangements of earlier western art music or extended compositions using the language and sounds of rock music, and jazz rock reached a wider audience than ever before through groups like Chicago; Weather Report; and Blood, Sweat, and Tears.

In the early 1980s, new-wave bands from Britain such as Police, Culture Club, and Eurhythmics were popular in the United States. This "second British invasion" was comparable to the one led by the Beatles during the mid-1960s. Though their styles varied, many British bands of this period, such as New Order and The Cure, made extensive use of electronic technology—synthesizers and computers—and often featured outlandish costumes. *Heavy metal* bands such as Quiet Riot, Iron Maiden, and Guns 'n' Roses played a type of basic rock with sexually explicit lyrics, bizarre costumes, and tremendous volume. The musical style of these heavy metal bands was greatly influenced by earlier recordings by Led Zeppelin and Black Sabbath.

During the later 1970s and 1980s, groups such as the Talking Heads, Peter Gabriel, and the Police—including Sting's solo recordings—also drew increasing inspiration from "exotic" sources, including African music and Jamaican reggae. Paul Simon's album *Graceland*, recorded in 1986 with South African musicians, also helped increase worldwide interest in African popular music. Four years later, Simon released *Rhythm of the Saints* (1990), an album incorporating west African, Brazilian, and zydeco elements. Another significant trend of the 1980s was increased awareness of "world music" in general and African popular music specifically. Youssou N'Dour of Senegal, whose music combined traditional African styles with contemporary European-American pop accompaniments, became an international star. His rise to stardom was helped by his tours for Amnesty International with such rock icons as Bruce Springsteen and Sting.

Interest in world music was not limited to African popular music. There was also an interest in other styles that combined traditional musical forms from around the world with the sounds of contemporary American and European popular music. Zouk, for example—a hybrid of Parisian and French Caribbean dance music—experienced widespread international appeal.

Among young urban blacks, *rap* developed. It began as a kind of rhythmic talking accompanied by a disk jockey who manipulated recordings on two turntables to create a collage of rhythmic effects. First popularized in black neighborhoods of east coast American cities, rap often depicts the anger and frustration of urban black youth. Rap is part of the *hip-hop* culture that also includes breakdancing and graffiti.

Heavy metal and rap continued to grow in popularity throughout the 1980s and into the 1990s. The audience for heavy metal has been, since its beginnings, mainly white working-class adolescents. Rap, on the other hand, had by 1990 adopted stylistic features that clearly distinguished it from other forms of popular music and had begun to attract a wider audience, crossing over ethnic and social lines. Some of the most successful rap artists of this period were Chuck D, Dr. Dre, Snoop Doggy Dogg, Ice Cube, Ice-T, and Scarface. An interesting hybrid of heavy metal and rap emerged in the early 1990s when Bodycount was formed by the rapper Ice-T. This group combined speed metal guitar riffs with rapped lyrics, initiating a period during which many groups, including Rage Against the Machine, Limp Bizkit, and Linkin Park, adopted a similar sound. By the end of the 1990s, rap and rap-flavored rhythm and blues moved into the mainstream and dominated the recording charts. Particularly influential were Dr. Dre, Tupac Shakur, Missy Elliot, and the Detroit rapper Marshall Mathers (Eminem). Recordings of the controversial *gangsta rap*—with its deliberately antisocial and sexually explicit lyrics—had enormous sales.

Many young people who had become disenchanted with the polished sounds of mainstream rock of the early 1990s embraced the brash grinding guitar sounds and angry lyrics of despair inherent in the music of alternative rock bands. One of the centers of alternative rock was the Seattle *grunge* scene from which Nirvana, Pearl Jam, Soundgarden, and Alice in Chains emerged. These groups encompassed a wide range of styles, although they were all influenced by 1970s punk, hard rock, and heavy metal. The continued success of alternative rock in the 1990s was confirmed by the popularity of such new bands as Smashing Pumpkins, Nine Inch Nails, and the female-led groups Belly and Hole. By the mid-1990s, this success engendered a punk resurgence with the success of Green Day, No FX, and System of a Down.

At the end of the twentieth century, interesting trends included the emergence of Latino artists who incorporated pan-Latin influences in their music (Gloria Estefan and Ricky Martin); the appearance of crossover artists from the world of country music (Garth Brooks, and more recently, Tim McGraw), and a renewed interest in music from the 1970s.

Throughout the history of rock, superstars have struck it rich through record royalties, movie contracts, and astronomical concert fees. However, many leading rock performers also give concerts to benefit various social causes. In 1985, 45 well-known performers joined together to record "We Are the World," a song and video that raised about $45 million for the victims of famine. That same year, a 16-hour Live Aid concert for African famine relief was telecast to an international audience of about 1.5 billion people. Recently, the Live 8 concerts of July 2005, held in 10 cities throughout the world and watched by an estimated audience of 3 billion, were designed to pressure the leaders of 8 major industrialized nations to do more to combat poverty in Africa. Performers included Paul McCartney, Madonna, Elton John, Mariah Carey, and Sting.

Elements of Rock

Tone Color

Having briefly examined the development of rock, we'll now consider its musical elements. Though some early rock performers used piano-based instrumentation, it was the electric guitar sound of rock that contrasted most with the brass-woodwind sound of the "big band" heard in earlier popular music. Rock music is powerfully amplified, and the guitar—typically the leading instrument—is often manipulated electronically to produce a wide range of tone colors. Along with singers (who often also play instruments), a rock group typically includes two electric guitars (lead and rhythm), electric bass, percussion, and keyboard instruments such as piano, electric piano, and synthesizer. Some groups also include one or more trumpets, trombones, or saxophones.

As rock evolved during the 1960s, a wide range of instruments—from the harpsichord to the Indian sitar—were occasionally added to the basic rock group, particularly for recording sessions. Rock recordings use such diverse sounds as electronic blips, crowd noises, and a fifty-piece orchestra. During the 1970s and 1980s, rock musicians such as Keith Emerson (Emerson, Lake & Palmer) exploited the ever-expanding capacities of synthesizers and computers. Sophisticated electronic technology made it possible for a few performers to sound like a large ensemble. In the 1990s and early 2000s, the development of the MIDI (musical instrument digital interface) standard and digital sampling technology made it possible for a even a single performer to sound like a huge performing ensemble. As a result, for many rock groups the personal computer has become an integral part of live performance and the recording studio.

The singing style of rock is drawn largely from black, folk, and country-and-western music. Although singing styles vary, they are all different from the crooning sound cultivated by earlier popular vocalists. Rock singers shout, cry, wail, growl, and use guttural sounds, as well as *falsetto,* a method of singing used by males to reach notes higher than their normal range. Nonsense syllables and repeated chants (such as *Yeah! Yeah! Yeah!*) are also featured.

The Beatles have so far been the most influential performing group in the history of rock.

Rhythm

Most rock is based on a very powerful beat in quadruple ($\frac{4}{4}$) meter with strong accents on the second and fourth beats of the bar. The rhythmic excitement is heightened because each beat is usually subdivided into 2 equal notes. This produces 8 faster pulses, which are superimposed on the 4 basic beats. To get the effect, count out the following: 1–and–**2**–and–3–and–**4**–and. Rock of the 1960s and 1970s often combined complicated rhythms with this basic pattern; for example, drummers typically emphasize the offbeats (the *ands*), known as the backbeats.

Form, Melody, and Harmony

The earliest rock music was often in 12-bar blues form (see Section 18), in 32-bar A A B A form, or in a variant of these forms. Other common popular music structures include strophic and verse-chorus forms. Strophic form (see page 220), in which the musical accompaniment remains the same for each stanza of the lyrics, is commonly found in folk music. Since the accompaniment is repeated, the listener's attention is drawn to the words, which are particularly important both in folk music and in its rock-oriented derivation known as *folk rock*. Verse-chorus form, a variant of strophic form, is very commonly used in popular music. (The Beatles' song *Lucy in the Sky with Diamonds*, studied below, is in verse-chorus form.) In this musical structure, each verse, or stanza, is followed by a chorus, or refrain. In the verse sections, the different stanzas of text are set to a repeated melody and accompaniment, as in strophic form. In the chorus, however, both text and music are repeated. The chorus typically includes a "hook line," a repeated lyric and melody that become the most memorable part of the song.

Earlier popular songs usually consisted of 4- or 8-bar phrases, but rock melodies sometimes contain phrases that are irregular in length. Rock songs tend to have short melodic patterns that are repeated or varied (or both) several times. They are occasionally built on modes, rather than on traditional major or minor scales.

The harmonic progressions of rock are usually quite simple, often consisting of just three or four basic chords. Sometimes the harmony can be restricted deliberately to only two chords, as in *Eleanor Rigby*, by John Lennon and Paul McCartney. However, by the mid-1960s, the Beatles, the Beach Boys, and other innovative artists began using chord progressions that were rarely found in earlier popular music.

Lucy in the Sky with Diamonds, from *Sgt. Pepper's Lonely Hearts Club Band* (1967), by the Beatles

Sgt. Pepper's Lonely Hearts Club Band, a landmark of rock, was one of the first rock music recordings to be presented as a "concept album": its thirteen songs are linked by the ruling idea of a music hall show with a dazzling succession of acts. The sense of continuity is heightened by the varied reprise of the opening song *(Sgt. Pepper's Lonely Hearts Club Band)* as the next-to-last song on the recording. The impact of this record comes largely from its tremendous range of sounds and electronic effects—audience noises, barnyard sounds, weird orchestral tone clusters, and instruments such as the harpsichord, harp, and sitar. There is also a wide range of musical styles, including traditional rock and roll (the Sgt. Pepper theme), a parody of a 1920s music-hall tune *(When I'm Sixty-Four)*, an old-fashioned melodramatic ballad *(She's Leaving Home)*, and the exotic sounds of Indian music *(Within You, Without You)*.

Lucy in the Sky with Diamonds, the third song of the cycle, evokes a world of daydream and fantasy. But the dreamlike mood is shattered by a brusque refrain. After the introduction, *Lucy in the Sky with Diamonds* is in verse-chorus form. The verse, which consists of subsections A-B *(Cellophane flowers)*, is relatively soft, gently pulsating, and in triple meter. In contrast, the chorus, or refrain, section C *(Lucy in the Sky)*, is loud, heavily accented, and in quadruple meter. The song can be outlined as follows:

Introduction

1. A-B *(Cellophane flowers)* C *(Lucy in the Sky)*
2. A-B *(Newspaper taxis)*   C
3. A   CC (fade-out at end)

Nonwestern Music

VII

"The highest aim of our music is to reveal the essence of the universe it reflects . . . through music one can reach God."

RAVI SHANKAR

1 Music in Nonwestern Cultures

2 Music in Sub-Saharan Africa

3 Classical Music of India

All over the world, music is closely linked with religion, dance, and drama. Shown here is a gamelan, an Indonesian orchestra.

Nonwestern Music

Nonwestern music reflects and expresses the diversity of the world's languages, religions, geographical conditions, social and economic systems, values, beliefs, and ways of life. Each culture has its own characteristic instruments, performance practices, tonal systems, and melodic and rhythmic patterns. Nonwestern societies also differ in their range of musical styles: some have only folk music, some have both folk and popular music, and some have complex classical music as well. Thus nonwestern music can offer a wide range of listening experiences and cultural insights. Moreover, nonwestern traditions were an important source of inspiration for twentieth-century western music. For example, they influenced the French composer Claude Debussy, the British rock star George Harrison, and the African American jazz artist John Coltrane.

Women of the Bamileke people of Cameroon singing and dancing. African music is closely associated with dancing. While moving, a dancer oftens sings or plays an instrument.

The koto, a plucked string instrument, is important in traditional Japanese music.

 # Music in Nonwestern Cultures

Characteristics of Nonwestern Music

Although nonwestern music is extremely varied, some features are common to most traditions: music is closely linked with religion, dance, and drama; it can be both entertainment and an accompaniment to everyday activities, magic rites, and ceremonies; and it is often used to communicate messages and relate traditions.

Oral Tradition

Nonwestern music is usually transmitted orally from parent to child or from teacher to student. Compositions and performance techniques are learned by rote and imitation. Music notation is far less important in nonwestern than in western culture: many musical cultures do not have notation; and when notation exists, it traditionally serves only as a record, not for teaching or performance.

Improvisation

Improvisation—usually based on traditional melodic phrases and rhythmic patterns—is basic to much nonwestern music. Often, it is a highly disciplined art that requires years of training. Indian and Islamic musicians, for instance, create music within a framework of many types of melodies, each type associated with a specific mood, a specific set of tones, and characteristic phrases. Although in some cultures the traditional songs and instrumental pieces are performed similarly from generation to generation (as in Japan, where improvisation in classical music is practically nonexistent), in other cultures pieces are treated with great flexibility (in Iran and sub-Saharan Africa, performers freely vary melodies and add sections).

Voices

In most nonwestern cultures, singing is the main way of making music. Each tradition has its own preferred vocal timbres: for example, middle eastern and north African singers cultivate a nasal, intense, strained tone while singers in sub-Saharan Africa prefer a more relaxed, open-throated sound. Vocal techniques include shouting, crying, whispering, sighing, humming, yodeling, and singing through the teeth.

Instruments

Nonwestern instruments produce a wealth of sounds and come in many sizes, shapes, and materials. Scholars usually group these instruments into four categories, based on what actually generates the sound:

1. *Membranophones* are instruments—basically, drums—whose sound generator is a stretched skin or some other membrane.

2. *Chordophones* are instruments—such as harps—whose sound generator is a stretched string.

3. *Aerophones* are instruments—such as flutes and trumpets—whose sound generator is a column of air.

4. *Idiophones* are instruments—such as bells, gongs, scrapers, rattles, and xylophones—whose own material is the sound generator (no tension is applied).

The musical style of a culture is an important factor in its choice of instruments. For example, chordophones (strings) are prominent in Islamic and Indian classical music, in which highly ornamented melodies require instruments with great flexibility of pitch. Idiophones and membranophones (such as bells, rattles, and drums) are typical in sub-Saharan Africa, where rhythm is strongly emphasized and music is closely linked with dancing.

A second factor is geography, which determines the availability of raw materials. Bronze idiophones are prominent in southeast Asia; Indonesian orchestras (gamelans) include bronze gongs, chimes, and xylophones. Instruments made of animal skins and horns are common in parts of sub-Saharan Africa, where these materials are easily found. Among the Aniocha Ibos of Nigeria, for example, drums are made of animal skins, and some aerophones (winds) are made from elephant tusks. Where raw materials are scarce, as in the deserts of Australia, instruments may be few.

A third factor in choice of instruments is religion: often, instruments are symbolic and are linked with specific gods and goddesses (for instance, they may be shaped like birds, animals, or fish).

Melody, Rhythm, and Texture

In Asia, the near east, and north Africa, most music emphasizes melody and rhythm, rather than harmony or polyphony. Texture is often monophonic: the melody is unaccompanied, or it is supported by percussion or (in India and the near east) by a drone—one or more sustained tones. In some regions (such as north Africa, the middle east, southeast Asia, and the far east) all parts may perform the same basic melody, with differing ornamentation or rhythm—a texture called *heterophony.* Homophonic and polyphonic textures tend to be more common in sub-Saharan Africa than in Asia.

Many scales are used in nonwestern music. Most often, they contain five, six, or seven tones. Nonwestern melodies commonly have intervals smaller or larger than those standard in the west. Microtones—intervals smaller than the western half step—are frequent in India and the near east. And much nonwestern music has very complex rhythms; drummers in India and sub-Saharan Africa spend years learning their sophisticated art.

Interaction between Nonwestern and Western Music

Because of increased urbanization, adoption of western technology, and access to radios, films, recordings, and western instruments, twentieth-century nonwestern music was influenced by American and European music. In large cities in Africa, Asia, and the near east, western elements often appear in popular music—such as west African *high life,* which combines European instruments with the characteristic African steady rhythm. Some composers combine traditional elements with western forms and styles. And in many areas, western and traditional music exist side by side. Yet there are vast areas where traditional music still prevails, and many governments subsidize traditional performers to preserve their heritage.

In the following sections, traditional music of sub-Saharan Africa and India will be studied as a sample of the wealth of nonwestern music.

 Music in Sub-Saharan Africa

The African continent can be subdivided into north Africa (Morocco, Algeria, Tunisia, Egypt, etc.) and sub-Saharan Africa, the area south of the Sahara Desert (Ghana, Nigeria, Mozambique, Angola, and many other countries). North Africa is predominantly Muslim and Arabic-speaking, and its music is closely related to that of the middle east. This section focuses on the music of sub-Saharan Africa, sometimes called "black Africa"; throughout the section, the word *Africa* generally refers to sub-Saharan Africa.

Sub-Saharan Africa, which is environmentally and culturally diverse, has several thousand peoples with different religions, different customs, and over 700 different languages. Though urban growth and industrialization are now transforming sub-Saharan Africa, many Africans still hold to traditional ways of life. Most are polytheists, live in villages, and have traditional occupations like agriculture and raising cattle.

Though the music of sub-Saharan Africa is as diverse as its people, most of it features complex rhythms and polyrhythms, percussive sounds, and a wide variety of instrumental ensembles. Vocal music is often performed by a soloist and a responding chorus. Of course, the different cultures of Africa have influenced each other. For example, in parts of sub-Saharan Africa, such as Ghana and northern Nigeria, musical styles have been influenced by Arabic culture.

Music in Society

Music permeates African life. It is used to entertain; as part of dances, plays, religious ceremonies, and magic rites; and to mark such events as birth, puberty, marriage, and death. There are work songs; specific songs or dances to treat the ill; litigation songs; songs praising leaders, criticizing authority, and recounting history; and many songs for particular occasions (for example, among

Singing and playing instruments are interwoven into African life.

the Fon—a people in Dahomey in west Africa—children sing a special song when they lose their first tooth). Singing and playing instruments are so interwoven into life that the abstract word *music*—as understood in the west—is not used by most African peoples, though there are words for *song, dance,* and *poetry.*

African music is closely associated with dancing; both arts are basic to many ceremonies, rituals, and celebrations. Dancers often sing or play rattles or other idiophones that are held or tied to the body.

African music is also intimately linked with language. Many languages are "tone languages," in which a word can have several different meanings, depending on its relative pitch. Tone languages permit the use of music for communication: drummers, trumpeters, and other musicians convey messages and tell stories by imitating the rhythms and pitch fluctuations of words. "Talking drums"—capable of two or more different pitches—are often used to send musical messages.

In Africa, music is a social activity in which almost everyone participates. It is usually performed outdoors, and there is spontaneous music making as well as performances by social and music groups at ceremonies and feasts. There is no musical notation; musical tradition, like folklore and history, is transmitted orally.

Elements of African Music

Rhythm and Percussion

Rhythm and percussion are highly emphasized in African music, reflecting the close link between music and dance. African music tends to feature complex polyrhythms; usually, several different rhythmic patterns are played simultaneously and repeated over and over, and each instrument goes its own rhythmic way. Dancers may choose to follow any of several rhythmic patterns—one dancer may follow the pattern played by a bell while a second follows a rattle and a third follows a drum.

Percussion ensembles consist mainly of drums, xylophones, or rattles carefully chosen to provide contrasts of tone color and pitch. The human body itself is often used as a percussion instrument—hand clapping, foot stamping, and slapping the thigh or chest are common.

Vocal Music

African singers use a wide variety of sounds. Even within a single performance a singer may shift from an open, relaxed tone to one that is tighter and more constricted. Singers may whisper, hum, grunt, shout, imitate animal noises, and yodel (move quickly from a chest voice to a falsetto).

In a characteristic performance style known as *call and response,* the phrases of a soloist are repeatedly answered by those of a chorus. An exciting overlap often results when the leader resumes singing before the chorus has finished responding. Singers are often accompanied by percussion ostinatos (repeated rhythmic patterns). Typically, short musical phrases are repeated over and over to different words.

Texture

African music (unlike that of many other nonwestern cultures) is often homophonic or polyphonic. Several voice parts may sing the same melody at different pitch levels, occasionally producing a series of parallel chords. Some African peoples also perform polyphonic music in which the different melodic lines are quite independent.

African Instruments

A great variety of instruments and instrumental ensembles are found in Africa. Ensembles have two to twenty or more players and may consist of instruments of indefinite pitch (bells, rattles, log drums), definite pitch (flutes, trumpets, xylophones, plucked lutes), or a combination of both (flutes, drums, bells).

Idiophones

The most common instruments in Africa are idiophones, such as bells, rattles, scrapers, xylophones, and log drums. Most are struck or shaken, but others are scraped, rubbed, plucked, or stamped against the ground. Many—like rattles, bells, and stone clappers—are instruments of indefinite pitch. A few—like the xylophone and *mbira,* or *thumb piano*—are tuned instruments.

Xylophones are particularly important; they are played solo, in small groups, and in larger orchestras and exist in different sizes ranging from soprano to double bass (in some areas, one large xylophone is played by several performers simultaneously). Xylophones have from about ten to over twenty slats, sometimes with gourd resonators. Spiderwebs are often placed over small holes in the resonators to create a buzzing sound.

The *mbira* (*sansa, kalimba,* or *thumb piano*) is a melodic idiophone that can produce elaborate melodies; vocalists often use it to accompany themselves. Eight to more than thirty metal or bamboo tongues, attached to a sounding board or box, are plucked with the thumbs and forefingers.

Another important idiophone is the slit drum, a hollowed-out log with a long slit on top used as both a "talking drum" and a musical instrument. Some slit drums are small enough to be held in the hand, while others are tree trunks over 20 feet long. Variations in the width of the slit allow two and sometimes four different tones to be produced.

Membranophones

Drums with stretched skins or other membranes are extremely important in African culture. They are essential to many ceremonies; they are used for dancing and regulating the pace of work; "talking drums" are used to send messages; and drums are often considered sacred or magical. The manufacture of drums is usually accompanied by special rites, and drums are sometimes housed in special shrines, given food, and offered sacrifices. Drums are often regarded as the property of a group, not an individual, and they often symbolize power and royalty.

Drums are usually played in groups of two to four, though some ensembles are made up of as many as fifteen drums, played by four to six performers. The drums are often tuned to different pitches and create melodic music similar to that of xylophone ensembles. The chief drummer is typically free to improvise within a traditional framework; the other drummers repeat certain rhythmic patterns. African drummers are among the most sophisticated in the world, producing complicated rhythms and a wide range of tone colors and pitches.

Drums come in many sizes, shapes, and forms. There are drums shaped like cones, cylinders, kettles, barrels, goblets, and hourglasses. They are made from logs, gourds, and clay. They may have one or two drumheads made from animal skins. Some drums produce a single sound; others—like the hourglass-shaped *pressure drum* (which often imitates the spoken "tone language")—can produce a variety of pitches. Devices used for special effects include seeds or beads inside a closed drum and pieces of metal or small bells attached to a drum's rim.

Aerophones and Chordophones

The most common African aerophones (winds) are flutes, whistles, horns, and trumpets. Reed instruments are less widespread. Flutes are usually made of bamboo, cane, or wood; horns and trumpets are made from animal horns, elephant tusks, wood, bamboo, and gourds.

Most chordophones (strings) are plucked or struck, perhaps because percussive sounds are preferred. One of the most widely used chordophones is the musical bow, whose string is plucked or struck with a stick. Some musical bows have a gourd resonator; with others, the player's mouth is the resonator.

Ompeh

Brief Set:
CD 4 [66]

Basic Set:
CD 8 [58]

Percussive sounds, complex polyrhythms, and a call-and-response pattern are featured in *Ompeh,* a song from the central region of Ghana, recorded by the ethnomusicologist Roger Vetter in 1992–1993. "Within this area," Vetter observes, "are to be found several ethnic/linguistic identities and a colorful palette of musical instruments, ensembles, and repertoires that fulfill the musical needs of small and large communities alike." *Ompeh* is performed by a recreational amateur ensemble of singers and percussionists who specialize in *ompeh,* a type of music of the Akan-speaking peoples in Ghana.

In the performance, brief solo melodies for male voice are each followed by longer responses from a chorus singing mostly in thirds. (From *do* to *mi* in the scale is an interval of a third.) Each choral response is introduced by a single held tone sung by a higher solo male voice. We also hear a percussion ensemble—consisting of a bamboo slit drum, pan rattles (made from aluminum pie plates), a two-headed cylindrical drum *(ogyamba),* a large barrel-shaped hand drum *(ompehkyen),* and metal bell *(afirikyiwa)*—producing a variety of rhythms, pitches, and tone colors. The metal bell serves as the timekeeper of the group. Its repeated rhythm reflects the influence of *high life,* a type of popular music from Ghana.

Listening Outline to be read while music is heard   Brief Set: CD 4   Basic Set: CD 8

Ompeh

2 solo male voices, chorus, bamboo slit drum, metal bell, pan rattle, cylindrical drum, large barrel-shaped hand drum

(Duration, 2:08)

[66] [58]	0:00		**1. a.** Bamboo slit drum, followed by metal bell, pan rattles, cylindrical drum.
	0:14		**b.** Solo vocal melody joins.
	0:23		**c.** Higher solo voice introduces choral response in thirds.
	0:34		**d.** Barrel-shaped bass drum joins accompaniment to chorus, percussion continues throughout.
[67] [59]	0:51	0:00	**2. a.** Solo vocal melody.
	1:00	0:09	**b.** Higher solo voice introduces choral response in thirds.
	1:25	0:34	**c.** Percussion alone.
[68] [60]	1:31	0:00	**3. a.** Solo vocal melody.
	1:40	0:09	**b.** Higher solo voice introduces choral response in thirds.
	2:04	0:33	**c.** Percussion alone closes segment.

Classical Music of India

The musical traditions of India, which include folk and popular music, date back over 3,000 years and are thus among the oldest in the world. Between the twelfth and sixteenth centuries, Indian classical music developed two distinct traditions: *Karnatak music,* of south India; and *Hindustani music,* of north India (an area that now includes Pakistan). The centers of north Indian music were the princely courts, whereas south Indian music was performed in temples. The music of north India absorbed many Persian elements because many of its rulers came from Persia and were Muslims. The music of south India developed more along its own lines.

When India came under British rule during the nineteenth century, north Indian classical music was still performed mainly for small, elite audiences at princely courts. But aristocratic patronage declined during the twentieth century as India made the transition from British rule to independence. Many musicians lost their jobs around 1947—the date of India's independence—when almost 600 princely states of India were abolished as political units and merged with neighboring territories. Indian performers turned to the general public for support, just as European musicians did during the eighteenth and nineteenth centuries.

Today, Indian musicians broadcast on radio and television, make recordings, and compose music for films. Some teach in colleges or give concerts for large audiences. Many Indian artists now travel and give concerts throughout the world.

Performers

Indian performers consider their music spiritual in character. "We view music as a kind of spiritual discipline that raises one's inner being to divine peacefulness and bliss," writes Ravi Shankar (b. 1920), one of the most important Indian musicians. "The highest aim of our music is to reveal the essence of the universe it reflects; . . . through music, one can reach God." This spiritual emphasis is reflected in the texts of south Indian songs, which have religious associations. Indian musicians venerate their *guru* (*master* or *teacher*) as representative of the divine. A special initiation ceremony usually occurs when a guru accepts a disciple. The student is then expected to surrender his or her personality to the guru.

Musical traditions are transmitted orally from master to disciple, who learns by imitation, not by studying textbooks or written music. For example, Indian music students imitate their teacher phrase by phrase at lessons and sing or play along at concerts. Although India has various systems of musical notation, they give only the basic melodic and rhythmic elements. The development of these elements—the essential ornaments and musical elaborations—cannot be notated and must be learned from a teacher.

Improvisation

Improvisation has an important role in Indian music. In few other cultures is improvisation as highly developed and sophisticated. The improviser is guided by complex melodic and rhythmic systems that govern the choice of tones, ornaments, and rhythms. Before being allowed to improvise, young musicians must study for years and practice many hours a day mastering basic rules and techniques. Improvisations are generally performed by a soloist and a drummer. They last anywhere from a few minutes to several hours, depending on the occasion and the mood of the performers and audience. Both vocalists and instrumentalists improvise.

Elements of Indian Classical Music

Indian music is based on the human voice—so much so that the pitch range of all Indian music is restricted to less than 4 octaves. Instrumentalists often imitate a vocal style of performance. Composed pieces are songs performed by a singer or an instrumentalist, with the instrumentalist imitating vocal styles. And songs are used as a springboard for improvisation.

There have been many composers in south India, producing thousands of songs. The greatest composers were Tyagaraja (1767–1847), Muthuswamy Dikshitar (1775–1835), and Shyama Sastri (1762–1827). These three musicians were born in the same village and were contemporaries of Haydn, Mozart, and Beethoven; they are called the "musical trinity."

Highly embellished melody—both vocal and instrumental—is characteristic of Indian music. Melodies often move by microtones (intervals smaller than a half step). Melodic lines are subtly embellished by microtonal ornaments, tiny pitch fluctuations around notes. Slides of pitch provide graceful transitions from one note to another.

Indian melodies are almost always accompanied by a drone instrument that plays the tonic and dominant (or subdominant) notes throughout the performance. The basic texture of Indian music, therefore, consists of a single melody performed over an unchanging background. Rather than the harmonic progression and polyphonic texture of western music, Indian music has melodic and rhythmic tension and relaxation. The main drone instrument is the *tambura,* a long-necked lute with four metal strings that are plucked continually in succession. The constant sound of the drone contributes vitally to the atmosphere of the music. Besides the soloist and the tambura players, there is a drummer who maintains the rhythmic structure and may also perform rhythmic improvisations.

Melodic Structure: Raga

In Indian classical music, melody is created within a melodic framework called *raga.* A *raga* is a pattern of notes. A particular raga is defined partly by the number of its tones and the pattern of its intervals. Each raga has an ascending and descending form with characteristic melodic phrases and tonal emphases. Particular ornaments and slides from one note to another give each raga its individuality.

The term *raga* comes from a word meaning *color* or *atmosphere,* and an ancient saying describes raga as "that which colors the mind." Ragas have many extramusical associations. Each raga is linked with a particular mood, such as tranquillity, love, or heroism. Ragas are also associated with specific gods, seasons,

The sitarist Ravi Shankar is accompanied here by a tabla (a pair of single-headed drums) and a tambura (a drone instrument).

festivals, and times of day or night. They involve so many dimensions that Indian musicians spend a long time learning each one. Some distinguished musicians restrict themselves to performing only about a dozen ragas. Within the framework of a raga, great artists can create and improvise a limitless variety of music.

Rhythmic Structure: Tala

Rhythm is organized into cycles called *talas*. A **tala** consists of a repeated cycle of beats. Although beat cycles range from 3 to more than 100 beats in length, the most common cycles have 6 to 16 beats. A cycle is divided into groups of beats. For example, the 10-beat tala called *jhaptal* is divided 2–3–2–3, while the 10-beat tala called *shultal* is divided 4–2–4:

Jhaptal

|1   2 |3   4   5 |6   7 |8   9   10|

Shultal

|1   2   3   4 |5   6 |7   8   9   10|

Each beat in a tala may be divided into smaller time values, just as a quarter note in western music may be divided into eighth or sixteenth notes. The most important beat of the tala cycle is the first. The soloist usually plays an important note of the raga on the first beat. Apart from the main beat, other beats receive secondary accents at the beginning of each group division. Singers and members of the audience often keep time with hand and finger movements on accented beats and hand waving on less important ones. Talas are performed in a variety of tempos ranging from slow to very fast.

The rhythm of Indian music is remarkably complex and sophisticated. Young drummers spend years with a master drummer memorizing hundreds of talas and their variations. Drummers and instrumental soloists sometimes have exciting dialogues in which rhythmically intricate phrases are rapidly tossed back and forth.

Instruments

Although the most important performing medium in India is the voice, there are a dazzling variety of instruments of all kinds. In north Indian classical music, instruments have become about as popular as the voice. Many instruments are associated with specific gods and goddesses. For example, the flute is associated with the Hindu god Krishna, and the *vina*—a plucked string instrument—is linked with Sarasvati, the Hindu goddess of wisdom. We will describe only a few of the best-known instruments.

The *sitar* is the most popular chordophone of north India. It is a long-necked lute with nineteen to twenty-three movable frets. There are seven strings, which are plucked: five are used for melodies, and two supply drone and rhythmic effects. The sitar also has nine to thirteen sympathetically vibrating strings that give the instrument its characteristic sound. These strings lie under the frets, almost parallel to the plucked strings. The most famous sitarist today is Ravi Shankar.

The *vina* is the most ancient plucked string instrument of south India. It has four strings for playing melodies, and three strings at the side of the fingerboard can be used for drone and rhythmic effects.

The *sarod* is a north Indian string instrument plucked with a plectrum of ivory or coconut shell. It has six main strings: four for melodies and two for drones and rhythm. Eleven to sixteen other strings vibrate sympathetically.

The *mridangam* is a two-headed barrel drum popular in south India. It is played with the open hands and fingers. The right drumhead is tuned to the tonic, and the left head functions as a bass.

The north Indian counterpart of the mridangam is the **tabla,** a pair of single-headed drums played by one performer. The right-hand drum is generally tuned to the tonic note, and the left-hand drum functions as a bass drum. These drums, which are played with the hands and fingers, can produce a wide variety of pitches and tone colors. The tabla is vital to north Indian concerts and is used for solos as well as accompaniments.

Maru-Bihag, by Ravi Shankar

Brief Set:

CD 4 69

The performance here is an improvisation by the sitarist Ravi Shankar on the evening raga *Maru-Bihag*. As usual, the sitar is accompanied by a pair of drums (tabla) with a *tambura* (a drone instrument) in the background. In his spoken

Basic Set:
CD 8 62

69 62

introduction to the recorded performance, Ravi Shankar illustrates the raga pattern and the tala (beat cycle) used as a basis for this performance. The ascending and descending melodic forms of *Maru-Bihag* are as follows:

Raga *Maru-Bihag*

The tala, played by the tabla, consists of 10 beats divided to give 2–3–2–3. In the illustration as well as the performance, it is not easy to perceive the beats. Each one is often subdivided into shorter drum strokes, and accents often come off the beat.

70 63

The performance opens with an *alap*, a rhapsodic introductory section in which the sitar is accompanied only by the tambura playing the tonic and dominant notes of the raga pattern. The sitarist plays in free rhythm, without regular beat or meter. Ravi Shankar conveys the basic mood and character of the raga by gradually unfolding its melodic pattern, characteristic phrases, and important tones. There are many long notes, microtonal ornaments, and slides from tone to tone. After opening with a downward glissando (glide) across the sympathetic strings, Ravi Shankar first explores the lowest notes of the melody and then plays slightly higher ones. In this performance the introductory section (alap) is 2 minutes in length. (In other performances, however, the alap can last as long as an hour.)

71 64

The entrance of the tabla playing the tala (beat cycle) marks the second phase of the performance. Ravi Shankar presents the *gat*, a short composed phrase that recurs many times. Between these recurrences, there are longer sections of improvisation. As the improvisation progresses, Ravi Shankar generates excitement by using increasingly rapid notes and by moving through the low and high registers of the sitar. This performance is a spectacular display of virtuosity and musical imagination.

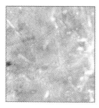

Glossary and Example Locator

Note: Musical examples are given for most of the terms in the glossary. Examples indicate (as appropriate) composer; title; movement (mvt); page (p) where discussed or page where listening outline (LO) or vocal music guide (VMG) appears; item on listening outline; words in vocal text; compact disk (CD) and track numbers (track numbers are in small boxes; light boxes for the brief set; dark boxes for the basic set). **Boldface** is used for the **brief** set of five CDs and lightface is used for the basic set of nine CDs. Additional abbreviations are: first, second, third, fourth, etc. = 1st, 2d, 3d, 4th, etc.; mvt = movement.

A B form See *two-part form.*

A B A form See *three-part form.*

Absolute music Instrumental music having *no* intended association with a story, poem, idea, or scene; nonprogram music.

A cappella Choral music without instrumental accompaniment.

> **Example** Josquin Desprez, *Ave Maria*; VMG; p. 82; VMG; **CD 1** 56 ; CD 1 74

Accelerando Becoming faster.

> **Example** Schoenberg, *A Survivor from Warsaw*, starting at *They began again*; p. 326; VMG; **CD 4** 26 ; CD 7 29

Accent Emphasis of a note, which may result from its being louder, longer, or higher in pitch than the notes near it.

Accompanied recitative Speechlike melody that is sung by a solo voice accompanied by the orchestra.

> **Example** Handel, *Messiah, Comfort Ye*, starting at *The voice of him*; CD 2 53

Accordion Instrument consisting of a bellows between two keyboards (piano-like keys played by the right hand, and buttons played by the left hand) whose sound is produced by air pressure which causes free steel reeds to vibrate.

Adagio Slow.

> **Example** Dvořák, Symphony No. 9, 1st mvt, slow introduction; p. 258; LO 1; **CD 3** 41 ; CD 6 8

Aerophone Any instrument—such as a flute or trumpet—whose sound is generated by a vibrating column of air.

Aleatory music See *chance music.*

Allegretto Moderately fast.

> **Example** Mozart, *Eine kleine Nachtmusik*, 3d mvt; p. 169; LO; **CD 2** 38 ; CD 3 46

Allegro Fast.

> **Example** Vivaldi, *La Primavera (Spring)*, Concerto for Violin and String Orchestra, 1st mvt; p. 126; LO; **CD 2** 1 ; CD 2 22

Alto (contralto) Female voice of low range.

Andante   Moderately slow, a walking pace.

> **Example** Haydn, Symphony No. 94, 2d mvt; p. 166; LO; **CD 2** 32 ; CD 3 **40**

Answer   Second presentation of the subject in a fugue, usually in the dominant scale.

> **Example** Bach, Organ Fugue in G Minor; p. 109; LO 1*b*; **CD 1** 68 ; CD 2 **14**

Aria   Song for solo voice with orchestral accompaniment, usually expressing an emotional state through its outpouring of melody; found in operas, oratorios, and cantatas.

> **Example** Puccini, *La Bohème, Che gelida manina*; p. 272; VMG; **CD 3** 52 ; CD 6 **23**

Arpeggio   See *broken chord*.

Art song   Setting of a poem for solo voice and piano, translating the poem's mood and imagery into music, common in the romantic period.

> **Examples** Schubert, *Erlkönig (The Erlking)*; p. 223; VMG; **CD 3** 12 ; CD 4 **48**
> Clara Schumann, *Liebst du um Schönheit*, p. 230; VMG; **CD 3** 22 ; CD 5 **8**

Atonality   Absence of tonality, or key, characteristic of much twentieth-century music.

> **Example** Schoenberg, *Pierrot lunaire, Mondestrunken*; p. 324; VMG; **CD 4** 24 ; CD 7 **27**

Augmentation   Variation of a fugue subject in which the original time values of the subject are lengthened.

Bandoneon   Square accordion used in tango bands, operated entirely with buttons.

> **Example** Piazzolla, *Fugata*; p. 364; LO 1.c.; **CD 5** 7 ; CD 8 **30**

Bar   Another term for *measure*, often used in jazz.

Baritone   Male voice range lower than a tenor and higher than a bass.

> **Example** Schubert, *Erlkönig*, (The Erlking); p. 223; VMG; **CD 3** 12 ; CD 4 **48**

Baritone horn   Brass instrument similar in shape to the tuba, with a higher range, commonly used in bands.

Bass   (1) Male voice of low range. (2) See *double bass*.

> **Example** Mozart, *Don Giovanni*, Introduction, Leporello's *Notte e giorno faticar*; p. 181; VMG; **CD 3** 1 ; CD 3 **60**

Bass clarinet   Member of the clarinet family, having a low range. Its shape is curved at the end before flaring into a bell.

Bass clef   Symbol on the staff indicating relatively low pitch ranges, such as those played by a pianist's left hand.

Bass drum   Percussion instrument of indefinite pitch, the largest of the orchestral drums.

> **Example** Britten, *The Young Person's Guide to the Orchestra*; p. 28; LO variation 13a; **CD 1** 29 ; CD 1 **36**

Bass fiddle   See *double bass*.

Basso continuo   Baroque accompaniment made up of a bass part usually played by two instruments: a keyboard plus a low melodic instrument. (See also *figured bass*.)

> **Examples** Monteverdi, *Orfeo, Tu se' morta*; p. 119; VMG; **CD 1** 71 ; CD 2 **17**
> Bach, Suite No. 3, bourrée; p. 133; **CD 2** 10 ; CD 2 **40**

Basso ostinato See *ground bass.*

Bassoon Double-reed woodwind instrument, made of wood, having a low range.

> **Example** Britten, *The Young Person's Guide to the Orchestra*; p. 28; LO variation 4;
> **CD 1** 20 ; CD 1 **27**

Baton Thin stick used by many conductors to beat time and indicate pulse and tempo.

Beam Horizontal line connecting the flags of several eighth notes or sixteenth notes in succession, to facilitate reading these notes.

Beat Regular, recurrent pulsation that divides music into equal units of time.

Bebop (bop) Complex jazz style, usually for small groups, developed in the 1940s and meant for attentive listening rather than dancing.

> **Example** Parker, *Bloomdido*; CD 8 **53**

Bitonality Approach to pitch organization using two keys at one time, often found in twentieth-century music.

Blues Term referring both to a style of performance and to a form; an early source of jazz, characterized by flatted, or "blue," notes in the scale; vocal blues consist of 3-line stanzas in the form a a' b.

> **Examples** Smith, *Lost Your Head Blues*; p. 375; VMG; **CD 4** 57 ; CD 8 **45**
> Ellington, *C-Jam Blues*; p. 9; LO; **CD 1** 3 ; CD 1 **10**

Bop See *bebop.*

Bow Slightly curved stick strung tightly with horsehair, used to play string instruments.

Brass instrument Instrument, made of brass or silver, whose sound is produced by the vibrations of the player's lips as he or she blows into a cup- or funnel-shaped mouthpiece. The vibrations are amplified and colored in a tube that is flared at the end.

Break In jazz, a brief unaccompanied solo.

> **Example** Ellington, *C-Jam Blues*; p. 9; LO 3, 4, 5, 6, 7; **CD 1** 3 ; CD 1 **10**

Bridge (transition) In the exposition of the sonata form, a section which leads from the first theme in the tonic, or home, key to the second theme, which is in a new key.

> **Examples** Mozart, Symphony No. 40 in G Minor, 1st mvt; p. 164; LO exposition 2; **CD 2** 24 ;
> CD 3 **11**
> Beethoven, Symphony No. 5 in C Minor, 1st mvt; p. 199; LO exposition 2; **CD 2** 46 ; CD 4 **24**

Broken chord (arpeggio) Sounding of the individual tones of a chord in sequence rather than simultaneously.

> **Example** Beethoven, Symphony No. 5 in C Minor, 3d mvt (opening six notes); p. 202;
> **CD 2** 59 ; CD 4 **37**

Cadence (1) Resting place at the end of a phrase in a melody. (2) Progression giving a sense of conclusion, often from the dominant chord to the tonic chord.

> **Example** Mozart, *Eine kleine Nachtmusik*, 3d mvt; p. 169; LO 1, end of stately melody;
> **CD 2** 38 ; CD 3 **46**

Cadenza Unaccompanied section of virtuoso display for the soloist in a concerto, usually appearing near the end of the first movement and sometimes in the last movement.

> **Example** Mozart, Piano Concerto in A Major, K. 488, 1st mvt; p. 189; LO recapitulation 5c; **CD 3** 11; CD 4 **7**

Call and response (1) In jazz, a pattern in which one voice or instrument is answered by another voice, instrument, or group of instruments. (2) Performance style in which the phrases of a soloist are repeatedly answered by those of a chorus, often found in African and other nonwestern music.

> **Examples** Smith, *Lost Your Head Blues*; p. 375; VMG; **CD 4** 57; CD 8 **45**
> *Ompeh*, p. 411; **CD 4** 66; CD 8 **58**

Camerata In Italian, *fellowship or society;* a group of nobles, poets, and composers who began to meet regularly in Florence around 1575 and whose musical discussions prepared the way for the beginning of opera.

Cantata Composition in several movements, usually written for chorus, one or more vocal soloists, and instrumental ensemble. The church cantata for the Lutheran service in Germany during the baroque period often includes chorales.

> **Example** Bach, Cantata No. 140, p. 137; **CD 2** 12, 15; CD 2 **44**, **47**, **50**

Castrato Male singer castrated before puberty to retain a high voice range; the most important category of vocal soloists in opera during the baroque period.

Celesta Percussion instrument of definite pitch, with metal bars that are struck by hammers controlled by a keyboard.

Cello (violoncello) String instrument with a range lower than that of the viola and higher than that of the double bass.

> **Example** Britten, *The Young Person's Guide to the Orchestra*; p. 28; LO variation 7; **CD 1** 23; CD 1 **30**

Chamber music Music using a small group of musicians, with one player to a part.

Chance (aleatory) music Music composed by the random selection of pitches, tone colors, and rhythms; developed in the 1950s by John Cage and others.

Chimes Percussion instrument of definite pitch, with suspended metal tubes that are struck with a hammer.

> **Example** Berlioz, *Fantastic Symphony*, 4th mvt *(March to the Scaffold)*; p. 249; **CD 3** 30; CD 5 **32**

Chorale Hymn tune sung to a German religious text.

> **Example** Bach, Cantata No. 140, 7th mvt; p. 137; **CD 2** 15; CD 2 **50**

Chorale prelude Short composition for organ, based on a hymn tune and often used to remind the congregation of the melody before the hymn is sung.

Chord Combination of three or more tones sounded at once.

> **Example** Bizet, *Farandole* from *L'Arlésienne* Suite No. 2, p. 51; LO 1a (opening chord); **CD 1** 37; CD 1 **53**

Chordophone Instrument—such as a harp or lute—whose sound is generated by a stretched string.

Chorus (1) A group of singers performing together, generally with more than one to a part. (2) In jazz, a statement of the basic harmonic pattern or melody.

Chromatic harmony Use of chords containing tones not found in the prevailing major or minor scale but included in the chromatic scale (which has twelve tones); often found in romantic music.

Chromatic scale Scale including all twelve tones of the octave; each tone is a half step away from the next one.

> **Example** Purcell, *Dido and Aeneas, Dido's Lament*, repeated descending chromatic scale in bass; p. 121; VMG; **CD 1** 73 ; CD 2 **19**

Church modes Scales containing seven tones with an eighth tone duplicating the first an octave higher, but with patterns of whole and half steps different from major and minor scales; used in medieval, Renaissance, and twentieth-century music and in folk music.

> **Example** *Alleluia: Vidimus stellam*; p. 68; VMG; **CD 1** 47 ; CD 1 **63**

Clarinet Single-reed woodwind instrument with a beak-shaped mouthpiece, cylindrical in shape with a slightly flared bell.

> **Example** Copland, *Appalachian Spring*, Section 7: Theme and Variations on *Simple Gifts*; p. 348; LO theme; **CD 4** 41 ; CD 8 **12**

Clavichord Baroque keyboard instrument in which sound is produced by means of brass blades striking strings, capable of making gradual dynamic changes, but within a narrow volume range.

Clef Symbol placed at the beginning of the staff to show the exact pitch of notes placed on each line and space.

Climax Highest tone or emotional focal point in a melody or a larger musical composition.

> **Example** Purcell, *Dido and Aeneas, Dido's Lament*, climax on *remember*; p. 121; VMG; **CD 1** 73 ; CD 2 **19**

Coda In a sonata-form movement, a concluding section following the recapitulation and rounding off the movement by repeating themes or developing them further.

> **Examples** Mozart, Symphony No. 40 in G Minor, 1st mvt; p. 164; LO coda; **CD 2** 31 ; CD 3 **18**
> Beethoven, Symphony No. 5 in C Minor, 1st mvt; p. 199; LO coda; **CD 2** 52 ; CD 4 **30**

Complete cadence Definite resting place, giving a sense of finality, at the end of a phrase in a melody.

> **Example** Mozart, *Eine kleine Nachtmusik*, 3d mvt; p. 169; LO 1, end of stately melody; **CD 2** 38 ; CD 3 **46**

Computer Tool used to synthesize music, to help composers write scores, to store samples of audio signals, and to control synthesizing mechanisms.

Computer music Composition including sounds generated and manipulated by computer.

Concert overture Independent composition for orchestra in one movement, usually in sonata form, often found in the romantic period.

> **Example** Tchaikovsky, *Romeo and Juliet*; p. 261; CD 5 **46**

Concertmaster Principal first violinist in a symphony orchestra.

Concerto Extended composition for instrumental soloist and orchestra, usually in three movements: (1) fast, (2) slow, (3) fast.

Concerto grosso Composition for several instrumental soloists and small orchestra; common in late baroque music.

> **Examples** Bach, *Brandenburg* Concerto No. 5 in D Major; p. 105; LO; **CD 1** 63 ;
> CD 2 1 , 6 , 11
> Zwilich, *Concerto Grosso 1985*, 1st mvt; p. 368; **CD 4** 51 ; CD 8 35

Conductor Leader of a performing group of musicians.

Consonance Tone combination that is stable and restful.

Contrabassoon Double-reed woodwind instrument with a register one octave lower than that of the bassoon.

Contralto See *alto.*

Contrast Striking differences of pitch, dynamics, rhythm, and tempo that provide variety and change of mood.

Cool jazz Jazz style related to bebop, but more relaxed in character and relying more heavily on arrangements; developed around 1950.

Cornet Brass instrument similar in shape to the trumpet, with a mellower tone.

Countermelody Melodic idea that accompanies a main theme.

> **Example** Haydn, Symphony No. 94, 2d mvt; p. 166; LO variation 3; **CD 2** 35 ; CD 3 43

Counterpoint Technique of combining two or more melodic lines into a meaningful whole.

Countersubject In a fugue, a melodic idea that accompanies the subject fairly constantly.

> **Example** Bach, Organ Fugue in G Minor; p. 109; LO 1*b*; **CD 1** 68 ; CD 2 14

Crescendo Gradually louder. (Often abbreviated *cresc.*)

> **Example** Bizet, *Farandole* from *L'Arlésienne* Suite No. 2, p. 51; LO 2*a*; **CD 1** 39 ;
> CD 1 55

Cymbals Percussion instrument of indefinite pitch, consisting of a pair of metal plates, played by striking the plates against each other.

> **Example** Britten, *The Young Person's Guide to the Orchestra*; p. 28; LO variation 13a;
> **CD 1** 29 ; CD 1 36

Da capo From the beginning; an indication usually meaning that the opening section of a piece is to be repeated after the middle section.

> **Examples** Mozart, *Eine kleine Nachtmusik*, 3d mvt; p. 169; LO minuet (A); **CD 2** 40 ;
> CD 3 48

Da capo aria Aria in A B A form; after the B section, the term *da capo* is written; this means *from the beginning* and indicates a repetition of the opening A section.

Decrescendo Gradually softer.

> **Example** Berlioz, *Fantastic Symphony*, 4th mvt; p. 249; LO 2*a*; **CD 3** 31 ; CD 5 33

Development Second section of a sonata-form movement, in which themes from the exposition are developed and the music moves through several different keys.

> **Examples** Mozart, Symphony No. 40 in G Minor, 1st mvt; p. 164; LO development; **CD 2** 28 ; CD 3 **15**
>
> Beethoven, Symphony No. 5 in C Minor, 1st mvt; p. 199; LO development; **CD 2** 50 ; CD 4 **28**

Diminuendo See *decrescendo.*

Diminution Variation of a fugue subject in which the original time values of the subject are shortened.

Dissonance Tone combination that is unstable and tense.

Dixieland jazz Jazz style originating in New Orleans, in which the front line, or melodic instruments, improvises several contrasting melodic lines at once, supported by a rhythm section that clearly marks the beat and provides a background of chords; usually based on a march or church melody, a ragtime piece, a popular song, or 12-bar blues.

> **Example** Armstrong, *Hotter Than That*; p. 380; LO 1 and 6b; **CD 4** 63 ; CD 8 **52**

Dominant chord Triad built on the fifth note of the scale, which sets up tension that is resolved by the tonic chord.

> **Example** Vivaldi, *La Primavera (Spring)*, Concerto for Violin and String Orchestra, 1st mvt; p. 126; LO 1*a*, end of first phrase; **CD 2** 1 ; CD 2 **22**

Dotted note Note with a dot to the right of it. This dot increases the note's undotted duration by half.

Dotted rhythm Long-short rhythmic pattern in which a dotted note is followed by a note that is much shorter.

> **Example** Chopin, *Revolutionary* Étude in C Minor; p. 234; LO; **CD 3** 29 ; CD 5 **29**

Double bass (bass) Largest string instrument, having the lowest range of the string family.

> **Example** Britten, *The Young Person's Guide to the Orchestra*, LO variation 8; p. 28; **CD 1** 24 ; CD 1 **31**

Double-reed woodwinds Instruments whose sound is produced by two narrow pieces of cane held between the player's lips; these pieces vibrate when the player blows between them.

Double stop See *stop.*

Downbeat First, or stressed, beat of a measure.

> **Example** Bizet, *Farandole* from *L'Arlésienne* Suite No. 2; p. 51; LO 1*a*, opening chord; **CD 1** 37 ; CD 1 **53**

Drone Long, sustained tone or tones accompanying a melody.

> **Example** Hildegard of Bingen, *O successores*; p. 70; VMG; **CD 1** 50 ; CD 1 **66**

Duple meter Pattern of 2 beats to the measure.

> **Example** Tchaikovsky, *Nutcracker* Suite, *Dance of the Reed Pipes*; p. 54; LO; **CD 1** 42 ; CD 1 **58**

Dynamics Degrees of loudness or softness in music.

Electronic instrument Instrument whose sound is produced, modified, or amplified by electronic means.

English horn Double-reed woodwind instrument, slightly larger than the oboe and with a lower range, straight in shape with an egg-shaped bell.

> **Example** Tchaikovsky, *Nutcracker* Suite, *Dance of the Reed Pipes*; p. 54; LO 1*c*; **CD 1** 42; CD 1 58

Ensemble In opera, a piece sung by three or more solo singers.

> **Example** Mozart, *Don Giovanni*, Introduction, andante, starting at *Ah, soccorso*; p. 181; VMG; **CD 3** 3; CD 3 62

Episode Transitional section in a fugue between presentations of the subject, which offers either new material or fragments of the subject or countersubject.

> **Example** Bach, Organ Fugue in G Minor; p. 109; LO 1*e*; **CD 1** 68; CD 2 15

Étude In French, *study*; a piece designed to help a performer master specific technical difficulties.

> **Example** Chopin, *Revolutionary* Étude in C Minor; p. 234; LO; **CD 3** 29; CD 5 15

Euphonium Brass instrument similar in shape to the tuba and the baritone horn, with a higher range than the tuba's, commonly used in bands.

Exoticism Use of melodies, rhythms, or instruments that suggest foreign lands; common in romantic music.

Exposition First section of a sonata-form movement, which sets up a strong conflict between the tonic key and the new key; and between the first theme (or group of themes) and the second theme (or group of themes).

> **Example** Mozart, Symphony No. 40 in G Minor, 1st mvt; p. 164; LO exposition; **CD 2** 23; CD 3 10

Expressionism Musical style stressing intense, subjective emotion and harsh dissonance, typical of German and Austrian music of the early twentieth century.

> **Example** Schoenberg, *Pierrot lunaire, Mondestrunken*; p. 324; VMG; **CD 4** 24; CD 7 27

Figured bass Bass part of a baroque accompaniment with figures (numbers) above it indicating the chords to be played. (See also *basso continuo*.)

Film music Music synchronized with images on a movie screen; it provides momentum and continuity, and it suggests mood, atmosphere, character, and dramatic action.

Flag Wavy line attached to the stem on a note, indicating how long that note is to be held relative to the notes around it.

Flat sign Symbol which notates a pitch one half step lower than the pitch that would otherwise be indicated—for example, the next lower key on the piano.

Flute Woodwind instrument, usually made of metal, with a high range, whose tone is produced by blowing across the edge of a mouth hole.

> **Example** Tchaikovsky, *Nutcracker* Suite, *Dance of the Reed Pipes*; p. 54; LO 1*b*; **CD 1** 42; CD 1 58

Form Organization of musical ideas in time.

Forte (*f*) Loud.

> **Examples** Mozart, *Eine kleine Nachtmusik*, 3d mvt; p. 169; LO 1; **CD 2** $\boxed{38}$; CD 3 ◼46
> Vivaldi, *La Primavera (Spring)*, Concerto for Violin and String Orchestra, 1st mvt; p. 126;
> LO 1*a*; **CD 2** $\boxed{1}$; CD 2 ◼22

Fortepiano Eighteenth-century or early-nineteenth-century piano, which differs from the modern piano in sound and construction.

Fortissimo (*ff*) Very loud.

> **Example** Stravinsky, *The Firebird*, Scene 2; p. 8; LO 2a; **CD 1** $\boxed{2}$; CD 1 ◼9

Fourth chord Chord in which the tones are a fourth apart, instead of a third; used in twentieth-century music.

Free jazz Jazz style that departs from traditional jazz in not being based on regular forms and established chord patterns; developed during the 1960s.

French horn Brass instrument of medium range, whose tube is coiled into a roughly circular shape and fitted with valves; commonly used in symphony orchestras and in bands. (Sometimes called simply a *horn*.)

> **Examples** Stravinsky, *The Firebird*, Scene 2; p. 8; LO 1a; **CD 1** $\boxed{1}$; CD 1 ◼8
> Britten, *The Young Person's Guide to the Orchestra*, LO variation 10; p. 28; **CD 1** $\boxed{26}$; CD 1 ◼33

French overture Common opening piece in baroque suites, oratorios, and operas; usually in two parts: the first slow, with characteristic dotted rhythms, full of dignity and grandeur; the second quick and lighter in mood, often starting like a fugue.

> **Example** Handel, *Messiah*, Sinfonia (Overture); CD 2 ◼51

Front line In New Orleans or Dixieland jazz, the group of melodic instruments which improvise on a melody, supported by the rhythm section.

Fugue Polyphonic composition based on one main theme, or subject.

> **Example** Bach, Organ Fugue in G Minor; p. 109; LO; **CD 1** $\boxed{68}$; CD 2 ◼14

Fusion See *jazz rock.*

Glissando Rapid slide up or down a scale.

> **Example** Piazzolla, *Fugata*; p. 364; LO 6*b*; **CD 5** $\boxed{7}$; CD 8 ◼31

Glockenspiel Percussion instrument of definite pitch, made up of flat metal bars set in a frame and played by striking with small metal hammers.

Gong (tam-tam) Percussion instrument of indefinite pitch, made up of a large flat metal plate that is suspended and struck with a mallet.

> **Example** Britten, *The Young Person's Guide to the Orchestra*, LO variation 13d; p. 28;
> **CD 1** $\boxed{32}$; CD 1 ◼39

Grand staff Combination of the treble and bass staves, used in keyboard music to encompass the wide range of pitches produced by both hands.

Grave Very slow, solemn.

> **Example** Beethoven, Piano Sonata in C Minor, Op. 13 *(Pathétique)*, slow introduction; CD 4 ◼8

Gregorian chant Melodies set to sacred Latin texts, sung without accompaniment; Gregorian chant was the official music of the Roman Catholic church.

> **Example** *Alleluia: Vidimus stellam*; p. 68; VMG; **CD 1** $\boxed{47}$; CD 1 ◼63

Ground bass (basso ostinato) Variation form in which a musical idea in the bass is repeated over and over while the melodies above it constantly change; common in baroque music.

> **Example** Purcell, *Dido and Aeneas, Dido's Lament*; p. 121; VMG; **CD 1** ⬚73⬚; CD 2 ■19■

Guitar Plucked string instrument with six strings stretched along a fretted fingerboard.

> **Example** Armstrong, *Hotter Than That*; p. 380; **CD 4** ⬚60⬚, ⬚61⬚; CD 8 ■49■, ■50■

Half step Smallest interval traditionally used in western music; for example, the interval between *ti* and *do.*

Harmonics Very high-pitched whistle-like tones, produced in bowed string instruments by lightly touching the string at certain points while bowing.

Harmony How chords are constructed and how they follow each other.

Harp Plucked string instrument, consisting of strings stretched within a triangular frame.

> **Example** Britten, *The Young Person's Guide to the Orchestra*, LO variation 9; p. 28; **CD 1** ⬚25⬚; CD 1 ■32■

Harpsichord Keyboard instrument, widely used from about 1500 to 1775, whose sound is produced by plectra which pluck its wire strings. The harpsichord was revived during the twentieth century.

> **Example** Bach, *Brandenburg* Concerto No. 5 in D Major, 1st mvt; p. 105; LO 8c; **CD 1** ⬚67⬚; CD 2 ■5■

Heterophonic texture (heterophony) Simultaneous performance of the same basic melody by two or more voices or instruments, but in versions that differ in ornamentation or rhythm; common in nonwestern music.

Home key See *tonic key.*

Homophonic texture Term describing music in which one main melody is accompanied by chords.

> **Example** Chopin, Nocturne in E Flat Major, Op. 9, No. 2; p. 232; LO; **CD 3** ⬚26⬚; CD 5 ■12■

Horn See *French horn.*

Idée fixe Single melody used in several movements of a long work to represent a recurring idea.

> **Example** Berlioz, *Fantastic Symphony*, 4th mvt; p. 249; LO 5d; **CD 3** ⬚33⬚; CD 5 ■35■

Idiophone Instrument—such as bells, a gong, a scraper, a rattle, or a xylophone—whose sound is generated by the instrument's own material (no tension is applied).

Imitation Presentation of a melodic idea by one voice or instrument that s immediately followed by its restatement by another voice or instrument, as in a round.

> **Examples** Josquin Desprez, *Ave Maria*, opening words *Ave Maria*; p. 82; **CD 1** ⬚56⬚; CD 1 ■74■
> Bach, Organ Fugue in G Minor; p. 109; LO 1; **CD 1** ⬚68⬚; CD 2 ■14■
> Piazzolla, *Fugata*; p. 364; LO 1a–d; **CD 5** ⬚7⬚; CD 8 ■30■

Impressionism Musical style that stresses tone color, atmosphere, and fluidity, typical of Debussy (flourished 1890–1920).

> **Example** Debussy, *Prelude to The Afternoon of a Faun*; p. 309; LO; **CD 4** ⬚9⬚; CD 7 ■1■

Improvisation Creation of music at the same time as it is performed.

> **Examples** Ellington, *C-Jam Blues*; p. 9; LO 3–6; **CD 1** `5` to `8`; CD 1 **12** to **15**
> Shankar, *Maru-Bihag*; p. 416; **CD 4** `70`; CD 8 **63**

Incidental music Music intended to be performed before and during a play, setting the mood for the drama.

Incomplete cadence Inconclusive resting point at the end of a phrase which sets up expectations for phrases to follow.

> **Example** Vivaldi, *La Primavera (Spring)*, Concerto for Violin and String Orchestra, 1st mvt; p. 126; LO 1*a* (end of opening phrase); **CD 2** `1`; CD 2 **22**

Interval "Distance" in pitch between any two tones.

Inversion Variation of a fugue subject in which each interval of the subject is reversed in direction.

Jazz Music rooted in improvisation and characterized by syncopated rhythm, a steady beat, and distinctive tone colors and performance techniques. Jazz was developed in the United States predominantly by African American musicians and gained popularity in the early twentieth century.

Jazz rock (fusion) Style that combines the jazz musician's improvisatory approach with rock rhythms and tone colors; developed in the 1960s.

> **Example** Davis, *Miles Runs the Voodoo Down*; p. 384; CD 8 **54**

Kettledrums See *timpani*.

Key (tonality) Central note, scale, and chord within a piece, in relationship to which all other tones in the composition are heard.

Key signature Sharp or flat signs immediately following the clef sign at the beginning of a piece of music, indicating the key in which the music is to be played.

Keyboard instrument Instrument—such as the piano, organ, or harpsichord—played by pressing a series of keys with the fingers.

Keynote (tonic) Central tone of a melody or larger piece of music. When a piece is in the key of C major, for example, C is the keynote.

Largo Very slow, broad.

> **Example** Chopin, Prelude for Piano in E Minor; p. 44; **CD 1** `36`; CD 1 **52**

Leap Interval larger than that between two adjacent tones in the scale.

> **Example** Chopin, Nocturne in E Flat Major, Op. 9, No. 2, upward leap at beginning of main melody; p. 232; LO 1*a*; **CD 3** `26`; CD 5 **12**

Ledger lines Short, horizontal lines above or below the staff, used to indicate a pitch that falls above or below the range indicated by the staff.

Legato Smooth, connected manner of performing a melody.

> **Example** Bach, Organ Fugue in G Minor; p. 109; LO 1*a*; **CD 1** `68`; CD 2 **14**

Leitmotif Short musical idea associated with a person, object, or thought, characteristic of the operas of Wagner.

> **Example** Wagner, *Die Walküre*, Act I, love scene, *sword*; p. 282; VMG; **CD 4** `6`; CD 6 **31**

Librettist Dramatist who writes the libretto, or text, of an opera.

Libretto Text of an opera.

Lute Plucked string instrument shaped like half a pear; used in Renaissance and baroque music.

Madrigal Composition for several voices set to a short secular poem, usually about love, combining homophonic and polyphonic textures and often using word painting; common in Renaissance music.

> **Example** Weelkes, *As Vesta Was Descending*; p. 87; VMG; **CD 1** 62 ; CD 1 80

Major key Music based on a major scale.

> **Examples** Mozart, *Eine kleine Nachtmusik*, 3d mvt; p. 169; LO; **CD 2** 38 ; CD 3 46
> Contrast between major and minor keys is illustrated in Tchaikovsky, *Nutcracker* Suite, *Dance of the Reed Pipes*; p. 54; LO 1, 2; **CD 1** 42 and 43 ; CD 1 58 and 59

Major scale Series of seven different tones within an octave, with an eighth tone repeating the first tone an octave higher, consisting of a specific pattern of whole and half steps; the whole step between the second and third tones is characteristic.

> **Example** Handel, *Messiah*, *Ev'ry Valley Shall Be Exalted*, downward major scale on first appearance of *-ley shall be exalted*; p. 144; VMG; **CD 2** 16 ; CD 2 55

Mass Sacred choral composition made up of five sections: Kyrie, Gloria, Credo, Sanctus, and Agnus Dei.

> **Examples** Machaut, *Notre Dame* Mass, Agnus Dei; p. 78; VMG; **CD 1** 53 ; CD 1 71
> Palestrina, *Pope Marcellus* Mass, Kyrie, p. 85; VMG; **CD 1** 59 ; CD 1 77

Mass ordinary Roman Catholic church texts that remain the same from day to day throughout most of the year: Kyrie, Gloria, Credo, Sanctus, and Agnus Dei.

Measure Rhythmic group set off by bar lines, containing a fixed number of beats.

Melody Series of single tones that add up to a recognizable whole.

Membranophone Instrument—basically, a drum—whose sound is generated by a stretched skin or another membrane.

Meter Organization of beats into regular groups.

Meter signature See *time signature*.

Metronome Apparatus that produces ticking sounds or flashes of light at any desired constant speed.

Mezzo forte (*mf*) Moderately loud.

> **Example** Copland, *Appalachian Spring*; section 7, Theme and variations on *Simple Gifts*; p. 348; LO Variation 4; **CD 4** 45 ; CD 8 16

Mezzo piano (*mp*) Moderately soft.

> **Example** Still, *Afro-American Symphony*, 3d mvt; p. 344; LO 2a; **CD 4** 39 ; CD 7 56

Mezzo-soprano Female voice of fairly low range, though not so low as alto.

> **Example** Crumb, *From Where Do You Come, My Love, My Child?* CD 8 32

Microtone Interval smaller than a half step.

Middle C Note C nearest to the center of the piano keyboard, notated as the pitch on the ledger line below the treble clef and above the bass clef.

Minimalist music Music characterized by steady pulse, clear tonality, and insistent repetition of short melodic patterns; its dynamic level, texture, and harmony tend to stay constant for fairly long stretches of time, creating a trancelike or hypnotic effect; developed in the 1960s.

Example Adams, *Short Ride in a Fast Machine*, p. 370; **CD 4** 53; CD 8 37

Minor key Music based on a minor scale.

Examples Purcell, *Dido and Aeneas, Dido's Lament*; p. 121; VMG; **CD 1** 72; CD 2 18
Contrast between minor and major keys is illustrated in Bizet, *L'Arlésienne* Suite No. 2; p. 51;
LO 1, 2; **CD 1** 37, 39; CD 1 53, 55

Minor scale Series of seven tones within an octave, with an eighth tone repeating the first tone an octave higher, composed of a specific pattern of whole and half steps; the half step between the second and third tones is characteristic.

Example Berlioz, *Fantastic Symphony*, 4th mvt, *March to the Scaffold*, downward minor scale at opening of first theme; p. 249; LO; **CD 3** 31; CD 5 33

Minuet and trio (minuet) Compositional form—derived from a dance—in three parts: minuet (A), trio (B), minuet (A). Often used as the third movement of classical symphonies, string quartets, and other works, it is in triple meter ($\frac{3}{4}$ time) and usually in a moderate tempo.

Example Mozart, *Eine kleine Nachtmusik*, 3d mvt; LO; p. 169; **CD 2** 38; CD 3 46

Moderato Moderate tempo.

Example Tchaikovsky, *Nutcracker* Suite, *Dance of the Reed Pipes*; p. 54; LO; **CD 1** 42; CD 1 58

Modified strophic form Form in which two or more stanzas of poetry are set to the same music while other stanzas have new music; found in art songs of the romantic period.

Example Clara Schumann, *Liebst du um Schönheit*, p. 230; VMG; **CD 3** 22; CD 5 8

Modulation Shift from one key to another within the same piece.

Example Mozart, Symphony No. 40 in G Minor, 1st mvt; modulation from G minor to B flat major; p. 164; LO exposition 2, 3; **CD 2** 24, 25; CD 3 11, 12

Monophonic texture Single melodic line without accompaniment.

Example *Alleluia: Vidimus stellam*; p. 68; VMG; **CD 1** 47; CD 1 63

Motet Polyphonic choral work set to a sacred Latin text other than that of the mass; one of the two main forms of sacred Renaissance music.

Example Josquin Desprez, *Ave Maria*; p. 82; VMG; **CD 1** 56; CD 1 74

Motive Fragment of a theme, or short musical idea that is developed within a composition.

Example Beethoven, Symphony No. 5 in C Minor, 1st mvt, first four notes; p. 199; LO exposition 1*a*; **CD 2** 45; CD 4 23

Movement Piece that sounds fairly complete and independent but is part of a larger composition.

Musical (musical comedy) Type of American theater created to entertain through fusion of a dramatic script, acting, and spoken dialogue with music, singing, and dancing—and scenery, costumes, and spectacle.

Example Bernstein, *West Side Story*, *Tonight* ensemble; p. 390; LO; **CD 4** 64; CD 8 56

Musical texture Number of layers of sound that are heard at once, what kinds of layers they are, and how they are related to each other.

Mute Device used to veil or muffle the tone of an instrument. For string instruments, the mute is a clamp which fits onto the bridge; for brass instruments, it is a funnel-shaped piece of wood, metal, or plastic which fits into the bell.

Nationalism Inclusion of folk songs, dances, legends, and other national material in a composition to associate it with the composer's homeland; characteristic of romantic music.

Natural sign Symbol used in notation of pitch to cancel a previous sharp or flat sign.

Neoclassicism Musical style marked by emotional restraint, balance, and clarity, inspired by the forms and stylistic features of eighteenth-century music, found in many works from 1920 to 1950.

> **Example** Stravinsky, *Symphony of Psalms*, 1st mvt; CD 7 26

Nocturne In French, *night piece*; a composition, usually slow, lyrical, and intimate in character, often for piano solo.

> **Example** Chopin, Nocturne in E Flat Major, Op. 9, No. 2; p. 232; LO; **CD 3** 26; CD 5 12

Notation System of writing down music so that specific pitches and rhythms can be communicated.

Note In notation, a black or white oval to which a stem and flags can be added.

Oboe Double-reed woodwind instrument with a relatively high range, conical in shape with a small flared bell.

Octave Interval between two tones in which the higher tone has twice the frequency of the lower tone.

> **Example** Handel, *Messiah*, *Hallelujah* Chorus, downward and upward octave leaps to the words *God omni(potent)*; p. 146; VMG; **CD 2** 18; CD 3 5

Opera Drama that is sung to orchestral accompaniment, usually a large-scale composition involving vocal soloists, chorus, orchestra, costumes, and scenery.

Oratorio Large-scale composition for chorus, vocal soloists, and orchestra, usually set to a narrative text, but without acting, scenery, or costumes; often based on biblical stories.

Organ (pipe organ) Keyboard instrument with many sets of pipes controlled from two or more keyboards, including a pedal keyboard played by the organist's feet. The keys control valves from which air is blown across or through openings in the pipes. (The *electric organ* is an electronic instrument that is sometimes designed to imitate the sound of a pipe organ.)

> **Example** Bach, Organ Fugue in G Minor; p. 109; LO; **CD 1** 68; CD 2 14

Organ point See *pedal point*.

Organum Medieval polyphony that consists of Gregorian chant and one or more additional melodic lines.

Ostinato Motive or phrase that is repeated persistently at the same pitch, used in twentieth-century music to stabilize a group of pitches.

> **Examples** Stravinsky, *The Rite of Spring, Introduction* and *Omens of Spring*; p. 316; LO 2*b*; **CD 4** 17; CD 7 16
> Piazzolla, *Fugata*; p. 364; LO 5*a*; **CD 5** 7; CD 8 31

Overture (prelude) Short musical composition, purely orchestral, which opens an opera and sets the overall dramatic mood. Orchestral introductions to later acts of an opera are called *preludes.*

Passacaglia See *ground bass.*

Pedal point (organ point) Single tone, usually in the bass, which is held while the other voices produce a series of changing harmonies against it; often found in fugues.

Pentatonic scale Scale made up of five different tones, used in folk music and music of the far east.

Percussion instrument Instrument of definite or indefinite pitch whose sound is produced by striking by hand, or with a stick or hammer, or by shaking or rubbing.

Performer Person who plays or sings music.

Phrase Part of a melody.

> **Example** Vivaldi, *La Primavera (Spring)*, Concerto for Violin and String Orchestra, 1st mvt, opening phrase of ritornello; p. 126; LO 1*a*; **CD 2** 1 ; CD 2 **22**

Pianissimo (*pp*) As softly as possible.

> **Example** Haydn, Symphony No. 94 *(Surprise)*, 2d mvt; p. 166; LO theme, section a repeated; **CD 2** 32 ; CD 3 **40**

Piano Widely used keyboard instrument of great range and versatility, whose sound is produced by felt-covered hammers striking against steel strings.

> **Example** Chopin, Nocturne in E Flat Major; p. 232; LO; **CD 3** 26 ; CD 5 **12**

Piano (*p*) Soft.

> **Example** Brahms, Symphony No. 3 in F Major, 3rd mvt; p. 265; LO 1a; **CD 3** 48 ; CD 6 **15**

Piccolo Smallest woodwind instrument, having the highest range; a smaller version of the flute.

> **Example** Britten, *The Young Person's Guide to the Orchestra*, p. 28; LO Concluding section a; **CD 1** 35 ; CD 1 **42**

Pipe organ See *organ.*

Pitch Relative highness or lowness of a sound.

Pitch range Distance between the highest and lowest tones that a given voice or instrument can produce.

Pizzicato Means of playing a string instrument by which the strings are plucked, usually with a finger of the right hand.

> **Example** Tchaikovsky, *Nutcracker* Suite, *Dance of the Reed Pipes*, p. 54; LO 1*a-b*; **CD 1** 42 ; CD 1 **58**

Plectrum Small wedge of plastic, leather, or quill used to pluck the strings of certain instruments, such as the guitar and harpsichord. (Plural, *plectra.*)

Polonaise Composition in triple meter with a stately character, often for piano solo; originally a Polish court dance.

> **Example** Chopin, Polonaise in A Flat Major, Op. 53; p. 235; CD 5 **16**

Polychord Combination of two chords sounded at the same time, used in twentieth-century music.

Polyphonic texture Performance of two or more melodic lines of relatively equal interest at the same time.

Examples Bach, Organ Fugue in G Minor, illustrates polyphonic texture based on imitation; p. 109; LO; **CD 1** [68]; CD 2 **14**

Bach, Cantata No. 140, 4th mvt, starting with entry of tenors, illustrates polyphonic texture based on simultaneous presentation of different melodies; p. 141; VMG; **CD 2** [13]; CD 2 **48**

Polyrhythm Use of two or more contrasting and independent rhythms at the same time, often found in twentieth-century music.

Polytonality Approach to pitch organization using two or more keys at one time, often found in twentieth-century music.

Postlude Concluding section; the section at the end of an art song which sums up its mood, played by the piano or orchestra, without the voice.

Example Clara Schumann, *Liebst du um Schönheit*; p. 230; VMG; **CD 3** [25]; CD 5 **11**

Prelude (1) Short piece usually serving to introduce a fugue or other composition; a short piece for piano. (2) See *overture*.

Examples Bach, Prelude in C Minor, from *The Well-Tempered Clavier*, Book I; CD 2 **31**

Chopin, Prelude in E Minor for Piano; p. 44; LO; **CD 1** [36]; CD 1 **52**

Prestissimo As fast a tempo as possible.

Example Beethoven, String Quartet in C Minor, Op. 18, No. 4, 4th mvt; p. 171; LO 7; **CD 2** [44]; CD 3 **52**

Presto Very fast tempo.

Primitivism Evocation of primitive power through insistent rhythms and percussive sounds.

Example Stravinsky, *The Rite of Spring, Omens of Spring—Dances of the Youths and Maidens*; p. 316; LO 3; **CD 4** [18]; CD 7 **17**

Program Explanatory comments specifying the story, scene, or idea associated with program music.

Program music Instrumental music associated with a story, poem, idea, or scene, often found in the romantic period.

Program symphony Symphony (a composition for orchestra in several movements) related to a story, idea, or scene, in which each movement usually has a descriptive title; often found in romantic music.

Example Berlioz, *Fantastic Symphony*, 4th mvt; p. 249; LO; **CD 3** [30]; CD 5 **32**

Progression Series of chords.

Prompter Person who gives cues and reminds singers of their words or pitches during an opera performance. The prompter is located in a box just over the edge of center stage, which conceals him or her from the audience.

Quadruple meter Pattern of 4 beats to the measure.

Example Vivaldi, *La Primavera (Spring)*, Concerto for Violin and String Orchestra, 1st mvt; p. 126; LO; **CD 2** [1]; CD 2 **22**

Quadruple stop See *stop*.

Quintuple meter Pattern of 5 beats to the measure.

Quotation music Works that make extensive use of quotations from earlier music; common since the mid-1960s.

Example Zwilich, *Concerto Grosso 1985*, 1st mvt; p. 368; LO; **CD 4** 51 ; **CD 8** 35

Raga Pattern of notes serving as a melodic framework for the creation of an improvisation, characteristic of Indian classical music.

Example Shankar, *Maru-Bihag*; p. 416; **CD 4** 69 ; **CD 8** 62

Ragtime Style of composed piano music, generally in duple meter with a moderate march tempo, in which the pianist's right hand plays a highly syncopated melody while the left hand maintains the beat with an "oom-pah" accompaniment. Ragtime was developed primarily by African American pianists and flourished from the 1890s to about 1915.

Example Joplin, *Maple Leaf Rag*; CD 8 41

Range See *pitch range.*

Recapitulation Third section of a sonata-form movement, in which the first theme, bridge, second theme, and concluding section are presented more or less as they were in the exposition, with one crucial difference: all the principal material is now in the tonic key.

Example Mozart, Symphony No. 40 in G Minor, 1st mvt; p. 164; LO recapitulation; **CD 2** 29 ; **CD 3** 16

Recitative Vocal line in an opera, oratorio, or cantata that imitates the rhythms and pitch fluctuations of speech, often serving to lead into an aria.

Example Mozart, *Don Giovanni*, introduction; p. 181; VMG; **CD 3** 4 ; **CD 3** 63

Recorder Family of woodwind instruments whose sound is produced by blowing into a "whistle" mouthpiece, usually made of wood or plastic.

Reed Very thin piece of cane, used in woodwind instruments to produce sound as it is set into vibration by a stream of air.

Register Part of the total range of an instrument or voice. The tone color of the instrument or voice may vary with the register in which it is played or sung.

Repetition Reiteration of a phrase, section, or entire movement, often used to create a sense of unity.

Requiem Mass for the dead.

Example Mozart, Requiem, *Dies irae*; CD 3 70

Resolution Progression from a dissonance to a consonance.

Rest In notation of rhythm, a symbol to indicate the duration of silence in the music.

Retrograde Variation of a fugue subject in which the subject is presented by beginning with its last note and proceeding backward to the first.

Rhythm Ordered flow of music through time; the pattern of durations of notes and silences in music.

Rhythm section Instruments in a jazz ensemble that maintain the beat, add rhythmic interest, and provide supporting harmonies. The rhythm section is usually made up of piano, plucked double bass, percussion, and sometimes banjo or guitar.

Example Ellington, *C-Jam Blues*; p. 9; LO; **CD 1** 3 ; **CD 1** 10

Riff In jazz, a short repeated phrase that may be an accompaniment or a melody.

Ritardando Becoming slower.

Example Chopin, *Revolutionary* Étude in C Minor; p. 234; LO 2*e*; **CD 3** `29`; CD 5 `15`

Ritornello In Italian, *refrain;* a repeated section of music usually played by the full orchestra, or tutti, in baroque compositions.

Example Bach, *Brandenburg* Concerto No. 5 in D Major, 1st mvt; p. 105; LO 1*a*; **CD 1** `63`; CD 2 `1`

Ritornello form Compositional form usually used in the baroque concerto grosso, in which the tutti plays a ritornello, or refrain, alternating with one or more soloists playing new material.

Example Bach, *Brandenburg* Concerto No. 5 in D Major, 1st mvt; p. 105; LO; **CD 1** `63`; CD 2 `1`

Rock First called *rock and roll,* a style of popular vocal music that developed in the 1950s, characterized by a hard, driving beat and featuring electric guitar accompaniment and heavily amplified sound.

Rondo Compositional form featuring a main theme (A) which returns several times in alternation with other themes, such as A B A C A and A B A C A B A. Rondo is often the form of the last movement in classical symphonies, string quartets, and sonatas.

Examples Beethoven, String Quartet in C Minor, Op. 18, No. 4, 4th mvt; p. 171; LO; **CD 2** `41`; CD 3 `49`
Beethoven, Piano Sonata in C Minor, Op. 13 *(Pathétique)*, 3d mvt; CD 4 `19`

Rubato Slight holding back or pressing forward of tempo to intensify the expression of the music, often used in romantic music.

Example Chopin, Nocturne in E Flat Major, Op. 9, No. 2; p. 232; LO 2*a*; **CD 3** `28`; CD 5 `14`

Saxophone Family of single-reed woodwind instruments.

Example Ellington, *C-Jam Blues*; p. 9; LO 5; **CD 1** `7`; CD 1 `14`

Scale Series of pitches arranged in order from low to high or high to low.

Scat singing Vocalization of a melodic line with nonsense syllables, used in jazz.

Example Armstrong, *Hotter Than That*; p. 380; **CD 4** `60`; CD 8 `49`

Scherzo Compositional form in three parts (A B A), sometimes used as the third movement in classical and romantic symphonies, string quartets, and other works. A scherzo is usually in triple meter, with a faster tempo than a minuet.

Example Beethoven, Symphony No. 5 in C Minor, 3d mvt; p. 202; **CD 2** `59`; CD 4 `37`

Score Notation showing all the parts of a musical ensemble, with a separate staff for each part, and with simultaneously sounded notes aligned vertically; used by the conductor.

Secco recitative Speechlike melody that is sung by a solo voice accompanied only by a basso continuo.

Example Mozart, *Don Giovanni*, introduction; p. 181; VMG; **CD 3** `4`; CD 3 `63`

Septuple meter Pattern of 7 beats to the measure.

Example Brubeck, *Unsquare Dance*; CD 1 `48`

Sequence In a melody, the immediate repetition of a melodic pattern on a higher or lower pitch.

> **Examples** Mozart, Symphony No. 40 in G Minor, 1st mvt; p. 164; LO 1*a;* **CD 2** 23 ; CD 3 **10**
> Beethoven, Symphony No. 5 in C Minor, 1st mvt; p. 199; LO 1*a;* **CD 2** 45 ; CD 4 **23**

Serenade Instrumental composition, light in mood, usually meant for evening entertainment.

> **Example** Mozart, *Eine kleine Nachtmusik*, 3d mvt; p. 169; LO; **CD 2** 38 ; CD 3 **46**

Serialism Method of composing that uses an ordered group of musical elements to organize rhythm, dynamics, and tone color, as well as pitch; developed in the mid-twentieth century.

Series See *tone row.*

Set See *tone row.*

Sextuple meter Pattern of 6 beats to the measure.

Sharp sign Symbol which notates a pitch one half step higher than the pitch that would otherwise be indicated—for example, the next higher black key on the piano.

Side drum See *snare drum.*

Single-reed woodwinds Instruments whose sound is produced by a single piece of cane, or reed, fastened over a hole in the mouthpiece. The reed vibrates when the player blows into the mouthpiece.

Sitar Most popular chordophone of north India. It is a long-necked lute with nineteen to twenty-three movable frets. Seven strings are plucked and nine to thirteen strings vibrate sympathetically.

> **Example** Shankar, *Maru-Bihag;* p. 416; **CD 4** 69 ; CD 8 **62**

Snare drum (side drum) Percussion instrument of indefinite pitch, in the shape of a cylinder with a stretched skin at either end. A "snare" of gut or metal is stretched below the lower skin and produces a rattling sound when the drum is struck.

> **Example** Ravel, *Bolero;* CD 7 **8**

Sonata In baroque music, an instrumental composition in several movements for one to eight players. In music after the baroque period, an instrumental composition usually in several movements for one or two players.

> **Example** Beethoven, Piano Sonata in C Minor, Op. 13 *(Pathétique);* CD 4 **8** , **15** , **19**

Sonata form Form of a single movement, consisting of three main sections: the exposition, where the themes are presented; the development, where themes are treated in new ways; and the recapitulation, where the themes return. A concluding section, the coda, often follows the recapitulation.

> **Examples** Mozart, Symphony No. 40 in G Minor, 1st mvt; p. 164; LO; **CD 2** 23 ; CD 3 **10**
> Beethoven, Symphony No. 5 in C Minor, 1st mvt; p. 199; LO; **CD 2** 45 ; CD 4 **23**

Sonata-rondo Compositional form that combines the repeating theme of rondo form with a development section similar to that in sonata form, outlined A B A—development—A B A.

> **Example** Haydn, Trumpet Concerto, 3d mvt; p. 176; CD 3 **53**

Song cycle Group of art songs unified by a story line that runs through their poems, or by musical ideas linking the songs; often found in romantic music.

Soprano Female voice of high range.

> **Example** Purcell, *Dido and Aeneas, Dido's Lament*; p. 121; VMG; **CD 1** 72 ; CD 2 18

Sound Vibrations transmitted, usually through air, to the eardrum, which sends impulses to the brain.

Sprechstimme In German, *speech-voice*; a style of vocal performance halfway between speaking and singing, typical of Schoenberg and his followers.

> **Example** Schoenberg, *Pierrot lunaire, Mondestrunken*; p. 324; VMG; **CD 4** 24 ; CD 7 27

Staccato Short, detached manner of performing a melody.

> **Example** Tchaikovsky, *Nutcracker* Suite, *Dance of the Reed Pipes*; p. 54; LO 1*b*; **CD 1** 42 ;
> CD 1 58

Staff In notation, a set of five horizontal lines between or on which notes are positioned.

Stem Vertical line on a note indicating how long that note is to be held relative to the notes around it.

Step Interval between two adjacent tones in the scale.

Stop (double, triple, quadruple) Means of playing a string instrument by which the bow is drawn across two, three, or four strings at the same time or almost the same time.

Stretto Compositional procedure used in fugues, in which a subject is imitated before it is completed; one voice tries to catch the other.

String instrument Instrument whose sound is produced by the vibration of strings.

String quartet Composition for two violins, a viola, and a cello; usually consisting of four movements. (*Also,* the four instrumentalists.)

> **Example** Beethoven, String Quartet in C Minor, Op. 18, No. 4, 4th mvt; p. 170; LO; **CD 2** 41 ;
> CD 3 49

Strophic form Vocal form in which the same music is repeated for each stanza of a poem.

> **Example** Clara Wieck Schumann, *Liebst du um Schönheit (If you love for beauty)*; varied strophic form; p. 230; **CD 3** 22 ; CD 5 8

Style Characteristic way of using melody, rhythm, tone, color, dynamics, harmony, texture, and form in music.

Subdominant Fourth note *(fa)* of the scale, or the triad (chord) based on this note.

> **Example** Smith, *Lost Your Head Blues*, repetition of the words *I was with you baby*; p. 375; VMG; **CD 4** 57 ; CD 8 46

Subject Theme of a fugue.

> **Example** Bach, Organ Fugue in G Minor; p. 109; LO 1*a*; **CD 1** 68 ; CD 2 14

Suite In baroque music, a set of dance-inspired movements all written in the same key but differing in tempo, meter, and character.

> **Example** Bach, Suite No. 3 in D Major; p. 133; **CD 2** 10 ; CD 2 38 , 40 , 42

Swing Jazz style that was developed in the 1920s and flourished between 1935 and 1945, played mainly by "big bands." *Also,* verb for what jazz performers do when they combine a steady beat and precision with a lilt, a sense of relaxation, and vitality.

Swing band Typically, a large band made up of fourteen or fifteen musicians grouped in three sections: saxophones, brasses, and rhythm. They play swing, a jazz style (*see* above).

> **Example** Ellington, *C-Jam Blues*; p. 9; LO; **CD 1** 3 ; CD 1 **10**

Symphonic poem (tone poem) Programmatic composition for orchestra in one movement, which may have a traditional form (such as sonata or rondo) or an original, irregular form.

Symphony Orchestral composition, usually in four movements, typically lasting between 20 and 45 minutes, exploiting the expanded range of tone color and dynamics of the orchestra.

Syncopation Accenting of a note at an unexpected time, as between two beats or on a weak beat. Syncopation is a major characteristic of jazz.

> **Example** Still, *Afro-American Symphony*, 3d mvt; p. 344; LO 1*b*; **CD 4** 37 ; CD 7 **54**

Synthesizer System of electronic components which can generate, modify, and control sound; used to compose music and to perform it.

Tabla Pair of single-headed drums in which the right-hand drum is generally tuned to the tonic note and the left-hand drum functions as a bass drum; the most important percussion instrument in north Indian music.

> **Example** Shankar, *Maru-Bihag*; p. 416; **CD 4** 69 ; CD 8 **62**

Tala Repeated cycle of beats organizing the rhythm in Indian classical music.

> **Example** Shankar, *Maru-Bihag*; p. 416; **CD 4** 69 ; CD 8 **62**

Tambourine Percussion instrument of indefinite pitch, consisting of a skin stretched across a shallow cylinder, with small circular plates set into the cylinder which jingle when the skin is struck or the cylinder is shaken.

> **Example** Britten, *The Young Person's Guide to the Orchestra*; p. 28; LO variation 13*b*;
> **CD 1** 30 ; CD 1 **37**

Tambura Long-necked lute with four metal strings that are continually plucked in succession; the main drone instrument in Indian music.

> **Example** Shankar, *Maru-Bihag*; p. 416; **CD 4** 71 ; CD 8 **64**

Tam-tam See *gong*.

Tango Argentinian dance in quadruple meter for couples in close embrace.

> **Example** Piazzolla, *Fugata*; p. 364; **CD 5** 7 ; CD 8 **30**

Tape studio Studio with tape recorders and other equipment used to create electronic music by modifying and combining recorded sounds.

> **Example** Varèse, *Poème électronique*; p. 362; **CD 4** 49 ; CD 8 **26**

Tempo Basic pace of the music.

Tempo indication Words, usually at the beginning of a piece of music, often in Italian, which specify the pace at which the music should be played.

Tenor Male voice of high range.

> **Examples** Handel, *Messiah, Ev'ry Valley*; p. 144; VMG; **CD 2** 10 ; CD 2 **55**
> Puccini, *La Bohème, Che gelida manina (How cold your little hand is)*; p. 272;
> **CD 3** 52 ; CD 6 **23**

Terraced dynamics Abrupt alternation between loud and soft dynamic levels; characteristic of baroque music.

> **Example** Vivaldi, *La Primavera (Spring)*, Concerto for Violin and String Orchestra, 1st mvt; p. 126; LO 1*a*; **CD 2** ☐1☐; CD 2 **22**

Thematic transformation Alteration of the character of a theme by means of changes in dynamics, orchestration, or rhythm, when it returns in a later movement or section; often found in romantic music.

> **Example** Berlioz, *Fantastic Symphony*; compare *idée fixe* in: 4th mvt; p. 249; LO 5*d*; **CD 3** ☐33☐; CD 5 **35**; 5th mvt; p. 251; LO 2*b*; CD 5 **37**

Theme Melody that serves as the starting point for an extended piece of music.

> **Example** Mozart, Symphony No. 40 in G Minor, 1st mvt; p. 164; LO 1*a*; **CD 2** ☐23☐; CD 3 **10**

Theme and variations Form in which a basic musical idea (the theme) is repeated over and over and is changed each time in melody, rhythm, harmony, dynamics, or tone color. Used either as an independent piece or as one movement of a larger work.

> **Examples** Haydn, Symphony No. 94 in G Major *(Surprise)*, 2d mvt; p. 166; LO; **CD 2** ☐32☐; CD 3 **40**
>
> Copland, *Appalachian Spring*, section 7, theme and variations on *Simple Gifts*; p. 348; LO; **CD 4** ☐41☐; CD 8 **12**

Three-part form (A B A) Form that can be represented as statement (A); contrast (B); return of statement (A).

> **Examples** Tchaikovsky, *Nutcracker* Suite, *Dance of the Reed Pipes*; p. 54; LO; **CD 1** ☐42☐; CD 1 **58**
>
> Brahms, Symphony No. 3 in F Major, 3rd mvt; p. 265; LO; **CD 3** ☐48☐; CD 6 **15**

Through-composed form Vocal form in which there is new music for each stanza of a poem.

> **Example** Schubert, *Erlkönig (The Erlking)*; p. 223; VMG; **CD 3** ☐12☐; CD 4 **48**

Tie In notation of rhythm, an arc between two notes of the same pitch indicating that the second note should not be played but should be added to the duration of the first.

Timbre See *tone color.*

Time signature (meter signature) Two numbers, one above the other, appearing at the beginning of a staff or the start of a piece, indicating the meter of the piece.

Timpani (kettledrums) Percussion instruments of definite pitch, shaped like large kettles with calfskin or plastic stretched across the tops, played with soft padded mallets.

> **Example** Britten, *The Young Person's Guide to the Orchestra*, variation 13*a*; p. 28; **CD 1** ☐29☐; CD 1 **36**

Tonality See key.

Tone Sound that has a definite pitch, or frequency.

Tone cluster Chord made up of tones only a half step or a whole step apart, used in twentieth-century music.

Tone color (timbre) Quality of sound that distinguishes one instrument or voice from another.

Tone-color melody Succession of varying tone colors serving as a musical idea in a composition, used by Schoenberg and his followers.

> **Example** Webern, *Five Pieces for Orchestra*, 3d piece; p. 333; LO; **CD 4** 36 ; CD 7 53

Tone poem See *symphonic poem.*

Tone row (set, series) Particular ordering of the twelve chromatic tones, from which all pitches in a twelve-tone composition are derived.

> **Example** Schoenberg, *A Survivor from Warsaw*, to the Hebrew words of *Shema Yisroel*; p. 326; VMG; **CD 4** 27 ; CD 7 30

Tonic See *keynote.*

Tonic chord Triad built on the first, or tonic, note of the scale, serving as the main chord of a piece and usually beginning and ending it.

> **Example** Bizet, *L'Arlésienne* Suite No. 2, *Farandole*, opening chord; p. 51; LO 1*a*; **CD 1** 37 ; CD 1 53

Tonic key (home key) Central key of a piece of music, usually both beginning and ending the piece, regardless of how many other keys are included.

Transition See *bridge.*

Treble clef Notation on a staff to indicate relatively high pitch ranges, such as those played by a pianist's right hand.

Tremolo Rapid repetition of a tone, produced in string instruments by quick up-and-down strokes of the bow.

> **Example** Vivaldi, *La Primavera (Spring)*, Concerto for Violin and String Orchestra; 1st mvt; p. 126; LO 3*b*; **CD 2** 41 ; CD 2 25

Triad Most basic of chords, consisting of three alternate tones of the scale, such as *do, mi, sol.*

Triangle Percussion instrument of indefinite pitch, consisting of a triangular length of metal suspended from a hook or cord, played by striking with a metal rod.

> **Example** Smetana, *The Moldau*; p. 255; LO 4*a*; **CD 3** 37 ; CD 6 4

Trill Musical ornament consisting of the rapid alternation of two tones that are a whole or half step apart.

> **Example** Vivaldi, *La Primavera (Spring)*, Concerto for Violin and String Orchestra, 1st mvt; p. 126; LO 1*b*; **CD 2** 2 ; CD 2 23

Trio sonata Baroque composition with three melodic lines: two high ones, each played by one instrument; and a basso continuo, played by two instruments.

Triple meter Pattern of 3 beats to the measure.

> **Examples** Mozart, *Eine kleine Nachtmusik*, 3d mvt; p. 169; LO; **CD 2** 38 ; CD 3 46
> Brahms, Symphony No. 3 in F Major, 3rd mvt; p. 265; LO; **CD 3** 48 ; CD 6 15

Triple stop See *stop.*

Triplet In notation of rhythm, three notes of equal duration grouped within a curved line with the numeral 3, lasting only as long as two notes of the same length would normally last.

Trombone Brass instrument of moderately low range, whose tube is an elongated loop with a movable slide, commonly used in symphony orchestras, bands, and jazz ensembles.

Example Britten, *The Young Person's Guide to the Orchestra*, LO variation 12; p. 28; **CD 1** 28 ; CD 1 **35**

Trumpet Brass instrument with the highest range, commonly used in symphony orchestras, bands, and jazz and rock groups.

Example Copland, *Appalachian Spring*, Section 7, Theme and Variations on *Simple Gifts*; p. 348; LO variation 3; **CD 4** 44 ; CD 8 **15**

Tuba Largest brass instrument, with the lowest range, commonly used in symphony orchestras and bands.

Example Britten, *The Young Person's Guide to the Orchestra*, LO variation 12; p. 28; **CD 1** 28 ; CD 1 **35**

Tutti In Italian, *all;* the full orchestra, or a large group of musicians contrasted with a smaller group; often heard in baroque music.

Example Bach, *Brandenburg* Concerto No. 5 in D Major, 1st mvt; p. 105; LO 1*a;* **CD 1** 63 ; CD 2 **1**

12-bar blues In vocal blues and jazz, a harmonic framework that is 12 bars in length, usually involving only three basic chords: tonic (I), subdominant (IV), and dominant (V).

Examples Smith, *Lost Your Head Blues;* p. 375; VMG; **CD 4** 57 ; CD 8 **45** Ellington, *C-Jam Blues;* p. 9; LO; **CD 1** 3 ; CD 1 **10**

Twelve-tone system Method of composing in which all pitches of a composition are derived from a special ordering of the twelve chromatic tones (tone row or set); developed by Schoenberg in the early 1920s.

Example Schoenberg, *A Survivor from Warsaw;* p. 326; VMG; **CD 4** 25 ; CD 7 **28**

Two-part form (A B) Form that can be represented as statement (A) and counterstatement (B).

Examples Beethoven, Contradance No. 7; p. 55; LO; **CD 1** 45 ; CD 1 **61** Haydn, Symphony No. 94 in G Major *(Surprise)*, 2d mvt, theme; p. 166; LO theme; **CD 2** 32 ; CD 3 **40**

Unison Performance of a single melodic line by more than one instrument or voice at the same pitch or in different octaves.

Examples Handel, *Messiah, Hallelujah* Chorus, to the words *For the Lord God;* p. 146; VMG; **CD 2** 18 ; CD 3 **5** Beethoven, Symphony No. 5 in C Minor, 1st mvt; p. 199; LO 1*a;* **CD 2** 45 ; CD 4 **23**

Upbeat Unaccented pulse preceding the downbeat.

Example Chopin, Nocturne in E Flat Major, Op. 9, No. 2, opening note; p. 232; LO 1*a;* **CD 3** 26 ; CD 5 **12**

Variation Changing some features of a musical idea while retaining others.

Vibraphone Percussion instrument of definite pitch with metal bars, similar to the marimba, with tubular metal resonators driven by electronic impulses.

Vibrato Small fluctuations of pitch which make the tone warmer, produced in string instruments by rocking the left hand while it presses the string down.

> **Example** Mendelssohn, Concerto for Violin and Orchestra in E Minor, 1st mvt; p. 241; LO;
> **CD 5** ☐1☐; CD 5 ■26■

Viol Member of a family of bowed string instruments popular during the Renaissance, having six strings and a fretted fingerboard.

Viola String instrument with a lower range than the violin and a higher range than the cello.

> **Example** Britten, *The Young Person's Guide to the Orchestra*, LO variation 6; p. 28;
> **CD 1** ☐22☐; CD 1 ■29■

Violin String instrument with the highest range of the string family.

> **Examples** Britten, *The Young Person's Guide to the Orchestra*, p. 28; LO variation 5; p. 28;
> **CD 1** ☐11☐; CD 1 ■28■
> Mendelssohn, Concerto for Violin and Orchestra in E Minor, 1st mvt; p. 241; LO; **CD 5** ☐1☐;
> CD 5 ■26■

Violoncello See *cello.*

Virtuoso Performing artist of extraordinary technical mastery.

Vivace Lively tempo.

Voice categories of opera Voice ranges which include coloratura soprano, lyric soprano, dramatic soprano, lyric tenor, dramatic tenor, basso buffo, and basso profondo, among others.

Whole step Interval twice as large as the half step; for example, the interval between *do* and *re.*

Whole-tone scale Scale made up of six different tones, each a whole step away from the next, which conveys no definite sense of tonality; often found in the music of Debussy and his followers.

Woodwind instrument Instrument whose sound is produced by vibrations of air in a tube; holes along the length of tube are opened and closed by the fingers, or by pads, to control the pitch.

Word painting Musical representation of specific poetic images—for example, a falling melodic line to accompany the word *descending*—often found in Renaissance and baroque music.

> **Example** Weelkes, *As Vesta Was Descending*; p. 87; VMG; **CD 1** ☐62☐; CD 1 ■80■

Xylophone Percussion instrument of definite pitch, consisting of flat wooden bars set in a frame and played by striking with hard plastic or wooden hammers.

> **Example** Britten, *The Young Person's Guide to the Orchestra*, LO variation 13c; p. 28;
> **CD 1** ☐31☐; CD 1 ■38■

Acknowledgments

Musical Excerpts and Musical Texts

Bach, Johann Sebastian. Cantata No. 140, *Wachet auf, ruft uns die Stimme*. English translation by Gerhard Herz. From *The Norton Scores* by Roger Kamien, editor. Copyright © 1970 by W. W. Norton & Company, Inc. Used by permission of W. W. Norton & Company, Inc.

Berg, Alban. *Wozzeck*. English translation courtesy of RM Associates. Used by permission.

Hildegard of Bingen. *O successores*. English translation. Copyright Peter Dronke. Reprinted by permission.

Machaut, Guillaume de. *Puis qu'en oubli*. English translation by R. Barton Palmer. From Guillaume de Machaut, *La Messe de Nostre Dame; Songs from Le Voir Dit*. Oxford Camerata, Jeremy Summerly, Director. Naxos 553833. Reprinted by permission of R. Barton Palmer.

Penderecki, Krzysztof. *Threnody to the Victims of Hiroshima*. © 1961 (Renewed) EMI DESHON MUSIC, INC. and PWM EDITIONS. All Rights Administered by EMI DESHON MUSIC, INC. (Publishing) and ALFRED PUBLISHING CO., INC. (Print). All Rights Reserved. Used by Permission.

Schoenberg, Arnold. *A Survivor from Warsaw*, Op. 46. Used by permission of Belmont Music Publishers.

Schubert, Franz. *Erlkönig*. From *The Ring of Words: An Anthology of Song Texts*, translated by Philip L. Miller. Garden City, NY: Doubleday, 1963. Reprinted by permission of Robert M. Kuehn, executor of the estate of Philip L. Miller, New York.

Schumann, Clara Wieck. *Liebst du um Schönheit*. English translation by Rufus Hallmark. Reprinted by permission of Rufus Hallmark.

Verdi, Giuseppe. "La donna è mobile" from *Rigoletto*. From *Verdi Librettos*, translated by William Weaver. Copyright © 1963 by William Weaver. Reprinted by permission of William Morris Agency, LLC on behalf of the Author.

Wagner, Richard. *Die Walküre*. English translation by William Mann. © William Mann. Commissioned and originally published by The Friends of Covent Garden. Reprinted by permission of Erika Mann.

Literary Acknowledgments

Considine, J. D. "Viva Santana: The Man, the Myth, the Legend—gazing into the spiritual eye of the Latin guitar great, Carlos Santana," http://www.guitarworld.com/artistindex/9704.santana.html

Ellis, Andy. "Carlos Santana on Spirit Guides, Rainbow Music & Passionate Guitar," *Guitar Player*, August 1999.

Gorin, Natalio. *Astor Piazzolla: A Memoir*, translated, annotated, and expanded by Fernando Gonzalez. Portland, OR: Amadeus Press, 2001, pp. 62, 71.

Holsinger, Bruce W. *Music, Body, and Desire in Medieval Culture: Hildegard of Bingen to Chaucer*. Stanford, CA: Stanford University Press, 2001, p. 113.

Page, Christopher. *Voices and Instruments of the Middle Ages: Instrumental Practice and Songs in France, 1100–1300*. Berkeley: University of California Press, 1986, pp. 59–60.

Pavarotti, Luciano, and William Wright. *Pavarotti: My World*. New York: Crown, 1995.

Pavarotti, Luciano, and William Wright. *Pavarotti: My Own Story*. Garden City, NY: Doubleday, 1981.

Reich, Steve. Comments in interview with D. Sterritt, "Artists and Their Inspiration: Tradition Reseen," *Christian Science Monitor*, October 23, 1980.

Santana, Carlos. Liner notes to the album *Dance of the Rainbow Serpent*.

Shankar, Ravi. *Raga Mala: The Autobiography of Ravi Shankar*, edited and introduced by George Harrison. New York: Welcome Rain Publishers, 1999.

Stravinsky, Igor. *Chronicle of My Life*. London: Gollancz, 1936.

Stravinsky, Igor, and Robert Craft. *Expositions and Developments*. Garden City, NY: Doubleday, 1962.

Zwilich, Ellen Taaffe. Comments on *Concerto Grosso*.

Photo Credits

Preface

Page xxiii: AFP/Getty Images; **p. xxiv:** © Kasskara. Photo courtesy of Deutsche Grammophon

Part 1

p. xxxiv: © Brian Duffy; **p. 2 (top):** © John Henley/Corbis; **p. 2 (bottom):** © Ron Sherman/Stock Boston, LLC; **p. 3 (top):** Mark Mainz/Getty Images; **p. 3 (middle):** STR/AFP/Getty Images; **p. 3 (bottom):** © Odile Noel/Lebrecht Music; **p. 11:** Graham Salter/Redferns; **p. 14 (top left):** © Alex Irvin Photography; **p. 14 (top right):** © Steve J. Sherman; **p. 14 (bottom left):** Steve J. Sherman; **p. 14 (bottom right):** © Joe D. Myers; **p. 15 (left):** Chris Stock/Lebrecht Music; **p. 15 (right):** © Lorenzo Agius/Sony Classical; **p. 16 (left):** © David Young-Wolff/PhotoEdit, Inc.; **p. 16 (right):** © Steve J. Sherman; **p. 17 (Top left):** Chris Stock/Lebrecht Music; **p. 17 (top right):** Chris Stock/Lebrecht Music; **p. 17 (bottom left):** Chris Stock/Lebrecht Music; **p. 17 (bottom right):** © David Redfern/retna; **p. 18 (Top left):** © Steve J. Sherman; **p. 18 (top right):** David Redfern/Redferns; **p. 18 (bottom left):** Wladimir Polak/Lebrecht Music; **p. 18 (bottom right):** © David Redfern/retna; **p. 19 (left):** © Retna Pictures L.; **p. 19 (right):** © Lawrence Migdale/Photo Researchers, Inc.; **p. 20 (left):** Kate Mount/Lebrecht Music; **p. 20 (right):** Graham Salter/Lebrecht Music; **p. 21 (Top left):** © Tony Freeman/PhotoEdit, Inc.; **p. 21 (bottom left):** © PhotoDisc/Getty Images; **p. 21 (right):** Wladimir Polak/Lebrecht Music; **p. 22 (top left):** Wladimir Polak/Lebrecht Music; **p. 22 (right):** © PhotoDisc/Getty Images; **p. 22 (bottom left):** © ArenaPal/opham/The Image Works; **p. 23 (top left):** Graham Salter/Lebrecht Music; **p. 23 (top right):** Richard Haughton/Lebrecht Music; **p. 23 (middle left):** Wladimir Polak/Lebrecht Music; **p. 23 (middle right):** Leon Morris/Redferns; **p. 23 (bottom):** © Bill Gallery/Stock Boston, LLC; **p. 24:** © Steve J. Sherman; **p. 25 (top):** © Larry Kolvoord/The Image Works; **p. 25 (bottom):** © Lawrence Migdale/Photo Researchers, Inc.; **p. 26:** © Mark Burnett/Stock Boston, LLC; **p. 40:** John Stanton/Getty Images; **p. 42:** Courtesy Roger Kamien

Part 2

p. 58: © Visual Arts Publishing Ltd./Art Resource, NY; **p. 60 (top):** Heidelberg University Library/akg-images; **p. 60 (bottom left):** © Art Resource, NY; **p. 60 (bottom right):** © Royalty-Free/Corbis; **p. 61 (left):** © Scala/Art Resource, NY; **p. 61 (right):** © Birdgeman-Giraudon/Art Resource, NY; **p. 62 (left):** Hervé Champollion/akg-images; **p.62 (right):** Enthroned Madonna and Child © Board of Trustees, National Gallery of Art, Washington; **p. 63 (left):** © Art Resource, NY; **p. 63 (right):** © Royalty-Free/Corbis; **p. 64 (top):** © Erich Lessing/Art Resource, NY; **p. 64 (bottom):** © Erich Lessing/Art Resource, NY; **p. 66:** © The Pierpont Morgan Library/Art Resource, NY; **p. 71:** Heidelberg University Library/akg-images; **p. 73:** © Royalty-Free/Corbis; **p. 77:** Courtesy Jonathan Wentworth Associates Ltd.; **p. 83:** Bibliotheque Royale Albert, 1er; **p. 88:** © The Pierpont Morgan Library/Art Resource, NY

Part 3

p. 90: © Hendrick ter Brugghen, 1588–1629, The Concert, Oil on canvas, 99.1 X 116.8cm. NG6483 Image © 2000 National Gallery, London; **p. 92 (top)** Scala/Art Resource, NY; **p. 92 (bottom left):** akg-images; **p. 92 (right):** akg-images; **p. 93 (left):** Judith and Holofernes (panel), Gentileschi, Artemisia (1597–c.1651) / Museo e Gallerie Nazionali di Capodimonte, Naples, Italy/The Bridgeman Art Library; **p. 93 (right):** © Scala/Art Resource, NY; **p. 94 (top):** Nicolas Poussin, Mars and Venus, c.1630. Museum of Fine Arts, Boston/Augustus Hemenway Fund and Arthur William Wheelright Fund 40.89; **p. 94 (bottom):** © Scala/Art Resource, NY; **p. 95 (top):** © Rembrandt van Rijn (Dutch 1606–1669), 'Self-Portrait', 1659 oil on canvas, 33¼ × 26,/Board of Trustees, National Gallery of Art, Washington/Andrew W. Mellon Collection/Photo: Richard Carafelli; **p. 95 (bottom):** © Royalty-Free/Corbis; **p. 101:** Réunion des Musées Nationaux/Art Resource, NY; **p. 115:** © Scala/Art Resource, NY; **p. 117:** akg-images; **p. 118:** © Erich Lessing/Art Resource, NY; **p. 120:** National Portrait Gallery, London; **p. 124:** akg-images; **p. 128:** © Dean Macdonell/Courtesy Tafelmusik Baroque Orchestra and Chamber Choir, Toronto; **p. 130:** akg-images; **p. 141:** akg-images

Part 4

p. 148: © Erich Lessing/Art Resource, NY; **p. 150 (top left):** akg-images; **p. 150 (top right):** © Geoffrey Clements/Corbis; **p. 150 (middle left):** akg-images; **p. 150 (middle right):** © Réunion des Musées Nationaux/Art Resource, NY; **p. 150 (bottom left):** akg-images; **p. 150 (bottom right):** © Erich Lessing/Art Resource, NY; **p. 151:** © Geoffrey Clements/Corbis; **p. 152 (top):** The Death of Socrates, 1787 Jacques-Louis David (French, 1748–1825) Catharine Lorillard Wolfe Collection, Wolfe Fund, 1931 (31.45); **p. 152 (bottom):** © PhotoLink / Photodisc / Getty Images; **p. 153 (top):** © Réunion des Musées Nationaux/Art Resource, NY; **p. 153 (bottom):** © Erich Lessing/Art Resource, NY; **p. 158:** akg-Images, London; **p. 175:** akg-images, London; **p. 178:** akg-Images, London; **p. 180:** © Jack Vartoogian/FrontRowPhotos; **p. 192:** © Steve J. Sherman; **p. 193:** akg-images, London

Index

Italicized page numbers indicate material in captions. Page numbers followed by (LO) indicate Listening Outlines. Page numbers followed by (VMG) indicate Vocal Music Guides.